The

BEGUINE,

The

ANGEL,

and the

INQUISITOR

The

BEGUINE,

The

ANGEL,

and the

INQUISITOR

The Trials of Marguerite Porete and Guiard of Cressonessart

SEAN L. FIELD

University of Notre Dame Press

Notre Dame, Indiana

Manufactured in the United States of America

Library of Congress Cataloging-in-Publication Data

Field, Sean L. (Sean Linscott), 1970–
The beguine, the angel, and the inquisitor : the trials of Marguerite Porete
and Guiard of Cressonessart / Sean L. Field.
p. cm.
Includes bibliographical references (p.   ) and index.
ISBN 978-0-268-02892-3 (pbk. : alk. paper) —
ISBN 0-268-02892-3 (pbk. : alk. paper)
EISBN 978-0-268-07973-4
1. Inquisition—France.   2. Church history—Middle Ages, 600–1500.
3. Porete, Marguerite, ca. 1250–1310.   4. Guiard, of Cressonessart.
5. Porete, Marguerite, ca. 1250–1310. Miroir des simples âmes.
6. Mysticism—France—History—Middle Ages, 600–1500.   I. Title.
BX1720.F54   2012
272'.2092—dc23

2012003446

For Cecilia and Romare

Look in the mirror, tell me what do you see . . .

—R. Emmett, *Ordinary Man*

CONTENTS

ACKNOWLEDGMENTS

The research and writing of this book were supported by a grant from the American Philosophical Society and by grants from the College of Arts and Sciences and the Office of the Vice President for Research at the University of Vermont. The final stages of writing were carried out in the idyllic surroundings of the Camargo Foundation in Cassis, France. I am grateful for this support, and particularly to the directors and staff of the Camargo Foundation and the fellows in residence there in spring 2010. I thank also the direction and staffs of the Bibliothèque nationale de France, the Archives nationales de France, the Institut de recherche et d'histoire des textes, and the Bibliothèque Mazarine in Paris, as well as of the University of Vermont Bailey/Howe Library (especially Barbara Lamonda and the staff of Interlibrary Loan). Ghislain Brunel, conservateur en chef of the Section ancienne at the Archives nationales, merits special gratitude for graciously facilitating access to original documents.

Cecilia Gaposchkin (my partner in Capetian crime) read and improved the first draft of the entire book and never failed to keep up her end of our sanity-preserving virtual chatter. Robert E. Lerner meticulously critiqued the penultimate draft. More than that, his support of this project from beginning to end was essential, as was his generosity with sources, insights, and bibliography. Elizabeth A. R. Brown answered countless questions and went over my translations of the trial documents with a fine-toothed comb, saving me from many errors in the process. Suggestions and criticisms from the two anonymous readers for the press were also greatly appreciated. Others who kindly read chapters include Charles F. Briggs, William J. Courtenay, Jennifer K. Deane, Larry F. Field, Walter Simons, Julien Théry, and Ian Wei. My colleagues in the Department of History at UVM read the introduction for a faculty research seminar and improved it with their comments. I owe many thanks to other scholars as well for their help and advice, including Christine Caldwell Ames, Nicole Bériou, John Bollweg, Louisa Burnham, Olivier Canteaut, Anne Clark, Olivia Remie Constable, Xavier Hélary, William C. Jordan, Kathryn Kerby-Fulton, Deeana Klepper, Zan Kocher, Pascal Montaubin, Sébastien Nadiras, Barbara Newman, Mark Pegg, Sylvain Piron, Jenny Sisk, and Justine Trombley. I particularly thank Larry Field for translation advice and for a prosecuting attorney's perspective on these trials. Whatever strengths the book possesses are due in great measure to these scholars' generosity. Only its shortcomings are uniquely my own.

A version of chapter 3 was presented to the Group de Travail sur les Derniers Capétiens at the Université de Paris-Sorbonne in April 2010. I thank Xavier Hélary for the invitation, and the members of this group for their criticisms. Work in progress was also presented to the Colloque internationale Marguerite Porete, held at Paris from 30 May to 1 June 2010. I thank the participants of this conference for stimulating discussion. A volume based in part on this conference is forthcoming, from which I am grateful to have been able to consult prepublication versions of William J. Courtenay's "Marguerite's Judges: The University of Paris in 1310" and Robert E. Lerner's "Addenda on an Angel."

I also thank the students in my 2005, 2007, and 2009 History 224 seminars at the University of Vermont, who enthusiastically entered the world of Marguerite Porete. In a very real way, their questions and insights helped to shape this book, and their enthusiasm for the subject convinced me that it was worth writing.

At the University of Notre Dame Press I owe a great deal to Barbara Hanrahan, who supported this project from its inception. Stephen Little stepped in at a crucial moment and saw it through to publication. Rebecca DeBoer and the entire editorial and production team have long had my respect and thanks, and Elisabeth Magnus strengthened the book with fine copyediting.

Finally, my family. My parents Larry and Tammy Field and my brother Nicholas have given me their unflagging support. Kristen Johanson, I hope, knows just how much of this book belongs to her. And perhaps Cecilia and Romare will read it some day (or at least stumble across the dedication) and think back to that spring semester by the sea.

ABBREVIATIONS

AN	Archives nationales de France, Paris
BAV	Biblioteca Apostolica Vaticana, Vatican City
BMaz	Bibliothèque Mazarine, Paris
BnF	Bibliothèque nationale de France, Paris

Introduction

Modern and Medieval Contexts

On 31 May 1310, at the Place de Grève in Paris, the Dominican inquisitor William of Paris read out a sentence that declared Marguerite "called Porete" to be a relapsed heretic, released her to secular authority for punishment, and ordered that all copies of a book she had written be confiscated. William next consigned Marguerite's would-be supporter, Guiard of Cressonessart, to perpetual imprisonment. Guiard was not an author, but rather what might be termed an apocalyptic activist, charged in his own mind with an angelic mission to defend the true adherents of the Lord—including Marguerite—as the time of Antichrist grew near. The inquisitor's sentences also sketched the bare outlines of Marguerite's and Guiard's stories. Marguerite had earlier been detained by a bishop of Cambrai, her book had been burned at that time, and she had been released with a warning never again to write or speak about the ideas contained there. She chose to ignore this order, however, and communicated her book to others, including a neighboring bishop. This audacity landed her before an inquisitor and the next bishop of Cambrai, and eventually led to her incarceration under William of Paris's jurisdiction by fall 1308. It was at this point that Guiard appeared in Paris and attempted to defend Marguerite in some way. He was also promptly imprisoned, and the two remained uncooperative until spring 1310. Over several months, William of Paris then conducted inquisitorial processes against them, complete with multiple

1

consultations of experts in theology and canon law. Under threat of death, Guiard at last consented to testify, perhaps shocking his interrogators with the news that he considered himself to hold the office of "Angel of Philadelphia." Marguerite, however, remained uncooperative to the bitter end. Nothing further is known about Guiard's fate after the sentencing of 31 May, but Marguerite went to her execution the next day.

Contemporary chroniclers recorded Marguerite's death and Guiard's imprisonment as among the most noteworthy events of 1310. But memory of the trials faded over time, and these two were largely forgotten. Marguerite's book, however, lived on. Although the trial documents never gave it a title, modern scholarship has identified it as the swirling exploration of spiritual nonbeing known as the *Mirror of Simple Souls (Mirouer des simples ames)*,[1] which circulated in unattributed copies of the original Old and then Middle French, and in translations into Middle English, Latin, and Italian, until Romana Guarnieri reconnected it to Marguerite's name in 1946.[2] This announcement led in turn to a wave of scholarly interest in Marguerite Porete as an author and thinker. The unique surviving Middle French manuscript of her book was edited by Guarnieri in 1961 (and in a more widely available edition of 1965) and then reprinted alongside Paul Verdeyen's edition of the Latin version in 1986. Modern translations into English, French, Italian, German, Spanish, and Catalan have followed, along with a torrent of linguistic, theological, philosophical, and literary studies that shows no sign of slowing down.[3] Historians, however, have written comparatively little about Marguerite since the 1970s, perhaps out of a sense that she and her book were best left to scholars of literature and theology. Guiard, for his part, has drawn relatively little interest after the thorough article by Robert E. Lerner in 1976 that made the facts of his case available to the scholarly world.[4]

The Curse of the Burned Beguine?

Although this study focuses equally on William of Paris, Guiard of Cressonessart, and Marguerite Porete, it is the latter who undoubtedly stands as the riveting figure at the center of the book. As the author of a sophisticated spiritual treatise, a woman undaunted in her determination to write in spite of repeated official condemnation, and a seemingly fearless opponent of inquisitorial persecution who went to her death without ever deigning to testify at her own trial, in recent decades Marguerite has earned an ever-increasing number of admirers, scholarly and otherwise.[5]

The stark fact is that Marguerite Porete was the first female Christian mystic burned at the stake after authoring a book—and the book's survival makes the case absolutely unique. Indeed, the import of this moment extends beyond a history of misogynistic censorship. Taken from a northern French perspective, the sentencing of 31 May was, as Henry Charles Lea famously put it, "the first formal *auto de fé* of which we have cognizance at Paris."[6] In the history of book burning, it is the first known instance of an inquisitorial procedure ending with the burning of both a book and the accused author.[7] If one thinks in terms of a history of violent intellectual repression, Marguerite has been described as "the only medieval woman, and possibly the only author of either sex, who died solely for a written text."[8] No matter what perspective is applied, the execution of Marguerite Porete marks a historical watershed.

And these events had wider consequences, since the church fathers at the Council of Vienne in 1311–12 almost certainly drew on extracts from Marguerite's book in crafting the decree *Ad nostrum,* which set in motion decades of inquisitorial persecution of beguines and beghards accused of being antinomian "heretics of the Free Spirit."[9] Pope Clement V and the churchmen gathered at Vienne may also have had Marguerite in mind as an example when they constructed the decree *Cum de quibusdam,* which attempted to legislate against communities of problematic beguines. Thus, as recent work has shown, 1310–12 marked a turning point not only in the whole beguine movement but in the way churchmen regarded female authors and ecstatically devout women more generally.[10] Guiard's case has not generally been thought of in such dramatic terms, but I will suggest that it can be seen as a step toward the crackdown on Joachite-inspired apocalypticism that culminated in condemnations and executions under Pope John XXII by the 1320s.[11]

Given the great interest of these trials, it is startling to note how frequently errors concerning some of the basic facts have been made and repeated. Indeed, this pattern is so striking that one might be tempted (tongue firmly in cheek) to imagine Marguerite as a forerunner of the Templar grand master Jacques of Molay, who supposedly hurled curses from the pyre in Paris in 1314.[12] But rather than calling her contemporary antagonists to a reckoning in the next world as Jacques is rumored to have done, perhaps Marguerite—always distrustful of arrogant scholars—placed a more subtle malediction on all those who would dig to the bottom of carton J428 in the Archives nationales de France, where the trial documents are now found.[13] This supernatural hypothesis, fanciful though it is, would at least offer some explanation for why scholars have so resolutely persisted in repeating misinformation about her trial.

For the most concrete example, consider several problems with chronology. In 1887 the American medievalist Henry Charles Lea (really his paid copyist) misdated a crucial document to 30 May instead of 9 May 1310, and thereby had a panel of canon lawyers declaring Marguerite a relapsed heretic only the day before her sentencing.[14] Lea can be forgiven for occasional lapses in his pioneering work—carried out by "remote control" from Philadelphia—but the effects of this error have nevertheless continued to linger right up to the present.[15] Not only was his erroneous date repeated when it was quickly reprinted in Paul Fredericq's still widely used collection of sources, but a recent translation into English of several of the documents from Marguerite's trial (available on the World Wide Web) is based on Lea's edition and hence continues to propagate it as well.[16] This error matters, for it fundamentally misrepresents the inquisitor's timetable and obscures the relation between Marguerite's trial and other events occurring in Paris in May 1310.

The great French medieval historian Charles-Victor Langlois, for his part, not only followed Lea's mistake in 1894 but added another layer of confusion by shortening Marguerite's life by one day, claiming that she was burned on 31 May.[17] Twentieth-century scholars as accomplished as Herbert Grundmann, Romana Guarnieri, Robert Lerner, Kurt Ruh, and Miri Rubin have inadvertently repeated the latter error.[18] A single day may not seem enormously important, but the correct date of Marguerite's death has continued to elude historians, appearing as early as 1 May 1310 in one influential work and as late as 1311 in another.[19]

Yet curses (even imaginary ones) run their course, scholarship marches on, and all the trial documents were at last correctly dated by

Lerner in 1976.[20] One might have hoped, therefore, that subsequent scholarship would no longer be plagued by these factual errors. Unfortunately, several more recent publications have once again muddied what should have been clearing waters. Most importantly, Paul Verdeyen in 1986 published an article with the laudable goal of bringing together for the first time all the Latin trial documents pertaining to Marguerite and Guiard.[21] Yet precisely because this work was intended to provide the definitive critical edition of the entire proceedings, any misinformation it conveyed was bound to be widely repeated. It is thus particularly lamentable that Verdeyen misread the date of the document in which twenty-one masters of theology condemned extracts from Marguerite's book as 11 April 1309 instead of 11 April 1310 and that he then compounded this error by repeating it in his short introduction to what has become the standard multilingual edition of Marguerite's work.[22] In this telling, the theological condemnation of the book would have been the very opening of the process, taking place a whole year before any further action occurred and coloring the rest of the process accordingly. Given this mistaken idea, Verdeyen's analysis of the subsequent course of the trial could not avoid conveying some misleading assumptions about the way William of Paris had approached his task.[23]

Another influential account of Marguerite's life, the introduction to the most recent English translation of Marguerite's *Mirror,* by Edmund Colledge, J. C. Marler, and Judith Grant, does get the date of 11 April 1310 correct but still indicates that this is the earliest document from the process (neglecting documents dated 3 and 9 April), then states that four canon lawyers were called in to consult on Marguerite's legal status "seven weeks later"—which, in fact, brings us right back to Lea's original misdating of 30 May for that document![24] If the standard edition of the trial documents, the critical edition of the *Mirror of Simple Souls,* and the most recent English translation of that work all contain such chronological errors, it can hardly be surprising that others who have summarized the trial have often repeated one or more of these mistakes.

Nor does the problem with accurate dating stop at the trial documents themselves. For example, Marguerite Porete first ran afoul of ecclesiastical authority when her book was condemned and burned by Guido of Collemezzo, bishop of Cambrai. This event must have occurred between 1296 and 1306, because those are the years in which

Guido held the bishopric of Cambrai. But over time, on the basis of no additional evidence, some scholars have inadvertently slipped into stating that the condemnation occurred "in 1306" or a similar formulation.[25] Again, the point matters, because if indeed Marguerite's first encounter with ecclesiastical censure happened only in 1306, then her path to inquisitorial arrest afterward was short and direct, whereas an earlier date would have allowed her time to mull over her response.

The first goal of this study, therefore, is to get the facts straight, where they can be established. These facts then provide the starting point for further analysis of actions, choices, and motivations. I hope that in many instances a clear grasp of the data allows me to offer interpretations that can be supported with contextual evidence or at least persuasive argumentation. At other points, however, the fragmentary documentary record permits only pure hypotheses. I have tried to make these two registers clear to the reader—if the speculative moments are marked by the use of words such as *perhaps* and phrases such as *might have*, these cumbersome formulations at least preserve the line between what I take to be established facts and what should be understood as more subjective interpretation.

In sum, this study analyzes the trials of Marguerite Porete and Guiard of Cressonessart in new detail and from previously unconsidered perspectives. I also hope it tells a compelling story and illuminates issues in a way that will be informative to scholars, students, and general readers alike. I therefore explain ideas and events throughout the book without assuming specialized knowledge. With this goal in mind, I now turn to an elucidation of the larger issues (most of which will be familiar to specialists) essential for understanding the context of the trial.

Intellectual Context: Beguine Mystics

Although it was her book that first got Marguerite Porete in trouble, simply writing a controversial book, even one in French expressing daring theological ideas, was not enough to land a woman in an inquisitorial prison and certainly not in itself sufficient to justify her execution by the secular authorities. To the contrary, the *Mirror of Simple Souls* was part of a wider flowering of a new kind of text—religious literature written in vernacular languages by thirteenth-century women,

sometimes nuns but frequently beguines or others on the edges of organized religious communities (chapter 1 will examine what it meant to
be called a *beguina*).[26] Many of these texts reported visions or mystical
experiences, most asserted theological truths of some kind, and virtually all were vibrantly original.[27] These works encompassed several
genres: for instance, the beguine Hadewijch wrote Flemish poetry, letters, and vision literature; Beatrice of Nazareth's Dutch *Seven Manners of Loving* more closely resembled a didactic treatise; Mechthild of
Magdeburg's German *Flowing Light of the Godhead* was a sprawling
spiritual diary of sorts; the Carthusian prioress Marguerite of Oingt
wrote a *Mirror* and a life of her fellow nun Béatrice of Ornacieux in
Franco-Provençal (and other works in Latin); and the Provençal beguine Felipa of Porcelet and the northern French Franciscan abbess
Agnes of Harcourt authored vernacular lives of their communities'
founders (Douceline of Digne and Isabelle of France respectively).[28]

In short, Marguerite had plenty of company as a thirteenth-century
woman writing in the vernacular about religious subjects. Her book,
moreover, had much in common with some of these texts. Like the
Flowing Light of the Godhead, the *Mirror of Simple Souls* was its author's life's work, a nonlinear narrative encompassing everything learned
over years of reflection. And like Hadewijch, Beatrice, and Mechthild,
Marguerite treated love, in various ways and multiple manifestations,
as the central subject of the text. Thus Marguerite's project sits com-
fortably among the texts of an emerging group of "beguine mystics"
or within the overlapping genre of *mystique courtoise.*[29] Hadewijch
and Mechthild in particular were at times as daring as Marguerite, but
while there are indications that they had to deal with various sorts
of suspicion, they did not face inquisitorial persecution. The brand of
love-drenched vernacular theology that these women favored may have
been provocative, but it was not necessarily heretical.

In other respects, however, Marguerite and her *Mirror* did stand
out from the contemporary crowd. One important difference from
many medieval female-authored works on religious subjects is that
Marguerite did not base her message on visionary authority. Only as a
seeming afterthought did she briefly report having had conversations
with God.[30] Marguerite did not claim that God spoke through her or
that what she knew came from a mystical access to the divine that others lacked. In fact, she did not deign to explain how she knew what she

knew at all. More broadly, first-person experience is only rarely lo-
catable in the text, and the *Mirror* almost entirely lacks the kind of so-
matic suffering and bridal imagery that characterizes many writings
about and by contemporary women.[31]

Instead, Marguerite employed a dialogue form in which numerous personified qualities and "characters" such as Love, the Soul, and
Reason ask and answer questions about the state of nonbeing, annihilation in love, and destruction of the will that allows the simple soul to
be nowhere and nothing and hence in a state of nondifference with
God, who is All. Such perfect, annihilated souls leave behind not only
reason but also the need to pursue pious activities such as penances,
fasts, or masses—or even the virtues themselves. The book is aimed at
once at those who have already attained the noble status of annihilation and at those "forlorn" souls who still strive for it. The perfect love
(fine amour) at play here is not a meditative longing for the crucified
Jesus but an impossible, self-destroying descent into an abyss of humility so profound that from its depths no self remains to impede God's
self-recognition there. In form, the *Mirror* is a mix of meditation, poetry,
and instruction, oscillating in mood from exaltation to despair, scold-
ing to mockery, and humility to haughtiness. It can, at first reading, seem
chaotic in the way it drops themes, picks them up much later, contra-
dicts itself, and generally proceeds along anything but a straight line.
Its culmination, however, comes at chapter 118 (in the Middle French
manuscript), which outlines a seven-step descent to annihilation in God;
and what unifies the book is the idea that elite, annihilated souls—who
have and will and know both everything and nothing, who are both
impossibly distant from and utterly united to God—follow a spiritual
path that transcends the more common road of Christian charity and
good works.

Although nothing can replace the experience of reading the *Mirror* oneself, a nearly random excerpt from the middle of the book (chapter 46 in the Middle French manuscript) will serve to provide the flavor
for those who have not yet read it:[32]

> Now [says Love], has this Soul fallen and come to knowledge
> of the more—indeed, only insofar as she knows nothing of God
> in comparison with his all.

O, alas, says Reason, dare one really call that nothing, that thing which is of God?

Ah alas, says this Soul, how else should one call it? Truly it is really nothing, whatever is given or shall be given to us from him. Indeed, even if he gave us the very same thing which is said above in this writing—by comparison, even if it could be that which was truth—still it would be nothing compared with a single spark of his goodness, which remains in his knowing, beyond our knowing.[33]

The role Reason plays here is characteristic, acting the dunce and waiting to be corrected by Love, while the Soul seeks its way to simplicity. Reason is no fool, however; he asks logical questions, but this rational approach is repeatedly slapped down as indicative of blindness to higher truths.

It can readily be imagined that not all churchmen would have appreciated this didactic technique. Moreover, the author's underlying message in a work with this format could be difficult to understand, and uncharitable readers could easily take particular remarks ascribed to particular personifications out of context. Still, caution is required before assuming that specific elements of the way Marguerite constructed or justified her text explain why her work was condemned, since there is no record of any contemporary churchman noting these points, approvingly or disapprovingly.

Equally important to Marguerite's treatment by authorities may be the fact that she had no known confessor to help shield her from suspicion. A fruitful strand of recent scholarship has analyzed the way such male confidants could influence their female charges, present them within an orthodox context, and bask in their spiritual glow.[34] Again, however, this lack of a prominent confessor cannot wholly explain why Marguerite alone among her peers went to the stake. For one thing, Marguerite did receive encouragement from some churchmen, including Godfrey of Fontaines, so she cannot be seen as an utterly lone figure (as she is too often portrayed).[35] Moreover, Hadewijch is not known to have had a confessor who promoted her writings, yet she did not suffer the same inquisitorial persecution as Marguerite. It is therefore necessary to expose Marguerite's specific actions and the context in which they were made in order to explain her fate. As Barbara Newman nicely puts it: "Medieval heresy was a juridical concept. Books or beliefs could not be heretical in the abstract; they became heretical only when authoritative churchmen—popes, synods, individual bishops, or inquisitors—pronounced them so. As for the human beings who wrote the books and adhered to the beliefs, they could be executed for the crime of heresy only if they proved 'obdurate' or 'relapsed,' that is, if they either refused to abjure their heretical views or did so under pressure but later recanted or resumed their prior activities."[36] Accordingly, it will be necessary to investigate exactly how and why a bishop pronounced Marguerite's book heretical and what subsequent "obdurate" behavior led to her execution.

Intellectual Context: Joachite Apocalypticism

If a woman writing about "annihilated souls" can sometimes be hard to contextualize, it is even more difficult to convince a modern audience that a man claiming to be the "Angel of Philadelphia" was anything other than deranged. Yet Guiard of Cressonessart was working with ideas that were very much in the air around 1300. Most generally, the claim that the time of Antichrist was near was no novelty in the later Middle Ages, and the idea that the Book of Revelation, with its seven churches, seven angels, and other recurring symbols, foretold in some mysterious manner the events that would accompany the last times was equally accepted.

More specifically, Guiard's testimony shows him to have been an intellectual heir of Joachim of Fiore (ca. 1135–1202), an Italian abbot whose formulations about the relationship of the Christian past to the Christian future were immensely influential.[37] Joachim's writings proposed a fundamentally new way of understanding God's plan for the full scope of Christian history. In several interlocking major works written between the 1170s and his death, Joachim combined meticulous reading of the Old and New Testaments with flashes of revelatory insight to offer his vision of the future. One of his "big ideas" was the "concordance of testaments," essentially that the Old Testament offered a guide to interpreting the second half of Christian history from the Incarnation to the Last Judgment. Read correctly, the Old Testament not only foretold events from the time of Christ up to the (twelfth-century) present but also laid out what was to follow. An essential addition to this methodology was Joachim's strategy for reading the Book of Revelation. Traditionally, Christian scholars had seen Revelation as a repetitious description (with its recurring series of sevenfold symbols) rather than as a continuous narrative. Most importantly, St. Augustine had authoritatively asserted long ago that the passage (20:1–5) that speaks of a thousand-year reign of the saints with Christ referred to the Christian present (that is, the time after Christ's incarnation) and not to some future period of earthly bliss.[38] Joachim, however, read Revelation as representing a continuous history from the time of Christ to the Last Judgment and therefore posited a millennial reign of the saints to arrive after the time of Antichrist and before the Last Judgment. Furthermore, he argued that close study of the Bible revealed an unfolding pattern, with the Christian time line divided into three overlapping *status:* those of the Father, the Son, and the Holy Spirit. Since the third *status* was equated with the millennial Sabbath after Antichrist, signs in Revelation associated with the coming of Antichrist also heralded the imminent arrival of the *status* of the Holy Spirit.[39] In practical terms, this meant that for those influenced by Joachim's ideas, a fundamentally new dispensation of understanding, concord, and spiritual intelligence (the third *status*) awaited beyond the looming time of Antichrist.[40]

Guiard emerged from this tradition, but his thoughts must have been filtered through those of the many Joachite thinkers who developed these ideas over the course of the thirteenth century. Thinking or writing in this vein was not in and of itself heretical. It is true that one specific (and now lost) book by Joachim dealing with the Trinity was condemned by the Fourth Lateran Council in 1215,[41] but his works as a whole were not off limits to the faithful, and his ideas about the third *status* were never condemned. They could, however, be pushed too far, as when a Franciscan student at Paris, Gerardino of Borgo San Donnino, published a work known as the *Eternal Gospel,* which mixed his own comments with some of Joachim's authentic writings. Flush with millennial enthusiasm, Gerardino asserted that Joachim's works would be the Scripture of the third *status,* fulfilling if not superseding the Old and New Testaments, and that the Franciscan order would lead the way into the age of the Holy Spirit while much of the rest of the church hierarchy fell away. This was enough to get Gerardino imprisoned for life by his order, as he continued to adhere to these claims even after the pope ordered his book destroyed.[42] Despite this episode, Joachim remained a major inspiration to later thirteenth-century thinkers, especially within the Franciscan order.

This is not, of course, to say that there was nothing audacious or novel about Guiard's claims: by insisting that he himself *was* the Angel of Philadelphia, he was obviously crossing over into dangerous territory as far as church officials were concerned. Nevertheless, as with Marguerite, it is essential to realize that within contemporary intellectual currents Guiard was pushing boundaries of orthodoxy rather than inventing "heresies" out of whole cloth.

The Reach of Royal Power in the Reign of Philip IV

Unfortunately for Marguerite and Guiard, the France of Philip IV (r. 1285–1314) was not a promising atmosphere for pushing boundaries where royal interests were concerned; and increasingly the king and his men insisted that royal power was implicated in all questions of ecclesiastical authority within the realm. Over the course of the thirteenth century, the French royal family had presented itself as a holy lineage (*beata stirps*) with the Most Christian Kings ruling over a French "chosen people."[43] The crown's role as leader of crusades, defender of the papacy, guardian of the university, and keeper of Christ's crown of thorns merged with the king's unique anointing and reputedly miraculous healing touch to support this public image. More specifically, the lived sanctity of Louis IX and his sister Isabelle (both d. 1270) had helped to foster a public perception of a saintly royal family, which in succeeding decades provided an argument for the sanctity of the whole Capetian line.[44] As the French realm developed from a modest twelfth-century domain centered on the Île-de-France to the nascent nation-state of the early fourteenth century, this special aura of holy authority was essential to the king's ability to command the loyalty of his subjects.[45]

Philip IV's reign witnessed the medieval culmination of this "religion of royalty."[46] He not only worked for Louis's canonization in

1297 but also did everything possible to translate this royal reputation for piety into real political control over church affairs in his kingdom.[47] The best recent commentators have developed a picture of Philip as "a captious, sternly moralistic, literalistically scrupulous, humorless, stubborn, aggressive, and vindictive individual."[48] He adhered to "two religions": a conventional Christian piety and "the religion of monarchy," which merged in his outlook to make devotion to Christ nearly identical with respect for the crown.[49] As king of France, he was God's anointed on earth, the defender of the church in his kingdom, and responsible for dispensing divine justice. For Philip, "no true believer could fail to see that the interests of the French monarchy and the interests of the Church were identical."[50] Thus he could be a "constitutional king" but also "chase phantoms" with "an element of terror" and thereby rule over an era of "unceasing strife, unending fear."[51]

After 1295, conflict and controversies in ecclesiastical contexts multiplied, as Philip and the newly elected pope Boniface VIII (r. 1294–1303) descended into a test of wills. An initial struggle over Philip's right to tax the clergy of France was quickly settled more or less to Philip's satisfaction by 1297. The real battle was set off in 1301 by the case of Bernard Saisset, bishop of Pamiers.[52] Bernard, a southerner with little love for the "French" of the North, was accused of making derogatory remarks about the king, insulting royal officials and northerners generally, and conspiring to see Languedoc removed from the crown's control. The bishop was arrested and sent north to Senlis, where, at an assembly of churchmen, the royal court added charges of heresy and simony to the list of accusations. Philip sought a quick ecclesiastical condemnation, hoping Bernard could then be handed over to secular officials for punishment (a draft memorandum specifically mentioned execution).[53] But Boniface ordered that Bernard be turned over to him and that the bishopric's seized revenues and temporal goods be restored. The propaganda contest that ensued far surpassed the specifics of this case to lay out with increasing intransigence the cases for royal and papal supremacy over the church in France (or more specifically, over ecclesiastical temporalities in the realm). It was in November 1302, in the heat of this contest, that Boniface published the famous bull *Unam sanctam,* probably the most extreme claim of universal papal sovereignty ever put forward.

In response, a French contingent headed by Philip's increasingly powerful advisor William of Nogaret (a former professor of law) embarked on an audacious plan.[54] In March 1303 Nogaret described Boniface in terms reminiscent of the propaganda concerning Bernard Saisset, painting him as a false pope, simoniac, and blasphemer. He now proposed to bring Boniface to account for these crimes by taking him into French custody and convoking a council that would judge and presumably depose him.[55] In June, at a public gathering at the Louvre, a royal group led by William of Plaisians, Nogaret's "right-hand man," read out a list of accusations against Boniface that now included corruption, atheism, sodomy, possessing a private demon, having clerics killed, and hating the French and their king.[56] Over the next weeks, royal officials pressured the clerics of the realm to sign letters of "adhesion" stating their support for the king.[57] William of Nogaret meanwhile set off for Italy. He may originally have been charged with more general negotiations, but by the end of June he must have received instructions to put in motion a plan very much along the lines of what he had originally proposed back in March.[58] When he learned that Boniface was about to excommunicate the king, on 7 September he and a small, armed group controlled by the Colonna family (mortal enemies of Boniface VIII) broke into the papal palace at Anagni and arrested the elderly pope. But as some of the attackers threatened to execute Boniface on the spot, the townspeople of Anagni rallied and freed him on 9 September. Nogaret beat a hasty retreat, and Boniface was able to return to Rome. But the pope was a broken man, physically and mentally incapable of any official actions after this point. He died on 11 October.[59]

These dramatic events coincided with a favorable turn in Philip's military fortunes. An ongoing war in Flanders had been proceeding very badly, with the low point being a humiliating defeat at Courtrai in 1302. But a reassuring victory at Mons-en-Pévèle in 1304 was followed by a favorable peace treaty in June 1305. Combined with the election of the more compliant French pope Clement V that same month, Philip seemed to have emerged triumphant in his major military, political, and ecclesiastical battles. Just as importantly, Philip's political operatives had perfected their signature techniques of defaming the crown's perceived enemies: paint the accused as a demonic heretic and threat to the Christian people of France, convoke public assemblies to clamor in favor of these accusations, and pressure church and lay assemblies to formally support the king. As the drive to amass more effective control over the kingdom continued, this three-step process would serve the king's interests well.

In 1306–7 the king launched two new assaults, which were—if possible—even more audacious than the attack on Boniface VIII. On 22 July 1306, after a month of secret planning, Philip's men arrested all the Jews of the kingdom (some one hundred thousand people), while the crown confiscated their goods and claimed the right to collect the principal of all debts owed to Jewish moneylenders. By October, all Jews had been expelled from the realm. In adopting this method of raising funds, Philip was following in the footsteps of his great-great-grandfather Philip II and emulating the more recent model of Edward I of England, who had similarly expelled the Jews from England in 1290. Thus after the summer of 1306 France was theoretically a "pure" Christian land, with only those Jews who had chosen to convert to Christianity remaining. The crown had again buttressed its image as defender of the faith, while enriching itself and demonstrating a remarkably disciplined ability to carry out a mass arrest and deportation.[60]

The following year Philip and his advisors put this experience to use in their infamous attack on the Knights Templar. The Templars were a military order founded in the twelfth century as monk-warriors dedicated to combating "Saracens" for control of the Holy Land.[61] By the thirteenth century, however, they had houses all across Europe, and many members had never seen the Holy Land or engaged in combat with an infidel. Indeed, most Templars in Europe were not knights at all. Particularly after the fall of the last crusader outpost at Acre in 1291, there were questions about whether the military orders were still necessary, suggestions that the Templars should be combined with the Hospitallers in a single, leaner order, and rumors about moral laxity. But the Templars' international organization had also made them a convenient network within which to transfer funds from place to place, and Templar commanderies often functioned as repositories for the wealth of nobles and kings. In fact, the Templars of Paris acted (at times) as treasurers to King Philip in the last years of the order.[62] Historians have recently veered away from simplistic arguments that would portray

Philip as coveting only the wealth of the order.[63] The fact remains, however, that Philip was chronically strapped for cash, and the existence of an order of dubious necessity, with extensive revenues and little reason to respect French royal sovereignty, was a temptation for a crown recently experienced in mass arrests and confiscations.[64]

To accuse an entire order of heresy and apostasy was unprecedented, but this is exactly what Philip and his men did. At several points this book will have to examine elements of this affair in some detail, for the "trial of the Templars" intersects with those of Marguerite and Guiard in important ways. Suffice it to say here that according to the crown, witnesses had denounced the Templars for crimes including spitting on the cross, denying Christ, idolatry, sodomy, and other immoral acts associated with a supposed secret portion of their initiation rite. It was not just that individual brothers had sinned; rather, the whole order had become an anti-Christian bastion of blasphemy and unbelief. These charges were wildly implausible,[65] yet Philip and at least some of his advisors may well have convinced themselves that the Templars' crimes were real. This was, after all, a king who perceived anti-Christian plots all around him and could not abide rival sources of authority. The more such rivals could be painted as heretics, the more clearly Philip could present himself as the shining beacon of faith standing between the Christian people of France and their enemies. Thus in late 1307 Philip ordered all Templars in France arrested, a command that was again carried out with impressive secrecy and frightening efficiency. Many Templars spent the next four years imprisoned, most confessed under torture, and eventually the order was suppressed by the Council of Vienne in 1312—but not before this affair again developed into a test between royal and papal authority, as Philip and Clement V maneuvered to control the proceedings.[66]

It might seem as though this would be all the scandal that Paris could deal with, but the trials and attacks continued up through 1310 and beyond. For example, Guichard, bishop of Troyes, had been the subject of several scandals going back to 1301, but after accusations in early 1308 the royal court accused him of sorcery, devil worship, usury, illicit sexual relations, and murder, including causing the death of Philip's queen, Jeanne of Navarre (d. 1305). The papal commission inquiring into his case formally began its work on 7 October 1308, but the process was allowed to drag on without ever reaching a conclusive resolution (eventually in 1313 Guichard was released to papal custody and then transferred to a far-off see in Bosnia).[67] Finally, there was the ongoing attempt to launch a posthumous heresy trial of Boniface VIII. Philip had insisted on such a trial early in the pontificate of Clement V, and Nogaret continued to push the idea as a way of vindicating his personal role in the "outrage at Anagni." Clement at last agreed to consider the list of articles against Boniface in 1310, and witnesses testified about a familiar cluster of accusations, including heresy, hatred of the French, blasphemy, and rejection of Christ.[68]

Taken together, the affairs of 1301–12 are an essential background to our story.[69] Over and over again enemies were created and cast in a common mold, only so that their destruction could redound to the glory of the Most Christian King. If the French crown was the defender of the faith, then its enemies must be heretics.[70] Conversely, anyone accused of heresy must be an enemy of the crown, according to the logic by which Philip sought to make himself (in Julien Théry's stark phrase) "pope in his kingdom."[71] In the Saisset affair, Nogaret argued that "what is committed against God, against the faith, or against the Roman Church, the king considered committed against himself."[72] The king and his men were thus "pontificalizing" the presentation of royal power, explicitly taking formulations used by popes going back to Innocent III to equate heresy with lèse-majesté, and in a newly literal way portraying the king as the aggrieved party in any case of heresy within his realm. To be accused of heresy in the France of Philip the Fair was to be accused of a direct attack on the king, making any heresy trial by definition an affair of royal interest.

Moreover, several semireligious women had recently run afoul of the royal court. According to contemporary chronicles, in 1304 a *pseudo-mulier* (pseudo- or false woman) originally from Metz but living among beguines in Flanders had gained influence over Philip IV and his wife, Jeanne of Navarre, through her prophecies. But this woman's malignant ways were supposedly exposed after she tried to poison the king's brother Charles of Valois. When Charles had her captured and tortured, she admitted to her *maleficia* (though she was eventually freed).[73] Four years later, in the trial of Guichard of Troyes, two of the star witnesses against the bishop were the *devineresse* Margueronne of

Bellevillette (also called Marguerite of Bourdenay) and the midwife Perrote of Pouy.[74] These women supposedly had helped Guichard to poison the queen and also attested to his plot to murder this same Charles of Valois. To judge from these episodes, the king and his family may have been on guard for attacks of such *pseudo-mulieres*—the very term with which a chronicler later labeled Marguerite Porete.

At the same time, however, the foregoing survey of these many "affairs" of the reign of Philip IV highlights ways in which the trials of Marguerite and Guiard were different. Unlike Bernard Saisset, Guichard of Troyes, or even Boniface VIII, neither Marguerite nor Guiard was accused of any direct attack on the king or kingdom (though such an idea might lurk beneath the surface of the charges), and neither was accused of anything like sorcery or invocation of demons. And both Marguerite and Guiard, to some degree, forced themselves onto inquisitorial attention—there was no need to drum up a list of wild accusations against them, since their own actions formed the basis of their convictions. The question of just exactly how the patterns of royal politics shaped the trials will require careful investigation.

Dominicans, Inquisitors, and the Crown

The link between the court and the trials of Marguerite and Guiard, however, is not in doubt. Not only did the surviving records end up in the possession of Nogaret and Plaisians (see Epilogue I), but the inquisitor, William of Paris, was also Philip's Dominican confessor. Thus a final element is necessary to add here—the rise of papal inquisitors and the ties between inquisitorial office, the Dominican order, and the French crown.

"The Inquisition" with a capital "I" is more a product of the modern imagination than a reflection of medieval reality.[75] No such "monolithic medieval institution" existed in the thirteenth or fourteenth century.[76] By the 1230s, however, the first papal inquisitors of heretical depravity were indeed carrying out their work. The impetus for the emergence of this office went back to the twelfth century, as the church responded to the challenge posed by popular "heresies" such as the Waldensians (or Poor of Lyons) and the (so-called) Cathars of southern France. These groups attracted laypeople desiring to live the life of the apostles, wandering and preaching in poverty and simplicity. The church's uneasy response was ultimately twofold: on the one hand increasingly strident attempts to suppress unlicensed preaching and doctrinal deviation by laypeople, but on the other—under Innocent III (r. 1198–1216)—the incorporation of the new Mendicant orders (those that begged for their existence) as an acceptable embodiment of these newly influential impulses.[77] The order of Lesser Brothers *(Ordo fratrum minorum)* of St. Francis and the order of Preachers *(Ordo praedicatorum)* of St. Dominic are better known simply as the Franciscans and Dominicans. Both orders were dedicated to itinerant lives of preaching and poverty, while Dominic in particular intended his order to be preachers who would combat the heretics of southern France.[78]

During these same decades from the mid-twelfth to the mid-thirteenth centuries, canon and civil lawyers developed the new (or newly rediscovered) trial procedure of *inquisitio.*[79] As opposed to an accusatorial system, where an accuser had to come forward to present a case against a defendant, in the inquisitorial system of justice an investigating judge was empowered to inquire into the truth of the matter where well-established public opinion, or *fama,* reported that a crime had been committed.[80] If that *fama* identified an individual as the likely guilty party, the judge could then proceed to a specific inquiry against this person. The adoption of inquisitorial procedure increasingly characterized secular as well as ecclesiastical justice in thirteenth-century continental Europe. Louis IX, for example, empowered *enquêteurs* to investigate charges of official corruption in France from the 1240s on (his saintly reputation and the use of the French term tends to obscure the fact this was a secular use of inquisitorial procedure),[81] and this form of governmental inquiry continued under the later Capetians.[82] Similarly, popes used inquisitorial procedure when investigating defamed bishops or other church officials.[83]

Regarding heresy specifically, it was first bishops who were instructed to conduct inquiries in their dioceses in 1184 and 1215. In the wake of the Albigensian Crusade, however, Gregory IX sought to deploy a more flexible and mobile kind of agent—the first papally empowered inquisitors of heretical depravity. From 1209 to 1229 northern French knights had answered the papacy's call to stamp out heresy in the South.[84] The result was both a vast increase in the power of the French crown in Languedoc and the destruction of organized religious life of the rebellious "good men" and "good women" of the region, dualist-leaning dissidents usually labeled by historians as Cathars. The task now was to pressure all those leaders, believers, and supporters of the heretics. Beginning in the 1230s, the pope turned to the order that had been created to fight heresy in the region, the Dominicans. In succeeding decades, ad hoc episcopal inquisitions continued to function, and Franciscans and other friars could be appointed inquisitors in specific regions. But it was the Dominicans whose identity as an order became increasingly bound up with the office of inquisitor.[85]

Dominican brothers were usually commissioned as inquisitors for a specific region by the order's provincial, who in turn was given this power by the pope. Thus there was no "Inquisition" with an international or national structure, and no "Head" or "Grand Inquisitor" in Paris or Rome.[86] There was no bureaucratic organization, hierarchy, or permanence to the office, only individuals with a few notaries and minions as aides, empowered for a specific region and heavily reliant on both parish priests and secular authorities to carry out their work. To the extent that semipermanent offices of inquisition were taking root in places like Toulouse and Carcassone, this was a function of Dominican brothers passing on their records, circulating their manuals, and employing the same notaries and assistants over time. In some cities of Languedoc, the presence of inquisitors might indeed have begun to seem very much like a permanent fact of life by 1300. Nothing similar, however, could be found for the Île-de-France, where historians have had trouble even tracing the existence of specific inquisitors between the 1270s and the time of William of Paris in the early fourteenth century.[87]

Wherever he was assigned, the inquisitor's job was to convert heretics to orthodoxy. If *fama* reliably indicated to an inquisitor that a person within his jurisdiction was a heretic or a supporter of heresy, he could charge the defendant, develop a list of accusations, and proceed to an inquiry that gathered witnesses and interrogated the suspect, who would have to swear an oath to tell the truth about the charges. Unless a criminal had been caught in the act, however, a conviction could come about only from the testimony of multiple witnesses, or through confession. Torture was a newly accepted (if still exceptional) method of extracting confessions in thirteenth-century French courts,[88] and it could be used in inquisitions where vehement suspicion of heresy lacked other proofs. The admission of guilt would then have to be repeated "without coercion" on a following day. Theoretically, suspects were allowed to know the charges against them, to defend themselves, and even to have legal counsel.[89] In practice, however, inquisitors of heretical depravity might or might not adhere to such legal restrictions, and the evolving practice of the office, embodied in a string of ever more elaborate manuals for inquisitors after 1248, often counted for more than the letter of canon law.[90] Moreover, the early inquisitorial campaigns were aimed at breaking up established (or imagined) groups of heretics, not at idiosyncratic individual thinkers.[91] This meant both that "secret crimes" that might exist only in the mind of an individual were not the intended target of inquisitors and that the exact procedure to be followed in a unique individual case might not always be clear, even to an inquisitor wishing to proceed with scrupulous legality.[92] In such cases, recourse to legal experts was a common expedient.

Confession and penitence were the desired ends of a heresy *inquisitio*. A contrite offender would be assigned a greater or lesser penance and reconciled to the church, generally in a public ceremony involving elaborate staging and a procession of those being sentenced to specific categories of heretical crimes.[93] The burning of an unrepentant heretic was a failure of sorts—perhaps necessary but brought on (according to this rationale) only by the victim's own unreasoning refusal to choose the salvation offered to him by the church and its inquisitors.[94]

Executions for heresy were thus the exception rather than the rule. For example, the early Dominican inquisitors Bernard of Caux and John of Saint-Pierre questioned at least 5,471 men and women of the Lauragais region in 1245 and 1246. Although only 207 sentences from this "great inquisition" survive, not one of these was a death sentence.[95] Later and more complete evidence comes from a recent analysis of the registers of Bernard Gui, one of the best-documented southern French Dominican inquisitors of the early fourteenth century, and shows that 6.5 percent of his sentences resulted in burning at the stake (41 out of 633 cases).[96] Far more frequent were penitential sentences ranging from the wearing of yellow crosses and undertaking of pilgrimages to perpetual imprisonment. Inquisitors generally looked to break up associations and change behaviors, and they used coercive interrogation, imprisonment with greater or lesser deprivation, and visible penances to these ends.[97] Executions that did occur were generally of those who had "relapsed." The legal principle was that after someone had been properly penitent and readmitted to communion with the church, any return to heresy was a sign of hardened obduracy and rendered the offender liable to "relaxation to the secular arm," which inevitably meant death by fire.

If Dominicans were the most prominent inquisitors of heretical depravity, they were also particularly close supporters of the French crown.[98] Most evidently, Philip's confessors were all Dominicans—William of Paris was the third man from his order to hold that position (after Nicholas of Gorran and Nicholas of Fréauville). Philip was also able to count on Dominican masters of theology at the University of Paris for intellectual support. The Parisian Dominican convent of Saint-Jacques (so named for its location on the rue Saint-Jacques) housed friars who had come to study at the university from all over western Europe, but the French delegation there, at least, provided some of Philip's strongest ecclesiastical supporters when loyalties were tested in the battle with Boniface VIII.[99] The "ablest" polemical treatise supporting Philip's theoretical position versus Boniface VIII, for example, was the work of the French Dominican master of theology John of Paris (or John Quidort).[100]

This intellectual relationship between Dominican masters and the royal court was part of a wider process by which Philip repeatedly sought public support from the masters of theology at the University of Paris. The university—a corporate entity comprising multiple faculties and possessing the right to grant teaching licenses—took clear shape only in the early thirteenth century.[101] The faculty of theology at Paris was unrivaled for prestige, and by the middle of the century Franciscan and Dominican masters were among its most influential members. Moreover, in the first years of the fourteenth century the university was becoming a "new source of authority,"[102] as the king asked the masters to provide formal opinions on questions around the dispute with Boniface VIII and the trial of the Templars. Though there were deep rivalries between Mendicant and secular masters, competition between students of various teachers, and a wide variety of opinions expressed on nearly every controversial question of the day, the court hoped that university masters would speak with one voice in supporting royal policy.

Philip IV thus looked to Dominicans to act as his confessors, to take the lead in promoting royal ideology within university circles, and to combat heresy within the realm as inquisitors. These roles, however, did not always mesh seamlessly, since not all Dominican masters were as thoroughly proroyal as John of Paris, and not all papally empowered inquisitors could be counted on to do the royal will. But for friars like William of Paris who tied their careers to the royal court, supporting the Most Christian King merged easily with inquiring into heresies that threatened the kingdom.

The Sources

To return from context to evidence, the primary source base for this study is at once quite wide and very narrow. The *Mirror of Simple Souls* itself provides some evidence for its author's experiences, and a large number of extant letters, testaments, accounts, chronicles, and other texts sheds light on subjects such as the career of William of Paris, the political context at the court of Philip IV, and the public perception of the trial. The "Continuer of William of Nangis," for example, is the best of our narrative sources for the trial and its aftermath (the relevant passages are translated in Appendix B of this book). William of Nangis had been a monk at Saint-Denis, the Benedictine abbey just north of Paris well known for its position as "custodian and interpreter of royal history" in medieval France.[103] In addition to biographies of Louis IX and Philip III, William compiled a universal Latin chronicle that traced events in France up to his death in 1300.[104] After 1300, other unidentified monks of Saint-Denis continued the work, and these chronicle entries provide crucial testimony at various points throughout the present book.

On the other hand, this study rests, at heart, on a very close analysis of just seven documents preserved on six pieces of parchment, prepared in 1310 as part of the trials of Marguerite and Guiard. There must once have been additional documents, so it should not be thought that these are the "complete" records of the trials. Moreover, some documents as they now survive are official, notarized copies, intended to stand as formal legal records, while others are unnotarized copies made either as preliminary records or as additional, informal copies for royal or inquisitorial officials. These documents are translated into English in Appendix A, where they are presented in chronological order. Here, however, it is worth listing them in the order in which they are found folded up in the bottom of carton J428 in the Archives nationales de France in Paris.[105]

> *No. 15* is a large piece of parchment preserving two discrete notarized documents. The first, shorter, text is properly dated 11 April 1310 and summarizes how twenty-one masters of theology condemned extracts from an unnamed book. The second, longer, text is dated 31 May and gives the final sentences of both Marguerite Porete and Guiard of Cressonessart.

> *No. 16* is the most complex document. Another large piece of parchment, it contains a single notarized document that reflects several earlier stages of composition. It relates how theologians and canon lawyers were called together in March 1310 to consider the case of Guiard of Cressonessart and then incorporates a decision by the canon lawyers, dated 3 April, that Guiard may be considered a recalcitrant heretic. The entire narrative, however, is preserved within a framework added when this actual document was copied and notarized, 4 October 1310. Thus this document mentions the earliest stage of the trial (March) but may have been the last to be actually copied (October) in its current form.

> *No. 17* is an unnotarized copy of the same 3 April decision by the canonists that is incorporated into no. 16.

> *No. 18* is an unnotarized copy of the canonists' 9 April decision on the case of Guiard of Cressonessart after he decided to testify. This document contains our only summary of what Guiard actually said under interrogation.

> *No. 19* is an unnotarized copy of the canonists' decision concerning Marguerite Porete, dated 3 April and nearly exactly parallel to no. 17 on Guiard of Cressonessart.

> *No. 19bis,* dated 9 May, is an unnotarized copy of the further decision by the canonists that, in light of her whole history, Marguerite Porete may be considered a relapsed heretic.

At various points in the book, the production of each of these texts will be the subject of analysis. I hope that one of the contributions made here is a clearer understanding of these documents in and of themselves—how, when, and why they were produced and copied, what choices they reflect, what preparatory stages they reveal, what perspectives they privilege, and (very often) what problems they attempt to hide with their silences.[106] Moreover, I hope that the English translations in Appendix A will make this evidence more readily usable to students and nonspecialists and will allow readers to decide for themselves how persuasive they find the interpretations advanced here.

Plan of the Book

My analysis of this evidence takes the form of a chronological narrative. The first three chapters set up the trial analysis by investigating events before 1308. Chapter 1 gleans what little information survives about the lives of Marguerite and Guiard before their first encounters with church authorities. Chapter 2 pieces together Marguerite's story from the time she first was arrested by the bishop of Cambrai until she was turned over to William of Paris. Chapter 3 then turns to the inquisitor and presents the first substantial study of William's career up to 1308. The next four chapters focus on the trial itself. Chapter 4 examines William of Paris's first legal moves and the intervention of the masters of canon law from March to 3 April 1310. Chapter 5 is devoted to Guiard of Cressonessart, examining in detail his testimony and the canonists' response of 9 April. Chapter 6 focuses on the masters of theology who were asked to weigh in on extracts from Marguerite's book on 11 April. Chapter 7 centers on the 9 May decision by the canonists, the 31 May sentencing, and the executions of the next day. The book concludes with three brief epilogues: the first traces the end of William of Paris's career; the second focuses on Arnau of Vilanova's intriguing "Letter to Those Wearing the Leather Belt"; and the third steps back to consider the way these trials affected decisions made at the Council of Vienne and beyond.

Thus the book follows several narratives simultaneously as it shifts from the perspective of Guiard and Marguerite to that of William of

Paris and others involved in the trial. Running throughout, however, is my primary argument that Guiard of Cressonessart and Marguerite Porete were caught up in a highly contingent series of events, where their own choices combined with the specific political situation and limited legal options of their inquisitor to drive them toward perpetual incarceration and the stake. The constraining factor in these individual choices was the political context at Paris by 1310. Guiard and Marguerite were processed by Philip IV's political machine, where all stories and all fights were ultimately about royal power. The individuals entered this machine through their own choices but were then ground down by the larger forces at play. Marguerite was drawn in from Hainaut and eventually executed not so much for her ideas as for her stubborn refusal to submit to episcopal and inquisitorial demands for obedience; in Philip IV's Paris a rebellious "heretic" was an affront to the crown and could be treated only as part of a wider contest for political power. Guiard threw himself into the gears of the machine in an attempt to announce his own rival eschatological narrative, but there was room for only one defender of the "true adherents of the Lord" in Philip the Fair's kingdom.

In a certain sense, William of Paris also paid for his close association with the royal court. He was both the willing instrument and the convenient scapegoat (in papal eyes) for the most brazen of Philip's moves, the attack on the Templars. But by the time he was conducting Marguerite and Guiard's trials, William had been sidelined from the grand events of the Templar affair and may have been something of a liability in Philip's ongoing negotiations with Clement V. His extremely careful handling of the trials of Marguerite and Guiard, I shall argue, resulted from this weakened position and his need to reestablish a creditable position for himself as a papal inquisitor at Paris. Certainly there can be no moral equivalency between the man who read out the sentence on 31 May 1310 and those who suffered its punishments. Nevertheless, William too may have found that his initial choices led him toward a diminishing range of options as the trial gathered momentum in the spring of 1310. In this sense all three historical actors at the center of this story were swept up in the ideological juggernaut that a decade of unrelenting royal propaganda had set in motion.

CHAPTER 1

Background to a Beguine, Becoming an Angel

One of the trial documents from 1310 refers to Guiard of Cressonessart as "arising from himself," presumably as a way of attributing his "heresy" to his own stubborn imagination. The description seems strangely appropriate, however, given how little is known about the lives of Marguerite Porete and Guiard of Cressonessart before they came into conflict with ecclesiastical authority. But the bits and pieces of evidence that survive do establish certain facts and help to contextualize the religious, social, and political settings from which Marguerite and Guiard emerged.[1]

Background to a Beguine

The *Mirror of Simple Souls* conveys the sense that its author felt herself to have passed from youth to maturity,[2] so a reasonable estimate might put Marguerite's birth sometime near 1260. The trial records state unequivocally that she came from the county of Hainaut. More specifically, by the time her book was burned she almost certainly lived in or near the town of Valenciennes. For one thing, Guido of Collemezzo, the bishop of Cambrai, chose to burn her book there (rather than in the city of Cambrai itself), probably out of a desire to make its condemnation known to inhabitants of her hometown. A Franciscan who

commented on her book at around this time probably came from Qué-
rénaign, a mere eight kilometers south of Valenciennes.[3] Just as significant may be the mounting evidence that this area was an early center
for the circulation of manuscript copies of the *Mirror*.[4] Finally, Jean
Gerson was probably thinking of the author of the *Mirror of Simple
Souls* when he referred to "Marie of Valenciennes" in 1401.[5] Though the
latter is a late and secondhand indication, Gerson presumably had some
basis for employing this designation.

Valenciennes was located on the Escaut (or Scheldt) River just at
the point where it became navigable for medieval boats heading to the
North Sea.[6] It is today a French city, but the medieval political context
was more complex. The Escaut marked the border between the counties of Flanders and Hainaut; the former was theoretically dependent
on the kingdom of France, and the latter on the empire. However the
Ostrevant—a little sliver of territory on the left bank of the Escaut—
was controlled by the counts of Hainaut after 1257. What makes these
details relevant is the fact that Valenciennes actually straddled the Escaut. Most of the medieval city was on the right bank and hence part
of Hainaut and presumably an imperial city. Yet the left bank section
of Valenciennes could be considered part of the Ostrevant, and thus
theoretically on the "French" side of the Escaut. This same river was
also an ecclesiastical boundary, with only the right bank pertaining to
the bishop of Cambrai and the left to Arras.[7] Valenciennes thus was a
potential trouble spot where larger questions of political control could
be fought out. The French crown had involved itself in disputes between
Flanders and Hainaut over Valenciennes and the Ostrevant since the
days of Louis IX; in the early fourteenth century this was just the kind
of area where Philip IV was seeking to impose his authority during his
long wars with Flanders.[8]

If Marguerite's geographic origins are fairly certain, nothing is
known about her family. The epithet "Porete" does not tell us anything
concrete.[9] Although this last name does show up in both the Low
Countries and Paris at this time, in Marguerite's case it was probably a
recent nickname, not an indication of deep family affiliation, since the
trial documents usually refer to her as "Marguerite called Porete" and
not simply "Marguerite Porete."[10] In Old French *poret* meant "leek,"
and figuratively could refer to any object of little value, in phrases such

as "that's not worth a *poret.*"[11] Perhaps the nickname therefore tells us something about Marguerite's self-image or reputation, consistent with her apparent reference to herself as a onetime "mendicant creature" in the *Mirror.*[12]

There are, however, reasons to suspect that Marguerite emerged from the urban patriciate (the wealthy and politically active urban class), if not the lower aristocracy.[13] First, the *Mirror of Simple Souls* projects an image of self-consciously aristocratic haughtiness, though transferred into spiritual imagery.[14] Second, she seems to have enjoyed impressive access to resources. She must have been able to pay for writing materials and perhaps scribes in order to copy and circulate her writings. Moreover, it has recently been argued that she may have owned a book of hours, a possession generally appropriate to the upper classes.[15] More broadly, the *Mirror* reflects a deep familiarity with the vocabulary of courtly romance.[16] While nothing prevented literate people of any background from reading such material, or illiterate people from hearing and absorbing it, there is still a distinct projection of upper-class tastes in Marguerite's brand of *mystique courtoise.*[17] Finally, her access to important churchmen such as Godfrey of Fontaines (to be investigated in the next chapter) indicates that she may have enjoyed a certain social standing.

Related to the question of status is that of education.[18] Authorship of the *Mirror* is self-evident testimony to her high degree of vernacular literacy. There is no doubt that Marguerite was also familiar with secular romance literature: she refers in the *Mirror* to the *Romance of Alexander,* she probably knew the popular *Romance of the Rose,* and recent work has shown her familiarity with a rich body of trouvère songs, and perhaps Chrétien de Troyes.[19] More controversial is the question of Marguerite's level of Latin literacy. Her modern editors have found echoes of authors including Augustine, Bernard of Clairvaux, Bonaventure, Richard of Saint-Victor, William of Saint-Thierry, and pseudo-Dionysius in her book.[20] Although some of these authors may have been known to Marguerite at second hand, and some were being translated into French by the end of the thirteenth century, it is at least possible that she encountered them in the original Latin. The *Grandes chroniques de France* labeled her a beguine "clergesse," which points in the direction of (at least perceived) Latin literacy.[21] Similarly, the

Mirror contains numerous biblical echoes (the majority from the New Testament).[22] Again, some of these probably entered Marguerite's vocabulary through liturgical repetitions, sermons in the vernacular, and perhaps personal conversations with churchmen; yet it is also possible that she had a basic familiarity with the Latin Bible.

Exactly how Marguerite acquired her learning is unclear. Contacts with a larger beguine community *(béguinage)* suggest one explanation, since many did offer instruction to young girls, sometimes including Latin and Bible study as well as vernacular reading and writing.[23] For example, a school existed from at least 1267 at St. Elisabeth's in Valenciennes,[24] and in the fifteenth century (admittedly late evidence) boys and girls received education there, with both male instructors and beguines teaching reading and writing, including Latin grammar.[25]

This possibility of ties to a beguinage raises the question of just what the trial records and other contemporary witnesses meant when they labeled Marguerite a *beguina*.[26] The French term *béguine* or the Latin *beguina* generally designated an unmarried laywoman leading a devout religious life in the world, but it could convey a wide range of fluid and overlapping meanings. In the larger communities of the Low Countries (modern Netherlands, Belgium, and a part of northern France), such laywomen began to gather into new kinds of pious communities in the first half of the thirteenth century. These *beguinae* (the Latin plural) could live in individual houses or could gather together in medium-sized convent-style arrangements or in larger "court" settings that had their own church and even formed their own parishes.[27] Life in any of these forms of beguinage "offered single women of all ages an opportunity to lead a religious life of contemplation and prayer while earning a living as laborers or teachers."[28]

Beguines had both supporters and detractors among churchmen from their very beginnings. But while early thirteenth-century sympathizers provided practical care and textual promotion, by the last quarter of the thirteenth century many churchmen increasingly regarded them with growing skepticism and suspicion, as unclassifiable elements that destabilized the boundary between lay and religious life and spread confusion with their unauthorized preaching and teaching.[29] The most often cited example is the Franciscan Gilbert of Tournai, who complained in 1274 that beguines needed to be regulated or suppressed because of the dangers inherent in their unsupervised reading, translating, and interpreting of Scripture and theological texts.[30] The hostility that Marguerite and her writings encountered certainly fits into this pattern.

The trial documents not only label Marguerite a *beguina* but also suggest her ties to a wider circle of semireligious (asserting her stubborn efforts to circulate her book "to simple people, beghards and others"). Moreover, the *Mirror of Simple Souls* reveals familiarity with organized beguine life.[31] It would therefore seem safe to refer to Marguerite as a beguine from the vicinity of Valenciennes.[32] Some scholars, however, have questioned whether she was "really" a beguine at all. One version of this argument was based on a circular logic that echoed that of her eventual accusers: since churchmen were troubled by the idea of wandering, unstable, "false," beguines, whom they accused of circulating suspect ideas, and since Marguerite was accused of circulating suspect ideas, then she must have been a wandering, morally questionable, unregulated woman—and thus not a "real" beguine like those in more stable communities.[33] More recently, other scholars have made the related claim that since Marguerite's accusers meant the term *beguina* in a hostile and pejorative sense, it cannot be taken at face value.[34] Still others have thought that Marguerite's writings somehow lack the essential qualities of beguine literature, so she must not have been a proper beguine.[35] All of these strands of doubt can also cite a statement in the *Mirror of Simple Souls* itself that includes beguines among those who will say that the author errs.[36]

These arguments, however, all contain their own flaws. For instance, there is in fact no evidence to indicate that Marguerite was a wanderer.[37] And the idea that *beguina* had become such a loaded term of opprobrium as to render its use by hostile authorities meaningless is an oversimplification: it has recently been pointed out that clerics and university masters at the very time and place of Marguerite's trial portrayed beguines in a variety of ways, from models of humility, piety, and visionary mysticism to charlatans and arrogant spiritual rebels.[38] Indeed, if there was one city in which beguines had unusual claims to respectability, it was the Paris that Marguerite's judges inhabited. The several hundred beguines living in the *grand béguinage* there enjoyed a special veneer of respectability because their house had been founded (before 1264) by the revered Louis IX and continued to be supported by the royal family over the next decades.[39] Indeed, practical care for this community was assigned by the crown to the canons of the Sainte-Chapelle (a royal institution founded by Louis IX to house precious relics of the Passion),[40] university masters routinely preached there, and Parisian Dominicans provided pastoral care as early as 1301.[41] Other Parisian beguines, many of them successful workers in the luxury silk trade, lived in scattered individual houses in the university quarter.[42] So when Parisian churchmen called a woman a *beguina,* they spoke from firsthand knowledge of the possible spectrum of beguine living arrangements and were familiar with a range of positive and negative images of these women. Finally, there is no reason why one beguine could not fear that other beguines would misunderstand her,[43] and the idea that Marguerite's writings do not satisfactorily fit some modern definition of what beguine-authored texts "should" be is too self-evidently problematic to require refutation.

More fundamentally, the very fluidity of the label renders moot an argument about whether Marguerite was "really" a beguine. In contemporary common parlance, the word could say as much about a layperson's religious self-presentation as about her relationship to a formally constituted community. In this looser sense, a beguine was someone who claimed special contact with God, acting and dressing in ways that set her apart. But depending on the observer's perspective these claims to divine knowledge could be true or false, and ostentatiously pious actions and dress could be sincere or deceiving. A *beguina* could thus be a woman of saintly life or a false prophet. Just as Nicole Bériou asserts for the terms *preudhomme* and *béguin,* being a *beguina* was a "way of existing in society . . . a way of being named and therefore judged by others."[44] As a status, it rested on a woman's public presentation but existed also in the mind of the beholder. Thus, when trial documents and chronicle entries labeled Marguerite Porete a *beguina,* they were simply stating what seemed a readily apparent fact—that Marguerite was a laywoman offering a manifest self-projection of uncommon religious devotion while insinuating a special knowledge of God. She might have had some link to a beguine community, or she might not. The label in its context is neutral on the question.[45]

How likely is it, then, that Marguerite had ties at some point to St. Elisabeth's, the main beguinage in Valenciennes? This was one of the best established court beguinages in the southern Low Countries, with origins stemming back to the bishop of Cambrai's approval of a hospital staffed by brothers and sisters in 1239. The community enjoyed Dominican support and consistent patronage from the local aristocracy.[46] At least by the 1260s (and probably earlier) multiple residences had developed around the original hospital, forming a larger court structure substantial enough to constitute its own parish. It is impossible to generalize about what kind of woman could have been a beguine there because living arrangements varied so widely, reflecting the varying economic backgrounds of the beguines and the differing vocations possible within the community.[47] A charitable fund to support poor beguines is attested from at least 1273,[48] but other beguines bought and sold land or left sizable bequests that demonstrate their high status.[49] A beguine named Elekine de Biausart, for example, left her house to her two sisters and her daughters Marie and Marguerite in 1254.[50] From the 1260s there was also a specific convent for the *béguines au sac,* who adopted a stricter form of voluntary poverty and followed their own rule,[51] while some beguines actually staffed the hospital and lived communally.[52] One early document refers to those "who live in the hospital and other religious women called beguines who lived in the same street and in the neighborhood *[voisinage]* who follow the path of a religious life."[53] All of these women were part of St. Elisabeth's, but the differences between the various kinds of lives lived there (rich and poor, communal and individual, "truly" poor and voluntarily poor) are striking. There is no single profile of a beguine at St. Elisabeth's, and thus no reason to insist that Marguerite could not at some point have fit into this diverse community.

If, on the other hand, Marguerite did not have ties to St. Elisabeth's, the most likely alternative scenario would be to imagine her as a beguine living elsewhere in or near Valenciennes. Given patterns in neighboring towns and Valenciennes' status as the largest city in the region, there must have been other centers of beguine activity in other parishes not associated with St. Elisabeth's.[54] Virtually nothing is known about them, however, because the research in the local archives remains to be done.[55] Thus several of the most astute recent commentators on Marguerite's life have considered it most likely that she would have lived as an "independent" beguine in Valenciennes or a neighboring town.[56]

Becoming an Angel

Guiard of Cressonessart's background is even less clear than that of the woman he would eventually attempt to shield from inquisitorial persecution. Small clues, however, provide some interesting indications about his life. Most concretely, the trial documents refer to him as a *beguinus* (or once as a *pseudo-religious*) from the Diocese of Beauvais. Although English usage usually translates *beguinus* (or *beghardus*) with the more Germanic term *beghard,* it should be noted that contemporaries labeled Marguerite and Guiard with gendered versions of exactly the same Latin word: *beguina/beguinus.*

Male *beguini* have been much less studied in recent years than female *beguinae.*[57] Though beghards could form communities roughly analogous to female beguinages, in the course of the fourteenth century *beguinus* (*béguin* in French) increasingly became a catchall term referring to ardent or hypocritical zealots standing outside the organized church.[58] In the South of France, moreover, the labels *béguin/béguine* and *beguinus/beguina* were just beginning at this time to be applied to the dedicated lay followers of the Franciscan Peter of John Olivi (1248–98),[59] increasingly under suspicion for their beliefs on absolute poverty and its relationship to the imminent coming of Antichrist. Though Guiard was a northerner, his ideas were related to Peter's (as we shall see), which adds another level of possible meaning to the use of the term.[60] This label is thus in some ways even less definite than the feminine *beguina.* It can only be taken to indicate that Guiard's accusers understood him to be, like Marguerite, projecting a conspicuous image of spiritual superiority.

If Marguerite and Guiard were living lives similar enough to warrant the use of an identical label by their inquisitor, there were nevertheless some obvious differences between their backgrounds. The most striking may be Guiard's clerical status. At his final sentencing, it was ordered that he be stripped of clerical insignia before being imprisoned, which would indicate that at some point he had taken at least minor orders. This does not necessarily imply that he was ordained a priest; many men became clerks in order to study at a university or otherwise enjoy the protections of ecclesiastical status. But new evidence (cited in chapter 5) that Guiard was literate in Latin further indicates the reality of his clerical status. Apparently Guiard had at one point begun an education aimed at a career in the church but had instead gravitated toward a life that ecclesiastics perceived as that of a *beguinus.*[61]

Guiard was also more mobile than Marguerite. Since the trial documents identify him as from the Diocese of Beauvais, he must truly have come from the hamlet of Cressonessart, or Cressonsacq as it is known today.[62] This little village, situated forty kilometers east of the cathedral town of Beauvais and some ninety kilometers north of Paris, had a recorded population of 215 in 1303 and still has fewer than 400 inhabitants today.[63] Guiard's roots were thus farther south than Marguerite's and were located more firmly in the Capetian heartlands. Yet Guiard's own testimony shows that he traveled fairly widely, substantiating other evidence—much of it hostile—that *beguini* did sometimes lead itinerant lives.[64]

In 1310, when he finally consented to explain his self-conception to his inquisitor, Guiard stated that he had realized approximately four years earlier that he had been given the office of "Angel of Philadelphia." Since he revealed that he had experienced this flash of insight while in the lower chapel of the Sainte-Chapelle in Paris, by 1306 he must have traveled from his native area to the Île-de-France. He further confessed that he had risked his safety on behalf of the true adherents of the Lord in Reims by opposing the Franciscans and Dominicans there before similarly exposing himself to danger on behalf of Marguerite Porete in Paris. He gives no overt dating for these events, but since it seems clear that he took up his active mission of defending the Lord's adherents only after 1306, he must have traveled from Paris to Reims and back again between 1306 and the fall of 1308.[65] Moreover, Guiard testified that the quintessential representatives of the current age of the church were "runners" who had given up everything to uphold evangelic rigor. This description sounds as though Guiard pictured himself as following an apostolic model of itinerant poverty.

His reference to the lower chapel of the Sainte-Chapelle deserves further attention. This was the marvelous chapel built by Louis IX between 1239 and 1248 to hold the crown of thorns and other relics newly purchased from the emperor of Constantinople (mentioned above because its canons were given practical care of the Parisian grand beguinage). The upper chapel is the stunningly beautiful space that still draws tourists today with its glowing stained glass and magical ambience. The lower chapel now (rather disappointingly) contains a gift shop, but it constituted an important liturgical site in the early fourteenth century. There is some evidence for how and when the lower chapel was used—for instance, on Pentecost, the Feast of the Dedication (April 26), and Maundy Thursday for specific rituals involving ecclesiastics, "the people," and even the king. But on the whole, "the extent to which the upper and lower chapels were used as distinct spaces, and for whom, remains unclear."[66]

What *is* clear is that the Sainte-Chapelle was the preeminent site linking Christ and the Passion to the French monarchy. As recent scholarship has shown, at certain points in time it would not have been unusual to find a large, mixed crowd of pilgrims gathered there. In addition to its function as a private chapel, the Sainte-Chapelle was a site where the royal court could display its self-conception as a divinely ordained and saintly family. Thus multiple papal and episcopal letters offered indulgences to pilgrims who visited on various feast days.[67] For instance in 1298 and 1300 indulgences for visiting on the feast day of the newly canonized St. Louis (25 August) were added, and then in 1300 and 1306 for the translation of his relics (17 May, or the Tuesday after Ascension).[68] It is interesting that St. Louis and his relics were the new attraction at about the time that Guiard's revelation must have occurred. Yet perhaps the most likely time for him to have found himself at the Sainte-Chapelle in 1306 was during Easter week, when a particular stress was laid on liturgical processions that brought king and people together.[69] Indeed, since Guiard testified on 9 April 1310, his reference to "four years earlier or more," if taken to imply any exactitude, would indicate a date very close to Holy Week 1306 (Easter Sunday fell on 3 April in 1306), a time of heightened eschatological awareness as the faithful contemplated the mystery of the Resurrection.

The Sainte-Chapelle was a monument to the ideals of Capetian sanctity, as the juxtaposition of the relics of St. Louis with the crown of thorns demonstrates. Guiard, however, absorbed the Christological dimensions of this highly charged space and refashioned them in his own idiosyncratic manner. The flash of insight he experienced there caused him to imagine himself, not the French monarchs, in direct relation to Christ. In a certain sense it was this act of apocalyptic reimagining that set him on a collision course with the royal confessor, William of Paris.

Guiard does not say whether he formed part of a group that day in the Sainte-Chapelle, but he did, apparently, have associates or even followers. At least when his interrogators asked him if those who wore tabards were "of his society," he responded that only those were who also wore a long tunic and a leather belt, particularly the latter. He also stated that there were others who knew of his calling, and he spoke of warning some of these associates not to take on a new habit without proper approval. At least in his own mind, Guiard was not a lone wanderer but a leader of a spiritual movement.[70]

Guiard was thus a *beguinus,* probably in minor orders, who traveled (at least) within the geographic triangle formed by Cressonessart, Reims, and Paris. In spite of his ties to other like-minded men, this description makes him sound like a marginal figure. Intriguingly, however, it is possible that Guiard actually came from the seigniorial family of Cressonessart, which had been particularly tied to the Capetians for over a century. Dreux I of Cressonessart was an associate of Louis VII; his son Dreux II participated in the Fourth Crusade; and his grandson Thibault I of Cressonessart fought in the Albigensian wars.[71] Indeed, the family's control over their domain continued up into the fourteenth century: Thibault II appears in documents from the 1240s and 1250s; Anselm seigneur of Cressonessart is documented in 1281, and two more Thibaults show up as lords of Cressonessart in 1286 and 1317.[72] The family also rose to considerable eminence within the church. Thibault I's brother Robert of Cressonessart was bishop of Beauvais from 1237 to 1248 and died in Cyprus after taking the cross as part of Louis IX's crusade.[73] This pattern was repeated in the next generation as Thibault II's brother Robert became bishop of Senlis in 1260, remaining in this position to at least 1282 (when he testified at the inquiry into Louis IX's sanctity).[74] Moreover, in Paris, Agnes (of Mauvoisin), widow of Dreux II of Cressonessart, was an important early patron of the Cistercian abbey of Saint-Antoine-des-Champs, making substantial bequests to that community beginning as early as 1206 before entering the community herself in 1214 and perhaps later serving as abbess.[75] Indeed, her descendants continued to patronize this important house for generations.[76]

Unfortunately, no documentary evidence indicates whether the "de Cressonessart" label reflects Guiard's membership in this seigniorial family or merely his place of origin. A century earlier, such a label would almost certainly have reflected noble status. But it was just at the end of the thirteenth century that Frenchmen systematically began to turn names of villages into lasting family names.[77] Still, there is at least a possibility that Guiard's origins lay with some collateral branch of the noble family—a possibility again enhanced by the Latin education revealed by his testimony.[78] Moreover, such a background would fit well with the audacity and sense of mission displayed in his eventual public opposition to the inquisitor William of Paris.[79]

Nothing more is known about Guiard until his dramatic attempt to come to Marguerite Porete's defense in 1308. The trial documents and the text of the *Mirror of Simple Souls,* however, provide tantalizing clues about Marguerite's experiences in the first years of the fourteenth century. It is to this evidence that we now turn.

CHAPTER 2

Seven Churchmen and a Beguine

Marguerite Porete has often been portrayed as a solitary figure whose stubborn disdain for churchmen set her on a certain path to the stake. The evidence, however, reveals another picture. Although the hostility of some ecclesiastics certainly contributed to her arrest, trial, and death, the positive reactions of others are also well attested. This chapter will trace her encounters with churchmen in the decade before 1308. Two bishops of Cambrai, a bishop of Châlons-sur-Marne, and an inquisitor of Lorraine were among those whose opposition led to her eventual incarceration, while a Franciscan, a Cistercian, and a secular master of theology were willing to praise her book. A close examination of Marguerite's interactions with these seven men reveals something of the mental framework within which she must have conceptualized her Parisian trial. By the time she was in the custody of William of Paris in 1308, she would have been well aware of the danger that some churchmen saw in her writings. But she also had good reason to know that more positive interpretations were possible as well.

An Italian Bishop in Cambrai

The first of the seven churchmen was Guido of Collemezzo, bishop of Cambrai. His burning of Marguerite's book is, in fact, the earliest concrete event that can be documented for her career. Recent work on

Guido allows some reasonable inferences about how he would have perceived a book such as the *Mirror of Simple Souls,* and a close reading of the evidence reveals unexpected nuances in Marguerite's own response to his condemnation.

A study by Pascal Montaubin has shed new light on Bishop Guido's background and political loyalties.[1] Guido of Collemezzo came from an Italian family, based in the Diocese of Anagni, that had produced a string of successful churchmen, most notably Peter of Collemezzo, archbishop of Rouen and then cardinal before his death in 1253. Our Guido of Collemezzo is probably the same *magister* who taught canon law at the university of Naples and in 1276 was named a counselor to Charles of Anjou, the king of Sicily. It is certain that he was well connected to the papal court by 1290 and enjoyed the patronage of the Franciscan cardinal Matthew of Acquasparta. Like others in his family before him, he accumulated ecclesiastical preferments in a French context, being named treasurer of Thérouanne in the 1270s, then by 1290 archdeacon of Arras, canon of Paris, and canon and treasurer of Noyon. In spite of his French positions and prebends, he seems to have remained primarily in Italy through 1295, since he is found acting as notary of Boniface VIII's chancery in June of that year.[2]

Boniface VIII promoted Guido to the See of Cambrai on 21 October 1296. In making this appointment, Boniface was imposing his own man against the will of the cathedral chapter, which had tried to elect a local candidate, Gerard of Relingues. After several months of wrangling, Guido was consecrated bishop of Cambrai sometime between 21 December 1296 and 1 January 1297, and arrived in his diocese by 26 July 1297. (Gerard was mollified by being given the diocese of Metz in April 1297.) The arrival of an "outsider" such as Guido was a particularly dramatic shift, since his predecessor had been William of Avesnes, brother of the Count of Hainaut. Guido was in fact part of a sizable Italian contingent at Cambrai whose orientation and loyalty was toward Boniface VIII and Rome.[3] Guido was not politically foolish enough to present himself as an overt opponent of Philip IV, but there is no doubt that he was Boniface VIII's protégé.[4]

Guido needed whatever political skills he possessed to manage his new diocese. On an ecclesiastical map, the Diocese of Cambrai was subject to the archbishop of Reims and therefore within a French orbit. Politically, however, it lay almost entirely in imperial territory, covering both the county of Cambrai (where the bishop was also count) and the larger county of Hainaut. Thus Guido occupied a precarious perch between the counties of Flanders, Hainaut, and Artois, balanced (as it were) on the line between the Empire and the Kingdom of France. In addition to negotiating the difficult waters of Philip IV's battles with Boniface VIII, Guido's hands were full on a local level, as a long-running contest between the bourgeoisie and the cathedral chapter of Cambrai culminated in the years 1298–1313. In dealing with open revolts of 1298, 1302, and 1305, Guido seems to have played peacemaker between town and chapter, while protecting church privileges. One intriguing episode in this battle may be particularly relevant: on 29 June 1304, Guy was forced to rescind his previous banishment from Cambrai of a beguine named Marion de Fayt, daughter of Gillon de Fayt (chaplain of the church of Notre-Dame of Cambrai), after admitting that her case pertained to the chapter's jurisdiction rather than his own.[5] Though Marion's offense is not specified, and there is no way to link this episode directly to Guido's handling of Marguerite Porete, it does show that at least one other controversial beguine drew his public disapproval.

As a canon lawyer and apostolic notary, Guido's outlook was probably more administrative and legalistic than theological.[6] His likely attitude toward an author such as Marguerite may be inferred from a legal reference book, known as the *Summa Innocenti abbreviati*, that he wrote before he became bishop.[7] This work was a simplified summary of Pope Innocent IV's *Apparatus* (ca. 1251), itself a commentary on Gregory IX's authoritative collection of canon law known as the *Liber extra*.[8] Guido's book was thus a contribution to the long tradition of academic commentary on church law, intended to clarify scholars' understanding of an ever-growing body of papal decrees. Given the number of surviving manuscripts and their geographic dispersion, this text must have been fairly popular.[9]

All known manuscripts of this *Summa* carry a prologue, in which Guido explained why he thought it necessary to offer this short guide to Innocent's authoritative canon law commentary:

I, Guido of Collemezzo, treasurer of Noyon,[10] have often considered Pope Innocent IV's published *Apparatus on the Decretals* to be of great profit to experts. Three reasons can be stated to all, however, why it might be rather unhelpful to some people: first, because in such a treasury of knowledge the amount of material is often detrimental to beginners; second, because it collects such a diversity of opinions that many people do not know in which one Innocent's approved opinion actually lies; third, because he has "ploughed the seashore" [i.e., wasted his time] by writing materials extraneous to their own headings, since the young with their weak memories will not have gotten to know [the collection] through protracted study. And therefore, after examining this [collection] as diligently as I could, I was eager to compose the present book, in which no material would appear unnecessarily [and] the true opinion of Innocent is always laid bare, with superfluous things cut away. And thus all the things which have been approved by the same Innocent, but are scattered across the larger volume, are rightly situated [here] under the appropriate titles.[11]

Guido here displayed a striking determination to stick to the most straightforward presentation of legal truths. Even when considering an ordered, approved, and learned legal commentary—composed by a pope no less—Guido still feared the dangers inherent in exposing the impressionable minds of students to controversial ideas. The safest course was to specify the approved ecclesiastical stance on any given point of canon law while cutting away all the clutter of contrasting opinions.

Though these ideas were expressed well before Guido encountered Marguerite Porete, they contextualize his eventual response to her work. If he feared the effects of a pope presenting several possible legal interpretations, Marguerite's mocking debates between Holy Church the Little and Perfect Love would surely have outraged him. More fundamentally, Guido was simply not the man to read a daring, controversial work with a sympathetic eye—let alone one written in French by a laywoman. Everything about Guido's orientation predisposed him to be suspicious of a book such as the *Mirror*. As a recent arrival from Italy, he can have had little experience with written expressions of beguine spirituality;[12] as a canon lawyer he was probably inclined to see problems in terms of the proper application of ecclesiastical authority; as an embattled administrator he must have had limited patience with anything perceived as a challenge.

We have only the briefest of indications as to when, why, and how Marguerite came to Guido's attention. It must have been between summer 1297 (when Guido arrived in his new diocese) and autumn 1305 (there is no evidence for his presence in Cambrai after October of that year). Further details are found in two terse passages in Marguerite's later trial documents. This is of course a version of events supplied by her eventual inquisitor, William of Paris. Although William states that his facts are based on the "depositions of many witnesses," they obviously form a highly selective account and must be used with care.[13] In later chapters it will be necessary to determine what this account reveals about William's own agenda. Here the bare outline of his narrative can be extracted to attempt to reconstruct these early events.

The first document (AN J428 no. 19bis) records the advice given by a team of canon lawyers to William on 9 May 1310. As a preamble to this advice, the canonists first related the facts as William had supplied them. According to this narrative, Marguerite "had composed a certain book containing heresies and errors, which had been publicly and solemnly condemned and burned by order of the reverend father lord Guido, former bishop of Cambrai."[14] The second account (AN J428 no. 15b) is found in Marguerite's final sentence, which William read out on 31 May 1310. Addressing Marguerite directly, it states that "you composed a certain pestiferous book containing heresy and error. For this cause the said book was condemned by Guido of blessed memory, then bishop of Cambrai, and by his order burned at Valenciennes, in your presence, publicly and openly."[15]

Among the things these passages do not state is exactly how Guido became aware of Marguerite and her book. There is no evidence that Guido was an active heresy hunter, so perhaps Marguerite and her book were thrust upon him in some way. Her teachings may have been denounced by a hostile churchman, for instance. But it is also quite possible that Marguerite deliberately sought the bishop's attention, given the evidence (discussed below) for subsequent actions of exactly this kind. Nor do we know the specific reasons why Guido found this book theologically objectionable—what "damnable material" "jumped out" at him (to paraphrase his fears about the effects of Innocent's *Apparatus*) is nowhere recorded.

Though Guido's actions are better documented than his thoughts, there are questions here too. It is clear that he forced Marguerite to watch her own book burn—perhaps she even had to consign it to the flames with her own hands.[16] But was Guido himself present in Valenciennes at this moment? It seems probable, but the texts only say the burning took place at his orders. Did he even ever meet with Marguerite face to face? Again, it seems likely that he would have interrogated her personally, but this is not spelled out, and the task could have been delegated to a subordinate. And if there was such a meeting, did it take place in Valenciennes, or was she first detained in Cambrai and only then sent to Valenciennes for the book burning? Neither document provides answers to these questions.

Guido's warnings to Marguerite, however, were clear. Returning to the same two documents, the first (J428 no. 19bis) records that "by a letter of the aforesaid bishop it was ordered that if she should again attempt by word or in writing any things like those contained in the book, he was condemning her and relinquishing her to be judged by secular justice."[17] In the second (J428 no. 15b), William of Paris recounted, "You were expressly prohibited by this bishop, under pain of excommunication, from composing or having again such a book, or using it or one like it. The same bishop added and expressly stated in a certain letter sealed with his seal that if you should again use the aforesaid book, or if you should attempt again by word or in writing those things that were contained in it, he was condemning you as heretical and relinquishing you to be judged by secular justice."[18] Thus Marguerite was forbidden not only from circulating her book again but from writing or speaking about the ideas it contained. The order did not entirely prohibit her from writing again on any subject,[19] but obviously any future authorial activity would run a grave risk of being perceived as returning to the ideas that had been condemned in her book.

These warnings in themselves reveal further interesting details. First, there is the existence of a formal, sealed letter. Such a document has never been found, either in the surviving trial records or in the various archives of the Diocese of Cambrai. Nevertheless, there is no reason to doubt that Guido did put his warning to Marguerite in writing. For one thing, although William of Paris does not actually say he held it in his hands, he implies that he has had access to this letter. Moreover, there seem to be structural and grammatical traces left in William's Latin that indicate copying from another text, showing that he may have taken his version of Guido's warning directly from the letter in question.[20] Thus it seems that Guido kept a record of his condemnation and preserved it carefully enough that it was retrievable by William of Paris in 1310.

Second, Bishop Guido made a fine distinction here between condemning a book and condemning a person. Guido condemned and burned Marguerite's book as "heretical" and containing "errors." His threat was that if Marguerite showed herself to be persistent in flouting ecclesiastical authority he would take the separate step of condemning her in her person as a contumacious heretic, which would likely result in her death at the hands of the secular authorities. The wording—at least as William of Paris later related it—implies that Guido considered this to be a sentence that would automatically take effect if Marguerite was found to have disobeyed his orders. This rather delicate phrasing, however, does not state that Marguerite herself was personally labeled a heretic at this time.[21] Indeed, the single most striking thing about this encounter is that Marguerite walked away from it personally unharmed. Her release indicates that she must have shown some level of cooperation and expressed contrition and willingness to obey in the future—otherwise she would surely have faced personal excommunication and condemnation. Even if she had been convicted of heresy but reconciled through sincere penance, some kind of punishment would probably have been imposed (imprisonment, pilgrimage, wearing of distinctive markings). The lack of any indication of such punishment suggests that she was able to convince the bishop that she herself was not a heretic.

This moment has not been fully factored into most accounts of Marguerite's career. Her later refusal to cooperate with her inquisitor has become the enduring image with which historians evoke her resistance to ecclesiastical authority. At this point, however, there can be no question of her having remained mute. She must have given Guido some reason to believe that she had learned her lesson.[22] As to why she might have adopted a contrite attitude at this juncture, it is possible that she was simply intimidated or frightened. She may have been subjected to harsh imprisonment or other pressure as Guido mulled over her case, though there is no specific evidence one way or the other. But it is also possible that she was temporarily willing to reassess the legitimacy of her writing and ideas in the face of a bishop's censure.

Polishing the Mirror

If Marguerite had indeed promised not to recopy her book or write further in the same vein, she broke that promise in short order. The same two trial documents continue (William's version of) the story, though again only in the most laconic language. The first (J428 no. 19bis) tells it this way:

> And this same inquisitor [William] also found that she acknowledged in court—once in the presence of the inquisitor of Lorraine and once in the presence of the reverend father Lord Philip, then bishop of Cambrai—that after the aforesaid condemnation she had possessed the said book and others. This same inquisitor also found that the said Marguerite, after the condemnation of this book, had communicated the said book, one similar to it containing the same errors, to the reverend father Lord John, by the grace of God bishop of Châlons-sur-Marne, and not only to the said lord but to many other simple people—*begardis* and others—as a good book.[23]

The second (J428 no. 15b) accuses Marguerite in very similar terms:

> After all these things, against the said prohibition, you several times had and several times used the said book, as is evident from your acknowledgments, made not only in the presence of the inquisitor of Lorraine, but also in the presence of the reverend father and lord, Lord Philip, then bishop of Cambrai and now archbishop of Sens. After the aforesaid condemnation and burning, you even communicated the said book, as though good and licit, to the reverend father Lord John, bishop of Châlons-sur-Marne, and to certain other people, as is clear to us from the evident testimonies of many witnesses worthy of faith who have sworn concerning these matters in our presence.[24]

The most basic fact that emerges from this account is that Marguerite subsequently circulated her book not only to "simple" people, including "beghards," but also to at least one other bishop. This course of action must indicate that she hoped to find a more sympathetic response from other readers and generally sought a fresh appraisal of her work.

As part of this campaign, it is highly probable that during this period Marguerite made additions and revisions to her book. Indeed, if one imagines Marguerite recreating from memory the contents of a burned book, then common sense would suggest that the result would have to have been something significantly different from the earlier version. But even if—as seems likely—copies of her first text survived, the process of copying and circulating would tend to produce additions and changes. Specifically, scholars have generally agreed that at least the final seventeen chapters of the *Mirror,* those numbered 123–39 in the Middle French manuscript, were probably added on after Marguerite's first brush with authority.[25] The authorial perspective and tone of the *Mirror* change abruptly at this point. Starting with chapter 123, the text employs less dialogue, shifts dramatically to an authorial first-person voice, and at least initially focuses on devotional and hagiographic material that seems comparatively uncontroversial. If indeed these chapters were added after the book's first condemnation, then this material offers important evidence for Marguerite's reaction to adversity. Rather than accept the idea that her book contained "heresy" and "errors," she sought to clarify and restate her ideas for the benefit of those who had not understood her properly the first time.

After chapter 122, where the Latin word *Explicit* ("The End") is found in the Middle French manuscript, there is an additional heading (not a chapter title but a unique, larger section break) that reads, "Here follow some considerations for those who are in the state of being of forlorn-ness, who ask the way to the land of freedom." These seven considerations make up chapters 123–28, on the apostles, Mary Magdalene, John the Baptist, the Virgin Mary, her Son, the suffering of Christ, and the Seraphim. Quite in contrast to most of the *Mirror,* Marguerite here employs an undisguised first-person voice, while limiting herself to what is essentially biblical commentary. This little section ends with a summary recounting the seven considerations and then flows into chapters 130–32, where Marguerite tells of her own spiritual journey through the land of the forlorn and of the considerations she dwelled on at that point. Again in sharp contrast to the rest of the book, here Marguerite herself speaks to God, and God to her. At the culmination of the section, Marguerite relates three paradoxical questions posed to her by God: How would I fare if I knew he could be better pleased that I should love another better than him? . . . if it could be that he could love another better than me? . . . if it could be that he would will that someone other would love me better than he?" She states that as a result of her inability to answer, her will was "martyred," bringing her out of her spiritual "childhood."[26]

What is so distinct about these related chapters (123–32) is not just the emergence of the authorial voice but its use in addressing directly those who have not yet reached the state of the free, annihilated soul—that is, those who do not yet understand her message because they are yet "forlorn." The author has redirected her attention to those who might like to understand but have not done so as of yet. This sustained shift in emphasis is the best argument for seeing these additions as having been made after the book's initial condemnation.[27]

With these additions, Marguerite attempted to show an imagined audience of dubious churchmen that she understood the kind of straightforward relation to the saints and the Scriptures that they might like to see in a devout woman,[28] and she came as close as she ever did to arguing that her knowledge came at least in part through conversation with God. Thus she made more clear her credentials as both a textual scholar and a mystic.

To cap off this concluding section, however, Marguerite returned to some of her more audacious statements, as though she could not resist restating them after providing a new grounding in textual exegesis and spiritual experience. Dialogue returns briefly for chapter 133, with Marguerite reformulating some of her riskiest ideas. "Divine Love," for instance, here addresses the "Soul," saying: "I have found many who have perished in the affection of the spirit, through works of virtue, in the desire of a good will; but I have found few who were nobly forlorn, and I have found fewer still who are free without fail . . . such as this book asks for; that is, who have one single will which *fine amour* causes them to have. For *fine amour* causes one to have one love and one will, and so my will has become a non-will."[29] The offhand equation of "works of virtue" with those who "have perished" (or "are lost") was exactly the sort of passage that would ultimately be held against Marguerite.

At the very end of the book, two different endings survive, since chapters 137–39 show significant differences between the Middle English version on one hand and the French and Latin on the other. It may be that the earlier ending is the Middle English's brief "gloss of this song," which offers a surprisingly optimistic coda affirming that in spite of the paradoxical nature of the three questions that have martyred her will, God loves no one more than her (as chapter 136 has already asserted) and must be joined to her.[30] The French and Latin versions, by contrast, present three completely different chapters, entitled (in the Middle French) "How this soul is professed in her religion and how she has guarded well her rule," and then "How the soul returns to her first state of being," and "How nature is subtle in several ways." Particularly in the very last chapter, Marguerite slips into much darker tones, complaining of how "wily" nature is, lamenting, "I have experienced this to my great misfortune." Overall these last seventeen chapters are a confident culmination of the work; perhaps, however, at the very last, they offer a glimpse of Marguerite's fears that her tribulations were not over.

Seeking Support: A Friar, a Monk, and a Master

Having attempted to clarify her ideas, it was probably at this time that Marguerite showed her book to three further churchmen and recorded their positive assessments as a new epilogue to her book. Although the unique surviving French manuscript of the *Mirror* does not preserve this material, both the English and the Latin versions of the *Mirror of Simple Souls* carry a short section that cites the "witness" of the "clerks" who have read the book. The first of these men was a Franciscan "of great name, of a life of perfection," called John "of Querayn"; the second was Dom Franc, chanter of the Cistercian abbey of Villers; and the third was the well-known secular master of theology, Godfrey of Fontaines.[31] Marguerite's interaction with these men again provides essential evidence for reconstructing her mind-set in the years before her Parisian trial.

Geographically, these three all came from near Marguerite's base around Valenciennes. It is possible that she was randomly soliciting the support of whomever she could contact and that it just so happened that these were the three men who gave her the positive responses she sought. Upon close inspection, however, there is a logic to the sequence. For one thing, these consultations are listed in chronological order: "The first was" John, and "after him" Frank read it, and "after him" Godfrey. Each figure also gets a little farther removed from Valenciennes, and a little more exalted in status. The Franciscan John "of Querayn" was probably from Quérenaing, a village only some eight kilometers south of Valenciennes.[32] His home friary was very likely that of Valenciennes. Thus it makes perfect sense that Marguerite would show the work first to a local friar, perhaps one accustomed to providing pastoral care to beguines. If John was really "of great name," then perhaps Marguerite hoped his renown for a "life of perfection" would reflect well on her book.

From there, Marguerite sought the support of a senior Cistercian (the office of chanter ranked only behind those of abbot and prior) of Villers, a community some ninety kilometers distant from Valenciennes.[33] Invoking ties to Villers suggests that Marguerite saw herself as part of the tradition of holy beguines with which this abbey had long associated itself through authorship of *vitae*, liturgical veneration, and burial. Thirteenth-century women in this tradition included Ida of Nivelles, Marie of Oignies, and Juliana of Mont-Cornillon.[34] Indeed, the author of Ida of Nivelles's life, Goswin of Bossut, had been Franc's predecessor as chanter of Villers in the 1230s.[35] Thus, although neither John nor Franc is a well-known figure today, their positive assessments would have gone a great distance toward convincing Marguerite that her book could be appreciated by influential friars and monks. In turn, she could have expected that the inclusion of their praises would have inspired confidence in the readers who encountered them.

With these encouraging reactions secured, Marguerite then turned to the most imposing of her three referees. The praise of Godfrey of Fontaines must have been the glittering jewel in Marguerite's array, for Godfrey was among the best-known theologians of his age. If a master of his stature could praise the *Mirror*, then Marguerite might reasonably have hoped that Bishop Guido's condemnation was simply wrong.[36] Stemming from a noble family in the Liège region (some 170 kilometers east of Valenciennes), Godfrey held canonries in Liège, Paris, and Cologne and was regent master of theology at Paris from at least 1285 to approximately 1299.[37] After travels that probably included an extended stay in the Low Countries, he returned to his chair as regent master in Paris by 1303. The last secure documentary evidence for his life places him in Paris in February 1304, and the necrology of the Sorbonne records his date of death as 29 October, but without a year.[38] Thus he may have died as early as October 1304, but there is some reason to suspect that he lived until at least 1306, or even a few years longer.[39]

These dates offer only some wide parameters as to when this meeting would have taken place. It must have been after he assumed his chair as regent master at Paris around 1285 and before Marguerite was imprisoned in autumn 1308 (since it is unclear exactly when Godfrey died, this factor does not usefully narrow down the possibilities). The years between 1300 and 1303 might have offered the best opportunity, since this was the period when Godfrey seems to have been in the Low Countries most steadily. But his encounter with Marguerite could also have been during one of the many times that he must have passed through Valenciennes as he traveled between Liège and Paris.[40]

What was the nature of the interaction between Marguerite and her three "clerks," and what did the latter actually have to say about the *Mirror*? The only direct evidence comes from the report given by the author herself. This "record of the clerks that have read this book" is found in its fullest version in the Middle English version and given in a literal modern English translation here:[41]

> The first was a Franciscan of great name, of a life of perfection. He was called John "of Querayn", who said, "We send you this by these letters of love, receive them out of courtesy, for love prays this of you, to the worship of God and of them that have been made free of God, and to the profit of them that are not, but if God wills, may yet be." He said truly that this book is made by the Holy Ghost, and even if all the clerks of the world were to hear it, unless they understood it, that is to say, unless they have high spiritual feelings and this same working, they would not understand what it meant. And he prayed for the love of God that it be wisely kept, and that only a few should see it. And he said thus, that it was so high that he himself might not understand it.

And after him a Cistercian monk read it, called Dom Franc, chanter of the abbey of Villers. And he said that it was proved well by the Scriptures, that it is all truth that this book says.

And after him read it a master of divinity who is called master Godfrey of Fontaines. And he blamed it not, no more than did the others. But he said this, that he did not counsel that many should see it, because they might leave their own workings and follow this calling, to which they would never come; and so they might deceive themselves, for it is made by a spirit so strong and perceptive that there are but few such, or none. And therefore the soul never comes to divine usages until she has this usage, for all other human usages are beneath these usages. This is divine usage and none other but this.

For the peace of listeners was this proved. And for your peace we say it to you, for this seed should bear holy fruit to them that hear it and are worthy. Amen.[42]

We have only the author's word for what these men said or wrote to her, and she may have been highly selective in choosing what to include. Particularly in the case of her very brief treatment of Dom Franc, it is tempting to speculate that what she left out may have been much more extensive than what she put in. Nevertheless, it is unlikely that she falsified these comments outright, since circulating her book with misattributed praise would have surely been counterproductive.

There are clues here as to the different kinds of interactions that Marguerite had with these three men. She seems to have met and spoken with all three, yet their responses were not based simply on her oral description of her ideas, since she refers to the three clerks who have "read" the book. With John of Quérenaing, Marguerite apparently was able to quote from a letter that he had written back to her: He said, "We send you this, these letters of love; receive them out of courtesy."[43] With Dom Franc and Godfrey, by contrast, Marguerite states that they read the text, but she then gives only references to what they "said," and no sense of quoting from a written report. Though these details may be mere coincidence, they suggest that Franc and Godfrey read her book but then gave their responses in face-to-face meetings. Nor would such meetings be extraordinary events in this context: Mendicants routinely offered pastoral services to beguines and laypeople, the Cistercians of Villers were well known for associating with local religious women, and university masters often preached to beguines in cities such as Paris (Godfrey of Fontaines was demonstrably aware of such preaching).[44]

These responses are often described as "approvals." But in fact the Middle English version (more detailed and reliable than the Latin) uses the verb *proved,* not the noun *approval,* to conclude the passage. By using this language, Marguerite was not suggesting semiofficial ecclesiastical approval but rather a "testing" of the book (*probatio* in Latin). The value or truth of the book, she claimed, had been proved or tested by these clerics' assessments, in the way that gold is proved in the fire, or revelations are proved to be from God, or saints are tested or proved by their trials.[45] Marguerite's language acknowledges possible controversy and the need for some kind of test of her book's orthodoxy, but she claims that these churchmen's readings offer exactly the necessary proofs.

Marguerite is most careful to stress the divine justification the men found for her writings. John says it is "made by the Holy Ghost," Franc "that it was proved well by the Scriptures," and Godfrey that it was "divine usage." But both of the two longer responses, by John and Godfrey, are in fact far more emphatic about cautioning that the book could also be easily misunderstood, and both men strongly urge her not to circulate it indiscriminately. John suggests that she should expect many churchmen not to understand it, even—with good Franciscan humility—admitting that he might not have understood it himself, and prays that "only a few should see it." Godfrey worries that the book might have negative effects, leading people away from the more straightforward path of everyday piety when they might never really understand the more difficult spiritual route laid out by the *Mirror.* Thus he "did not counsel that many should see it."

Marguerite, however, puts these mixed messages to good use. For instance, she begins her report of Godfrey's assessment with her own editorial statement: "He blamed it not, no more than did the others." This argument from silence suggests to the reader how to understand what follows, even though most of Godfrey's assessment stresses what he *cannot* do. What is notable is that Marguerite did not simply suppress these warnings. She must have felt that they highlighted the very reason why some readers did not approve of her ideas—because not everyone was cut out for the same daunting spiritual path. In turn, Godfrey's positive assessment of the "spirit" behind the book was a highly flattering reference to Marguerite. Thus these praises invited readers (or listeners) to identify themselves with Marguerite as among the elite souls with the spiritual understanding necessary to take in the book's teachings. At the same time, the warnings offered an explanation for why some churchmen could not understand that her book was "divine usage"; men such as Bishop Guido simply did not have the necessary "high spiritual feelings."

Chronology and Conclusions for 1297–1306

Thus Marguerite appears to have been a very busy woman during the period after her book's condemnation. Putting all the pieces of the puzzle together suggests at least a loose chronology of her activities. The dates of Guido's episcopal reign—with a slight contraction on each end due to his known travels—limit the possibilities for his first condemnation of the *Mirror* to 1297 to 1305. I would suggest the likelihood of a date around 1300, which would allow Marguerite to have had time to work on her additions and then to show the extended version of her book to her three recommenders roughly during the years 1300–1303 (based on the most likely time for her interaction with Godfrey of Fontaines). She then must have produced a new "edition" of the book, with the praises appended to the new concluding chapters, which would have circulated for several years before she was again detained sometime between early 1306 and mid-1308.[46]

Even if this chronology must remain tentative, the essential dynamic of these years is clear: a bishop unambiguously declared Marguerite's writings to be heretical, but a friar, a monk, and a renowned master of theology reached a different conclusion. Godfrey of Fontaines and his like-minded colleagues were willing to do what Guido of Collemezzo was not—apply a sympathetic reading that assumed Marguerite's good faith (literally) and construed her ideas in an orthodox light.[47] Thus Marguerite had perfectly reasonable grounds on which to hope that further circulation of her book could lead to a wider consensus of approval.

All of this evidence also suggests that Marguerite in these years was surrounded by books and in contact with like-minded men (and presumably women). The trial documents accuse her at this point of possessing her own book "and others," so apparently she had other texts at her disposal as she continued to think through and clarify her ideas. Indeed, this passage could be taken to indicate that Marguerite authored more than one book.[48] In any case, she must have produced in this period multiple copies of the *Mirror*. If she sent individual copies to John, Franc, and Godfrey, then later to "simple people" (plural) and the bishop of Châlons-sur-Marne, that would suggest that at least a half-dozen copies were circulating, to say nothing of earlier copies that might have still been floating about.

In turn, this has implications for Marguerite's access to wealth or other means of support. Either she was furiously making copies of her weighty book herself, or she was paying a scribe or scribes to do so. Either case would require substantial funds (parchment and writing supplies were not cheap).[49] She must therefore have had access to substantial sums of money either personally or through sympathizers. There is every reason to envision Marguerite—even after her book's first condemnation—as an established, perhaps fairly well-off, author at the center of a circle that included both local semireligious and the kinds of churchmen who had long been linked to holy women of the Low Countries.

1306–1308: Two Bishops and an Inquisitor

Three men played central roles in Marguerite's second clash with the ecclesiastical authorities: the bishop of Châlons-sur-Marne, an inquisitor for Lorraine, and the new bishop of Cambrai.

This next encounter took place after January 1306 (when Philip of Marigny became bishop of Cambrai) and before fall 1308 (by which time Marguerite was in William of Paris's custody). Though the trial records do not make this explicit, it seems probable that it was John of Châteauvillain, bishop of Châlons-sur-Marne, who took steps to ensure Marguerite's arrest. As we have seen, William of Paris reported that Marguerite sent Bishop John a copy of her book. The Latin verb used by William, *communico* (to share, communicate, or impart), could suggest that

Marguerite sought out John and spoke to him in Champagne or else-where,[50] but it seems more likely that she sent him a copy of the book via some kind of messenger. In any case, something must have led her to hope that this bishop would lend the book a sympathetic eye, as John, Franc, and Godfrey had done. She was to be greatly disappointed.

From a noble family of Champagne, John of Châteauvillain had held his see since 1285 and was a firm Capetian supporter.[51] For example, he was present at the Louvre in 1297 (alongside most of the French episcopate) with the king and the leading officials of the realm when a defiant letter from the Count of Flanders was read out, and again in June 1303 when William of Plaisians read heresy charges against Boni-face VIII.[52] More recently, he had been among the bishops invited to par-ticipate in Philip IV's translation of St. Louis's head-relic to the Sainte-Chapelle on 17 May 1306.[53] Marguerite's book must have come to his attention around the same time as his attendance at this visually power-ful demonstration of Capetian sanctity (and just about the time Gui-ard of Cressonessart had his epiphany in the same Sainte-Chapelle). But these ties to Philip IV were not without repercussions. Later that year the bishop of Châlons-sur-Marne found himself the target of a re-volt in his diocese when he attempted to implement Philip IV's un-popular revaluation of the royal currency (November 1306 into Janu-ary 1307). Both episcopal and royal officials were attacked and beaten in this violent uprising.[54] One can only surmise that John might not have been disposed to hear the appeal of a controversial beguine at just this moment.

The most likely scenario is that John received a copy of Margue-rite's book and realized that it had been previously condemned. If so, this would imply that Bishop Guido's condemnation was well known, either because Guido himself had circulated notices to regional church authorities or simply because the burning of Marguerite's book had attracted significant public attention.[55] Since John was not, however, Marguerite's ordinary (bishop with jurisdiction over her), it was not his case to handle. One avenue would therefore have been for him to notify the bishop of Cambrai of this troublesome challenge. It seems, however, that he turned first to the inquisitor of Lorraine, and that it was the latter who took Marguerite into custody before subsequently calling in the new bishop of Cambrai.

This sequence of events is hinted at by the trial documents. As cited above, one document (no. 15b) refers to Marguerite's testimony at this point "made not only in the presence of the inquisitor of Lorraine, but also in the presence of the reverend father and lord, Lord Philip then bishop of Cambrai and now archbishop of Sens." This wording is ambiguous, but the other document (no. 19bis) clearly indicates that she gave her testimony two separate times, "once in the presence of the inquisitor of Lorraine and once in the presence of the reverend father Lord Philip, then bishop of Cambrai." It would seem, moreover, that the inquisitor conducted the first session. Not only do both documents list him first, but the wording of the more explicit document strongly implies a temporal sequence.

But what was an inquisitor "of Lorraine" doing mixed up with the case in the Diocese of Cambrai? One answer is that if a papal inquisitor was going to be involved at all he would have had to be called in from a neighboring region, since there is no evidence that inquisitors were appointed specifically for Cambrai in this period.[56] By contrast, we do know that Dominicans acted as inquisitors in these years in the area that can loosely be called Lorraine. In June 1290 Pope Nicholas IV had asked the provincial prior of the Dominicans in France to appoint six of his brothers to act as inquisitors in France, and three more brothers to fill the same role for an eastern region designated as the cities and Dioceses of Geneva, Sion, Lausanne, Besançon, Toul, Metz, and Verdun.[57] The provincial, with the consultation of other discreet members of the order, was also empowered to replace these original appointees as necessary for any good reason or in the event of their deaths.

Almost certainly a man described as an inquisitor of Lorraine was a Dominican sent to deal with a perceived threat of heresy in the Dioceses of Toul, Metz, and Verdun.[58] These largely French-speaking lands were formally imperial territories, yet Philip IV cultivated a role as their protector (particularly west of the Meuse).[59] More immediately, they were within the Dominican province of Francia, so papal policy was simply aligning inquisitorial jurisdiction with Dominican regional organization.[60] Thus any inquisitor for this area would have been oriented toward Paris and might well have known John of Châteauvillain personally, especially since these dioceses bordered on Châlons-sur-Marne. For these reasons "the inquisitor of Lorraine" might have been the logical person for John of Châteauvillain to alert concerning Marguerite's flagrant disregard for authority.

Although it has not previously been noted, this inquisitor can almost surely be identified with the "Brother Ralph of Ligny" (*frater Radulphus de Lineyo)*, who called himself "inquisitor of heretical depravity by apostolic authority in the cities and Dioceses of Toul, Metz, and Verdun" in a letter to Philip IV dated 23 November 1307.[61] The inquisitor does not here specifically label himself a Dominican, but the *frater* (often used by the Mendicants) together with the Dominican authority to appoint inquisitors for these dioceses makes it almost certain that he belonged to this order. Ralph of Ligny is apparently an otherwise obscure figure,[62] yet the contents of this document do reveal something of his inquisitorial approach and his relationship to the royal court. On 25 October (twelve days after the arrests of the Templars all across France), two German Templars, the priest "lord Conrad of Mangoncia" and his associate Henry, were captured in the region of Chaumont as they fled Paris trying to reach imperial lands. Ralph questioned them and determined that they knew nothing about the crimes (renouncing Christ, spitting on the cross, and indecent kisses) attributed to the Templars. He specifically mentioned that he did not wish to torture Henry because the latter was very ill. Although Ralph had obtained no confessions and apparently regarded the two Templars as innocent, he nevertheless wrote directly to Philip IV to report the incident, at the urging of Henry of Clacy, a knight and Philip's appointed agent in the Templar matter for the region.[63] This inquisitor would thus seem to have been reluctant to personally employ harsh measures in questionable cases, yet willing to defer to royal officials.

Sometime just a few months before or after these events, Ralph must have summoned Marguerite to account for her actions. Presumably he traveled to Valenciennes to accomplish this step, though nothing in the trial documents specifies the location of this interview. The documents do assert, however, that Marguerite affirmed in this inquisitor's presence that she had again possessed her book "and others" in contravention of Guido of Collemezzo's explicit written orders. Interestingly, the documents do not actually say that Marguerite admitted to having sent the book to John of Châteauvillain or to anyone else— William of Paris presents this as information that he learned through the testimony of other witnesses. Still—although we have only William's word for it—it seems that Marguerite admitted to having recopied her book and kept it in her possession. Ralph of Ligny must have realized that this admission virtually ensured that Marguerite would be legally considered a contumacious heretic (it might have been less clear whether this admission would constitute in and of itself a "relapse" into heresy, if she had not personally been condemned before). Rather than take any immediate further steps himself, however, the inquisitor elected to act together with the episcopal authority that had initiated her case.[64]

By this time, however, Guido of Collemezzo was no longer on the scene. On 22 January 1306, Clement V had formally transferred him to the archbishopric of Salerno. Perhaps Guido had lobbied to return home to Italy, or perhaps Charles II of Anjou had requested his transfer. More likely, however, Philip IV of France had prevailed on the new pope, Clement V (elected June 1305 and consecrated in November), to put someone less independent in the See of Cambrai.[65] Guido did not, in any case, have long to ruminate on this change, since he died between 26 March and 4 June 1306 without ever having reached Salerno.[66]

His successor in Cambrai as of January 1306 was an entirely different sort of ecclesiastical officeholder.[67] Whereas Guido had risen through a legal career and loyalty to the papal curia, Philip of Marigny was the king's man. His rise to influence paralleled that of his older and better-known brother, Enguerran, who had entered the service of Philip IV's queen, Jeanne of Navarre, before 1298, was one of Philip IV's chamberlains by 1304, and eventually became the king's most powerful advisor.[68] But although this ascent was steady, it was only after about 1308 that Enguerran was even the most influential of the several royal chamberlains, and only after 1311 that he was truly at the apogee of power.[69] Philip of Marigny's early success cannot all be attributed to Enguerran's influence,[70] since Philip was already canon of Douai and a royal clerk overseeing acquisitions in the *prévôté* of Paris by 1301.[71] Very likely Nicholas of Fréauville, the Dominican confessor to the king and cousin to the Marigny brothers, helped Philip's career just as he is known to have promoted Enguerran's.[72] In any case, by 1306 the Marigny brothers had begun to create a network of church patronage that linked northern dioceses to Paris. Their younger half brother John, for instance, was chanter of Paris by 1306, but also provost of Saint-Amé in Douai (Diocese of Arras, close to Valenciennes) by 1309 (and archdeacon of Pont-Audemer and Sens by 1312 and bishop of Beauvais in January 1313).[73] Another half brother, Robert, likewise held a canonry in Cambrai by 1312 (along with others in Chartres, Auxerre, and Orléans).[74] Philip himself added prebends in Cambrai and Arras (as well as Bourges and Issoudun) to that of Douai by the time of his episcopal election.[75] The Marigny brothers were thus as attuned to events in the Dioceses of Arras and Cambrai as they were loyal to the king in Paris.

The passages quoted above assert that Marguerite repeated in Philip of Marigny's presence her confession of having possessed her book after its condemnation.[76] This second interrogation was a crucial moment in determining the future course of Marguerite's trial, for Philip of Marigny's perspective was fundamentally different from that of his predecessor. Guido had known how to negotiate the political environment of France, but by training and temperament he had been a canon lawyer steeped in the claims to papal supremacy advocated by Boniface VIII. The political winds in the Diocese of Cambrai had now shifted; once Marguerite was before Bishop Philip, her case was certain to be drawn into the political orbit of the royal court in Paris.

This is not to say, however, that Marguerite immediately became a pawn in a relentless royal plot. To the contrary, Philip of Marigny may not have known exactly what to do with this troublesome woman. Marguerite had now confessed, twice, to exactly the act she had been warned—on pain of punishment by the secular arm—not to repeat. Philip could thus have handled her case in the most summary manner.[77] Had she indicated repentance, he could perhaps have sentenced her to imprisonment or some other serious penance if he had seen fit to exercise mercy. Or, since there is no reason to think that she did appear penitent, he could simply have transferred her to the secular authorities for punishment as a contumacious heretic. Yet he took neither of these steps and instead turned her over to the jurisdiction of the inquisitor William of Paris by fall 1308. Why?

Several factors may have been at work. First, the earlier intervention of Marguerite's three recommenders, and particularly Godfrey of Fontaines, may have given Philip pause. If the bishop was aware—

and there may have been textual evidence to this effect in front of him—that a well-known master of theology such as Godfrey had recently praised the book, this fact might have been enough to make him decide that a fuller theological hearing (or refutation) was necessary.[78] Second, Philip of Marigny may simply have been eager to pass this problem on to someone else—after all it was not he who had first condemned the book, he was no theologian himself, and faced with an obviously unrepentant woman seemingly destined for a public execution, he may have wanted to extricate himself from a messy situation.

On the other hand, there is an overtly political interpretation available as well. The period 1307–8 was a precarious moment in terms of Philip IV's reputation as a defender of orthodoxy. The king's battles with the church had culminated in the arrest of all the Templars in France in October 1307, but the resulting process was not progressing entirely as the king would have liked (as the next chapter will show in more detail). Philip of Marigny, as a loyal supporter of Philip IV, may therefore have wanted to provide the court with a cut-and-dried case of heresy to handle publicly at Paris. These interpretations, moreover, are not mutually exclusive; Philip's lack of theological sophistication and his overt political orientation may have worked together to suggest that a high-profile inquisitorial trial in Paris was the best solution to this case that had been dropped in his lap.

Thus, sometime in fall 1308, Marguerite Porete was delivered over to William of Paris. What might her state of mind have been at this point? Any attempt to answer such a subjective question must be speculative, but the narrative traced here does allow some reasonable inferences. When Bishop Guido condemned her book, Marguerite may have been momentarily chastened, to judge by the fact that she offered some level of cooperation. The public burning of her book in her hometown can only have impressed the seriousness of this condemnation on her mind. Still, she lived to write another day, and after a certain amount of time had passed she apparently felt confident enough to confront her book's condemnation by adding new explanations and seeking new opinions. If Guido's grounds for his finding of "heresy" and "error" were explained to Marguerite, she may have itched to write further and show that her ideas had not been properly appreciated by those lacking her spiritual insight. Perhaps cautiously at first, she showed her revised work to a local Franciscan, then to a well-connected Cistercian, and finally to the illustrious Godfrey of Fontaines. If she was able to meet these men face to face and impress them with an aura of personal piety, the effect of this interaction may also help explain their granting of (very cautious) praise. These men repeatedly warned her not to show the book around, but she preferred to glean from their words a "proving" of the book's worth. And why not? Guido of Collemezzo had been an accomplished canon lawyer, but Godfrey of Fontaines was one of the great theologians of his generation. Was not the latter a better judge of orthodoxy than the former?

At this point, the transfer and death of Guido of Collemezzo may have triggered a new level of activity. With the specific man who had condemned her book removed from the scene, and with growing evidence in her own mind that the revised *Mirror* could be read as orthodox by local churchmen, was it not time to show that her earlier humiliation had been a mistake? Why she chose the bishop of Châlons-sur-Marne as a recipient for her book is a mystery. But even when this step led to new interrogations, she admitted her activities before an inquisitor, and again when turned over to the new bishop of Cambrai. Everything suggests that up to this point she was hoping for some kind of new hearing on her ideas. Again it is worth stressing that (in contrast to her later comportment) she was not silent. Her admissions may have been terse and defiant, or lengthy and spirited. But in any case, she was apparently not refusing all communication.

Perhaps, when she learned that she was to be turned over to the inquisitor William of Paris, she sensed that this was the end of her hopes. But on the other hand, a Parisian master of theology had been supportive before. Was it not possible that Paris might hold other sympathizers? Unfortunately for Marguerite, the inquisitor in Paris was a legalistic thinker like Guido of Collemezzo and an ardent royal loyalist like Philip of Marigny—from her perspective, the worst of both worlds. In William of Paris, Marguerite would run up against a man embroiled in larger events that would push him toward a meticulous prosecution of her case.

CHAPTER 3

The Inquisitor

While Marguerite Porete was battling church authorities in the Low Countries and Guiard of Cressonessart was developing his angelic mission, William of Paris was enjoying a steady ascent toward the upper echelons of the Capetian court.[1] Nothing is known of his family, except that a nephew appears in royal accounts for July 1307.[2] The "of Paris" label probably indicates that William was born in that city; he was certainly a Dominican resident at Saint-Jacques before March 1297,[3] when he is recorded as a chaplain to King Philip IV.[4] His ties to wider circles around the royal family are shown by the fact that he acted as an executor for the testament of Philip of Artois in August 1298, along with Durand of Champagne, the Franciscan confessor to Queen Jeanne of Navarre.[5] From this point he accumulated further royal and papal offices: confessor to the king's sons by 1299; papal inquisitor for the French kingdom from late 1303 or early 1304; Philip's own confessor by the end of 1305 or early 1306; and papal chaplain before fall 1307. He was in many ways the epitome of a successful Dominican: not only was his intellectual formation firmly in the traditions of his order, but the offices of confessor to the French king and of papal inquisitor were generally reserved for Preachers. Yet William was also venturing into uncharted territory, since no one had ever before held the two offices of royal confessor and papal inquisitor simultaneously. This new combination of powers in turn led to unforeseen results; at the moment when William's path crossed those of Marguerite and Guiard, he had just been through a year of tumultuous controversy.

A Dominican Intellectual

William's intellectual activities reveal, above all, his unwavering adherence to Dominican traditions. Although he was never a university master or even a lector within his order, his writings suggest that he was trained in canon law and (to a lesser extent) theology.

Most likely this training took place entirely within Dominican *scholae* and *studia.* Every Dominican priory had a *schola* with a lector who lectured on the Bible and the Sentences of Peter Lombard (the basic text for the study of theology) and presided over weekly disputations (formal determinations of theological questions). Every brother attended these lessons and thus acquired a basic theological education. Beyond this introductory level, by the third quarter of the thirteenth century a sophisticated system was in place whereby students showing exceptional promise moved up to *studia* at the provincial level for further training in advanced logic, Aristotelian natural philosophy, and (again) the Sentences.[6] At the end of these studies brothers were primarily expected to return to the priories as lectors.[7] Only a few eventually advanced to the highest level of theological study at one of the order's *studia generalia* in Paris, Montpellier, Bologna, Cologne, or Oxford. Graduates, again, would be expected to return to the priories and teach as lectors before a very select number would finally come back to one of the *studia generalia* as a bachelor to train to take over the position of regent master (teaching master holding a chair of theology).

For a Dominican resident at Paris, however, some of these lines were blurred. The order had controlled two university chairs of theology since at least 1230, so that students in the Dominican *studium generale* there were also part of the university. Moreover, at the priory of Saint-Jacques in the Left Bank university quarter, friars would have routinely rubbed shoulders with their order's masters of theology, and the lector and master of students at Paris were likely to be among the most qualified anywhere.

We would in any case expect William to display a high level of intellectual accomplishment on the basis of the profiles of the two Dominicans who had most recently served as confessors to Philip IV. Nicholas of Gorran, former prior of Saint-Jacques and Philip's confessor from 1285 to 1290, was known for his influential biblical commen-

taries *(Postillae)* as well as for his collection of *Distinctiones* and his sermons.[8] He was followed by Nicholas of Fréauville, who had exercised
the office of lector at several convents and who remained Philip's confessor until his promotion to the cardinalate in December 1305.[9] If the
king did not choose his confessors from the most rarefied intellectual
circles, he nevertheless expected them to be accomplished scholars.[10]

William seems to have been cut from the same cloth as these predecessors.[11] The evidence for his purchases, donations, and ownership
of books offers specific indications as to his intellectual orientation.
Royal accounts for 1299 and 1300 show him, as confessor to Philip IV's
children, purchasing Bibles for Princes Louis and Philip (the future
Louis X and Philip V), as well as a missal, a breviary, and the book *De
eruditione principum (On the Education of Princes)* for Louis.[12] A codicil to Philip IV's testament, issued 28 November 1314 (the day before
his death), also reveals that William had at some point given the king a
copy of Vincent of Beauvais's *Speculum historiale (Historical Mirror).*[13]
Sometime after 1305 William acquired a manuscript, still extant in the
Bibliothèque Mazarine, of Nicholas of Gorran's *Postillae super Lucam
(Commentaries on the Book of Luke).*[14] Finally, and most unexpectedly,
William gave a Hebrew Bible (or part of one) to the Dominican house
in Bologna in February 1310 or 1311.[15]

William of Paris was also himself an author, with at least one and
probably two extant works to his credit. The first, more certain, attribution is a practical index to key texts of canon law, known as the
Tabula juris (The Table of Laws) or the *Tabula super Decretales et Decreta (The Table on the Decretales and Decreta).*[16] Written before 1298
(there is no mention of Boniface VIII's *Liber sextus*) and widely copied
in manuscript, it has remained virtually unstudied by modern scholars.[17] This was in fact a two-part work, with one half providing an alphabetical guide to Gratian's formative twelfth-century compilation of
canon law, known as the *Decretum,* and the other to subsequent compilations of *Decretales* at least through the time of the second Council
of Lyon (1274).

Though the two "Tables" are reference works with no commentary, William's explanatory introduction still gives us some indication
of the way his mind worked.[18] This brief preface states that the reader
needs to know three things in order to profit from the book. The first

is that it proceeds by alphabetical order, which—he feels it necessary
to explain—means that the principal terms beginning with "a" will
come first, then "b," and so on.[19] Second, right after each case or question or sentence is mentioned, the principal texts of canon law that pertain to it will be listed, and a system of superscript letters will then explain where in the gloss or text itself the relevant information can be
found.[20] Finally, the beginning of each new heading for a main term
will include a cross-listing showing where it intersects with headings
for other terms.[21] What shows through here is the logical, analytic mind
of a man who took satisfaction from creating unified order out of disparate texts. The work suggests that William enjoyed teaching others
but not that he was a person of great imagination.

William is probably also the author of a work known as the *Dialogus de septem sacramentis (Dialogue on the Seven Sacraments)*. This
was an even more popular treatise, with nearly sixty medieval manuscripts extant and many editions printed between 1473 and 1580.[22] It
survives in two versions (a fact not generally noted by scholarship):
one is slightly shorter and written before 1298; the second was revised
and expanded after that date.[23] Although the attribution to William is
not entirely certain, it has been widely adopted by modern scholarship because he is the only plausible Dominican candidate,[24] while the
work's explicit reliance on the Dominican theologians Thomas Aquinas
(d. 1274) and citation of the *Summa de penitentia* by the Dominican
Raymond of Peñafort (d. 1275) suggest a Dominican author.[25] It does
seem likely that William wrote the first version, and he may also have
been responsible for later revisions.[26]

This work (in both versions) takes the form of a conversation
between a young priest named Peter and a more experienced teacher
"G" (Guillaume or Gilon), explaining church doctrine on the seven
sacraments and summarizing practical rules for administering them. It
continues the legalistic perspective of the *Tabula juris*—evident in numerous references to *decreta* and *decretales*—and applies it to questions of pastoral practice.[27] Peter asks questions, to which G provides
lengthy answers, often then breaking them down further into simple
components. To take one relevant example: in the chapter on the sacrament of penance, Peter asks about various conditions for granting absolution. In his response, G pauses at one point to enumerate situ-

ations in which a lowly priest should consult his superiors and then specifies cases that are usually reserved for bishops, including incest, deflowering of virgins, homicide, transgression of vows, divination and the invocation of demons, sacrilege, sodomy, lying, blasphemy, church burning, destruction of a fetus, heresy, adultery, and the act of striking a cleric. Peter then tersely demands, "Give me an exposition of these cases." G is happy to oblige, systematically giving further short definitions of each sin. When he gets to heresy, he explains that "one holding a false opinion against God, preaching [or] teaching openly or secretly against the articles of the faith, and all fautors and holders of similar opinions, are held to be heretics."[28] This sort of process is repeated dozens of times as G moves through the sacraments and sums up thirteenth-century canon law and scholastic opinion for his imaginary young priest.

Two conclusions emerge from this evidence concerning books and authorship. First, William's adherence to his Dominican intellectual training shapes all of these activities. The books that William purchased for and gave to his royal associates indicate that he carried out his role as confessor within the framework of his order's literary tradition. Vincent of Beauvais (d. 1264), for example, was among the most influential Dominican authors of the middle of the thirteenth century. Lector at the royal Cistercian foundation of Maubuisson, his *Speculum historiale* (part of his larger *Speculum maius*) was written at least partly with a royal audience in mind and was completed in its first form by 1244. It was a universal chronicle, meaning it began with Creation, but it was most detailed on recent political and sacred history. For instance, the penultimate section (book 30) covers roughly the years 1211 to 1243 and focuses not only on the deeds of Philip II, Louis VIII, and Louis IX but also on the lives of Saints Dominic, Francis, and Anthony of Padua, and—perhaps more interestingly here—the early "beguine" Marie of Oignies.[29] Book 31 then adds updates through about 1253, discussing Louis IX's departure for his crusade and details about the Mongol Empire, together with a long section on Saint Edmund of Canterbury and a shorter one on the Dominican saint Peter Martyr. This work was already well known to the Capetian court, but William ensured that this Dominican representation of sacred and secular history was called to Philip IV's immediate attention.[30]

The *De eruditione principum* that William bought for Prince Louis was most likely the work of that title compiled by the French Dominican William Peraldus (resident in Lyon) around 1265 for "a certain prince."[31] This was part of a longer Dominican tradition of mirrors for princes, since it incorporated parts of a treatise for Louis IX's children written by Vincent of Beauvais.[32] According to a recent analysis, the work is notable for advocating "a superior position for the Church and the clergy vis-à-vis secular politics" and for offering advice that is useful for all Christians, only secondarily detailing topics seen as particularly appropriate for princes. When it does express political ideas, the author's "sympathies are beyond any doubt with the common people."[33] This sympathetic stance does not extend to heretics, however, as Peraldus notes that no one should be moved if he sees heretics that appear abstinent or compassionate, since there are many people with those qualities among Catholics; and even if some Catholics are bad, there are also many truly bad heretics—only they hide their wickedness as much as possible, "and no wonder, since they hide themselves as well."[34]

Thus in these two works William provided Dominican teaching tools on history and morality for a royal audience. Once in the office of royal confessor, he acquired Nicholas of Gorran's *Postillae super Lucam,* an example of the latest Dominican theological output. Nicholas was not only William's predecessor as Philip's confessor but also the most important Parisian compiler of biblical scholarship since the appearance in the 1230s of the complete Dominican *Postillae* that passed under the name of Hugh of St. Cher.[35] This possession suggests that William kept abreast of theological work by leading scholars of his order.

All of this Dominican learning is similarly apparent in his own *Dialogue,* with its citations of Thomas of Aquinas and Raymond of Peñafort.[36] While relying on Thomas in particular was hardly a controversial choice, it should be remembered that he was not yet the quasi-official Catholic theologian he was to become in later centuries.[37] Thus when William, at the end of his treatise, simply referred the reader to the not-yet-sainted Thomas for any further questions, he was adhering to a developing conservative tradition within the order, presenting the most illustrious Dominican theologian as the ultimate guide for those seeking deeper knowledge.

The second conclusion concerns the nature of William's intellectual training. The author of the *Tabula juris* could only have been a serious student of canon law, given the extensive control of legal texts displayed there. His *Dialogue* also cites both specific decretals and wider collections of legal commentaries.[38] But William was acquainted with academic theology as well.[39] The *Dialogue* obviously relies on the writings of such church fathers as Augustine and Jerome,[40] but it also suggests knowledge of the most up-to-date disputes among Parisian academics. In fact (at least in some manuscripts), it cites none other than Godfrey of Fontaines, from a quodlibetal question published between 1295 and 1297, to call attention to a difference between Godfrey and Thomas Aquinas concerning the nature of just restitution within the sacrament of penance.[41] Further evidence for William's familiarity with university circles comes from the extant manuscript of Nicholas of Gorran that William once owned. Nicholas's *Postillae super Lucam* was available from the university stationers, according to a surviving list of 1304, and indeed William's manuscript bears *pecia* markings indicating that it must have been copied and purchased there.[42] Though William was not a university master himself, he was no stranger to university circles.

As an author, William was thus in some ways similar to Guido of Collemezzo; both men were legalistic thinkers with orderly minds who preferred to strip away scholastic debate in favor of straightforward answers to practical questions. He did share a preference for dialogue form with Marguerite Porete—but what a different sort of dialogue! In Marguerite's *Mirror* the competing voices of the text mock and challenge and circle each other; William's "Peter" serves only to offer up simple questions to his master and then to express satisfaction with the answers.

Confessor and Inquisitor

A royal letter of 16 December 1301 suggests the dynamic that underlay the development of William's career. This was a moment not only of heightening tension between Philip IV and Boniface VIII but of intense royal displeasure with Dominican inquisitors in southern France. The trouble started in Carcassonne, where townspeople antagonistic toward local Dominican inquisitors found a leader for their cause in the incendiary Franciscan Bernard Délicieux. By 1301 Bernard had convinced two royal *enquêteurs* that Foulques of Saint-Georges, Dominican inquisitor for Toulouse and a former inquisitorial official in Carcassonne, was incarcerating and torturing honest people merely because they were loyal to the king. In October Bernard and his entourage traveled north to Senlis to present their allegations to Philip IV. Although Foulques and other important Dominicans, including Nicholas of Fréauville, arrived to defend themselves, Bernard succeeded in convincing the king that Foulques was abusing his inquisitorial powers. Philip ordered that from then on inquisitors would work with bishops and royal officials in making arrests, with problems to be resolved through recourse to panels of local Dominican and Franciscan priors, guardians, and lectors. More specifically, the king asked the Dominican order to relieve Foulques of his inquisitorial office. Dominican leaders in Paris, however, refused to carry out this request immediately.[43]

In December, in the midst of this impasse, Philip wrote to his Dominican chaplain William of Paris.[44] Regarding "the discussion, held lately in the convent of the Dominicans of Paris concerning the business of inquisition and the person of Brother Foulques," the king had heard many things that "incline more to our dishonor and the disgrace of all the people, than to the utility of the church and the punishment of excesses committed." The prior and brothers were insisting that Foulques remain in his inquisitorial office, at least until the middle of the following Lent and in conjunction with another brother, so that he could pass sentence on unfinished cases. This recalcitrance, according to Philip IV, was "increasing our dishonor and by no means impeding the grave danger and general scandal which may follow from things committed in this manner." Philip then lamented in rather ominous fashion: "Who would believe, Brother William, that, by whatever daring, the [Dominican] provincial of our kingdom and all the brothers of your order, in our time, would presume to support a person so detestable and defamed in our eyes by such opprobrium and division, against our opinion and that of all the people, as they have done lately in this way?" Philip directed William to strive to change the minds of the provincial and the brothers, again noting that because of his lifelong love of the order he never would have believed that its provincial and priors would keep a brother in office against the royal will.[45] Evidently the Dominican leadership in Paris wished to preserve its autonomy in appointing and removing inquisitors; just as clearly Philip believed William would side with royal interests in this dispute.

Although there is no evidence for any concrete steps William took at this moment, his unhesitating loyalty to the king is demonstrated by the list of Parisian Dominicans who signed the "letter of adherence" supporting Philip IV in his battle with Pope Boniface VIII on 26 June 1303.[46] In and of itself, his appearance on this list is not remarkable, since almost all the French Dominicans in Paris eventually adhered to the royal position (those who resided at Saint-Jacques but came from outside France, on the other hand, probably did not). But William's position near the top of the list (seventh on the list of 133 friars) shows that he adopted the royal position without delay, unlike the provincial and prior of Paris, who were part of a group that hesitated as long as possible.[47]

This loyalty was soon rewarded. Not long after William had been asked to exert pressure within his order to bring inquisitorial appointments in line with royal preferences, he himself was entrusted with the office of inquisitor.[48] The exact date of this appointment is not known, but Pope Clement V later referred to William's having received his inquisitorial commission from the pope's "predecessors."[49] William must therefore has been appointed before Clement ascended the papal throne, probably during the short reign of the Dominican pope Benedict XI (22 October 1303–7 July 1304).[50] William would have been appointed by the Dominican provincial in Paris, presumably with Philip's support and perhaps even at his direct request. This appointment might then have been explicitly confirmed by papal letters (as the passage seems to indicate), or perhaps Clement only meant to say that he knew William had been duly appointed through mechanisms set up by his predecessors. In any case, Clement's remark makes it clear that William's appointment to the office of inquisitor predated his own ascension to the papal throne.

If William indeed received his inquisitorial commission in 1303 or 1304, this timing would be significant, for it coincides with Philip's trip south to restore order in Languedoc. Although the king may first have intended to further rein in Dominican abuses of inquisitorial power, on his arrival in Toulouse he quickly became convinced that Bernard Délicieux and his allies were the real threat to order and royal authority. Moreover, the death of Boniface VIII meant that the king could now negotiate the question of inquisitorial authority with a new and per-haps more cooperative pope. Thus in January 1304 Philip began to shift his support back from Bernard Délicieux to the Dominican inquisi-tors in the South, issuing new regulations for inquisitors but mak-ing his belief in their utility clear.[51] This would have been an appro-priate moment for the king to have arranged for his loyal chaplain to be appointed a papal inquisitor of heretical depravity. In this manner, Phillip sought to open up a more effective avenue of influence over the Dominican inquisitors of the realm, even as he was reassuring them of his support.[52]

Given the close trust the king had already shown in him, it is on one level not surprising that William became Philip IV's confessor when Nicholas of Fréauville was promoted to the cardinalate on 15 December 1305.[53] The new appointment was, however, extraordinary, because there was no precedent for a papal inquisitor serving as royal confessor. Nei-ther Nicholas of Gorran nor Nicholas of Fréauville had been an inquisi-tor, and no such combination had existed under Philip III or Louis IX. Moreover, it must have been Philip who fostered this new combination of powers, for it was the king who chose to make the inquisitor his con-fessor, not the pope or Dominican provincial who made the royal con-fessor into an inquisitor.[54] The appointment of a newly visible inquisitor in Paris was not a response to any fresh heretical threat looming over the Île-de-France but rather part of the king's long-term campaign to gain more effective control over all aspects of church power in the realm.

Moreover, the very fact that an inquisitor was now so closely tied to the royal court was bound to give inquisitorial activities in the North a new prominence. There is very little evidence for any inquisitions against heresy in the Île-de-France in the decades preceding William's appointment, and none whatsoever for Paris itself. The Dominicans Simon Duval and William of Auxerre were active in the North around 1276–78 and 1285–86, with evident royal support.[55] But if there was a Dominican inquisitor with regional authority for the Île-de-France in the years just before 1303–4, no documentary trace of his activities has yet been found. Thus William was not simply stepping into an estab-lished office but rather helping to create a new source of authority cen-tered on the royal court. Indeed, for a papal inquisitor, charged with destroying heretical depravity in the Kingdom of France, to also be re-sponsible for hearing and absolving the king's sins suggests a new conceptual link between the spiritual safety of the realm and the personal salvation of the monarch.[56]

On the other hand, William was not occupying an office of "head inquisitor" or "grand inquisitor" for France, for no such office existed. Strictly speaking, William was only *one* papally appointed inquisitor with jurisdiction within the French kingdom. For example, the title that he gives himself in documents from 1307 to 1310, "inquisitor of heretical depravity in the Kingdom of France appointed by apostolic authority," is exactly the one used by his counterpart in Toulouse, Bernard Gui, in 1309 and 1310.[57] This is not to suggest that William was merely one inquisitor among many. He surely enjoyed a certain preeminence by virtue of his association with the court, and more generally because Dominican inquisitors for the province of France were appointed from Paris. As we shall see, Philip and William sought to use this informal prestige to their advantage in coordinating the attack on the Templars, and Pope Clement V could later write to William "and all the inquisitors of France" as though William in some sense stood in for the rest.

Nevertheless, what it meant to be simultaneously inquisitor in Paris and royal confessor was an open question. Nor would the practical aspects of this dual role be immediately worked out, since there is no record of William participating in any heresy trials before 1307. Several documents of that year, however, do show him seemingly secure in his enjoyment of royal and papal favor. The royal accounts, for instance, give us a glimpse of William acting on royal business in January 1307,[58] whereas in May Clement V granted him an indulgence, at Philip's request, allowing him to eat meat when his stays in the king's household necessitated it.[59] Later that same year William used the title "papal chaplain," although just when he acquired this title is unknown.[60] At this moment, however, Philip IV sought to take sudden and full advantage of William's dual office.

The Templar Affair

Philip IV's attack on the Templars put William's loyalties to the test. In theory William carried out his role in his capacity as papal inquisitor. In reality he was acting very much as Philip IV's man.[61] The attempt to implement royal orders while claiming to act on papal authority was an audacious gamble—one that would ultimately expose William to Clement V's ire.

On 14 September 1307 Philip issued letters ordering royal officials throughout the realm to prepare for a mass arrest of the Templars. The king first detailed at length the accusations—primarily that the Templars, upon entry to the order, were made to spit on an image of Jesus, deny Christ, and engage in illicit kisses. Philip, "assigned by God to the watchtower of royal eminence for the defense of the faith [and] of ecclesiastical liberty," announced himself persuaded by the "public infamy" and the "information" reported to him by "the beloved brother in Christ William of Paris, inquisitor of heretical depravity appointed by apostolic authority." The king, convinced of the legitimate "vehement suspicion" of the Templars, was therefore now "assenting to the just supplications of this inquisitor," who had "invoked the aid of our arm."[62]

William was thus fully implicated in this first, behind-the-scenes step in the arrest of the Templars. The king and his advisors used William's office to suggest that the arrest of the Templars would be a proper inquisitorial procedure and that the impetus had originated with the church and its inquisitor in Paris. Some of the language employed in this letter established the legal framework for an inquisition: public infamy (*fama*) had led to a preliminary inquiry, which in turn had produced a vehement suspicion of heresy. A legitimately appointed papal inquisitor had therefore decided that further judicial action was necessary, and the king was providing the assistance requested of him.

In the king's version of events, it was really William who had brought the whole matter to his attention; now that he had been called in by the inquisitor, the king was of course willing to carry out the actual arrests and make the suspects available for interrogation. The reality, however, was that Philip was acting on his own initiative (as the pope's incredulous response would soon demonstrate). William's active cooperation was essential to the facade of legitimacy, and he was apparently quite willing to go along with the charade and use his papal appointment as cover for the king's actions.

A week later William took an even more active role in the secret planning for the arrests. Characteristically, his impulse was to turn to the brothers of his order. On 22 September he wrote to the Dominican inquisitors of Toulouse and Carcassonne and to the priors, subpriors, and lectors of all the Dominican houses in France to urge their cooperation with the king.[63] He reminded them in his greeting that he was a fellow Dominican ("of the same order") who combined papal and royal authority as "chaplain of the lord pope, confessor of the most serene prince the lord king of France, and inquisitor of heretical depravity in the Kingdom of France appointed by apostolic authority."[64] He first repeated the accusations against the Templars, echoing the language of Philip's letter. As he recounted events, however, he assigned Philip a more active role than the king's own wording had done: "Therefore, the aforementioned lord the Most Christian King, after hearing those previously stated accusations, terrified with the stupor of wonder and burning with ardor of the faith, did not reject them, but diligently related the things he had heard both to us and to his secret counselors and to our most holy lord the highest pontiff, first at Lyon and then at Poitiers."[65] Thus William not only stressed Philip's active role but also suggested that the king had Clement V's backing. Although it is true enough that Philip did discuss his suspicions of the Templars with Clement and that the pope had recently indicated his intention of investigating the rumors of corruption, William must have known that he was being disingenuous with this formulation.[66]

"And soon," William continued, "having called us in, he inquired more diligently, and many trustworthy witnesses . . . were received judicially by us." Again, it is noteworthy that William suggested that it was Philip who had called for inquisitorial action, not the other way around. But since all these witnesses confirmed the foul customs of the Templar reception, "presumption against all [the Templars] was introduced." Therefore, after William and the king gathered all the archbishops, bishops, abbots, and other eminent churchmen together and received their counsel, "we have urged this same king for the necessary cause of the faith, that he deign to give us favor, support, and aid against each person of the said order of this kingdom vehemently suspected of the foregoing things, so that we will be able to have them for examination, as is fitting, concerning these things."[67] William was careful to add that this inquisition was not against an order as such—which would be beyond his authority—but merely against suspected individuals. Philip then, "hearing favorably our request," issued instructions for the Templars' arrest. William finally arrived at his message to his Dominican brethren:

We, however, not being able to come to diverse parts of the kingdom personally, due to the impediments of our many duties and the infirmity of our body, exhort you in the Lord, entrust to you by the tenor of the present letter, and depute you individually . . . that when the suspected persons will be shown to you by the men of the said lord king, you shall very diligently inquire on our behalf, or more accurately on apostolic behalf, into the truth of the aforementioned matters, with the depositions of these men to be written by a public person, if this can be done conveniently, or by two suitable men. And if you find that the foregoing crimes are true, be sure to lay bare this affair to wise men of the Franciscan order and other religious, so that with them and with the people scandal will not arise from this process, but rather the odor of good fame. And do not delay to send the depositions of such witnesses to the lord king and to us in France, closed under your seals and those of the men of the king of France who are sent specially for the aforesaid matters.[68]

This letter reveals a great deal about William. It not only fully establishes his complicity in the premeditated attack on the Templars but also demonstrates how far he would go to toe the royal line. It is always possible that William truly believed the accusations against the Templars. The instructions accompanying Philip IV's letter of 14 September, however, suggested that torture would be used to extract confessions, which in turn indicates that even the king's men knew that the case against the order would have to be created through intimidation and violence.[69] But whether or not William thought the Templars likely to be guilty, he was overtly duplicitous in twice suggesting that his letter reflected papal wishes. At best, he and Philip may have been betting that Clement would go along with a fait accompli once the arrests had been made and that these claims would in some sense become true after the fact. Even so, William's suggestion that the interrogations he was asking for would be "on apostolic behalf" can only be described as a patent distortion of the truth.[70] At the same time, William's attempts to place a large share of the responsibility on Philip's shoulders reveal something of his uneasy conscience. He understood full well that the legality of this undertaking was questionable, and he was not quite willing to take credit for the initial impetus in the way the king seems to have expected him to do.

Moreover, William's letter makes its explicit requests of other inquisitors and Dominicans without specifying the exact nature of the authority on which they rest. It was not at all clear that an inquisitor in Paris had any authority to command other inquisitors, and William held no position such as provincial prior that would have allowed him to issue orders to other French Dominicans. It was left to be understood that William represented the royal will and that as such it would be wise to carry out his "exhortations." Indeed, the ultimate authority for the investigation is underlined by William's concluding plea to send all depositions "to the king and us" by means of the king's messengers.

Thus the events of September 1307 demonstrate that William was willing to treat inquisitions as tools of royal policy. But they also placed William in a highly compromised position as soon as it became evident that Clement V was not afraid to challenge the royal version of events. At first, the process went as Philip and William had envisioned. On 13 October royal agents arrested the Templars with startling efficiency all across France. In Paris, many were incarcerated in the Temple itself, where questioning—and torture—began within a week.[71] From 19 to 26 October, William personally led the interrogation of the first thirty-seven Templars, including the grand master Jacques of Molay on 24 October.[72] Of the 138 Templars detained at Paris, 134 confessed by November, including Jacques and other leaders of the order.[73] It was essential, however, that these confessions be publicly broadcast. William therefore assembled a crowd of churchmen and some university personnel at the Temple on 25 October, and then again the next day a group augmented by many of the university's masters and bachelors in theology (a number of whom would later be called upon to advise William in the cases of Marguerite and Guiard) to hear Jacques of Molay and his brethren repeat their admissions of guilt.[74] These were powerful scenes indeed, as the Templars confessed in William's presence to most of Philip's charges. This dramatic performance was to be the high point of William's public involvement with the early phases of the trial, though he continued to lead questioning of Parisian Templars through at least 17 November.[75]

After this early success, things did not go as smoothly as Philip and William had planned, largely because of Clement V's unwillingness to endorse the fiction that papal authority lay behind the arrests. Although Clement had been given all the cover necessary to follow Philip's lead if he so desired, he instead reacted with outrage. As early as 27 October he wrote in strong terms to Philip, demanding that the Templars be turned over to papal legates sent for this purpose.[76] For Clement, the issue was less the Templars' innocence or guilt than it was Philip's obvious usurpation of papal authority. But now that the process was already under way, Clement's dilemma was how to wrest the impetus away from the French court.

On 22 November the pope ordered that since confessions had already been made, a trial would have to go forward, with Templars to be arrested all across Europe. The latter step was now carried out, whereas to this point most secular rulers outside France had declined to follow Philip's lead. The jockeying for position between pope and king over the next two months is known only through secondhand reports. What is clear, though, is that by January the pope had begun to doubt the basis of the entire affair after several important Templars, probably including Jacques of Molay, seized the opportunity to address a more open-minded papal audience and retracted their earlier confessions. As a result, sometime around February Clement suspended and revoked the powers of William, other French inquisitors, and French bishops and archbishops with regard to the Templar case.[77]

Over the next five months the proceedings ground to a halt, as the king and his advisors did everything possible to pressure Clement into reinstating the authority of the local inquisitors and bishops, including whipping up anonymous attacks on Clement and again attempting to enlist the support of the masters of theology at Paris. The masters were asked to decide seven (decidedly leading) questions concerning the proper role of a prince in a case such as this. This time, however, the theologians would not provide the desired result. The masters (again many of the same men who would judge extracts from Marguerite's book two years later) in their response of 25 March basically refused to approve of Philip's usurpation of the church's right to control heresy prosecutions. The Templars' guilt or innocence was not the primary question here; the issue was who could instigate proceedings for heresy. The theologians were clear in stating that this was beyond royal authority and belonged to the sphere of church power. Rebuffed but undaunted, Philip's men called an assembly of the "Estates" from throughout the realm that took place on 5–15 May at Tours, intended to crystallize public opinion and pressure the pope.[78]

Events came to a head when Philip and a large entourage then met with Clement at nearby Poitiers, beginning 26 May. In spite of several vehement and increasingly threatening speeches by William of Plaisians, Clement remained firm until a series of seventy-two Templars were brought from Paris and paraded in front of him to confess between 29 June and 2 July. This show finally caused Clement to relent.[79]

In two bulls issued 5 July, Clement at last allowed the bishops and inquisitors of France to proceed against individual Templars again. Here he recounts his own version of events and his perception of William's less than satisfactory role in them. The longer letter *(Subit assidue)* is addressed "to all the venerable brothers archbishops and bishops of the Kingdom of France, and the beloved son William and other inquisitors of heretical depravity generally appointed by apostolic authority in the same kingdom." After lamenting the sad state of affairs, Clement began to recount how things had gotten to this point:

> Some time ago we and our brothers [i.e., the cardinals], not unjustifiably grieving, took up the sudden seizure of the Templars. Common rumor had brought it to the hearing of our apostolic office and of our brothers, because the reasons and causes that were leading our dearest son in Christ Philip, the illustrious king of France, to a seizure of this kind—and were suggesting to you, William, that you should ask the king about this—lay concealed from our knowledge and from that of our brothers. Since nothing was made known to us by you, the aforementioned William, though you were—so to speak—at our very door, the stuff of great suspicion was aroused in our mind and in the minds of our brothers, concerning the proceedings against these same men that were held—and, as it was feared, needed to be held—by you with precipitous haste, concerning which an unheard-of public assertion came back [to us]. Because of this, suspending all the power which you had in the affair of this kind, with the counsel of the aforestated brothers, we ordered this same affair to be totally recalled to us.[80]

Clement then recounted how the king and bishops and William had repeatedly justified themselves by claiming that if the arrests had not taken place the Templars' crimes would have done irreparable damage to the faith. Clement stressed that he was not able to believe the evidence that was gathered "before the time of the suspension and revocation of the aforesaid proceedings, or at least before the suspension and revocation came to your notice."[81] But at last, after hearing the confessions of the Templars brought before him by the king, the pope began to change his mind. After the king and the bishops and William himself had beseeched him at length, Clement gave in and ordered the suspension lifted, with the qualification that the bishops, and the inquisitors "if you want to interest yourselves along with the archbishops and bishops," would have to work in tandem with other men assigned for the purpose by the pope.

The second bull is a terse and somewhat grudging letter *(Licet indignacionem)* addressed to William directly:

> Clement, bishop, servant of the servants of God, to his beloved son, Brother William of the order of Preachers, inquisitor of heretical depravity in the Kingdom of France generally appointed by apostolic authority, greetings and apostolic blessings.
>
> Although you ought to incur our not unjustified indignation for this fact—that you presumptuously proceeded against the brothers of the order of the Knights of the Temple, without seeking us out when we were so close by in the vicinity—wanting, however, to employ clemency rather than severity toward you in this regard, persuaded by the often repeated perseverance of our most beloved son in Christ Philip, illustrious king of France, out of apostolic kindness we concede to you that you may proceed against individual persons of these same Templars, together with prelates of the aforesaid kingdom and others associated with them by us, and not otherwise. And we concede this same thing to the other inquisitors of the said kingdom by the tenor of the present letter.[82]

Several points emerge from these two letters. First, it was not just William who was chastised, or just Dominican inquisitors. It was all the prelates and inquisitors of France who were temporarily suspended from the Templar prosecution. Clement had grown so distrustful that he suspected all French churchmen of being loyal to Philip rather than to him. But within this larger crisis of loyalty, William is the only one singled out by name. He is blamed repeatedly, in both letters, for having declined to inform Clement of his activities and colluded with the king to keep the pope in the dark even when he was near enough (at Poitiers) to make communication a simple matter. Even as he restored French prelates' ability to act against individual Templars, Clement was pointedly publicizing the fact that William had acted in a manner that flouted the pope's authority. In the second letter, Clement could not resist getting in one more dig, reminding William that he was still indignant at this behavior. These letters may have restored William to his full powers, but they hardly vindicated him or placed him in a good light.[83]

Second, these letters ensured that William's tenuous position with the pope would have been well known to fellow churchmen. It is likely that the French archbishops were sent copies of both of these letters—even the one ostensibly addressed to William personally—and that bishops saw them as well. At any rate the archbishops of Reims, Bourges, and Tours registered copies, and William le Maire, bishop of Angers, made a copy as well. French ecclesiastics were thus aware that while William of Paris was formally able once again to prosecute individual Templars, he was hardly in Clement's good graces.

Third, if William had indeed returned to the Templar case, his powers would have been severely curtailed. As both letters indicate, new ground rules were being laid down by the pope. Clement spelled out these instructions in a separate letter of 13 July, sent to the archbishops and bishops of France. Inquisitions against individual Templars were to be handled by the bishop, two members of the cathedral chapter, two Franciscans, and two Dominicans. William, if he had returned to a role in the Paris proceedings, would have been only one of seven men, perhaps merely as an adjunct to Bishop William Baufet of Paris.[84]

In fact, William of Paris played no further role in the trial(s) of the Templars. In addition to the reauthorized episcopal inquisitions of individuals, on 12 August Clement put in motion a new mechanism whereby eight papal commissioners would take on the question of the order's innocence or guilt as a whole, at the same time reserving the cases of the order's leaders to himself and calling for a general council to meet in Vienne in two years to settle the matter once and for all.[85] He then left Poitiers for Avignon, anxious to be away from Philip IV's heavy hand and incidentally settling into the town that would house the papacy for the next seven decades. William's name never appears in connection with the episcopal inquiries for the Archdiocese of Sens (to which we shall have to return) or in the records of the concurrent papal hearings that also began a year later in Paris in August 1309.[86] The Templar affair continued on its messy course, but for William it ended, for all intents and purposes, with the very document that ostensibly restored his powers.[87]

Inquisitor "against the Jews"

Thus William was no longer occupied with the Templar trials by the time Marguerite and Guiard entered his custody in fall 1308. It has not generally been remarked, however, that at just this moment he was also developing something of a specialty with cases of Jews who had converted and then returned to their ancestral faith.[88] While being Jewish was not a crime, leaving the Christian faith after accepting baptism was understood to constitute apostasy,[89] and in these cases inquisitors could involve themselves with the "heresy" of renouncing baptism and Christianity. And after the expulsion of 1306, in theory there were no Jews left in France—just a certain number of recent converts who might be regarded with a good deal of suspicion.

The "Continuer of William of Nangis" relates two such Parisian inquiries, immediately after recounting the arrest of the Templars in October 1307 and just before events assigned to January 1308. According to the "Continuer," a recent convert from Judaism named Proteus recognized "in the presence of the inquisitor of heretical depravity" that he had returned to Judaism at the urging of his brother Moses (*Moussetus*).[90] After questioning, however, he claimed that this confession had been a lie intended to defame Moses (who owed him money and had not wanted to repay it). But it was judged, with the counsel of experts and the assent of the bishop of Paris, that the first confession was more plausible and would stand. Proteus was therefore sentenced to perpetual imprisonment. But then "as he recognized in the presence of the aforementioned inquisitor," in prison he stated that he was "not a Christian but a Jew called Samuel, and that Christians ate their God," and that if he had to die he wanted to do it as a Jew. He was again judged with the counsel of experts and immediately handed over to the secular arm. This phrasing surely indicates that he died at the stake, though there is no evidence for the exact date or location of this execution.[91]

At about the same time (the chronicler continues), another convert to the faith named John confessed "in the presence of the aforesaid inquisitor" that he had openly and publicly declared that he was not a Christian but a Jew named Molot *(Mutlotus)*, that he had sinned in accepting baptism by water, and that he wanted to purge himself through fire.[92] But then he repented and requested mercy, claiming he had spoken through melancholy and "lightness of head." With the counsel of experts, an "exemplary punishment" was therefore imposed on him. Since this description does not mention turning him over to the secular arm, presumably the punishment was not death.[93]

Although the "inquisitor" in these two accounts is not named, there can be little doubt that it was William of Paris, the only person known to have been an inquisitor in Paris in 1307.[94] The same inquisitor is referred to in both cases, and the tales are related immediately after the arrest of the Templars, where the inquisitor under discussion was indeed William. Thus by the end of 1307 William had conducted multiple trials against recently baptized converts to Christianity, at least one of which had ended in execution.

This chapter can therefore conclude where it began, with one of William's books. William's role in inquisitorial trials of "relapsed" Jews after 1306 probably accounts for his presentation of a Hebrew Bible to the Dominicans of Bologna in 1310 (perhaps 1311 in modern reckoning). A note at the beginning of this volume read, "Brother William of Paris of the order of Brothers Preachers, confessor to the illustrious king of the Franks, gave this Hebrew Bible to the convent of Bologna for the common library of the brothers, out of reverence for the blessed Dominic, in the year 1310, the day before the Ides of February. May whoever reads it pray for him."[95] It is not difficult to imagine how "surplus" Hebrew volumes came to be in the possession of a Parisian inquisitor, since in 1306, Jewish possessions, including books, had been confiscated. Some of these books were destroyed; for instance, on Sunday, 7 December 1309, "three big full wagonloads" of books "which the Jews had compiled and made" were burned in Paris.[96] Others, however, probably ended up in the possession of royal officials (account books certainly did) and with the Franciscans and Dominicans of Paris and other French cities.

William's donation of this book was doubtless intended to make a timely contribution to his order's missionizing efforts. In the thirteenth century some Christian scholars were increasingly interested in Hebrew scholarship on the literal meanings of the Old Testament, but Dominicans particularly stressed the need to study Hebrew as an aid to attempts to convert Jews.[97] To this end, the Dominican general chapter meeting at Piacenza in June 1310 asked the master general to set up new *studia* for Hebrew, Greek, and Arabic so that "apt and intelligent students" might be sent there from any province.[98] The Council of Vienne in 1311 similarly resolved to found new chairs in these languages at Paris, Oxford, Bologna, Rome, and Salamanca. Though little ever came of these resolutions, a new desire for a missionizing knowledge of Hebrew was in the air in 1310, with Bologna one of the proposed centers for study. Thus William's gift of a Hebrew text probably ties into a Dominican sense of mission, providing a volume that would help his brothers confront Jews on their own scriptural turf. His donation out of "reverence for Dominic" surely recognized Dominic's personal association with Bologna and his death there; but with this gift William also wove biblical scholarship, language study, and Dominic's example together into the historical Dominican mission of preaching against nonbelievers.

In the fall of 1307 William had been spearheading the most audacious attack ever launched on a monastic order; a year later he had been publicly chastised and only grudgingly restored to papal grace. It may not be a coincidence that William's involvement with the Templar interrogations ended just at the moment that his known trials of "relapsed" Jews also concluded. After the summer of 1308 William was in a sort of limbo. He still held his position as royal confessor—Philip IV was known for his unshakable loyalty to his close advisors, and there is no indication that the king had lost confidence in him. He also continued to hold the powers of an inquisitor. But because Clement V had made his displeasure known in a very public fashion, any future activity William undertook specifically as an inquisitor "by papal authority" would have to be conducted in such a manner so as to withstand the closest scrutiny. It was at this moment in the fall of 1308 that the cases of Marguerite Porete and Guiard of Cressonessart were put into his hands.

CHAPTER 4

First Steps

Marguerite Porete and William of Paris had more in common in the fall of 1308 than one might think. Both must have felt deceived by recent events. Marguerite had patiently gathered support for her writings but then apparently miscalculated if she intentionally communicated her book to the bishop of Châlons-sur-Marne. William had garnered royal and papal office and carried off his assigned part in Philip IV's attack on the Templars but then suffered a public papal censure. In spite of these congruent trajectories, once Marguerite was in William's custody the contest between them would obviously be unequal. Marguerite did retain some ability to influence the course of events, or at least their pace. Other "heretics" might treat an inquisition as a chance to express their ideas,[1] but Marguerite chose the path of noncooperation. Such legal delaying tactics to put off the commencement of a process were not uncommon. The Templars gathered in Paris, for example, would stall by declining to appoint procurators,[2] and Clement V himself delayed Boniface VIII's posthumous heresy proceedings by refusing to consider deponents as formal witnesses.[3] Playing for time was a rational strategy when holding a weak legal hand—during a delay circumstances might change, opponents might die, the political winds might shift.[4] In the meantime, Marguerite's methods forced William of Paris to maneuver carefully, since neither a confession nor self-incriminating testimony would be forthcoming. For the inquisitor, the question at hand cannot have been primarily Marguerite's guilt or innocence, since he must have known that she had admitted to acts that virtually ensured her punishment as a recalcitrant heretic. Rather the issue was how to construct an airtight legal case and ensure that the ultimate sentence would be beyond any possible challenge. William therefore employed the utmost circumspection in pursing her process.

But it was also at this point that events took an unexpected twist with Guiard of Cressonessart's irruption onto the scene. The appearance of the self-proclaimed Angel of Philadelphia was probably as surprising to Marguerite as it was to William. It was the inquisitor, however, who would have to determine how to deal with Guiard. This complicating element must have further encouraged his caution. If this *beguina* from Hainaut could inspire sympathy from men ranging from the famous theologian Godfrey of Fontaines to a *beguinus* sent to "defend the adherents of the Lord," who could say what other supporters might be waiting in the wings?

Marguerite's Move to Paris

No evidence explains the physical process by which Marguerite got from the custody of the bishop of Cambrai to that of the inquisitor in Paris. The approximate date, however, is clear. Marguerite is described in several documents from early April 1310 as having been imprisoned under William's jurisdiction for almost a year and a half, so her incarceration in Paris must have begun sometime around October 1308.

It has sometimes been suggested that Marguerite could have traveled to Paris of her own free will and remained there, at large, until being arrested.[5] Although the trial documents at first glance seem to allow this possibility, on closer scrutiny this interpretation is impossible to sustain. After admitting several times that she had flagrantly violated an episcopal order to cease writing and teaching her condemned ideas, Marguerite could hardly have gone free, only to journey directly to Paris in time to be jailed by William in later 1308. The confusion stems from the way the trial documents draw on standard formats for uncooperative suspects, which were often those who attempted to evade summonses.[6] The wording of these texts was intended to establish precise legal grounds for subsequent actions, not to relate an exact course of events.

Specifically, one document (which must ultimately reflect wording crafted by William of Paris) says first that "a certain *beguina* named Marguerite Porete of Hainaut was suspected for various probable causes of the stain of heretical depravity" and that "after she many times contumaciously refused to appear, [William] caused this same woman to be personally brought into his presence."[7] A second trial document says Marguerite "was suspected for various probable causes of the stain of heretical depravity, and because of this was arrested by [William]."[8] In a third formulation, William directly recounts that "you, Marguerite of Hainaut, called Porete, were vehemently suspected of the stain of heretical depravity; because of this we caused you to be summoned, so that you might appear before us in judgment."[9] What each account emphasizes is that "suspicion" or "vehement suspicion" led to Marguerite's incarceration and appearance before the inquisitor. This was the crucial point; what mattered legally was the establishment of public ill-repute *(fama)* and justifiable suspicion.[10] The phrasing "many times contumaciously refused to appear" might sound as though Marguerite was strolling the streets of Paris, but here it must simply mean that she was refusing to be cooperative while already in custody. The fuzziness over whether Marguerite was "brought into [William's] presence" or "arrested" or "summoned" reflects the fact that detailing the exact physical manner in which she was detained was not essential to the legal case being documented here. This interpretation is borne out by the chronicle evidence of the "Continuer of William of Nangis," who states that Marguerite would not abjure her errors and endured excommunication for a year or more but still "did not want to appear in [William's] presence, although she had been sufficiently warned."[11] This passage strongly implies that her "refusal to appear" in William's presence occurred after she was taken into custody.

There are therefore two possibilities for how Marguerite arrived in Paris. One is that her interviews with the inquisitor of Lorraine and Philip of Marigny took place in Valenciennes or elsewhere in the Diocese of Cambrai. Then when she was turned over to inquisitorial jurisdiction in Paris, she would have been physically transported there in fall 1308. But there is another possibility, which is that when the inquisitor of Lorraine brought her before Philip of Marigny for episcopal questioning, Philip was residing in Paris for an extended stay, and the interview occurred there for his convenience. In that case, Marguerite would have arrived in Paris some weeks or months earlier.

There is, in fact, some evidence to support the latter scenario. Philip of Marigny must of course have been resident in his diocese frequently, but it is also certain that much of his attention continued to be directed toward the royal court and that he was frequently in Paris. Thus, shortly after his elevation, he was present in the Sainte-Chapelle at the king's request (with John of Châteauvillain) for the translation of St. Louis's head-relic in May 1306.[12] Then from at least late 1307 he was embroiled in a dispute with Countess Mahaut of Artois over the latter's rights to jurisdiction over part of the city of Cambrai.[13] On 23 December 1307 Philip of Marigny issued a document—notarized by Evens Phili, who would later handle some of the documents in the trials of Marguerite and Guiard—from the hôtel of the bishop of Cambrai in the Parish of Saint-Germain-l'Auxerrois in Paris (near the Louvre), which accepted Philip IV's arbitration in the dispute.[14] From this date until this legal squabble was resolved on 6 April 1308, Philip of Marigny may have wanted to be present frequently at court.[15] If the bishop of Cambrai was in Paris for some part of early 1308, it is possible that his interrogation of Marguerite took place there as well. In this scenario, turning her over to William of Paris would have been a simple matter of shifting jurisdictions, rather than a long-distance physical transfer.

In either case, all of the formulations from William's documents cited above stress his own action—his citation, summons, or arrest of Marguerite. William therefore made an active choice (presumably in consultation with Philip of Marigny) to inquire into Marguerite's case from Paris. As far as the extant documentation reveals, the inquisitor had undertaken no new inquiries after his suspension from the Templar process.[16] He now claimed jurisdiction over this inquisition into a new case of heretical depravity, one that in fact asserted his ability to draw in an accused heretic from the far northern reaches of the "*regno Francie*" for which he was commissioned. In political terms considering Valenciennes part of "France" was highly dubious; this extradition (to use an anachronistic term) to Paris was thus a more dramatic act than has often been realized. Indeed, Marguerite's arrival in Paris and her transfer to inquisitorial custody must have caused a stir, to judge by the way it drew the attention of the man who would prove to be her last defender.

Enter the Angel

Guiard of Cressonessart's dramatic intervention may be the most unexpected moment in this entire story. William of Paris can only have been taken by surprise at the appearance of such a "protester." As usual, the only available information comes from the trial documents' very brief description. Several documents recount that Guiard "came forth publicly, demonstrably, and notoriously in defense and aid of Marguerite."[17] In his final sentence, William modified this phrasing slightly to "you . . . notoriously fell into aid and defense of Marguerite" and then went on to say that he had warned Guiard not to impede him in his inquisitorial work, "nor provide defense, aid, counsel, or favor to the said Marguerite."[18] What exactly William meant to imply by the assertion that Guiard "came forth" is not clear, but evidently it was an action that was visible and public, calling attention to the injustice of Marguerite's incarceration. The documents suggest that William may have given him a warning to desist but met with stubborn persistence. Guiard was therefore arrested along with Marguerite. Since he, like Marguerite, is described in April 1310 as having been incarcerated for almost a year and a half, his demonstrations must have happened more or less immediately after Marguerite entered William's custody.

What had Guiard known of Marguerite before this point? The ideas he eventually explained to his inquisitor do not mark him as Marguerite's intellectual disciple. It is not impossible that he encountered her writings at some previous time, but on the whole it seems more likely that it was Marguerite's plight in and of itself that moved Guiard, not an abstract interest in her ideas. He probably had never met her at all before her entrance into Paris and can have had little opportunity to exchange ideas with her once she was imprisoned.

The Standoff

There is no evidence as to exactly where, within Paris, Marguerite and Guiard were held for their twenty-month ordeal. Nor is it clear whether they were kept in the same location or separately. It is quite possible that they did not meet at all during this entire process. There was no formally designated "inquisitorial jail" in Paris (unlike Carcassonne with its "Wall"),[19] and although royal and episcopal holding cells certainly existed, the haphazard nature of contemporary imprisonment is shown by the facilities in which the Templars were incarcerated at just this time. By February 1310, Paris was in fact overflowing with these prisoners. In addition to the seventy-five brothers confined in the Temple itself, others were being held in at least thirty different locations, including monastic settings, private houses, and episcopal residences. By March nearly six hundred Templars were imprisoned in Paris—it must, in fact, have been somewhat of a challenge to find space for Marguerite and Guiard.[20]

William explained in multiple documents how he went about his business between fall 1308 and March 1310. Here he is at pains to show that he followed proper legal procedure in both cases: he asked Marguerite and Guiard (separately and individually) to take an oath "concerning speaking truly about those things which had been reported and revealed about her/him." They each refused, though they did both acknowledge that William was a duly appointed inquisitor. William therefore placed them under major excommunication.[21] Over the course of eighteen months, he claims to have tried frequently to extract the necessary oaths, offering them absolution in return.[22] William gave slightly more detail in the final sentences, noting that the requested oath was "to tell the full, pure, and whole truth about yourself and others, regarding those things which are known to pertain to the office of inquisition committed to us," that the sentences of major excommunication were put in writing, and that this step had been taken with the counsel of many learned men.[23] Again, these documents served the legal purpose of establishing that the inquisitor had followed correct procedure; they were not intended to tell a full story of what occurred in these months. Nevertheless, they allow several points to be made, first about William's intentions, then about Marguerite and Guiard's.

William was playing things strictly by the book. When faced with someone who refused to take an oath, canon law and inquisitorial practice were both well established by this time. Since at least 1184, canon law had declared that suspects called before an inquisition (episcopal inquisitions at that early date) to answer legitimate, substantiated charges but refusing to swear an oath "are from that very circumstance to be adjudged heretics."[24] Dominican practice had refined the exact inquisitorial procedure to be followed in such cases, as laid out most fully just a few years later by William's Dominican contemporary Bernard Gui, in his *Practica inquisitionis heretice pravitatis* (finished by 1323). For those who refuse to give unconditional oaths,

> after a canonical admonition has been given, a written sentence of excommunication shall be imposed. . . . If, however, he incurs the sentence of excommunication and for some days bears it obstinately and with a hardened spirit, he shall then be called back into court and asked if he considers himself excommunicated and bound by this sentence. If he replies that he does not . . . it is then clear from this very fact that he scorns the keys of the church. This scorn is an article of error and a heresy, and anyone who obstinately persists in it is deemed heretical . . . and further legal action shall now be taken against him as far as the law permits, through canonical admonition, peremptory exhortation that he renounce this error and heresy and abjure it. And if he does not, he shall be judged to be a heretic, condemned, and as such transferred to the judgment of the secular court.
>
> It must be noted that in order to convict him of his wickedness . . . a fresh sentence of excommunication can be written against him, as one who is contumacious on a question of faith, that is, obstinately refusing to give a plain and absolute oath or even to respond to questions of faith or to abjure his exact error and heresy. In this he manifestly appears evasive, no less than one who is summoned and contumaciously absents himself. The sentence against him shall be clearly made known to him and written down. If anyone thus excommunicated for contumacy in matters of faith bears this sentence of excommunication with a stubborn spirit for more than a year, for this he ought to be legally deemed a heretic and can be condemned.[25]

In stressing that he offered the oath, then issued a written sentence of excommunication, then tried again patiently for at least eighteen months, William was simply filling in the legal blanks. He may not have adhered to Bernard's policy of asking the accused whether they considered themselves justly excommunicated, but in all other regards he might as well have been reading from Bernard's manual (or, to put it more accurately, the congruence of William's actions and Bernard's subsequent prescriptions demonstrates the development of consistent Dominican inquisitorial practice). Where Bernard speaks of suspects "bearing the sentence of excommunication for more than a year with a stubborn spirit" *(si dictam excommunicationis sententiam ultra annum sustinuerit animo pertinaci),* William describes Marguerite and Guiard as "bearing the aforesaid notification [of major excommunication] with a stubborn spirit for almost a year and a half" *(post notificationem predictam fere per annum et dimidium . . . sustinuisti animo pertinaci).*[26]

William may indeed have spent long hours trying to reason with these two, or he may have made only the most cursory of appearances to ask if they had changed their minds. The formulaic Latin of the documents does not specify.[27] What can be perceived, however, is William's extreme caution in handling these two cases. Other contemporary inquisitors, such as Bishop Jacques Fournier (the future Benedict XII), were occasionally willing to take unsworn statements in cases where defendants refused the oath.[28] For a high-profile case in Paris, however, William did not wish to see any legal loopholes emerge. Similarly, in her inquisitorial trial a century later, Joan of Arc negotiated at length over exactly what oaths and how many she would swear, but her episcopal and Dominican inquisitors would not proceed until she agreed to take an acceptable oath.[29] In a case that might come under scrutiny, the oath was essential. William had recently been stung by his overconfident attempt to manipulate inquisitorial proceedings against the Templars for royal benefit. He evidently decided that if Marguerite and Guiard would not swear, patience would be a virtue.

As for Marguerite and Guiard, there are several points to be made about their stubborn "silence" over a year and a half. First, the impression of an absolute refusal to communicate is probably illusory. It is not evident that they refused to utter a sound, only that they would not take a judicial oath. There may in fact have been substantial conversations between the detainees and their inquisitor. For instance, both are said to have "recognized" that William was an inquisitor performing the duties of his office. At the very least, the refusals they made concerning the oath were probably verbal. Granted that it is possible to imagine communication entirely through mute nods and silent shakes of the head, this would seem somewhat fanciful. The standard picture of Marguerite and Guiard disdainfully declining to speak to their captors is probably an exaggeration. What they did do was refuse, formally, to take the oath that would allow judicial proceedings to commence with their participation. This tactic forced the inquisitor either to ride roughshod over standard legal protections or to play a waiting game. Recalcitrance was thus an effective, if temporary, form of resistance. Moreover, in Marguerite's case, she had repeatedly seen that some churchmen found her book acceptable. She might have made a rational calculation that the longer she drew things out, the greater the chance that some new support would emerge. Second is the seemingly coordinated nature of this refusal to swear an oath. This is really the only evidence that suggests Marguerite and Guiard acting together in some way. Perhaps this concerted strategy does indicate that the two prisoners had some chance to communicate even while imprisoned.

How would William counter this strategy? One thing he did not do was employ torture. This omission may seem odd to modern audiences accustomed to equating "the Inquisition" with the ruthless application of pain. To be sure, inquisitors, like other ecclesiastical and secular judicial officials, could legally use torture to extract confessions within certain limits.[30] The evidence for their use of torture in this era, however, is actually slim.[31] It seems most often to have been employed in cases where inquisitors suspected that information gained could break up a larger conspiracy of some kind (not unlike the rationale claimed for the utility of torture by some agents of the American government in the early twenty-first century). Where it was assumed that a suspect really did know something concrete that he otherwise refused to tell, torture could elicit it. For example, many Templars in Paris were clearly tortured into false confessions at just this time (though this was done by royal agents). The point here was not so much to extract confessions of individual misbelief as to prove larger associations and reveal a web of heretical intrigue that could implicate an entire order. Similarly, Jews, lepers, and Muslims were tortured (again by secular officials) in southern France and Catalonia in 1320–21 when they were linked in a vast (and imaginary) conspiracy to poison wells.[32] Again, the goal was to determine who had participated in an alleged plot, rather than to force confessions of deviant thought. Medieval people were fully aware that subjects would say anything required of them under sustained torture.[33] Pain could be used to coerce a confession to a predetermined set of charges when a simple confession was all that was needed (as with the Templars); it could enforce conformity and change behaviors through the lingering fear it inspired;[34] but it could not be trusted to elicit anyone's innermost thoughts. The later trial of Joan of Arc again provides a useful comparison: her judges threatened her with possible torture, but after taking learned counsel on whether it would serve any purpose they decided against it as counterproductive.[35]

Even without resorting to means that would unequivocally be considered torture by modern standards, William could have attempted to coerce his recalcitrant suspects into quicker cooperation. Bernard Gui, for instance, allowed the possibility of extreme pressure being brought to bear on prisoners in just this situation: for a defendant refusing to swear an oath, after excommunication "witnesses may be called against him . . . or he may be constrained or restricted in diet, or otherwise [held] in confinement or fetters or even 'be questioned' on the advice of experienced persons . . . so that the truth may be forced out."[36] The Latin verb for "be questioned" used here, *quaestionari,* can also mean "be tortured,"[37] and that was indeed probably what Bernard intended to suggest (one of the only times he ever mentions torture). But even before arriving at that eventuality, he advocated severe measures to force the taking of the oath. Perhaps William did make the conditions of Marguerite and Guiard's imprisonment particularly harsh in this way; there is simply no evidence to tell us. What is clear is that William relied primarily on excommunication and extended incarceration to achieve his ends, instead of the application of extreme pain.

Why this patience? Since William was fully complicit in the campaign against the Templars, with its barely concealed application of torture, the answer cannot be that he had a principled aversion to the use of brute force. The simple fact is that he did not call for torture because he did not need to. In Marguerite's case, her previous contumacious behavior could be established independently, and the issue concerning her personal guilt was not, at heart, about her ideas so much as her actions. Torture could have been used to force her to admit that her ideas had been theologically wrong and that her behavior had been an affront to the church. But insincere confessions elicited through force had come back to haunt William with the Templars—such confessions could be recanted later and, as he now knew all too well, could serve to darken the reputation of the inquisitor. With Guiard, perhaps torture did seem like a viable option, and it is not impossible that he was threatened with it, since there are indications that William was interested in ascertaining whether he had followers. The fact that he was not tortured may again simply reflect the nature of his case.[38] William had evidence, based on firsthand knowledge, of Guiard's attempts to obstruct his inquiries—a confession from Guiard himself was not actually necessary for a conviction on this point.

Instead of resorting to the quick and dirty method of torture, William set about the basic legal work of gathering testimony against Marguerite (there is no evidence that additional testimony against Guiard was sought). For one thing, he does relate, without further detail, that he took the counsel of "many experts" *(de multorum peritorum consilio)* before excommunicating Marguerite and Guiard. Perhaps these were preliminary consultations with some of the same masters who would later give formal opinions. More specifically, William in his final sentencing of Marguerite recalled that "while you, Marguerite, were remaining obstinate in these rebellions, we—led by conscience, wanting to carry out the responsibility of our office committed to us—conducted an inquiry against you."[39] This inquiry seems to have involved the acquisition of at least some written evidence, since William then strongly implies that he had Bishop Guido's earlier letter at hand. It also apparently included the gathering of sworn testimony of witnesses. This would have been standard procedure for an inquisitor, to call in anyone who had knowledge of a case of heresy. But who were the "many witnesses" in this case? The most obvious, and well-informed, sources of information were John of Châteauvillain, Philip of Marigny, and the inquisitor of Lorraine. If William followed formal protocol, there should once have existed sworn depositions from these men.[40] John and Philip were frequently in Paris and could have come into William's "presence" there. William could also have traveled to Cambrai or Valenciennes, or sent minions there to gather testimony. Such an evidence-gathering mission might have been the source for his claim that Marguerite had "imparted" her book to "many simple people," including beghards, if witnesses in Hainaut were willing to swear to this fact.[41] But the testimony of John and Philip would have been quite enough to establish the relevant facts to William's satisfaction, and it is quite possible that these men alone constituted his "many witnesses." If so, this gathering of testimony could have been a fairly brief affair.

Through this inquiry William established the "facts" already covered in chapter 2: that Marguerite's book had been condemned once by Guido, bishop of Cambrai; that Guido had issued a written warning to desist or face punishment as a relapsed heretic; that she had nevertheless sent the book to others, including the bishop of Châlons-sur-Marne, and had confessed this before the inquisitor of Lorraine and the new bishop of Cambrai. If this narrative was sworn to by credible witnesses, it would have allowed William to proceed further against her, with or without her cooperation.

The extremely interesting fact, however, is that although William must have had this information at his disposal by March 1310, he kept his cards close to the vest.[42] Rather than immediately seek to convict Marguerite based on this entire history, he moved deliberately from one legal question to the next.

The First Consultations:
The March Meeting and the Opinions of 3 April

Even after the prescribed twelve months of excommunication were up (which would have been around October 1309 if the excommunications were issued right away), William still did not take any hasty steps.[43] Two external factors might have propelled the inquisitor to finally move forward in March 1310.

First, new developments in the Templar proceedings at Paris would have offered a strong spur. The papal commission charged with the inquiry into the guilt or innocence of the order as a whole had been impaneled under the presidency of Gilles Aycelin, who was archbishop of Narbonne but a member of Philip IV's inner circle of advisors.[44] This commission began its work by holding inconclusive hearings in November 1309 at Paris but then adjourned until 3 February 1310.[45] Philip IV, to this point, probably remained confident that Archbishop Gilles and his commission would continue to encounter only confessions from intimidated Templars. But by February some leaders of the order had begun to rally the brothers to a defense. In fact, over five hundred Templars brought from all over France now declared themselves ready to defend the order.[46] By 28 March, this surge of defiance reached the point where 546 Templars were gathered in the garden behind the bishop of Paris's residence (next to the cathedral of Notre-Dame) and asked to choose procurators to present their case.

William himself was no longer involved in these proceedings, yet his reputation was still tightly bound up in the question of the Templars' guilt. Although Gilles Aycelin had made his belief in the order's culpability well known, the strengthening Templar defense raised the possibility that the commission would eventually be forced to exonerate the order, in which case William's own part in the initial arrests would hardly have appeared in a positive light.[47] Thus the end of March would have been an opportune moment for William to generate a countering narrative highlighting the effective nature of inquisitorial proceedings carried out under his authority.

Second was the prospect of a posthumous heresy trial of Boniface VIII. This had been a contentious issue since the election of Clement V, but now the pope had agreed to hold a new round of formal hearings on the question of whether Philip IV's great opponent had in fact been a heretic. Several of Philip IV's key ministers took part in this process, which began March 16 at Avignon.[48] Notably, William of Nogaret and William of Plaisians were personally in Avignon from about 4 March until at least 17 May, and probably still in the South through much of the summer.[49] King Philip, however, remained in Paris throughout March and during an assembly of his barons in early April before departing for various travels that lasted until early July.[50] Though the proceedings against Boniface did not concern William of Paris so directly, they suggested the larger desirability of some public demonstration of the royal circle's effective prosecution of heresy. With Nogaret and Plaisians occupied elsewhere, William held center stage in Paris to orchestrate such a spectacle himself.

Against the backdrop of these larger events, William took his first concrete actions in March 1310. The document that records the initial steps (AN J428 no. 16) is actually a complex notarial instrument that requires two preliminary points. First, this single document reflects three distinct stages in its compilation. At its heart is an opinion issued by five regent masters of canon law, dated 3 April. Another copy of this opinion survives as well, in accurate but unnotarized form (AN J428 no. 17), and there was once a solemn original with the masters' seals attached. This record of the canonists' decision was then embedded in a second layer of text, which was a notarized document intended to convey the opinion of 3 April while explaining how it had come to be issued. This document was compiled and authenticated by the notary Evens Phili, either on 3 April or perhaps a few days later.[51] It is this second layer that narrates the larger gathering called together by William of Paris in March. Finally, the outermost layer in the document is a later collation whereby the notary Jacques of Vertus, with two other clerical witnesses, made a faithful copy on 4 October—four months after the completion of the trials.

Second, although this document relates specifically to debate about Guiard's case, almost certainly an analogous document concerning Marguerite must have been created at the same time. Though no such document is extant, it would be a mistake to think that Guiard's case was taken up first, independently of Marguerite's.[52]

The "second layer" of the surviving document tells us that on an unspecified date in March William called together an impressive group of masters of theology and canon law. The evidence for William's handling of cases concerning "relapsed" Jews shows that he made a regular practice of consulting experts before rendering judgments. This time fifteen masters of theology and five masters of canon law met at the Dominican house of Saint-Jacques in response to the inquisitor's request for advice. The notary Evens Phili was there to record the proceedings, and four of the masters of theology (listed separately) were asked to act as witnesses. Most likely Evens wrote up a record of the meeting at this time, into which the opinion of 3 April was later incorporated.

The narrative records that William did not want to proceed rashly against Guiard and so asked for counsel from the assembled masters as to "what was to be done" in this case. The masters of theology and canon law then deliberated and decided among themselves that the masters of canon law should handle this consultation. This was a fairly obvious conclusion, since Guiard had not yet expressed any theological opinions. The relevant issues were around legal interpretations of his actions and were hence best handled by the canonists.

Since the theologians declined to offer any opinion at this point, we will leave them aside for now. Here it was the canonists who gave crucial support to William. These five named regent masters of canon law (*magistri in decretis*) were William called "Brother," archdeacon of St. Andrews in Scotland (styled "master of both laws," i.e., canon and civil); Hugh of Besançon, canon of Paris; John of Thélus, canon of Saint-Quintin in the Vermandois; Henry of Béthune (called in another document "canon of Furnes"); and Peter of Vaux, curate of Saint-Germain-l'Auxerrois in Paris. This must have been a hand-picked group, probably chosen for their perceived reliability from among the fifteen to twenty masters of canon law resident in Paris.[53]

William called "Brother" was the senior member, a Scot who had benefited from the patronage of Philip IV since assuming his teaching chair around 1302.[54] But Hugh of Besançon is the only one of these men whose career can be traced in detail—and his example is instructive.[55] He was doctor of canon law at Paris at least by August 1302, canon of Laon sometime around 1303, canon of Notre Dame by November 1305, and canon of Besançon around the same time.[56] He was one of the university masters called by William of Paris to hear the confessions of Jacques of Molay and other Templars in October 1307, when he was referred to as "doctor of both laws."[57] A year later, in August 1308, he (along with many other churchmen) was given a payment by Clement V for services connected to the Templar trial.[58] Hugh was subsequently to become master of the grand chamber of the Parlement of Paris in 1316 and finally bishop of Paris from 1326 to his death in 1332. His success in these latter decades seems to have rested in part on his ties to Jeanne of Burgundy, wife of Philip V. She had been raised at the French court in anticipation of her marriage, and Hugh—who came from the same region—may have played a role in her education,[59] much as William of Paris had been confessor to her intended husband. Thus this future bishop of Paris was an effective careerist with strong ties to the French royal family. William of Paris must have known him well and would have had every reason to believe he could count on his support.

The canonists may have actually conferred and formulated their advice on the spot that day in March, but if so they adjourned without producing a written opinion. At least several days or weeks passed (depending on when in March this first meeting occurred) before these five issued their formal opinion on 3 April. They first repeated the facts of the case as William had provided them and then moved on to state their opinion: since Guiard's defense of Marguerite "passed over first into vehement and then into violent presumption of heresy," and since he was clearly rebellious and stubborn, he "must be considered a heretic and definitively condemned as a heretic and relinquished to secular authority" unless he quickly repented and abjured his errors, in which case he should be sentenced to life in prison.[60]

There was further legal paperwork to be done, however. Rather than simply securing a notarized copy of this opinion, William of Paris saw that it was inserted into the larger document narrating the meeting at the Dominican house in March. The notary Evens Phili states that he had been present at the meeting itself to record the original deliberation of the masters of theology and canon law and that he then "caused the letters of aforesaid consultation" from 3 April "sealed with the seals of the said masters, as they said, to be faithfully incorporated here, and having diligently collated them with the present instrument and found them to agree with each other, subscribed myself and added my customary sign." His notarized document was therefore a legal instrument that could be treated as evidence.

The notary also indicated that four of the masters of theology "consented and expressly acquiesced in the counsel of the said masters, as witnesses specially called and invited for this purpose." These were the Augustinian friars Alexander of Marcia (also known as Alexander of Sant'Elpidio) and Gregory of Lucca; the Cistercian Jacques of Dijon; and Ralph of Hotot, who is usually considered to have been a secular theologian but may possibly have been a Mendicant.[61] At first glance it is unclear why these men are listed as witnesses, separate from the eleven theologians presented as taking part in the initial deliberations. Most of these men were familiar with royal business and heresy proceedings, since Alexander, Ralph, and probably Jacques had signed the consultation on the Templars on 25 March 1308. It was certainly not a case of the less distinguished theologians being relegated to the status of witnesses—Alexander was already a senior member of the faculty of theology and was subsequently elected prior general of his order in 1312 and bishop of Amalfi shortly before his death in 1326. Although the others were slightly less experienced, Gregory eventually became bishop of Sorra (Sardinia) and then Belluno-Feltre by 1323, and Jacques served as abbot of Preuilly from 1312 to 1332.[62] (Ralph's subsequent career is more obscure.)[63]

Instead, it seems that the process of incorporating the later opinion back into a narrative about the March meeting produced some awkwardness in the notarial phrasing. The document as it was prepared by Evens Phili says these men were witnesses "present" "at the house of the Dominicans of Paris, in the year, indiction, month, day, and pontificate aforementioned," which should indicate the March date (not 3 April).[64] Yet they are described as having "consented and acquiesced in the counsel of the said masters," which must mean the opinion ultimately issued 3 April. What seems most likely is that the canonists gave their counsel first in verbal form at the March meeting and that these theologians represented the larger group in acting as witnesses at that time. The canonists may have preferred that their opinion then be recorded in their own formal, sealed document (or William of Paris may have asked for the production of such a document), which would have had to have been drawn up afterward. When Evens Phili received the 3 April opinion, he collated this sealed document with the earlier memorandum and thereby created the notarized instrument that guaranteed the authenticity of the entire proceedings.

As noted above, almost certainly the theologians and canonists were asked in March to consider the cases of both Guiard and Marguerite. This assertion is supported by the fact that on the same date of 3 April the same five canonists issued an opinion on Marguerite's case (AN J428 no. 19) that bears nearly identical wording and renders the same substantive decision as in Guiard's case. This is an unnotarized document, parallel exactly to the unnotarized form (J428 no. 17) that gives the bare decision about Guiard. So although in Marguerite's case the notarized document that would have integrated the opinion of 3 April into the larger narrative of the March meeting does not survive, the process of deliberation must have been concurrent and identical.

Concerning Marguerite, the canonists were again clear. Her stubborn refusal to cooperate, in and of itself, sufficed for her condemnation as a heretic and justified her relaxation to the secular arm for punishment. It is particularly interesting that in these documents the canon lawyers did not draw a distinction between the two cases. Guiard at this point could be convicted of nothing beyond his obstinacy and his obstruction of the inquisitor. For Marguerite, by contrast, this was

in a general sense her second strike, after her confession of having continued to circulate her book—or even her third, counting her initial
confrontation with Bishop Guido. There is no indication, however,
that the canonists had in fact been given Marguerite's entire history. At
least as far as the formal documentation demonstrates, they had been
told only of her arrest on strong suspicion of heresy and of her obstinate refusal to swear an oath. At this point, the inquisitor was only
posing the limited question of whether her actions since incarceration
sufficed to place her in the legal category of a contumacious heretic, and
he gave out only information pertinent to this issue. But this evidence
suggested only her "lapse" into heresy, not a relapse. The canonists
therefore included the same clause that they had inserted in their opinion regarding Guiard, which stated that if Marguerite repented in time
she should be sentenced to perpetual imprisonment. Indeed, it may be
that William was purposely holding open the possibility that Marguerite's trial might still end with her confession, reconciliation, and imprisonment. In any case, he had not yet publicized the information—
concerning her earlier brushes with church authority—that would have
virtually ensured her relaxation to the secular arm.

Was this consultation with the masters of canon law strictly necessary? In a purely legal sense, the answer is certainly no. The canonists were simply giving a stamp of approval to what was already clear
law—failing to cooperate with a proper inquisition, impeding such an
inquisition, and refusing to swear the oath were grounds for conviction
as a contumacious heretic. As the canonists indicated, William "sufficed" to make this ruling himself. William—the author of a widely circulated finding aid for canon law—was surely well enough informed to
know this. So why did he go to the trouble to convoke fifteen theologians and five canonists?

On one level, asking for expert opinion before taking a legal step
was just good policy.[65] But the specific nature of William's actions indicates something more than standard procedure. He was attempting to
demonstrate the university's support for his actions and to ensure that
his personal decisions would not be the sole justification for the process should any aspect of the trial prove problematic. This interpretation is borne out most clearly by William's attempt to involve the theologians at this stage. The masters of theology reached an immediately
obvious conclusion in declining to offer an opinion—there were no

theological issues involved with Guiard at this stage. Concerning Marguerite, the same thing in fact holds true. To condemn her book would indeed require theological judgment, but at this point William was presenting a very limited case against Guiard and Marguerite's persons.[66]

The large gathering William had summoned to Saint-Jacques by including the theologians was thus unnecessary in any strict legal sense. Indeed, it is more reminiscent of the way university masters, from across the faculties, were brought in to hear Jacques of Molay's staged confession at the Temple, not because their expertise was actually required, but to ensure the support of these influential intellectuals as the case unfolded. William's additional use of four masters of theology as witnesses for the Saint-Jacques meeting is probably best explained in this context as well: they were asked to witness the proceedings specifically so that there would still be some involvement from the faculty of theology, even though the theologians as a group had not given an opinion on the legal questions.

Finally, the way the document was drawn up is worthy of note. The notary public, Evens Phili of Saint-Nicaise, was a cleric from the Breton diocese of Quimper, with whom William had worked extensively in the early Templar depositions in 1307.[67] (We have seen that Philip of Marigny relied on his services as well.) In this case, there was no particular need to do anything other than record the sealed opinion of the canonists. Yet William made sure that the legal document recorded the involvement of the wider group of masters and made it clear how he had gathered them all together and sought their support. Indeed, Evens Phili's phrasing suggested that the theologians agreed to "stand behind" the canonists' decision, and the witnessing of that decision by some of them further emphasized the point. The structure of this document again indicates that William's primary purpose in March was to implicate the university in the textual record of the process.

Here matters stood as of 3 April 1310. William of Paris had secured learned legal confirmation that both Guiard and Marguerite could legitimately be handed over to the secular authorities for punishment if they remained impenitent. Had he wished to move directly to this denouement, he could have done so at any time. Yet he held off, probably waiting to see whether this clear threat of impending execution would convince his two charges to testify. In the case of Guiard, he was not to be disappointed.

CHAPTER 5

Philadelphia Story

William of Paris must surely have communicated the canonists' decision to Marguerite and Guiard and spelled out—if this was necessary—what the possibility of relaxation to the secular arm implied. There is no indication that the opinions of 3 April had any effect on Marguerite's conduct. Guiard, however, was not immune to this threat of impending execution. Within days he decided to answer the inquisitor's questions.

But William may have been under significant pressure himself in the first week of April if he was paying attention to the growing momentum of the Templar defense. Between 31 March and 7 April, Archbishop Gilles Aycelin's papal commission dispatched at least seven notaries to gather testimony from the Templars imprisoned in Paris who wished to defend the order.[1] Over the course of fifty-nine visits to thirty different places of detention, they recorded statements from 537 Templars, who defended the order's innocence with near unanimity.[2] In a sense, every brother who joined the chorus of voices claiming that their crimes had been fabricated and their confessions coerced was offering an indictment of William and his role in the royal attack on the order. This cannot have been an easy week for Philip IV's confessor.

Cressonessart Redux

Interestingly enough, among the most prominent leaders of the Templar defense was one Matthew of Cressonessart. Considering his place of origin, his story offers an appropriate window on the dramatic developments of the first week of April. According to his later deposition, Matthew was from the Diocese of Beauvais, and so certainly from the same village as Guiard. Matthew was born about 1275, entered the order in Paris around 1293, and eventually became the preceptor of the house of Bellinval in the Diocese of Amiens.[3] As early as 17 February 1310 he was among those coming forward to defend the order, and on 28 March he was part of the crowd of Templars gathered in the gardens of the bishop of Paris.[4] This Matthew had been held, along with ten of his brothers, under the guard of one Colart of Evreux. These eleven men were interviewed by the notaries on Wednesday, 1 April, and protested that their order was "good and holy and legal."[5] They refused to suggest procurators but asked to be able to consult with the order's leaders. Two days later, on the same 3 April on which the canon lawyers were issuing their opinions on Guiard of Cressonessart and Marguerite Porete, these eleven Templars sent a statement of defense, written in French, which Colart of Evreux carried to the commission for them. This statement again asked to consult with specific leaders of the order and requested that the eleven be allowed to come before the commission personally—or, if this were not feasible for the whole group, that Brothers Matthew of Cressonessart and André le Mortoier be allowed to represent them.[6] Evidently Matthew was a respected senior brother within this group (in both these documents he is listed second after the priest John Penet). More dramatically, his status within the order as a whole is shown by the fact that when nine brothers were chosen to represent all those Templars incarcerated in Paris, one of these men who finally stood in front of the commission in the episcopal chapel on 7 April was Matthew of Cressonessart. These brothers presented a vigorous defense, arguing that previous confessions had been obtained by torture, that the accusations against them were lies, that outside France no Templars had confessed, and that their order had always been holy and honest.[7]

Although evidence from his later testimony shows that Matthew was a sergeant rather than a knight in the order, his title as preceptor, his respected role as a leader chosen among all the nearly six hundred Templars in Paris, and his knowledge of Latin all suggest the possibility that he came from a branch of the noble family of Cressonessart.[8] Since it is not certain that Guiard also really was a member of this family, the question of whether or how these two men were related must remain open. Nevertheless, it is a striking fact that the very week when Guiard finally confessed, another man from his tiny hamlet was taking the lead in fighting the charges of heresy in the Templar case. These two may not even have been aware of each other's presence, but surely someone on the level of the papal commissioners would have noticed two sons of Cressonessart so prominently testifying in this first week of April. In any case, Matthew of Cressonessart's experience demonstrates that "in the first two weeks of April 1310 the prospects for the imprisoned Templars looked brighter than they had at any time during the two and a half years that the proceedings had continued."[9] These brightened prospects, in turn, shone an unflattering light on William of Paris.

The End of Silence

Guiard, for his part, evidently decided that he did not wish to go silently to his death. Sometime during the week between Friday 3 April and Thursday 9 April, he agreed to "confess and testify." Our evidence for this session comes from the document, dated 9 April, in which the group of regent masters of canon law at Paris offered a legal opinion on his testimony. The extant document is an unofficial (unnotarized) copy of the original, which had borne the canonists' seals.[10]

In giving his testimony, Guiard would have answered questions from William (there is no evidence of participation by associates). Such exchanges were normally conducted in the vernacular when a layperson was interrogated; the scribe or notary would then translate and record the responses in Latin. Guiard, however, was a cleric of some kind, and (as we shall see) there is good reason to suspect that his testimony was actually given in Latin. A concise version of the essential portions of his testimony would then have been written down (still in Latin) by the scribe or notary. The record might then have been read back to Guiard for his assent. This synopsis was then sent to the canonists, who recorded it as part of their response. Indeed, the canonists may have abbreviated the testimony even further as they incorporated it into their opinion. It is important to remember, therefore, that the extant document is hardly a verbatim record of a conversation. The inquisitor's specific questions are sometimes recorded and can often be inferred, but Guiard's answers have been boiled down into a form that could be used judicially.

Because Guiard's self-conception seems so bizarre to modern sensibilities, it is easy to assume that he spoke in non sequiturs. But very likely some of the seeming disjointedness in the record reflects the scribe's attempt to condense the testimony into only what was most relevant (to his mind) and the fact that the inquisitor may not have asked the questions that would have elicited Guiard's own understanding more clearly. Just as importantly, it is essential to remember that Guiard spoke under extreme pressure, with the threat of death hanging over his head. At times he attempted to explain why his ideas should not be understood as dangerous; he did wish to convey his "true" identity as the Angel of Philadelphia, but in a manner that he hoped his inquisitor would see as unthreatening to church authority. Though this may have been an impossible line to walk, it reminds us that he applied his own filters even before the scribe had a chance to add his.[11]

The document as it now exists (AN J428 no. 18) is written in the names of four of the five canonists who had issued the 3 April decisions. For unknown reasons, Henry of Béthune did not join his colleagues in considering Guiard's testimony. Most likely he was simply taken away from Paris by other business, unless the omission of his name was only a scribal oversight. The canonists' account briefly relates once more how Guiard (here called a "pseudoreligious") was arrested by William of Paris, refused to cooperate, but eventually consented to testify. It then provides the copy of his testimony upon which our analysis must be based.

An Angel's Ideas

The opening section of Guiard's testimony gives a good sense of the way questions, responses, and clarifications mix into the record. Indeed, the document seems to jump right into the middle of a discussion, as the shift from the canonists' preamble to the testimony itself commences with a present active participle.[12] Guiard testified "just as the said inquisitor related to us": "Saying, namely, that he is the Angel of Philadelphia. And explaining this term, he says that 'Angel' is the name of an office, not of a nature. And he interprets 'Philadelphia' as 'saving the adhesion of the Lord or one adhering to the Lord.' And thus 'I consider myself sent to save the adhesion of the Lord or one adhering to the Lord in the Church of God.'"[13] One gets the sense that after eighteen months Guiard must have been bursting with the necessity to declare his angelic mission!

Though the title "Angel of Philadelphia" will surely strike most modern ears as bizarre, many medieval Christians would have recognized the implications of Guiard's claim immediately. He was situating himself within the Apocalypse, the end-times scenario that would herald the rise of Antichrist, the Second Coming of Christ, and the Last Judgment. The final book of the New Testament—the Apocalypse of St. John or the Book of Revelation—provides the most vivid, if enigmatic, signs of what believers could expect as the time of Antichrist grew near. Its imagery works through a series of sevenfold symbols, including stars, candlesticks, lamps, spirits, seals, angels, trumpets, vials, and plagues. Most relevant here, however, are the seven churches and seven angels. The sixth church is the Church of Philadelphia (a city in Asia Minor), and hence the sixth angel is the Angel of Philadelphia. If all of the sevenfold series are understood as referring to the history of the church, with the seventh alluding to the time of the Second Coming, then the sixth angel stands on the cusp of these climactic events. Guiard was thus making a statement not only about his own importance to the unfolding of the divine plan but also about where all Christians were on God's time line. If the Angel of Philadelphia was walking the earth, Antichrist could not be far behind.

Did William have any inkling beforehand that Guiard would burst forth with this declaration of his angelic office? Perhaps he did, since it is possible that Guiard and Marguerite spoke freely to their inquisitor even while refusing to take the oath necessary for formal testimony. Guiard may also have proclaimed his mission at the time that he appeared to defend Marguerite in Paris. But it is also possible that William was struck rather suddenly with the realization of just what sort of character he was interrogating. After all, one does not interview the

Angel of Philadelphia every day, and nothing about Marguerite Porete or her book would have indicated that a supporter would bear this kind of apocalyptic message.

In any case, after Guiard's first words, very likely William asked him to explain his understanding of this initial, bold statement. The inquisitor, however, does not seem to have encountered much difficulty in extracting information. Now that the floodgates were open, Guiard wished to explain himself. He hastened to make clear that he did not in fact believe himself to possess the nature of an angel—the title "Angel of Philadelphia" was rather a description of his divinely appointed role or office. And he particularly wanted to make known what the word *Philadelphia* implied. The two-part definition given here ("saving the adhesion of the Lord or one adhering to the Lord") is subsequently repeated several times in the testimony, indicating that Guiard was attempting to give a precise indication of his thoughts. Interestingly, the testimony here slips into the first person for a moment ("I consider myself . . ."). This shift of perspective does not necessarily mean that Guiard's exact words are preserved. But at least there is some record of the scribe choosing to include a version of his direct statement.

From this point, the series of questions William posed can be reconstructed: By whom had Guiard been sent? Did he believe anyone else had been sent in the same way? What did he think the seven churches in the Book of Revelation designated? What was the Church of Philadelphia, since there was only one church? Were there others who knew about his "gift"? Were those wearing tabards (a loose, sleeveless garment) part of his society? These questions break down into two categories: the first is concerned with Guiard's self-understanding and its ecclesiological implications, the second with whether he was part of a larger group. Guiard seemed to do his best to answer the questions and then frequently went beyond what he was asked in order to offer additional information. To some degree, he was thereby able to shape the course of the questioning, as William occasionally followed a direction Guiard had imposed on the dialogue.

Guiard explained that he had been sent "by he who has the key of David."[14] His immediate reference thus continued to be to be the Book of Revelation (3:7), where "John" has a vision of Christ, who says, "And to the Angel of Philadelphia write: These things the Holy One and the True One says, he that has the key of David, he that opens and no man shuts, shuts and no man opens: I know your works. Behold, I have given before you an open door, which no man can shut."[15] Guiard continued, "explaining that by this he understands Christ, who has the key of excellence, and that his vicar the lord pope has the key of ministry."[16] To identify Christ with "he that hath the key of David" was unproblematic. But what of this reference to two keys?

In general, the "doctrine of the keys" rests on the passage in Matthew 16:19 where Christ gives the keys of the kingdom of heaven to Peter (the central text of papal claims to head the universal church on earth): "And I will give to you the keys of the kingdom of heaven, and whatever you shall bind upon earth, it shall be bound also in heaven; and whatever you shall loose on earth, it shall be loosed also in heaven." It was understood that Peter was the first bishop of Rome and that every succeeding pope inherited this power of the keys. Any discussion of "keys," therefore, spilled over quickly into questions about papal power. Yet these keys of Matthew 16:19 could be used in theological discussion to stand for various more specific powers within the larger idea of binding and loosing; depending on context, they could be endowed with a number of different labels and implications, and the exact theological understanding of the extent and nature of these powers was a subject of contemporary theological debate.[17]

What is particularly interesting about the division Guiard cited is the way it seems to stem from a discussion in the Sentence Commentary of the Dominican Thomas Aquinas. In using this vocabulary (key of excellence vs. key of ministry), Guiard was speaking a language familiar to academic theologians of the late thirteenth century, and particularly to Dominicans such as William of Paris.[18] Far from imposing a novel division, he was lining himself up with the most illustrious theologian of the inquisitor's own order. Thomas, in a long discussion of the "keys of the Church," had written that

> in corporeal things, an instrument which opens a door is called a key. However, the door of the kingdom is closed to us by sin . . . and so the power which removes such an obstacle to the kingdom, is called a key. This power is in the most holy Trinity by authority,

and so it is said by some that [the Trinity] has the key of authority. But in Christ as man was found this power to remove the aforesaid obstacle by the merit of the Passion, which is said to open the door. And so [Christ] is said to have the keys of excellence *(claves excellentiae),* according to some. . . . But the efficacy of the Passion remains in the sacraments of the church; and because of this, the power to remove the aforesaid obstacle remains in the ministers of the church, who are the dispensers of the sacraments, not by their own virtue, but by divine virtue, and the Passion of Christ. And this power metaphorically is called the key of the church, which is the key of ministry *(clavis ministerii).*[19]

Guiard was in fact doing little more than paraphrasing Thomas; both agreed that Christ had the key(s) of excellence (though Thomas hedged with "according to some"), and where Thomas said the "ministers" of the church had the key of ministry, Guiard specified that it was the pope who held this key. Guiard was if anything more clear than Thomas about the specificity of papal power!

Next Guiard revealed a bit about his personal history. He "added" (suggesting he was continuing on without being asked) that he had perceived the nature of his office four years ago (or more), when he was in the lower chapel of the Sainte-Chapelle in Paris, but that he believed it had actually been given to him twenty years before that time (or less).[20] This cryptic passage suggests that Guiard retrospectively decided that an event of around 1286–87 had been fundamental to his assumption of the office of Angel of Philadelphia but that two decades had elapsed after this moment before he fully understood his calling that day in the Sainte-Chapelle in 1306.

At that time, "the mode of perception and reception of this office and of the opening of the door was in a flash through the opening of the understanding of Scripture."[21] The "opening of the door" obviously refers back to the passage from Revelation 3:7–8 and continues with the theme of keys and doors. But Guiard wanted to explain further that this revelatory moment was about an instantaneous understanding. He did not relate any tales of visionary experience or direct commands from God; rather, all at once he came to understand the words of the Bible in a new, intuitive way. His claims, in the final analysis, were based on his interpretation of Scripture; but that interpretation in turn flowed from divine illumination.

There followed several short answers: only one Angel of Philadelphia could be sent at a time (if he failed another could be sent); there was only one church, but within it could be different *status* or states, and at various times the church might shine forth more in one *status* and take its name from it. Here Guiard began to reveal a chronological dimension to his ideas. The seven churches of the Apocalypse did correspond to different times. By implication, now had to be the time of the Church of Philadelphia—and hence the world must be in the sixth age and on the verge of the time of Antichrist.

The next question elicited a long string of explanations: "Since there is one church, what is the Church of Philadelphia?" Guiard tried to explain first by defining how the different *status* could give different characteristics to the church as they shone forth. There was a *status* of "runners" who cast away possessions, living in the rigor of the Gospels, and shone forth their inner ardor through outer actions. These were the origins of the Church of Philadelphia. And, he hastened to add, they did this without injury to the universal church. All good Christians could be saved, but these "runners" had a special role, and among them the Angel of Philadelphia had a special gift and mission from the Lord. Apparently beginning to pick up steam, Guiard continued by comparing his sufferings to those of Christ: just as Christ was struck down for the sins of man, so too the Angel might be struck down in a state of innocence for the crimes of the people. He was prepared to risk his own death to support the true adherents of the Lord, and he had done so in Reims against the Dominicans and Franciscans, and at Paris on behalf of Marguerite. He had taken these steps because his duty was to oppose those attacking the adherents of the Lord, when those who normally should have this office in the church were silent. William then added a question, asking him whether this role applied particularly to him. Guiard indicated that others might take this task up through zeal but that only he had it as an office.

Guiard was evidently attempting to explain himself fully, as shown by the way he seems to have run on with a stream of connected self-justifying thoughts here. He did want to insist that he and his fellow "runners" had a unique role to play as representatives of the "Church of Philadelphia" that set them apart from members of the institutional church. But at the same time, he hoped to convince William that they were not a threat to ordinary churchmen and that they were not questioning the salvation of other good Christians. Yet since Guiard could not resist pointing out the ways his office made him a Christ-like figure, the odds of him convincing an inquisitor of the merits of his claims would seem to have been extremely slim.

At this point William turned to the question of Guiard's associates. He picked up on Guiard's own language, asking if others knew of his "gift." Guiard affirmed this, saying he had spoken about "the opening of the door" to others "receiving the habit of Christ." The clause "understanding by this a habit such as he himself wore" seems to be a response to prodding for further clarification. Here Guiard asserted, in a roundabout fashion, that he had followers who imitated his attire and to whom he had revealed his mission. But again Guiard attempted to cover his tracks, insisting that he had warned these followers not to receive any unapproved religious dress (the habit of a new religion or order) but rather to take up a habit approved with the authority of Christ. No doubt he was referring to the prohibition on new religious orders theoretically in effect since the fourth Lateran Council of 1215 and renewed by the Second Council of Lyons in 1274.

This issue of church prohibitions evidently weighed on his mind, because he added (again seemingly of his own volition) that "because he cannot have a patron in the New Testament because of the prohibition of the church, he takes one in the Old, according to the admonition of the Savior giving and authorizing freedom."[22] The key to this cryptic comment may be found in the following, concluding passage: "Asked if those who wear tabards are of his society, he responds no, not with regards to all things, except those who have and wear a long tunic and leather belt *(zona pellicea)*, which belt is essential to the habit. However he believes that they are adherents to the Lord, even if they have a secular form in their habit."[23]

What did this "leather belt" signify? Two men wearing a *zona pellicea* appear in the Vulgate. In the Gospels of Matthew (3:4) and Mark (1:6), John the Baptist is described as dressed in "camel's hair with a leather belt *(zona pellicea)* around his loins" as he preached the coming of Christ, saying, "I have baptized you with water, but he shall baptize you with the Holy Spirit." But in the Old Testament (4 Kings 1:8), it is

Elijah who is seen "girded about the waist with a leather belt" *(zona pellicea)*, shortly before he is taken up in a fiery chariot "by a whirlwind into heaven" (2 Kings 2:11).

Of these two possibilities, Guiard would seem to have been explicitly claiming Elijah as his patron, since he is the Old Testament figure associated with the leather belt. At the same time, however, there is a hint that Guiard would like to have presented himself as a new John the Baptist but had been told that this was forbidden. His rebuttal was to claim that the Old Testament figure of Elijah would serve his purposes just as well. Indeed, this distinction changed little in Guiard's self-presentation because Elijah in the Old Testament was taken to be a figure for John in the New (an interpretation attributed to Jesus by Matthew, Mark, and Luke). The essential point is that whereas elsewhere Guiard presented himself as Christ-like in his mission and his suffering, here he adopted the slightly more modest position of a new Elijah or John the Baptist, one who would announce the Second Coming. The *zona pellicea* was the visible sign of this status.

His claim that he took this patron in the Old Testament "according to the admonition of the Savior giving and authorizing freedom" may be an oblique biblical reference as well. For instance, Paul in his letter to the Galatians lends himself an angelic tinge, saying, "You . . . received me as an angel of God, even as Christ Jesus" (4:14) and then launches into an allegory about the two sons of Abraham to show that Christians are allegorically the "free" heirs to Jerusalem "by the freedom with which Christ has made us free" (4:31).[24] Guiard may have had a passage such as this in mind in claiming Christ's "freedom" *(libertas)*, and he would certainly have liked to be received in Paris "as an angel." It is also possible, though, that Guiard was making only the more general claim that as long as he was following Christ he was "free" to imitate any legitimate models he might find in Scripture.

Thus Guiard and William at first seem to have been talking at cross-purposes as they discussed clothing. William was most interested in dress as a marker of transgression, a way of identifying *beguini* who had adopted a pseudoreligious role not sanctioned by the church.[25] Guiard's society as he described them might have resembled Augustinian friars, who also wore a leather belt,[26] and this kind of confusion was unacceptable to churchmen. For Guiard, however, the meaning of specific items of clothing was deeper, saturated with biblical resonances.

He seems almost impatient with William's specific question about tabards; it was the underlying meaning that he wanted to explain.

As Guiard's testimony unfolded, however, William must have picked up the significance of these sartorial markers to the Angel of Philadelphia. Indeed, there is additional evidence that Guiard really did cling to the leather belt as essential to identifying his mission and that his accusers eventually understood just how central this was to his self-conception. The "Continuer of William of Nangis" summed up Guiard's trial thus: "Then [there was] also a pseudoperson, by the name of Guiard of Cressonessart, who—calling himself the Angel of Philadelphia sent directly by God to comfort those adhering to Christ—was saying that he was not required by the order of the pope to take off the leather belt with which he was girded, nor the habit in which he was dressed; indeed he would sin by [following] the papal command."[27] The first sentence shows a strong understanding of Guiard's self-conception, particularly in using the phrase "those adhering to Christ." The additional information here may therefore be trustworthy. If Guiard really claimed that not even the pope could order him to take off his habit and leather belt, then clearly he felt this attire to be divinely commanded as part of his angelic office. But interestingly, the Latin vocabulary in this account (*cingulus* substituted for *zona*) severs the connection to Elijah and John the Baptist and thus obscures the specific eschatological significance of the belt.

The chronicle evidence combined with Guiard's own testimony produces a picture of a man who continued to believe in his divine mission, even after a year and a half in prison. It is not clear at what point he might have been refusing to take off the belt that defined his angelic identity, but his self-conception as the Angel of Philadelphia was still intact in early April. He had attempted to explain and even ingratiate, but he did not recant. Even as he tried to present himself in such a way as to give the least offense possible, he continued to cling to the understanding he had gained four years earlier in the Sainte-Chapelle.

Angels All around Us: The Sources for Guiard's Ideas

While William of Paris doubtless remained unconvinced by Guiard's claims, he would not have jumped to the conclusion most modern readers might favor—that Guiard was simply deranged.[28] Guiard, in fact, was thinking within a well-established tradition. As Robert Lerner has shown, what made Guiard so audacious was not his belief that the Angel of Philadelphia could be expected to play a role in an imminent battle with Antichrist, but only his claim that he himself *was* this angel.[29] The specific kind of speculation that inspired Guiard had grown out of the writings of Joachim of Fiore, had been picked up by Franciscans in particular, and had flourished in Paris and elsewhere in the early fourteenth century.

Joachim had proposed an interpretive hermeneutic that suggested all of Christian history (past and future) could be understood through the "concordance of testaments" and had also insisted on reading the Book of Revelation in a linear manner that hinted at a time of earthly bliss after Antichrist. This last era of human existence was furthermore to be equated with the third *status,* that of the Holy Spirit (after the first two *status* of the Father and the Son), when a new kind of spiritual intelligence would more fully reveal God's plan to all (Jews and Gentiles alike). Although Joachim had tentatively suggested that this transition might occur around 1260, after that date his intellectual heirs had no trouble adjusting the abbot's calculations and continued to treat the arrival of the third *status* as an imminent event.

Guiard's debt to Joachim can be readily perceived in his linear reading of Revelation and in his use of the term *status* (though by the latter term he does not seem to mean precisely the same thing as Joachim, since he never mentions a tripartite division). Joachim also preceded Guiard in using the "opening of the door" of Revelation 3:7–8 as the metaphor for his own moment of understanding and in highlighting the importance of Christ's "key of David" in his apocalyptic scenario. Most importantly, he had proposed a reading of Revelation that specified that the Church of Philadelphia represented the sixth of the seven ages of the church and marked the arrival of the third *status.*[30]

In spite of this discernible influence, it seems unlikely that Guiard read Joachim directly. Instead, he probably absorbed versions of Joachite ideas that developed in Franciscan circles and were disseminated in Paris.[31] The most insistent and specific interpreters of Joachim in the later thirteenth century tended to be Franciscans. Joachim's authentic writings had suggested that two new, more perfect monastic orders would herald the imminent arrival of the third *status,*[32] and an apocryphal Jeremiah commentary attributed to him in the 1240s developed a more explicit "prediction" about the coming of the Dominicans and the Franciscans. In the Jeremiah commentary, the Franciscans in particular were depicted as the primary participants in a climactic battle against Antichrist and hence as crucial agents in ushering in the third *status*. This attribution of a unique apocalyptic role for their order obviously appealed to many Brothers Minor.

The essential element in this larger story is the way Joachite-leaning Franciscans came to believe that St. Francis himself had been destined to play the role of "Angel of Philadelphia." To Franciscans, the Angel of the Sixth Seal "ascending from the rising of the sun, having the sign of the living God" (Apoc. 6:12, 7:2), could be identified with Francis. After all, given that he was held to have received the stigmata before his death, who could better claim to bear the "sign of the living God"? Bonaventure, Franciscan master of theology at Paris and then minister general of the order from 1257 to 1274, made this equation explicit in his widely disseminated official life of Francis (the *Legenda maior*).[33] And since the Angel of the Sixth Seal could be further understood as synonymous with the Angel of Philadelphia (the sixth church), it was but a short leap to the identification of Francis with Philadelphia. Again, Bonaventure, in his 1273 *Collationes in Hexaemeron*, made this connection explicit, demonstrating the mainstream nature of this thinking within the Franciscan order.[34] Indeed, Bonaventure further connected Elijah, John the Baptist, and Francis. As Lerner writes: "For Bonaventure all three were heralds of a new dispensation: Elijah and John of Christ's coming, and Francis of the coming of the final earthly age. Once more, it seems that Guiard merely transposed one of the terms in the equation, making himself the new composite Elijah and John the Baptist instead of Saint Francis."[35] Thus Guiard was following the lead of Franciscan thinkers but audaciously replacing Francis with himself in this established scenario.[36]

Between the time of Bonaventure's death and Guiard's own day, more radical Franciscan Joachites, and the "heretics" influenced by them, pushed these ideas even further. The controversial Franciscan theologian Peter of John Olivi, for example, specified that the "granting of the key of David to the Angel of Philadelphia" represented the beginning of the third Joachite *status*;[37] the renegade Franciscan Bernard Délicieux played with related images in predictions about the death of Pope Benedict XI;[38] and the Italian heretic Fra Dolcino in 1300 made similar (though not identical) claims about the eschatological importance of the arrival of the Angel of Philadelphia.[39]

Lerner has recently suggested one further source of Franciscan/Joachite inspiration for Guiard's self-conception, based on Guiard's insistence that he had been given the office of Angel of Philadelphia around 1286–87 (twenty years "or less" before 1306). Apparently at the time of his revelatory moment in 1306, something convinced Guiard that if he was indeed the Angel, then he had to have been holding this office—even without his own knowledge—for two decades. What would have caused him to reach this odd-sounding conclusion? A likely catalyst would be a prophetic text that pointed to 1286 or 1287 as the date of the opening of the sixth seal. It so happens that just such a source was at hand in Paris—the "Columbinus" prophecy, composed by an unknown author who was probably a Franciscan or tied to Franciscan circles. Not only did this text point to 1287 as the beginning of the tribulations associated with the opening of the sixth seal, but it was actually recorded in a royal register in Paris in 1306–7.[40] It is therefore tempting to imagine Guiard hearing or reading this prophecy after his revelatory moment in the Saint-Chapelle and drawing the conclusion that his newly revealed status must have been shadowing him since 1287. But whether or not it was this exact prophecy that sparked Guiard's interpretation, some similar retrospective explanation for the apocalyptic significance of 1286–87 must have been at work in his mind, and thus another source of his loosely Joachite self-conception.[41]

Thus Guiard's thinking worked along well-established paths, picking up ideas and adjusting them to his own ends. Indeed, it is the fact that his testimony appears to be so steeped in specific Latin theological and biblical terminology that suggests that he must have given his testimony in Latin.[42] It could be argued that his interrogators caught the drift of his thinking and purposely translated French answers into Latin phrases that drew on Franciscan discourse about Francis and Revelation, or on Thomas Aquinas's statements about the keys of excellence and ministry. But not only is it unclear why William of Paris would have wished to do this (or that his scribe would have been able to), but some distinctions in the testimony can really only reflect Guiard's own familiarity with established Latin theological terms. For instance when he clarified that "angel" referred to an office, not a nature, he was echoing an established distinction that went back to Augustine and Gregory but had recently been explicitly cited by at least one Franciscan university master while equating Francis with the Angel of the Sixth Seal.[43] There is little likelihood that a scribe would have replicated this exact language if he was quickly translating a vernacular answer into Latin. Similarly Guiard almost certainly must have used the specific biblical phrase *zona pellicea* in its Latin form and employed the Latin terms that seem to echo Thomas's Sentence Commentary. Finally, and perhaps most tellingly, Lerner has recently noted that Guiard's definition of Philadelphia as *salvans adhesionem Domini vel adherentem Domino* comes directly from the *Interpretationes nominum Hebraicorum* (a list, appended to some thirteenth-century Bibles, of Latin translations from Greek and Hebrew of biblical proper nouns).[44] These exact Latin words can only have come directly from Guiard's mouth. The weight of this evidence suggests that this *beguinus* was actually a theologically sophisticated cleric and that his testimony was given in Latin—the appropriate language for theological explication.

Finally, in considering the sources of Guiard's ideas, there is the question of whether Marguerite Porete's own writings had some influence on him. Some scholars have indeed claimed to find reflections of the *Mirror* in Guiard's statements.[45] This idea might make intuitive sense: If Guiard thought highly enough of Marguerite to risk his life in defending her, would he not have had some familiarity with her book? In fact, however, their ideas were fundamentally different. Marguerite's treatise on spiritual annihilation is simply not concerned with the same issues as Guiard's apocalyptic thinking. Guiard may have known about Marguerite's book; indeed, nothing proves that he did not read it or discuss it. But if so, her ideas did not have a discernible impact on his thought, and his desire to defend Marguerite was not the result of an intellectual affinity.[46] It is rather his mission as defender of the true adherents of the Lord that explains his involvement with Marguerite. As a *beguina* attacked by churchmen, Marguerite apparently fit this definition. In this sense, Guiard's defense shows that at least one onlooker in Paris perceived her mode of life as a devout, if not holy, "adherence to God."

The Canonists' Response

The canonists, after concluding their record of Guiard's testimony, indicated that William of Paris had not wished to proceed without legal advice and hence had sought their formal opinion. The counsel they now offered to him was straightforward: Guiard ought indeed to be considered, judged, and condemned as a true heretic. They did urge, however, that he not be handed over to the secular arm if he repented. In combination with their earlier opinion of 3 April, Guiard could now be treated not only as a contumacious heretic on the basis of his behavior but also as a "true heretic" by virtue of the ideas he had advanced. His fate—execution or imprisonment—would simply depend on whether he decided to repent.

The general verdict could hardly have been a surprise. But as the men charged with providing the actual basis in canon law for this condemnation, what specific legal grounds would the canonists cite? Considering the wildly inflammatory material they had read, their rationale for judging Guiard a heretic was dry as dust. They found that "he establishes a division in the church militant, indeed really establishes two churches militant—he himself wielding the keys of excellence of one, and the pope holding the keys of ministry of the other. And this same pope is not altogether the unique head of this church militant and is not able altogether to order it through himself and his ministers and his sacred canons and his statutes, all of which is heretical."[47] In other words, their finding was that Guiard had set himself up as a rival to the pope by claiming for himself the power of one of the keys.

The fascinating fact, however, is that Guiard never made this explicit claim in his recorded testimony. The lawyers, rather, seem to have found it implied between the lines of his statements. Guiard had indeed stressed that Christ possessed the key of excellence, and the pope only the key of ministry. But this distinction merely echoed Thomas Aquinas, and at least for William of Paris's Dominican order, Thomas's writings were virtually synonymous with orthodoxy. The four canonists now commenting on the testimony were not themselves Dominicans, but if they were knowingly attacking Thomas, this would hardly have been the response William sought. Indeed, it is quite possible that William was deeply uncomfortable with the direction this opinion was taking; after all, his own writings had used Thomas's Sentence Commentary to explain related ecclesiastical questions in an analogous fashion.[48] He may have been reassured, however, by the fact that this distinction in and of itself was not where the canonists alleged that Guiard's heresy lay. Rather, they went a step further in asserting that Guiard believed that he *himself* now wielded the keys of excellence. To make this assumption, they seem to have gone through a string of equivalencies: if Christ has the key of excellence, which is synonymous with the key of David that opens the door of Revelation 3:7–8, and if Guiard considers himself to have opened this door and to occupy an "office" that involves the opening of this door, he must be claiming to wield the key of excellence. The report by the "Continuer of William of Nangis" that Guiard had stated that even the pope could not order him to remove his belt may help explain the canonists' reasoning as well.[49]

This interpretation was probably further facilitated by the multiple ways in which Guiard suggested that he was like a new Christ and by the way he set the role of his office against the institutional church, insofar as it had failed to protect the true adherents of the Lord. The canonical texts the masters concluded by citing, therefore, generally deal with schism and false division in the church. In the grand scheme of things, the canonists may have been justified in treating Guiard as one who sought to separate a small group of followers from the main body of the church. The fact remains, however, that they convicted him of a claim that is not actually found in his testimony.

It is equally striking that they chose not to comment on any of his wilder statements.[50] In one sense, however, this restraint was quite logical. These men were, after all, lawyers and not theologians. Their job was not to comment on the theology involved in claiming an angelic office but merely to determine whether Guiard's ideas transgressed the less spectacular dictates of canon law (and no papal decree had ever defined the specific heresy involved in claiming to hold the office of an angel!). This observation in turn raises a further question: Why did William of Paris choose to consult canon lawyers at this point, rather than the masters of theology?

One possibility is that this path seemed safer. The smaller, probably hand-picked group of canonists could be counted on to define Guiard's ideas as a heretical challenge to church authority. Perhaps William was less certain what direction a larger meeting with the faculty of theology might take (a similar move had backfired for the royal court in March 1308 with the Templar questions). Yet William had attempted to enlist the theologians at the beginning of Guiard's process in March, and on 11 April the theologians would in fact be presented with extracts from Marguerite's book. Surely William had every reason to believe that these men would ultimately have provided a theological condemnation of Guiard's ideas, particularly given the extent to which he could control the evidence they were shown.

Another possibility is that a group of theologians did in fact consider Guiard's case, perhaps at the same time that they issued their 11 April condemnation of Marguerite's ideas. The best evidence for this possibility comes from Guiard's final sentence (31 May), in which William of Paris refers to the "counsel and concord of many learned men both in theology and in canon and civil law" that he received.[51] There is no specific record of theologians giving counsel on Guiard at any other time, though they were present originally at the March meeting where some did act as assenting witnesses. This reference might therefore reflect a meeting for which the documentation has not survived.

A final possibility, perhaps the most likely, is that Guiard indicated his willingness to repent shortly after April 9 and hence that further steps against him were deemed unnecessary. The canonists urged that Guiard not be turned over to the secular authority if he repented. Since he was not ultimately sent to the stake, he must in fact have offered his repentance and submission. Nothing in his recorded testimony suggests that Guiard had changed his mind by 9 April and no longer considered himself to be the Angel of Philadelphia. Only the concluding statement from the "Continuer of William of Nangis" indicates that "finally, in fear of the fire, taking off his habit and belt and finally recognizing his error, he was sentenced to be belted with perpetual imprisonment."[52] Exactly when between 9 April and his sentencing on 31 May he "recognized his error" is unclear. If it was relatively soon after 9 April, however, this would explain why William's further actions concerned only Marguerite and her book. In any case, the Continuer's pun on the Latin words *cingulum/praecingi* (belt, belted) shows the satisfaction of ecclesiastical observers at seeing the Angel's wings clipped.

No one had originally denounced Guiard; no one had particularly sought his arrest. His own actions had brought him to inquisitorial attention in a way that virtually demanded his detention. He had first been arrested not for his ideas but for his visible actions challenging church authority. As his testimony progressed, William of Paris seemingly wished to focus on practical questions about his followers and any similar challenges to authority that they might harbor. So far as the record reveals, he did not question Guiard about his relationship to Marguerite Porete, or as to whether he subscribed to any tenets found in her book. He did not press him on the issue of the "two keys," and he may well have found Guiard's testimony on this subject slightly embarrassing if he realized the relationship to Aquinas's Commentary. The canonists, for their part, simply ignored most of Guiard's testimony. Rather, they turned one brief statement into a rationale for making their own point about papal power. As Lerner long ago pointed out, this process generally allowed the royal court to portray itself as suppressing a "heretical" challenge to papal power in Paris at the very moment that the king and his men (in the Templar affair above all) were asserting the crown's right and ability to increase its control over ecclesiastical affairs in France. It also permitted William personally to show his respect for papal authority after his loyalty had been so publicly questioned in 1308. These goals were facilitated even more explicitly than has previously been realized, insofar as Guiard's testimony was twisted to construct him as a direct rebel against the pope. Guiard of Cressonessart, in these regards, proved the occasional utility of angels to kings and inquisitors.

CHAPTER 6

Twenty-One Theologians and a Book

Guiard's decision to testify and repent saved his life. But he had failed in his mission to defend Marguerite Porete. William of Paris, however, did not immediately take further steps concerning the issue of Marguerite's personal guilt. He turned, instead, to her book. To be sure, the question of the book's orthodoxy lay behind the origins of the Paris trial, but William had not overtly addressed it to this point. Yet if men such as Godfrey of Fontaines had been able to praise the *Mirror,* who was to say that Marguerite had not originally been unfairly arrested for defending an orthodox work? To erase this lingering question, William now turned to the authority of the masters of theology at Paris. His handling of this issue, however, was carefully managed so as to keep any debate over the book's orthodoxy quite separate from the establishment of Marguerite's personal culpability. In effect, the theologians were now asked to participate in a discrete inquisition against the book itself.[1]

11 April: The Consultation with the Masters of Theology

On Saturday, 11 April 1310, William of Paris gathered together twenty-one masters of theology at Saint-Mathurin, a church on the rue Saint-Jacques just north of the Dominican house and a frequent meeting place for university business.[2] Two notaries were present this time,

with Jacques of Vertus, from the Diocese of Châlons-sur-Marne, joining Evens Phili.[3] According to the terse record that Jacques prepared,
William asked for the masters' advice on what action should be taken
concerning "a certain book which he showed them, from which the several articles exhibited there had been extracted, which he had pointed
out to them, as he said."[4]

The group that gathered now included all fifteen theologians who
had earlier been present at the initial meeting called by William in March.
We have met the four who acted as witnesses to the canonists' decision
on that occasion (the Augustinian friars Alexander of Marcia and Gregory of Lucca; the Cistercian Jacques of Dijon; and the secular Ralph of
Hotot).[5] The others were Simon of Guiberville, Thomas of Bailly, and
John of Ghent (all secular canons of Notre Dame); the Benedictine Peter
of Saint-Denis; the Augustinian friar Henry of Friemar; the Augustinian
canons Gerard of Saint-Victor and John of Mont-Saint-Éloi; the secular John of Pouilly; Lawrence of Dreux, prior of Val-des-Écoliers; the
Dominican Berenger of Landora; and the Franciscan Jacob of Ascoli.[6]
To these fifteen were now added the seculars William Alexandri (canon
of Notre Dame) and Roger of Roseto; the Cistercian Jacques of Thérines; the Carmelite Gerard of Bologna; and the Franciscans John of
Clairmarais and Nicholas of Lyra.[7]

Many of these men were veterans of previous controversies. For
example, at least nine had been present on 25 or 26 October 1307 (or on
both days) when William of Paris had assembled the university to hear
Templar confessions, and an overlapping group of nine had formally
participated in the March 1308 opinion on the legality of Philip IV's
actions (five men had been present in October and had also responded
in March).[8] It was also a nearly complete gathering of the faculty of theology. Only a handful of masters known to have been resident in Paris
at this time are not accounted for in this list. Among these, the new
chancellor of the university, Francesco Caraccioli, was notably absent,
as was William of Paris's Dominican colleague Hervé Nédellec.[9] It is
always possible that these men preferred not to involve themselves for
personal or political reasons (Caraccioli, for instance, was not closely
tied to the royal court),[10] but more likely they simply happened to be
traveling or otherwise occupied.[11] In sum, this was as illustrious a mus-
tering of theological authority as it was possible to assemble in Paris.

Among the most important things that Jacques of Vertus's notarized account reveals is that William of Paris possessed a copy of Marguerite's book, which he brought with him to this meeting. This may have been the copy Marguerite sent to the bishop of Châlons-sur-Marne, or another copy that she had carried at the time of her arrest. William, however, did not give the theologians access to the entire book. Instead, he used its physical presence to suggest that he himself understood its contents, while "exhibiting" only extracts for their consideration. The theologians may have had a chance to consider these extracts previously.[12] But if so, there is no record of exactly when or where such a consideration might have taken place.

The silences of this document are even more striking than its opening statements. Most obviously, it does not mention Marguerite Porete by name or give the title of her book. These omissions might seem to slight Marguerite, but they can also be read as further evidence of William's careful conduct. At least as his notaries recorded the event, William did not emphasize that this was a work by a woman, let alone by a woman already liable to condemnation as a contumacious rebel. Moreover, the documentary record does not state that the theologians were informed about the book's previous condemnation. Of course, it would be hard to imagine that the theologians, many of whom had been called in only a few weeks ago to consult on Guiard (and almost certainly Marguerite) before deferring to the canonists in their March meeting, were wholly ignorant of the author's identity. The brief account of the meeting should not be mistaken for a transcription of everything that transpired there. Still, it is a striking fact that nothing in the 3 April decisions concerning Marguerite or Guiard had referred to Marguerite's authorship of a book, and nothing in the actual text of the 11 April document tied the book under consideration to Marguerite. As far as the trail of documents informs us, William was carefully keeping the theological judgment of these extracts separate from the issue of Marguerite's personal culpability. In limiting discussion to the abstract issue of the orthodoxy of the extracts, William was again effectively controlling how much information to give out to specific experts and how to present that information in the written record.

The masters were given at least fifteen excerpts to consider. The trial documents explicitly give the first and the fifteenth, and most scholars have assumed that these were intended to represent the first and last extracts; this is plausible but hardly certain. In any case, the two recorded extracts were written into the notarized document in Latin, which was surely the language in which William would have presented them to a body of university men.[13] Indeed, there is nothing to show for certain that the theologians even knew that the work itself was originally in French.

There is one more source of information on these extracts, since the "Continuer of William of Nangis" seems to convey a third article, which presumably (though, again, not certainly) would have been numbered between two and fourteen on the original list. Combining these sources of information, the three known excerpts are:

[1] That the annihilated soul gives license to the virtues and is no longer in servitude to them, because it does not have use for them; but rather the virtues obey [its] command.

[?] That the soul annihilated in love of the Creator, without blame of conscience or remorse, can and ought to concede to nature whatever it seeks and desires.

[15] That such a soul does not care about the consolations of God or his gifts, and ought not to care and cannot, because [such a soul] has been completely focused on God, and thus its focus on God would then be impeded.[14]

Just how fair was William in presenting these extracts? Although taking statements out of context in this manner might seem to slant the process against their author, this was standard contemporary practice in asking for learned judgment on a larger work suspected of heresy.[15] Moreover, as far as the extant three extracts indicate, William was not overtly distorting Marguerite's ideas in and of themselves. The first extract can be clearly identified with a passage in chapter 6 of the *Mirror,* and the unnumbered article given by the "Continuer of William of Nangis" seems to stem from chapters 9 and 17. The fifteenth extract echoes ideas in chapter 26 (and perhaps chapters 15 and/or 16), if not quite so clearly.[16] Indeed, the one passage where William has been accused of blatantly distorting the *Mirror*'s meaning may not be an example of his unfairness after all: in the existing French manuscript of the *Mirror* a passage that talks about giving to nature whatever it seeks and desires is followed by the disclaimer "But such Nature is so well ordered . . . that Nature demands nothing which is prohibited."[17] It has recently been shown, however, that this saving clause probably was not in the version or versions of the *Mirror* that existed at the time of Marguerite's death.[18]

Nevertheless, by translating the extracts into Latin and taking them out of Marguerite's dialogue format, with its multiplying explanations and mocking disputations, William made it much easier for his theologians to reach a clear decision. Moreover (as Kocher has remarked), since the known extracts all seem to come from the first twenty-six chapters of the *Mirror*, we cannot be sure that William even read the entire text, particularly the last section (after chapter 122) where Marguerite tried to clarify her ideas for doubters.[19] More broadly, it is obviously true that William's entire purpose was to select extracts that would be condemned. To judge by the three that are known, it would be hard to imagine the theologians declining to find them heretical. Without being couched in some form of explanation, the claim that the Christian virtues no longer applied to "annihilated souls," and that such souls could therefore do whatever they wished without remorse, would surely be interpreted as a dangerously amoral antinomianism.

After William's presentation of the extracts, the theologians may have withdrawn to confer among themselves. It is also possible, however, that they had reached agreement in advance and now offered their answer without delay. In either case, Master Simon of Guiberville, until recently chancellor of the university and now dean of the chapter of Paris, announced their unanimous opinion:[20] "That such a book in which the said articles are contained, should be exterminated as heretical and erroneous and containing heresy and errors."[21]

Unlike the canonists on 3 and 9 April, there is no indication that the masters of theology ever issued a separate document bearing their own seals. Rather, what survives is simply a record of their oral verdict, as prepared by Jacques of Vertus (with Evens Phili) and presented as a notarized public document to be made known to all, which was then later copied onto the same sheet of parchment with Marguerite and Guiard's final sentences. Both the masters of theology and the inquisitor are referred to in the third person (unlike the documents of 3 and 9 April, where the canonists write in the first person plural); it is only the notary's detached summary that we receive. In short, we have here a very selective account of events constructed by the notary to serve the legal purposes of William of Paris.

Again, the silences in the judgment are striking. Did any serious debate by the theologians lie behind their clear-cut condemnation? Since the masters seem to have been given access to the extracts in advance, did they in fact proceed to a systematic consideration of each of the propositions? If so, did they actually find them all to be heretical? The document does not answer these questions. The theologians could conceivably have found some extracts orthodox and others rash or dangerous but not heretical.[22] It is only certain that they condemned the two extracts recorded by Jacques of Vertus. Moreover, the theologians apparently preferred not to issue a solemn, sealed statement of their own. If such a document had ever existed, it would be odd that the notary made no mention of it (we have seen the lengths to which William and his notaries had gone to incorporate the canonists' sealed opinion into a notarized record of their meeting in March).[23] Instead, the account stresses the "harmonious" agreement of all the theologians, but only on the limited issue of two specific extracts, and with no indication of the thinking behind the condemnation.[24] In sum, William had obtained a clear but tightly circumscribed judgment from the theologians, recorded in a laconic document authenticated only by his own notary's attestation of his personal presence.

Something New

The gathering of 11 April was a rather remarkable moment, since a formal consultation of such a large group of masters of theology in the case of a layperson's writings was virtually unprecedented.[25] William can be viewed as acting on three levels simultaneously. From each of these perspectives, he was building on precedent but going well beyond it.

First and most overtly, he called the theologians together as an inquisitor asking for expert opinion to inform an impending judgment. In this sense he was continuing to follow standard inquisitorial practice but was pushing it to an unprecedented level of formal deliberation by bringing together almost the entire faculty of theology from the university to ask for a judgment on the writings of a laywoman.[26]

Second, he stood implicitly as a representative of the royal court (he was after all still the king's confessor), asking the university for its opinion on a controversial question. Philip IV had created a new relationship between court and university—and more specifically the faculty of theology—by calling for such consultations on high-profile issues such as his battle with Boniface VIII and then (in March 1308) the legality of his prosecution of the Templars.[27] Thus these masters would have expected to have their opinions solicited by the royal court from time to time. Again, though, the case of a specific woman's book was quite distinct from these towering issues of church and state. And the stakes were still high; as the rebuff on the Templar questions showed, the court could ask leading questions and apply various kinds of pressure, but in the end it could not control the opinions the masters might render. This move, in the case of a single text, was therefore a great deal of effort for a somewhat risky procedure.

Third, and perhaps most intriguingly, William's action to some degree resembled an internal university investigation into the orthodoxy of a theological proposition defended by a bachelor or master at Paris. This is not to suggest that the panel of theologians was confused about whether the extracts they were judging had come from a university context. Surely they were aware that this was not the case. Yet the very process they engaged in must have felt familiar. Masters of theology were used to participating in internal inquiries concerning the orthodoxy of a colleague's overly daring writings.[28] Such cases normally began with a complaint about the orthodoxy of a proposition recently defended in open academic debate, to be investigated by the chancellor and an appointed panel of masters. By introducing these Latin extracts from an unidentified book to a panel of masters of theology, William adopted a position reminiscent of the one usually occupied by the chancellor (interestingly absent from this panel) in cases of academic heresy. The masters, in turn, were asked to treat these writings in a fashion analogous to the ideas of one of their own.[29] In university inquiries, the scholar might be censored and forced to recant, but he would not be treated as a heretic in his person as long as he submitted to correction.[30] Those who remained obdurate after formal correction could be considered contumacious heretics, yet even then this sort of process would not lead an academic theologian to the stake in the fourteenth century.[31] By presenting these extracts to the theologians without explicitly tying them to Marguerite Porete, William allowed them the luxury of divorcing the question of their orthodoxy from the fate of their author. But even more interestingly, William chose not to present these extracts as the work of a woman who had just been labeled a contumacious heretic (on 3 April), or as coming from a book that had previously been condemned by a bishop. At this point he was rigorously holding the question of the book's orthodoxy separate from its author's guilt and even her identity. The theologians were thus ruling on an abstract intellectual question, not on any issue that would lead directly to the punishment of a person. In this sense, William allowed them to remain within the parameters of their professional expertise.

No matter what angle is considered, William's consultation of the theologians was something new. Part of the explanation for this innovation probably lies, again, in the inquisitor's need to cover all possible bases. He himself had not, at any point up to now, suggested a formal opinion on the orthodoxy of Marguerite's writings. The basis for the claim that her book contained heretical ideas was the judgment made originally by Bishop Guido of Cambrai. The entire sequence of events from that point was spurred on by Marguerite's concrete actions, not by any further formal condemnation of the contents of her book. Indeed, Marguerite in the meantime had probably gathered the three positive assessments by Low Country churchmen, complicating the question of her book's orthodoxy.

Specifically, the opinions of the Franciscan John of Quérenaing and the Cistercian Dom Franc might not have meant a great deal by this time, but the praise by Godfrey of Fontaines would have continued to carry weight in Paris. Indeed, no inquisitor had before faced this situation—the attempted condemnation of a book, written by a layperson but circulating with the explicit written praise of a regent master of theology at the university. And not just any master, for Godfrey until his recent death had been among the most important theologians of his generation. The scholars who examined extracts from Marguerite's book would virtually all have known him personally, and certainly by reputation. Many would have argued with and against him, and at least one, John of Pouilly, proudly called himself Godfrey's student. Indeed, William of Paris himself had apparently cited one of Godfrey's quodlibetal determinations in his *Dialogue on the Seven Sacraments* not many years before. In essence, if an eminent master of theology such as Godfrey had been willing to see spiritual value in the *Mirror*, William must have understood it as essential to provide overwhelming evidence that this was an aberration rather than a reflection of general theological opinion in Paris.[32] It was not necessary at this point to lay out a full case against Marguerite and all of her previous actions, only to establish the appearance of a unanimous condemnation of the book by the faculty of theology.

In addition, the theologians themselves may have been eager to have a voice in these proceedings. The best evidence for this might be the surprisingly large number of participants: twenty-one was a significant increase, for example, over the fourteen who had signed the opinion on the Templars in 1308. The Templar question was fraught with political peril; some masters might well have shied away from such a controversial encounter with the crown.[33] Now, however, the faculty of theology had every reason to see participation as setting an advantageous precedent; in a case involving novel theological ideas brought in from outside a university setting, the ultimate authority for any condemnation should come neither from an individual bishop nor from a single inquisitor but from the combined knowledge of the faculty of theology. Men like Godfrey of Fontaines himself had been explicit in claiming just this kind of theological authority over and against bishops.[34] Now, although his own positive opinion of the *Mirror* was emphatically overturned by this panel, Godfrey's larger position in this regard was vindicated by the importance William granted to the theologians in this case. In this sense, William's interests may have dovetailed with the theologians'.

Four Sketches

So far as is currently known, none of the twenty-one theologians involved ever offered any additional comments on the matter in their own writings. It is possible, however, to make some general observations about the perspectives they would have brought to the table. In some ways, these men shared a common intellectual outlook, due to their education and the habits of thought it formed. As scholastic theologians, they were trained to debate questions using the formal rules of Aristotelian logic, to consider arguments for both sides, and then to determine the truth of the matter and attempt to demolish opposing positions. In the most general sense, any academic theologian might therefore have had cause to be overtly hostile toward Marguerite's project (if he knew its full scope), with its mocking claim to treat truths lying beyond the understanding of those still chained to reason.

A preliminary example of this potential for an instinctive, dismissive antagonism comes from a man who was not part of the panel judging Marguerite's extracts at all. John Baconthorpe was an English Carmelite who began theological studies in Paris sometime after about 1312 and rose to become regent master of theology before 1324 (eventually provincial master for England, d. ca. 1348).[35] In his Sentence Commentary, first composed around 1320 and revised a few years later, John recalled that "a certain beguine, who had published a little book against the clergy, was burned near Paris."[36] Since he probably did not arrive in Paris until several years after 1310, John's recollection suggests that Marguerite's case interested masters and students for some time. It also shows just how easily Marguerite's ideas could be perceived as simply directed "against the clergy."

But individual masters of theology also had a great deal invested in an array of intellectually divisive issues related to Marguerite's writings. Beyond the apparent uniformity of their training, these men inhabited a fractious academic environment that pitted masters and their opinions one against another. Not only did academic theologians fall into a number of philosophical camps, but—like any other small world of competing professionals—they had their personal rivalries, their conflicting institutional loyalties, and their long-term ambitions beyond the academic world to consider. Each of them would have had a slightly different professional relationship to the issues raised by Marguerite's book.

What follows is a brief attempt to assess how the consultation on the extracts might have looked to the theologians involved. Since sketching all their careers is impossible here, I have chosen four men, not quite at random, to represent the group: Jacques of Thérines, Nicholas of Lyra, John of Pouilly, and Henry of Friemar.

Jacques of Thérines had already been a Cistercian monk at Chaalis, north of Paris and near his hometown of Thérines (indeed near Cressonessart), before being sent to Paris in the early 1290s to complete his studies. He was regent master of theology by 1305–6. His quodlibetal writings (formal determinations of questions on any topic that were posed to masters at Advent/Christmas and Lent) show that he was not afraid to criticize royal policy, such as the decision to expel the Jews in 1306. They also reveal that the nature of "virtue" was among his favorite topics to ponder.[37] He was present when the Templar leaders confessed before the university on 26 October 1307. The following March, however, he joined the opinion whereby the masters denied most of Philip's attempts to legitimate his actions,[38] and his later writings show that he grew increasingly unconvinced of the government's case against the Templars.[39] But spring 1310 saw a major milestone in his career. In early April he had just returned from Chaalis, where his confreres had elected him their new abbot. In fact, this trip to Chaalis probably explains his absence from the March meeting where theologians deferred to canonists on Guiard's case. When he now appeared along with other masters of theology at Saint-Mathurin, he was probably in Paris only to gather his belongings before transferring himself permanently to his abbey.[40] Jacques subsequently attended the Council of Vienne and went on to defend his order's interests as abbot of Chaalis and then (by 1318) of the more important house of Pontigny. Among the issues most important to him, as proven in multiple contexts, was the exemption of religious orders from the authority of local bishops.[41]

Since Jacques's writings and actions show that he was willing to oppose royal desires and also that he was no particular friend to the Mendicant orders, William of Paris's status as royal confessor and Dominican inquisitor would not automatically have moved him.[42] On the other hand, a scholar who had invested time in such quodlibetal questions as "whether justice is a more noble virtue than any other moral virtue" might have been particularly dismayed by the extracts he was shown insinuating that Marguerite's book urged taking leave of the virtues.[43] From another perspective, as someone who criticized episcopal pretensions to jurisdiction over exempt orders, he would have relished the chance to show that masters of theology, particularly those like him from exempt orders, were ultimately more important than bishops in deciding orthodoxy. Most subjectively (but intriguingly), one has to wonder just how his impending departure from the world of the university affected his approach to this consultation. He had missed one meeting called to discuss Marguerite and Guiard because his order's business had to be given priority in March; on 11 April he would have been preparing to leave Paris behind and adopt a position of authority in the wider monastic world. Perhaps this meeting was no more than an obligation to be gotten over with as quickly as possible before moving on to more pressing matters; or perhaps—as one of his last acts as a master at Paris—it held additional solemnity for the newly elected Abbot Jacques.

Our second example, the Franciscan Nicholas of Lyra, was and is regarded as the foremost biblical commentator of his age. His *Postilla litteralis* "became the standard work on the Bible in the late Middle Ages,"[44] largely because of his knowledge of the Hebrew Bible and ability to summarize rabbinic tradition into a literal reading acceptable to Christian audiences. From Normandy, he entered the Franciscan order around 1300 and was sent to Paris to study by 1301. He was present at the Templar confessions on 26 October 1307 along with Jacques of Thérines. He did not participate in the formal opinion of the following March, however, because he did not assume the Franciscan chair of theology as regent master until the academic year 1308–9.[45] He probably stepped down from this chair by 1310 (though it is possible that he served two consecutive years as regent), but he remained based in Paris for the rest of his life, even while serving as his order's provincial minister of Burgundy by 1324.[46] He was also much closer to the royal court than Jacques of Thérines. For example, Queen Jeanne of Burgundy (wife of Philip V and patron of Hugh of Besançon) named him an executor of her will, and he was present at an elaborate ceremony when Jeanne and Philip's daughter Blanche became a Franciscan nun at the royal foundation of Longchamp 1 February 1319.[47]

In 1309 Nicholas determined quodlibetal questions that focused on Jews and historical readings of the Old Testament, for instance asking whether the advent of Christ could be proved by Jewish Scripture and whether Jews could or should have recognized Christ as the Messiah during his lifetime.[48] These questions—debated while Marguerite and Guiard were imprisoned in Paris—suggest two ways that Nicholas might have perceived the extracts from Marguerite's work. Theologically, this expert on the literal meaning of Scripture would have been deeply skeptical of Marguerite's whole enterprise, which swept past the basic teachings of the Bible in its swirling rush down the path to spiritual annihilation. In this sense, the more Nicholas might have known about the thrust of Marguerite's ideas, the more he might have agreed with the contemporary *Grandes chroniques de France,* which summarized Marguerite's offenses by saying she "had transgressed and overstepped Divine Scripture."[49] But Nicholas's role as expert on "Jewish questions" might have lent him other perspectives on this process as well. We have seen that William of Paris had overseen two trials of "relapsed" Jews in late 1307, and we shall shortly see that in 1310 he was involved in a third such case. It has been suggested that perhaps Nicholas had some involvement in this case as a consultant to William;[50] if so, perhaps he was also among the "experts" William is recorded as having consulted in 1307. We would then have a picture of a friar who worked closely with royal patrons and was conferring with William on multiple cases. For these reasons, William of Paris would probably have been confident as to Nicholas's reaction to the extracts he was presented.

Our third theologian, John of Pouilly, was in his own way nearly as controversial as Marguerite Porete. As a self-proclaimed student of Godfrey of Fontaines and (before 1307) a canon of Saint-Géri of Cambrai, he was perhaps in a better position than any of the other theologians to have independent knowledge of Marguerite's interaction with Godfrey and of the local context from which she had emerged. He was also a supporter of Godfrey's stance on academic freedom and an opponent of the episcopal condemnations that had limited academic debate at Paris since 1277. He might therefore have had more reason than some of his colleagues to have felt sympathy for Marguerite.

Yet John had his own tendency to land himself in hot water. Indeed, his initial disputation upon becoming a master in 1306 had caused an academic uproar.[51] At this ceremony two senior masters (Henry of Friemar and Thomas of Bailly, both part of Marguerite's panel) had the role of posing arguments against the new master, who then offered his determination the next morning. At the heart of the question John addressed was the issue (in Ludwig Hödl's paraphrase): "Does what is (contingent) individual and future come to be, exist, and remain under a persistent essential form, the divine idea, or do only creatable-temporal circumstances meet the requirements of the free, time-bound choice of the will?"[52] Modern readers may or may not find this a scintillating topic for debate, but John's opponents—the followers of Henry of Ghent, who had been the longtime intellectual adversary of John's master Godfrey of Fontaines—were incensed by his answer, for philosophical reasons concerning the nature of human will. Masters who staked their careers on such questions might be less than enthusiastic about the *Mirror of Simple Souls*' attempt to wipe away reason and will simultaneously.

John was not listed as attending the Templar confessions of 25 or 26 October 1307,[53] and he was not one of the fourteen masters of theology appending their seals to the decision of March 1308 (almost certainly because he dissented from the findings recorded there).[54] He did, however, offer extended comments on the Templars affair, first in a quodlibet from December 1307 (or spring 1308) that seems wholly approving of Philip IV's actions.[55] More intriguing is John's account of how the bishops of the kingdom asked the doctors of theology to address several controversial questions about the Templars, especially whether those who had confessed and then retracted their confessions should be considered relapsed. Though he gave his version of this otherwise unrecorded consultation in a later quodlibet, it must actually have taken place in 1309 or early 1310.[56] In the event, only three of the masters of theology were willing to see the Templars as meeting the formal definition for relapse into heresy, while nineteen disagreed. John, however, was one of the three who supported a formal label of "relapse," marking him as one of the most ardent royal supporters on this issue.[57] He knew of the Templars' confessions in the presence of the university and had no doubt about their crimes. Whereas the subsequent retractions had shaken Jacques of Thérines's belief in the Templars' guilt, they had only solidified John of Pouilly's vision of them as hardened heretics. Accordingly, he continued to advocate the order's suppression at the Council of Vienne.[58]

John, however, was soon to find himself accused of defending heretical positions.[59] In an ongoing controversy, John had sided with seculars who argued that anyone confessing to a Mendicant still needed to confess to his or her parish priest at least once a year.[60] Many seculars, including Godfrey of Fontaines, had expressed similar criticisms of Mendicant privileges before, but John had a way of pushing his arguments too far. After inflammatory sermons at Cambrai, among other places, by 1318 he was called to Avignon to defend himself in front of John XXII. A list of thirteen errors (at least two fewer than Marguerite!) was drawn up from his writings. His great adversary at this point was another Parisian master of theology, the Dominican Peter de la Palu, who authored what amounted to a prosecutorial brief.[61] John was allowed to defend himself in a one-day hearing, in which he declared himself ready to submit to any final judgment (and hence not liable to being found a contumacious heretic). But the affair dragged on for another three years, at which point a second list of nine articles was presented against him. Finally, in July 1321, the papal court condemned three dangerous propositions attributed to John, who was forced to read a retraction in Paris in front of a large crowd. After this we know no more about his career or life, but there is no indication that he was forced to stop teaching or that he suffered other penalties before his death (perhaps around 1328).[62]

Thus John of Pouilly offers a fascinating example on several levels. His own trial provides some context for the way an academic theologian might encounter censure, in contrast to the summary procedure afforded Marguerite's extracts. But in 1310 he must also have had mixed feelings about his approach to the inquisitor's consultation. On the one hand, he was an avowed opponent of the Mendicants and the intellectual adversary of Dominican masters Hervé Nédellec (who was not present on Marguerite's panel) and Berenger of Landora (who was).[63] How much sympathy would he have had for the opinion of a Dominican inquisitor, particularly when the extracts he was being asked to condemn came from a book that had been praised by his former master, Godfrey of Fontaines?[64] Nor was John's antagonism limited to Dominicans; at various times he wrote specifically against Nicholas of Lyra, faced off repeatedly with John of Ghent, and sparred with other members of our group of twenty-one such as Ralph of Hotot and Jacques of Thérines.[65] On the other hand, he was a strong supporter of the royal attack on the Templars, and hence William's overt ally in this regard. And like Jacques of Thérines, he wrote a great many questions concerned with understanding the nature of the virtues.[66] In the end, he ultimately lent his name to the condemnation of the extracts. The many conflicting issues that would have pulled him in competing directions in this case, however, suggest the possibility that he had to struggle with this decision.

Our final example, the Augustinian friar Henry of Friemar ("the Elder," known to contemporaries in Paris as Henry the German), may have attended Godfrey of Fontaines's lectures as well (he was probably responsible for an abbreviation of Godfrey's quodlibets). He arrived in Paris to study for the doctorate in theology shortly after 1300 and held the order's teaching chair as regent master by 1307.[67] He was present at the Templar confessions on 25 and 26 October 1307 and was a signatory to the university opinion of March 1308.[68] He later attended the Council of Vienne and died around 1340.

Henry stands out as the author of a number of treatises that consider the nature of mystical unity with God;[69] these employ a language of negative theology that shares a great deal with the *Mirror of Simple Souls.* For example, in *On the Birth of the Word in the Soul* (*Tractatus de adventu Verbi in mentem*), a work written before 1309, Henry quotes from pseudo-Dionysius's *De mystica theologia* to describe "going away from yourself and everything, putting aside all things which are in the world and loosed from all of these things," and urges the reader to "turn the sharp eye of your mind to the divine darkness."[70] This Dionysian language of the "darkness" of God is very much in the same vein as Marguerite's descent into divine nothingness. In the same treatise, Henry explains how the soul can be transformed through love into a state of assimilation with the image of God: "It is characteristic of this love that the soul dissolves and melts from the magnitude of interior sweetness. . . . And from the effect of this love, the soul devoted in all its desires is transformed into this same uncreated image; such a soul seeks nothing, desires nothing, aims at nothing among transitory things, nor does it delight in anything apart from the divine good alone to which it is linked by intimate love."[71] Given his authorship of passages such as these, Henry would have found the *Mirror* intriguing.

Even more striking is the fact that Henry is also the author of a treatise *On the Seven Grades of Love* (*Tractatus de septem gradibus amoris*), probably also written before 1309. To be sure, this treatise took its inspiration from Bernard of Clairvaux's *Tractatus de caritate*, as well as from a longer tradition of Christian mysticism stretching back to Boethius and Augustine. Nevertheless, Henry's seven grades of love are not dissimilar to the seven states of being found in the *Mirror*'s chapter 118 (or to Beatrice of Nazareth's *There Are Seven Manners of Loving*). He lays out his progression thus:

> The first love can appropriately be called "cutting away," because it separates the soul from the dregs of temporal things. The second love is called "setting ablaze" because it inflames this same soul with the fire of divine love. The third can be called "wounding," because with its sweetness it wounds the heart of the lover. The fourth is called "binding," because it immobilizes the lover. The fifth is called "boiling over," because it raises up the one affected incessantly and indefatigably so that he can only taste the divine gift. The sixth is called "languishing," because it melts and dissolves the soul. The seventh is called "destroying," because it leads the soul into an eclipse and annihilation of itself.[72]

Henry later specifies that in this seventh grade of love, such annihilated souls "now do nothing of their own will, leave nothing to their own decision, but entrust everything to divine dispensation."[73]

Henry's step-by-step examination of divine love does not match up specifically with the way Marguerite constructs her own sevenfold division in chapter 118 of the *Mirror*. Yet the end point—the annihilation of the soul and the discarding of will—is broadly analogous to Marguerite's fifth and sixth stages. For example, she writes of the fifth stage: "Now the will sees, by the light of the spreading of divine light . . . that it cannot serve itself well if it does not depart from its own will. . . . For the soul . . . sees by this light that will has to will the divine will alone, without other will, and for this the will was given. And for this the soul departs from this will, and the will departs from such a soul."[74] As an academic theologian, Henry might have found technical reasons to dispute specific aspects of Marguerite's formulation. But as an expert on negative theology he had a large stake in just this sort of statement concerning the abnegation of the will and its relationship to the "annihilation" of the soul.

Of course, there is no evidence that Henry ever saw the *Mirror of Simple Souls* in its entirety. Perhaps if he had, he might have regarded Marguerite as a kindred soul. On the other hand, he might just as easily have been put off by Marguerite's vernacular dialogue—so far from his own ordered and subdivided scholastic approach. One of the ironies here is that because the theologians were given an orderly list of fifteen (or more) propositions in Latin, they were insulated from any immediately negative reaction that a vernacular, female-authored treatise might have produced before even being read.

Henry's fear regarding the extracts he was given may have been more general. His academic distinctions (just the kind of thing Marguerite impatiently waved away) could show concern for the way simpler people might misinterpret the idea of becoming one with God. For instance, in *On the Birth of the Word in the Soul,* Henry stipulates that unity with God "is not to be understood as an identity of real existence as certain erroneous ones maintain, but a certain similitude of conformity and transformation."[75] Could a trained academic theologian trust a layperson to stay on the right side of a subtle line such as this?

His caution about lay mysticism is further seen in his *Treatise on the Four Inspirations,* which has recently been studied as a forerunner to the "discernment of spirits" literature of the later fourteenth century, a genre often overtly misogynist in its suspicion of laywomen's spirituality.[76] Inspiration, according to Henry, could be divine or angelic, but also diabolical or simply natural. A layperson might think her or himself divinely inspired, but she or he would be unlikely to know the difference—it could be the disordered inspirations of the demonic, or simply the vain natural inclination to scholarly puffery. But since Henry may never have set eyes on Marguerite, he had no way of judging her personal comportment. And since he probably never read her entire treatise, he could not know whether she claimed some kind of divine or visionary inspiration or merely presented herself as writing on her own authority.

The most important point raised by Henry's example, however, is that the panel of experts who judged the extracts did contain at least one expert on negative theology. This master would not have been blindly hostile to the general line of thinking Marguerite pursued. He might well have expressed profound disagreement on details of her formulations, but he could not be accused of an inability to grasp the goal of her work. He would, however, likely have found laughable the idea expressed in the prefatory poem contained in the French manuscript of the *Mirror,* that "theologians and other clerics / you will have no understanding of [this book] at all . . . unless you shall proceed humbly / and Love and Faith together / cause you to rise above reason."[77] This was his professional territory; certainly in his own mind he would have felt eminently qualified to use his highly trained powers of "reason" to grasp and judge ideas so close to his own.

These sketches cannot explain exactly how these four men (or the seventeen who joined them) felt about the condemnation they endorsed. They do show, however, that the factors involved were more complex than they might seem at first glance. These men were more often at odds with each other than in agreement; they fell on different sides of questions such as the guilt of the Templars and the Mendicant/secular rivalry. Some of them were clearly allies of William of Paris in various ways, others had a long history of opposing the intellectual traditions of his order. The idea that they would have rallied around a professional and misogynist prejudice against the writings of a laywoman must be treated with care because of the way William chose to keep Marguerite's name and the nature of her treatise out of the formal written record. At the same time, any knowledge that they did have concerning Marguerite's overall stance toward the use of reason would assuredly have offended them. The documentation as it survives tells us only that the senior scholar Simon of Guiberville was able to express the group's unanimous opinion on two articles and hence to support the idea that the book merited destruction. It does not let us see what level of contention may have characterized any fuller debate over the other articles.

Nevertheless, if Marguerite had once been able to show that a Cistercian, a Franciscan, and a secular theologian had found her book praiseworthy, the names of Jacques of Thérines, Nicholas of Lyra, and John of Pouilly had now negated that breadth of approval. And with a list including approximately thirteen members of religious orders and eight seculars, the theologians who now condemned her ideas covered the whole spectrum of possible church affiliations. William of Paris now had all the theological support he needed to treat Marguerite's book as heretical.

Presumably William would have reported the outcome of his consultation with the theologians to Marguerite. If so, what might her reaction have been? It is entirely possible that even at this late date she had retained some hope of finding support among theologians—perhaps from someone such as John of Pouilly, who was heir to the intellectual positions associated with Godfrey of Fountaines; or Jacques of Thérines, who was not afraid to oppose the royal attack on the Jews; or Henry of Friemar, who seemed to share her general theological outlook. She might even have hoped that William would hold exactly this kind of consultation.[78] If so, her hopes were dashed by the theologians' verdict. Yet perhaps if she knew that only extracts had been fed to these twenty-one men, she might have retained to the end her conviction that, given a full hearing, her book would have been accepted as "divine usage."

CHAPTER 7

Toward the Stake

The 11 April condemnation of extracts from Marguerite's book had not materially altered the standing of the case against Marguerite in her person. Her status remained what it had been since 3 April, when the canon lawyers had judged her a contumacious heretic but left open at least the formal possibility that repentance could yet save her life. Just what the effect of sincere repentance at this point might have been is difficult to judge. It is possible that to this point William was purposely reserving to himself the option of a sentence short of death, or he may merely have wished to create this illusion as a way of pressuring Marguerite into testifying. But in either case, by early May her repentance was still not forthcoming. William thus had one more move left to make. What the inquisitor still wished to see confirmed was the final issue of whether, on the basis of her entire case (and not just her behavior since coming into his custody), Marguerite could and should be treated as one relapsed into heresy. In contrast to the open-ended suggestion of eventual repentance still envisioned in the 3 April opinion, a final finding of "relapse" would definitively bring the inquisition against Marguerite Porete to a close.

9 May: The Canonists Once More

William therefore once again called on his original group of five masters of canon law, with Henry of Béthune now rejoining William called

"Brother," Hugh of Besançon, John of Thélus, and Peter of Vaux. There is no indication of where these men met on this occasion, but presumably their deliberations took place on or shortly before 9 May, the Saturday on which they issued their judgment. The document as we now have it (AN J428 no. 19bis) is an unnotarized copy of the sealed original that the canonists produced.

This document is the first that specifically indicates that the canon lawyers were told Marguerite's whole history, a fact the masters themselves emphasized by stating that William had "newly" *(nuper)* made the results of his inquiries known to them.[1] Perhaps William's ongoing fact finding had been informally discussed before this point, but this wording suggests that Marguerite's fuller history really did now arrive as new information to the canonists.[2] In any case, the earlier opinions by the canonists and theologians (3 and 11 April) had been issued without any formal reference to this larger story. William must have purposely chosen to keep this information out of any of the earlier documents. Now at last he laid his cards on the table.

Thus the canonists now received William's report of how he had taken the "deposition of many witnesses" and his findings that Marguerite's book had been burned by Bishop Guido of Cambrai with the written warning that she not teach or write anything like what was in the book again; that she had nevertheless possessed the book again, admitting as much to the inquisitor of Lorraine and to Philip of Marigny; and that she had imparted the book to John, bishop of Châlons-sur-Marne, and other people. In the face of this damning testimony, the canonists, "assuming the truth of the preceding facts," wasted few words. Their verdict was that "this same *beguina* . . . is to be judged relapsed and deservedly relinquished to the secular court."[3]

Even as they received this longer history of Marguerite's life, the canonists were still given only the bare information necessary to induce them to reach the desired conclusion. It is now apparent why the inquisitor's account reveals so little of Marguerite's earlier life; any more detail at this point would only have muddied the legal waters. William was not about to bring forth the praises Marguerite's book had received or to offer any extraneous information that might engender sympathy for her. He wished to present only the "facts" that would lead to the desired opinion on the specific issue at hand. His narrative is only condemnation, disobedience, and admission of that disobedience. Once again, given the information they had to work with, the verdict by the canonists could hardly have been in doubt.

At the same time, it is striking that William limited his story here to Marguerite's own actions. The document makes no mention of the 11 April finding by the theologians concerning her book and does not even remind the canonists of their own 3 April judgment.[4] Again, the question of whether she should be considered relapsed was kept absolutely walled off from all other legal issues as William pursued his tightly controlled process.

This document sealed Marguerite's fate. The finding of 3 April that her rebellious behavior marked her as "lapsed" into heresy had still allowed the legal possibility of reconciliation and imprisonment. The 9 May designation of "relapsed," however, ensured that she would be relinquished to the secular arm for certain execution.

Did William need the canonists' confirmation on this point? At first glance it would seem not; if multiple witnesses confirmed that Marguerite had admitted to defying Bishop Guido's written orders, then her relapse into heresy might seem self-evident. But the exact parameters for applying the legal status of "relapse" had only developed over the thirteenth century and were still open to a certain amount of debate in the early fourteenth.[5] For example, the masters of theology at Paris had only recently (1309 or early 1310) been asked to determine whether Templars who had confessed and then defended the order were technically guilty of relapse, and their answer—as recalled by John of Pouilly—had not been unanimous.[6] Indeed, Marguerite's case does seem to have contained some ambiguity, for the documents do not quite specify that Guido of Collemezzo had convicted Marguerite of heresy in her person and then brought about her reconciliation with the church. Under those circumstances, a new offense would clearly have justified the finding of relapse, but William may not have been able to demonstrate the exact legal outcome of Marguerite's encounter with Guido (she was uncommunicative and Guido had since died). In any case, the account that William furnished to the canonists was vague on this point, opening up a question in need of expert interpretation. Perhaps for this reason, the canonists did not preface their judgment with the note that William "sufficed to complete the matter himself," as they had on 3 April. On the other hand, they did not find it necessary to explain their reasoning or to buttress their decision with the kinds of citations to legal texts that had concluded their verdict on Guiard's testimony a month earlier.

After securing the canonists' ruling, William had a definitive judgment in his inquisition against Marguerite. Yet still he waited several weeks before proceeding to the sentencing of Marguerite and Guiard on 31 May. These were hardly, however, uneventful weeks in Paris.

Paris in Flames

In the month between 11 April and 9 May, when William's case against Marguerite was completed, events in the Templar affair began to intersect with Marguerite's process in a newly direct manner. On 11 April the papal commission investigating the guilt or innocence of the order as a whole at last began to hear witnesses in Paris. In spite of the royal court's attempt to provide hostile witnesses first, the four senior Templars charged with the order's defense—Reginald of Provins, Peter of Bologna, William of Chambonnet, and Bertrand of Sartiges—vigorously challenged the legitimacy of the proceedings, proclaimed their order's innocence, and attacked the honesty of their detractors. Over the next four weeks (with a recess for Easter) the Templars had reason to hope that the hearings were veering in their direction. As momentum gathered, additional brothers even came forward to subscribe to the defense. These proceedings were allowed to continue up through 9 May.[7]

At this moment, however, events took a dramatic turn. It will be recalled that in July and August 1308 Clement V not only had empowered Gilles Aycelin's commission to look into the guilt or innocence of the order as a whole but had also allowed bishops and inquisitors in France once again to pursue heresy accusations against individual Templars. Accordingly, the archbishop of Sens now assembled a provincial council at Paris to judge individual Templars within his jurisdiction (which included Paris), set to open Monday, 11 May.[8] This was not only an ominous development for the individual Templars of the archdiocese but a move that linked the fate of the Templars directly to Marguerite's ongoing saga—for the new archbishop of Sens was none other than Marguerite's onetime accuser, the former bishop of Cambrai, Philip of Marigny.

Philip's star had continued to rise along with his brother's career. Enguerran of Marigny by this time had reached nearly the height of his influence at Philip IV's court—within a year he would clearly overshadow William of Nogaret as the king's most powerful advisor. At this point in the Templar affair (and the ongoing trial of Bishop Guichard of Troyes), it was essential that Philip IV have a man he could trust as archbishop of Sens. As early as 26 January 1309 Clement V had promised not to appoint anyone to this see without considering Philip's preferences. Thus when the preceding archbishop of Sens (Stephen Béquart) died 29 March 1309, Philip IV was virtually in a position to name his successor. Enguerran of Marigny, for his part, worked to make sure the nominee was his brother.[9] The exact date of Philip of Marigny's election and installation as archbishop is not clear, but by October 1309 the king could thank the pope for his compliance in this matter.[10] In dealing with the Templars, the king was now able to act through Philip of Marigny for his archdiocese, much as he had originally attempted to work through the papal inquisitor, William of Paris.

Philip of Marigny's provincial council left no extant records, so we can follow his actions only as they are reflected in other sources. On 9 May Philip was authorized to have a replacement carry out his pastoral visits because of "the services he was rendering to the king."[11] On Sunday 10 May the papal commission hastily convened (it did not normally do business on Sundays) at the Left Bank church of Sainte-Geneviève to hear an urgent plea from the four Templar representatives. These men informed the commissioners that the archbishop of Sens intended to move against a number of Templars to keep them from continuing to defend the order.[12] They asked the commissioners to intervene and formally appealed for papal protection. Archbishop Gilles Aycelin answered that his commission had no power to meddle in Philip of Marigny's proceedings and could only hear any defense the brothers cared to make. The Templars therefore deposited their written appeal and departed. The commissioners read it (and had it copied into their records), at which point Gilles, caught between his loyalties to king and pope, rather weakly announced that he had to "celebrate or hear Mass" and made an ignominious exit. The rest of the commissioners offered nothing concrete in their response later that evening.[13]

On Tuesday, 12 May, in the middle of their interviewing a witness, "it came to the notice" of the commissioners that fifty-four Templars "who had been said to present themselves in the presence of the same lords commissioners for the defense of the said order" were scheduled to be burned that very day.[14] The commissioners now did attempt to send officials to request that Philip of Marigny delay this action, particularly in light of the appeal that they had heard. The archbishop of Sens, however, turned a deaf ear. The fifty-four Templars were taken to a field outside the eastern city walls, near the convent of Saint-Antoine, and burned to death.

The legal pretext for these executions was that by first confessing and then rallying to the defense of their order these men had shown themselves to be relapsed into heresy.[15] The "Continuer of William of Nangis" reported that this decision was made "according to the counsel of men learned in both divine and canon law."[16] This was hardly a clear legal case; we have seen that in 1309 or early 1310 approximately nineteen out of twenty-two Parisian masters of theology refused to apply the label of "relapse" to the Templars. This decision, however, was never publicized,[17] and now Philip of Marigny and his council simply ignored it. If indeed Philip found legal and theological experts to support his actions, they must have been figures very like John of Pouilly—or perhaps even the same hand-picked canonists who had obligingly labeled Marguerite Porete relapsed only days earlier.

Philip of Marigny, acting for the royal court, had achieved his objective—the breaking of the Templar defense. The lone Templar interviewed by the papal commissioners on 13 May was clearly terrified.[18] More concretely, on 18 May three of the Templar leaders let the commissioners know that the fourth, Reginald of Provins, had been called in front of Marigny's council to defend himself (Provins was within the jurisdiction of the archbishop of Sens). The commissioners again appealed to Philip of Marigny to delay any action. His response, made through three representatives of his council later that day, is the closest we get here to a record of his thoughts: "Since two years had elapsed since the inquisition had begun against the said brother Reginald, as against an individual brother of the said order, concerning the crimes which were imputed to him and to the other brothers of the said order; and since they were gathered in Paris in council so that they could finish the said inquisition and others made against individual brothers of the Temple of the same province . . . and since the same lord archbishop could not gather the said council whenever he liked," his delegates were asking the papal commission what they meant by their request. After this feigned incomprehension, they asserted "that it was not the intention of the said lord archbishop of Sens, his suffragans and council to impede in any way the office of the aforesaid lord commissioners."[19] Philip was on solid legal ground in pointing out his authority to inquire against individual brothers of his diocese. But the petulant claim that he could not just convene a regional council whenever he wished and his statement that he did not mean to interfere with the commission's business were patently insincere.

This obfuscation evidently frustrated the commissioners, who responded that their request for a delay had been perfectly clear. In fact, Reginald was returned to the custody of the commissioners, but then one of the other main defenders, Peter of Bologna, disappeared without a trace. After this week of intimidation and death, the contest was over. On 19 May a number of brothers announced that they now wished to renounce their defense.[20] On 27 May five more Templars were burned outside Paris.[21] The remaining brothers were now cowed into silence or newly willing to admit their faults. Matthew of Cressonessart, for instance, who had been such an adamant defender of the order only a month ago, at about this time submitted to the archbishop of Reims and his council at Senlis (where nine more brothers were burned) and received absolution and reconciliation.[22] In these circumstances, the papal commissioners gave up, and on 30 May they adjourned until November.

It is always dangerous to assume that two events must be related to each other merely by virtue of their simultaneity. Yet in this case the congruent timing in the two Parisian trials is too striking to ignore. The papal commission on the Templars began hearing witnesses 11 April, the same day the theologians were gathered by William of Paris to consider extracts from Marguerite's book. It continued through 9 May, the day the canonists issued their final opinion and declared Marguerite relapsed. The very next day Philip of Marigny began to move against Templars of his diocese. After the burnings of 12 May, the commission continued to try to attend to its business up through 30 May. The very next day Marguerite and Guiard were sentenced. The two processes thus marched along in near-perfect synchronicity. Beyond the chronological parallels, the major involvement of Philip of Marigny suggests a larger coherence to the pace of both proceedings. The very man who had first seen to it that Marguerite was sent to Paris was now resident in that city and charged with demonstrating that royal patience with overly long inquisitions was at an end. The fact that both processes came to fiery conclusions within weeks of each other is more than a coincidence.[23]

This is not to say, however, that every event in Paris in the spring of 1310 was necessarily planned in advance detail by a single-minded royal court. The king himself surely had the greatest overall interest in the outcome of the Templar affair but probably did not manage the details of Philip of Marigny's regional council. As we have seen, Philip IV was traveling away from Paris for the second half of April and all of May, and his most strident advisors in ecclesiastical conflicts, Nogaret and Plaisians, were similarly occupied with Boniface VIII's trial in the South. Enguerran of Marigny may also have been at the king's side away from Paris; in any case, although his influence was sharply on the ascent, he did not share the shrill combination of legal intransigence and theological zeal that drove Nogaret, and these inquisitorial matters were not his signature area of competence.

If there was a specific collusion emanating from the royal court, it would have to have been an agreement between Philip of Marigny and William of Paris to coordinate their inquisitorial processes within the general framework suggested by the king's political demands. Both men had an evident interest in seeing the power of the papal commission broken. While William must have feared the commission's ability to cast his own earlier actions in a negative light, Philip had clearly been given the blunt task of using intimidation to stop its flow of defiant witnesses. Moreover, these two men were doubly linked: it was Philip who had first interrogated Marguerite and turned her over to William's custody, and William who had first led the arrest and interrogation of the Templars now in Philip's hands. They therefore shared a mutual interest in the outcome of both trials and could have coordinated their efforts in an attempt to seize the initiative away from the papal commission. The greatest congruence in this regard is the way Marguerite (9 May) and the 54 Templars (11 May) were judged relapsed within two days of each other.[24]

Whether or not Philip of Marigny and William of Paris were actually communicating at every step, these two loyal servants to the king must have been acting under broad royal orders, and within this framework their own interests would have driven them toward similar actions. Members of Philip IV's inner circle displayed unfailing loyalty to the king, yet were fully capable of keeping an eye on their own interests. Nogaret, for example, was at this moment pursuing the posthumous heresy trial of Boniface VIII at Philip's behest but with an overriding interest in seeing his own name cleared after the infamous events of Anagni. Similarly, Enguerran of Marigny would negotiate in Flanders in ways that were completely loyal to Philip IV but that still worked for his own aggrandizement.[25] William of Paris, for his part, was carrying out a course of action that furthered royal goals but also worked toward a rehabilitation of his own reputation. With a tarnished image after 1308, he matched the pace of his process to counter the Templar proceedings in 1310, so that every time a twist in the papal hearing might seem to place him in a negative light, a development in Marguerite or Guiard's trial would display his competence; and when the Templar defense was at last crushed, he was ready to step in with the triumphant end to his own proceedings. He thus pursued his own ends while acting in lockstep with the royal imperatives embodied in Philip of Marigny's move against the Templars at Paris.[26]

31 May: The Sentence

Was Marguerite tempted to break her silence in the weeks between 9 and 31 May? Her refusal to cooperate had been effective at slowing down the proceedings against her. But time was now up. If Marguerite had wished to preserve her life a little longer, offering to testify would now have been the logical course of action. Yet she remained uncooperative to the end. This fact, perhaps more than any other, gives her story its air of tragic dignity.

On Sunday, 31 May, William brought his two cases to a dramatic conclusion. Although the masters of theology and canon law were aware of developments as the trials neared their conclusion—and those who moved in university, Dominican, and royal circles must similarly have had some knowledge of how events were unfolding—for the wider public this would have been an extraordinary moment of unexpected drama. Inquisitorial "general sermons" might have become routine occurrences in Toulouse or Carcassonne, but hardly in Paris. Henry Charles Lea was quite right when he asserted that the public sentencing of Marguerite Porete and Guiard of Cressonessart constituted "the first formal *auto de fé* of which we have cognizance at Paris."[27] That is, this was the first time an inquisitor had brought forth multiple convicted heretics for a public ceremony in the heart of Paris that included sentencing, reconciling of the penitent, and relaxation to the secular arm for those abandoned by the church. In the South, Bernard Gui's contemporary handbook of inquisitorial practice demonstrates in detail how an inquisitor might stage a highly theatrical general sermon (the technical name for such an event), with dozens of sentences to be pronounced (and commuted), following a predictably ordered procession through various categories of offenses and punishments.[28] The population of cities like Toulouse knew where and when such events would take place and how they would unfold. By comparison, the affair of 31 May 1310 was brief, but it would have been entirely novel.

Indeed, the "ritual" itself had to be invented. William chose, as the place for the sentencing, the Place de Grève (the modern Place de l'Hôtel de Ville) on the Right Bank, where one could look across the Seine to the Île-de-la-Cité and the towers of Notre-Dame.[29] This was a logical spot, since it formed one of the few open areas in the maze of narrow streets that made up central Paris. The Place de Grève was then a gravely area sloping down to the Seine, where boats could unload passengers and merchandise, and also the heart of a lively parish centered on the nearby church of Saint-Jean-en-Grève. It had been used for public spectacles in the past. For example, books had been burned there before, such as copies of the Talmud in 1242.[30]

William now gathered there "a copious multitude of people" and "many processions from the city of Paris," and "the clergy and people of the said city" and a host of dignitaries and officials—eleven of whom are named in the notarized version of the final sentences. The reference to "processions" indicates a ritualized route through the city: perhaps from Notre Dame, over the Grand Pont and up the Right Bank, or more directly from wherever Marguerite and Guiard were imprisoned. There was probably some kind of raised platform from which a dozen dignitaries loomed over the unfortunates about to be sentenced. The men who gathered around William of Paris were all known royal supporters or officials. William Baufet, bishop of Paris, stood with the inquisitor as his main support (mentioned a total of five times in the document). This William was a longtime intimate of the royal court.[31] As bishop of Paris since 1305, he had just participated in Philip of Marigny's provincial council with its burning of local Templars (later Templar depositions relate being reconciled by him). A third William in attendance, of Chanac, had served as official of Paris (the bishop's chief administrator), and was later (1333–42) himself bishop of Paris. Also present were John of Forgetis, labeled here as the official of Paris; the royal masters of accounts John of Dammartin and Sanche of Charmoie; and the provost of Paris, John of Ploiebach.[32] William of Paris's sometime inquisitorial lieutenant, the Dominican Nicholas of Ennezat, was there as well. Nicholas had handled the early Templar interrogations along with William and in many ways appears to have been a similar figure in terms of his career and intellectual predilections.[33] The Franciscan bachelor of theology Martin of Abbeville, an adherent to the royal position in 1303 and later regent master from 1312–14, represented the other main Mendicant order and provided the only true theologian in attendance.[34] Notably, no masters of canon law or theology (neither those who had participated in William's consultations nor any others) are recorded as witnessing the event. The ever-present notary Jacques of Vertus was there, however, and surely would have included such illustrious figures in his account had they participated.

William of Paris read out his sentences. Presumably the copy he held was identical to the one that Jacques of Vertus later notarized and was written in Latin. Most likely, however, the sentences were actually proclaimed first in French and then Latin.[35] Unlike Bernard Gui, who made a policy of leaving cases of relaxation to the secular arm for last in his *sermones generales,* William dealt with Marguerite first. The sentence addressed her in the second person and recounted how she had refused to swear the oath and had endured excommunication for a year and a half, continuing in this state up to the present, "because of which, according to canonical sanction, we consider and must consider you as convicted and confessed and as lapsed into heresy or as a heretic."[36] William's language here emphasized his own lack of choice in the matter—her own actions had led to an inevitable result. The inquisitor then related how he had nevertheless carried out an inquiry, which had uncovered Marguerite's acknowledgment of continuing to possess copies of her book, made before the inquisitor of Lorraine and "lord Philip, then bishop of Cambrai and now archbishop of Sens." This invocation of Philip's current position was a vivid reminder that on his authority fifty-four Templars had been burned a mere three weeks ago. Though Philip was not actually present on 31 May (Jacques of Vertus would surely have noted his presence), his shadow hung over the proceedings.

There are also some small but interesting differences between the way Marguerite's earlier history had been recounted in the document sealed by the canonists 9 May and the public version William now delivered on 31 May. A few additional details were added, such as the fact that the first burning of Marguerite's book had taken place in Valenciennes and in her presence and that Guido's warning letter had been "sealed with his seal." William also now emphasized that his process was carried out according to legal forms and that his witnesses were "worthy of faith." These were little touches intended to strengthen a public case for listeners who might need convincing. But there was also one very noticeable omission—at no point in this document did William call Marguerite a *beguina*. Similarly, the male equivalent *beguinus/beghardus* was absent here. Not only was this label not used in Guiard's subsequent sentence, but when listing Marguerite's transgressions, William stated only that she had sent the book to the bishop of Châlons-sur-Marne and "certain other people," whereas the canonists (surely working from information William had provided) had said it was to the bishop and "many other simple people, *beghardis* and others."

The fact that William specifically chose not to use the word *beguina* in his final sentence shows that he was not making any overt attempt to use the crimes of Marguerite and Guiard to tarnish publicly other *beguinae* and *beguini* at this moment. This choice of language may have been once again intended to avoid controversy. Calling Marguerite a beguine would have raised possible questions in the minds of onlookers about her links to a specific beguinage or to Mendicants assigned to care for beguines (as the Dominicans were for the grand beguinage in Paris). In their internal discussions this had seemed a useful label to the canonists (who specifically employed it in their 9 May judgment); for the wider public it must have seemed to William counterproductive.[37]

At last William arrived at his specific sentence, taking care to make clear the consensus it represented: "Therefore, after diligent deliberation concerning all the aforestated matters and having received the counsel of many persons expert in both laws, having God and the sacred Gospels before our eyes, with the assent and counsel of the reverend father and lord, Lord William by the grace of God bishop of Paris, we condemn you by sentence, Marguerite, not only as one lapsed into heresy but as one relapsed, and we relinquish you to secular justice, asking it that short of death and mutilation of the body it act mercifully with you, as far as canonical sanctions permit."[38] The plea that her punishment by the secular arm be short of death was a standard clause, but this fact does nothing to lessen its striking insincerity.

Then, in what amounted to a separate condemnation, William turned to Marguerite's book—though it remained, to the last, without a title: "And the said book we condemn by sentence as heretical and erroneous, as containing errors and heresies by judgment and counsel of the masters of theology residing in Paris, and now we want it to be exterminated and burned, and strictly order that every and each person having the said book, under pain of excommunication, is required to turn it over without fraud to us or to the prior of the Preaching Brothers of Paris, our commissioner, before the next feast of the apostles Peter and Paul [i.e., 29 June]."[39] Although the sentence does not spell this out, very likely one or more copies of the book were in fact burned on the spot.[40] Penitent heretics were normally forced to throw their books into the flames themselves, and Marguerite may well have done this once before at Valenciennes. But this time, remaining staunchly impenitent, it seems unlikely that she could have been made to perform this act. Perhaps William of Paris fed the book to the fire with his own hands.

Significantly, William apparently believed that additional copies of the book were circulating in Paris. Had he thought himself to possess the only copy, he would have been unlikely to demand that "every and each person" having a copy turn it in to the Dominican prior. There is no record as to whether anyone came forth to surrender a banned copy over the next thirty days. But what is clear is the way the book was treated separately from Marguerite, right to the end.[41] It was condemned and burned on 31 May, and placed (so to speak) under the authority of the inquisitor and his Dominican brethren—just at the same moment that

Marguerite herself was released from inquisitorial custody into that of the secular arm.

William then turned to Guiard and ran through the same preliminary course of events—his arrest and stubborn refusal to swear the oath, his excommunication, and the finding of him to be "confessed and convicted of heresy and as a heretic." But, William continued, at last Guiard had appeared in his presence ready to testify and had asserted that he was the Angel of Philadelphia "sent directly by Christ, who has the key of excellence, not by the lord pope, who has only the key of ministry, as you said."[42] For this reason, he was convicted of proposing a division in the church. Following the lead given by the canonists 9 April, William stuck to the accusation that Guiard's heresy lay in having challenged papal authority. The wording here was not exactly faithful to Guiard's own testimony and once again conflated his several claims in order to make him seem to have more directly set himself up as a rival to the pope. Just as importantly, in this very short summary most of Guiard's more inflammatory ideas were kept out of public hearing.

Therefore, with the counsel of many learned men in theology and canon and civil law, and with the "counsel and assent of the reverend lord, Lord William by the grace of God bishop of Paris": "We condemn you by sentence, the aforesaid Guiard, as a heretic, declaring you deprived of all clerical privileges, [and] asking the aforesaid reverend father that he remove clerical insignia from you immediately. When these steps have been carried out, we condemn you by sentence to perpetual imprisonment, reserving to ourselves and our successors in the aforementioned office of inquisitor the power of mitigating, diminishing, changing, increasing, or completely absolving, as far as your merits will require and it shall seem proper to us and our successors in the aforesaid office."[43] There is no record of Guiard being made to demonstrate his penance in a visible fashion, or indeed of anything that happened to him from this point on. He presumably had all clerical insignia removed immediately by Bishop William.[44] His imprisonment would have remained, however, within an ecclesiastical context, since he was not turned over to secular authorities. As the sentence notes, this perpetual imprisonment could later have been altered at the discretion of the inquisitor. But after 31 May 1310 the Angel of Philadelphia simply disappears from the historical record.

1 June: The Stake

Here the dossier of trial documents ends. It is only several chronicle entries that record the last act in Marguerite's drama, most importantly the "Continuer of William of Nangis." This monk of Saint-Denis was not factually infallible; for instance, he dated Marguerite's execution to "around Pentecost," and since Pentecost fell on 7 June in 1310 this lack of precision suggests that his entry for 1310 was written down somewhat later, when memories were still fresh but not quite as sharp as they might have been in June. On the other hand, it should be recalled that one of the theologians who condemned extracts from Marguerite's book was Peter of Saint-Denis, a fellow monk who could have provided firsthand information about at least some parts of Marguerite's process.[45] Indeed, the theologians' perspective is particularly evident in this account, since the "Continuer" emphasizes that the book published by "a certain pseudowoman from Hainaut, named Marguerite called Porete" contained many errors and heresies in the judgment of all the theologians who examined it. After briefly recounting Marguerite's stubborn refusal to recant, he continues: "At the Place de Grève in the presence of the clergy and people specially assembled for this purpose, with the counsel of learned men, she was brought forth and handed over to secular justice. The provost of Paris, immediately taking her into his power, in the same place the next day caused her to be destroyed by fire."[46] From this passage we learn that it was John of Ploiebach, provost of Paris (essentially the royal official in charge of policing the city), who had custody of Marguerite the night of 31 May,[47] probably detaining her in the nearby Grand Châtelet or another royal prison. It was the provost who would then have determined the timing and details of Marguerite's impending execution.

The execution by fire on 1 June probably took place at the Place de Grève, "in the same place" as the sentencing. Though this square was later notorious as a site for public punishments, executions, and eventually the guillotine, in 1310 there was no single established spot in Paris for carrying out sentences of death. Other fourteenth-century executions did occur in the Place de Grève,[48] but hangings were staged at Montfaucon outside the Porte du Temple, burnings sometimes took place at the pig market beyond the Porte Saint-Honoré, and beheadings

could transpire at Les Halles in the heart of the city.[49] In any given instance secular officials might decide on whatever site seemed most useful for the lesson the execution was intended to teach. In 1306, for example, rioters had been hanged from four gates to the city.[50]

But, just as the ritual sentencing of 31 May was new for Paris, so
too the events of the next day were distinct from routine executions of
common criminals. It is true that heretics had been burned at Paris before: ten followers of the theologian Aumary of Bène were burned outside the walls of Paris in 1210, but presumably little public memory of
that event was operative a century later.[51] Moreover, although the trial
of the Aumaricians had employed a precocious inquisitorial procedure,
these executions occurred decades before the appearance of the first
papally appointed Dominican inquisitors. When such inquisitors did
begin their work in the 1230s, several hundred men and women—
including at least one beguine—were burned in northern France as the
Dominican Robert le Bougre moved across the Archdiocese of Reims
in 1236 and 1239.[52] But there is no evidence for executions for heresy in
Paris before the time of William of Paris. We have seen that at least one
relapsed Jew was burned in Paris in late 1307 or early 1308, but we do
not know exactly where. Most recently, of course, dozens of Templars
had just been executed after Archbishop Philip of Marigny turned them
over to secular authority. But they were hustled off to the field outside
town near Saint-Antoine on the very day of their condemnation, and it
is unclear which secular official oversaw their burning.

The choice of the Place de Grève therefore seems slightly unexpected as a site to execute heretics (so much so that one historian has recently questioned whether this was really where the execution occurred
at all).[53] On one hand, it might be explained by the same logic that eventually made this public square a frequent site of punishments—if the
goal was an exemplary spectacle for public consumption, this central
spot was ideal. But there may have been a more specific reason as well.
Places of execution often were intended to have some symbolic relationship to the crime being punished.[54] For Marguerite, whose book
had once been burned in Valenciennes under a similar logic, no location
in Paris held such a resonance. Tax records do show that a number of independent beguines lived on or near the Place de Grève,[55] but given that
William chose not to employ the word *beguina* in his sentence, this fact
does not seem significant.

The key to this choice of location may in fact have had nothing to do with Marguerite, for she did not go to her death alone that day. After describing Marguerite's fate, the "Continuer of William of Nangis" immediately (even before discussing Guiard of Cressonessart) goes on to relate that "on the same day, in the same place, a man some time ago converted to the faith from Judaism was cremated in the temporal fire, passing over to eternity, when again, like a dog returning to his vomit, in contempt of the blessed Virgin, he was trying to spit on images of her."[56] This is the sum total of what is known about this unfortunate man's tribulations. The two executions of 1 June, however, were certainly part of a single event. And although the "Continuer" does not spell this out, given that William of Paris had overseen the earlier trials of two "relapsed" Jews in 1307, it is virtually certain that he had similarly conducted the investigation of this third case in 1310 as well. This realization in turn implies that this nameless Jew may well have been part of the "auto-da-fé" of 31 May. His sentence must have been recorded separately and thus was not preserved along with the trial documents of Marguerite and Guiard.

From William's perspective, therefore, 31 May and 1 June 1310 saw the end not of two trials but of three. The fact that records survive from the trials of Marguerite and Guiard and not from that of the unnamed Jew creates the impression that the former were more important and elaborate than the latter. But this was at least the third case of "relapse" by a recent convert to the faith that had received substantial publicity since 1307, and all had almost certainly been handled by William of Paris. In this light, the unexpected title given to William in a later inquisitorial formulary makes sense: "Inquisitor against the perverse Jews and those who violate the ecclesiastical sacraments."[57] Though William could not have been granted an official papal title of inquisitor "against the Jews," he might well have been remembered this way after this trio of high-profile cases of "relapse."[58] Moreover, these acts of "apostasy" could be perceived as an attack on royal policy and prestige, given their relation to the expulsion of 1306. In light of the court's overriding desire to propagate the image of a most Christian king defending the faith within his realm, the recurring challenge of converts relapsing to their ancestral faith might have weighed especially heavily on the minds of the king's inner circle. Thus as the provost of Paris arranged these executions, it may have been the inclusion of this "relapsed" Jew that suggested the appropriateness of the Place de Grève. For this was a spot loaded with recent symbolism for the supposed crimes of the Jews.

Two decades earlier, Paris had seen a major landmark in emerging persecutions of Jews—the first documented accusation of host desecration. Related to the older "blood libel" (the claim that Jews engaged in ritual murder of Christian babies), in this 1290 episode a Jew was accused of bribing a Christian woman to give him a consecrated host, which he then supposedly tried to destroy in different ways. When he stabbed it, however, it miraculously bled, revealing its true nature as the body of Christ and the Jew's true status as persecutor of Christ. The Jew was executed (in the pig market outside the western edge of the city, according to one chronicler),[59] and his family may have converted. But as the event's fame grew, a new chapel was built on the site of his house to hold the knife he had used for his attacks (eventually the chapel des Billettes, where the oldest cloister in Paris still survives behind an unassuming doorway on the rue des Archives), while the miraculous wafer itself was displayed at the Church of Saint-Jean-en-Grève. Both sites were just off the Place de Grève and drew an increasing number of pilgrims to venerate these new relics.[60]

Before 1306 most Jews in Paris had lived in the neighborhoods immediately north and east of the Place de Grève,[61] and this quarter was now the center of remembrance of the Jewish "attacks" on the host in 1290. Burning a relapsed Jew here tied the problem of "false" conversions back to the idea of Jews as eternal enemies of Christ and in turn reinforced the idea of the king as his defender. Thus the place of Marguerite's execution may have been determined by the fate of a man whose separate trial simply happened to end at the same time as hers. The existence of two "heretics" awaiting execution suggested the utility of a larger spectacle where both would meet their fate, and the fact that one was a converted Jew "relapsed" into his old faith may have suggested the Place de Grève as the appropriate location.

The "Continuer of William of Nangis" finally relates, in a unique passage, something of how Marguerite appeared to onlookers in her final moments: "She showed many signs of penitence at her end, both noble and devout, by which the hearts of many were piously and tearfully turned to compassion, as revealed by the eyes of the witnesses who beheld this scene."[62] The monks of Saint-Denis were generally supporters of the royal court, but at times the "Continuer" was able to express independent convictions. For instance, just before this passage he notes that the fifty-four Templars burned on 12 May had maintained their innocence to the end, and he hints at doubts about their true guilt.[63] Although it is often said that all the evidence about Marguerite's trial is from hostile sources, the "Continuer" cannot be considered to have been entirely without sympathy for her plight.

What were these many "signs of penitence"? Did Marguerite at last speak? If so, should we imagine her, at the very end, expressing regret? For what? For having written her book? For having refused to defend it? It seems unlikely that she would have disavowed her book or her actions. Had she wished to repent, even a day earlier, she might have delayed her execution by offering to cooperate. Repentance, now that it was too late, would have served little practical purpose, and on the spiritual plane Marguerite seems to have been little concerned with the sacraments that could have been offered as an inducement. More likely these "signs of penitence" were more in the nature of a general comportment suggesting an aura of devoutness. To onlookers, Marguerite faced death as a woman who appeared to be pious rather than rebellious. If she did speak at last, she must have impressed the crowds with the sincerity of her words. More likely, however, the reference to "signs" indicates merely a projection of a "noble and devout" demeanor that brought tears to the eyes of those gathered to watch her fiery departure from the world.

In the End

Marguerite's long battles with authority had begun with her book. But for most of the intervening period it was her actions, not the ideas contained in her writings, that placed her at odds with bishops and inquisitors. Her defiance had been based on the entirely rational evidence of the praise given to her book by multiple churchmen, and very likely by the reactions of other "simple people" and "beghards" who had read or heard her ideas. Some of this defiance and even rational optimism could have continued right up into spring 1310 and the series of final judgments against her. But silence is hard to interpret, particularly at a distance of seven hundred years, and one can only speculate on what meaning she might have assigned to her ordeal as it neared its end. At some point in time she must have become deeply disillusioned with the intellectual rejection involved in her process. It might be expected, therefore, that the final condemnation of her book would have left her visibly bitter. Alternatively, it is possible to speculate that her apparent silence over a year and a half was never the noble defiance it might seem but merely the result of some kind of collapse or incapacity. Yet the chronicle evidence suggests neither an angry rebel nor a befuddled invalid, bur rather a "noble" woman able to go calmly to the pyre—one last surprise in an endlessly surprising career.

Marguerite's story contains its share of contradictions. She was a theologian of nonaction and nothingness, yet consistently active in seeking approval for these ideas. She gave at least the appearance of penitence once and may have communicated with her interrogators more than has generally been realized. She was, I think, a rational actor rather than either a wandering naif or a would-be martyr seeking literal "annihilation" at the hands of her inquisitor. Yet Marguerite also exhibited a "persistent complicity in her own demise" that prevents us from treating her as simply a victim of an intolerant and misogynist age.[64] Her own choices led her to the stake, as much as did the steps taken by her inquisitor. These contradictions and complexities only add to the extraordinary nature of her life and death.

Guiard's history does not offer quite the dramatic narrative that Marguerite's does, if only because he did at last save his life by testifying. It is hardly necessary to point out, however, that this instinct for self-preservation does not make him somehow less sincere in his beliefs than Marguerite. He sought open confrontation with authority in a way that has parallels to Marguerite's actions, but with less rational basis on which to think he might emerge triumphant. Probably nowhere in Guiard's background was there some equivalent to Godfrey of Fontaines—a leading churchman who might have encouraged him in his conviction that he held the office of an angel. Guiard's story also lacks the literary redemption of the *Mirror of Simple Souls'* miraculous survival. Guiard's ideas were not read and recopied down through the centuries. His attempt to defend Marguerite did bring him attention at the moment of his arrest and again at his sentencing, but even then his claims were probably never fully aired, since at his sentencing William of Paris did not give him the satisfaction of a long rehearsal of his ideas. He was treated as simply a rebel against the pope, which hardly did justice to his self-conception. Guiard was thus effectively silenced by his inquisitorial process. Whether he truly came to believe he had been misguided in his beliefs is impossible to say. If his repentance was less than sincere, then it must have been difficult to allow the inquisitor and his team of experts to recast his apocalyptic message into mere disobedience. One wonders whether even as he was led off to prison some part of Guiard remained convinced that this was all merely the most dire moment of persecution for an angel who would still somehow return to fulfill his functions at the time of Antichrist.

William of Paris, however, must have considered that his handling of this *beguinus* had reached a successful conclusion. Would he have said the same for the entire course of the two trials? William had done his job with meticulous care and according to scrupulous legal standards. Inquisitors were fully capable of rationalizing executions as not only sadly necessary but ultimately beneficial—to the wider Christian community and perhaps even to the soul of the executed heretic.[65] But generally speaking, their larger task was to induce repentance, to "cure" heresy as doctors of the soul. One would not want to veer too close to the opinion of the *curé* whom Marcel Pagnol remembered from his youth, who believed that if the "Holy Inquisition" had burned many Jews and scholars, it did so "with tears in the eyes, and to ensure them a place in paradise."[66] Yet it is true enough that an execution implied a failure of sorts for an inquisitor. Would William of Paris have had to acknowledge defeat in the case of Marguerite?

Perhaps not. William might have preferred to see Marguerite repent, but above all he was concerned with the way every step of the proceedings, including the eventual sentencing and execution, would appear to a wider public made up of lawyers, theologians, royal advisors, and papal officials. William of Paris had not initiated these proceedings against Marguerite. Her contest with authority had begun under the jurisdiction of Bishop Guido and then careered through the interventions of (probably) John of Châteauvillain, the inquisitor of Lorraine, and Philip of Marigny. By the time she was turned over to William of Paris, the possible outcomes were severely limited. Theoretically, a sudden and very convincing turn toward repentance could still have saved Marguerite's life, since before 9 May the canon lawyers treated her as contumacious rather than relapsed. In reality, however, this was never a likely outcome. Several bishops already knew the "facts" of the case, which showed Marguerite to have flouted a clear episcopal order never to circulate her book again. William would probably have had to actively and permanently suppress this information if he had wished to justify any sentence other than relaxation to the secular arm. The way he held back her whole story through early May suggests that he may have wished to keep this option open for a time, but once he introduced this information he must have known that the canonists would unhesitatingly place her in the category of a relapsed heretic. At this point her fate was certain, and William's final task was merely to construct a sentence that would make her execution seem not only justified but inevitable and fully supported by a range of experts.

On these terms, Marguerite's case was a success of sorts for William. The first inquisitorial general sermon ever held in Paris positioned William as the embodiment of formalized concern for legal processes. In the wake of the hastily arranged burnings of the Templars on 12 May, this event was an essential indicator that the intersection of royal and inquisitorial justice could produce results that were legally unimpeachable. On a more personal level, this dramatic public ceremony was William's rehabilitation. After the discrediting papal rebukes of July 1308, William returned to a visible position of public authority on 31 May 1310. This was—in a perverse but real way—his moment in the sun. Not only did he send one heretic away to prison and turn another over to the secular arm, but he staged the dramatic burning of a book judged heretical by the masters of theology, all actions demonstrating that an inquisitor in Philip IV's Paris could deal effectively and legally with heresy and heretics.

An Inquisition's End,
the End of an Inquisitor

By 1 June 1310 Marguerite Porete had been executed and Guiard of Cressonessart imprisoned. As anticlimactic as it might seem, however, our story does not end there, since these trials continued to make waves in the wider ecclesiastical waters of Europe. The epilogues concluding this book highlight several ways in which specific individuals used several aspects of the trial toward specific ends. Epilogue I first follows the documents that were prepared after the trial and then traces the last years of William of Paris's career. Epilogue II looks at one little-known indication of the hopes and fears inspired by the followers of the Angel of Philadelphia. Finally, Epilogue III turns to the events of the Council of Vienne and beyond.

The Archives of an Inquisition

Throughout the spring of 1310 the various trial documents were recorded, recopied, and sometimes integrated one into another. Though a number of sealed documents had been issued by the canonists, no sealed originals survive. The dossier as it now stands is composed only of notarized and unnotarized copies. But this process of writing and rewriting was not quite over as of 1 June. At least two stages remained.

The first saw the production of AN J428 no. 15, the large piece of parchment conveying notarized copies of two of the most important trial texts. At the top of this sheet is found the 11 April decision of the theologians regarding Marguerite's extracts; on the bottom three-fourths of the page are the formal sentences for Marguerite and Guiard. These two texts have generally been referred to as "15a" and "15b" because they represent copies of what were originally two different documents. But it is essential to realize that they survive only as they were copied onto this single sheet and individually notarized by Jacques of Vertus. The exact date of this instrument's preparation is not specified. In notarizing the 11 April decision, Jacques stated that he had been present personally, along with Evens Phili, and had written the document with his own hand, recorded it in public form, and added his customary sign. At the end of the sentences, Jacques again noted that he had been personally present at the Place de Grève and that he had "made and published this public instrument and signed it with my sign." Normally the notary would indicate that he had seen and collated the original texts, in order to verify that the newly produced copy could be treated as authenticated by his sign. In both cases here Jacques omits this language and seems to be asserting that his personal presence in and of itself provides this assurance. In spite of this omission, the process by which these final copies were created seems clear. There must once have been an earlier version of the 11 April judgment that Jacques prepared on that date or immediately afterward.[1] Then, on or after 31 May, Jacques copied out the extant version before proceeding on the same sheet of parchment to reproduce and notarize William's sentences. These sentences also must have existed in an earlier version, presumably the one the inquisitor held in his hand at the time of the sentencing. Because Jacques writes about the sentencing in the past tense and can list all the witnesses that were there, it is certain that he made this notarized version after the event. It could, however, have been as soon as later that day, and in fact Jacques's omission of any additional date in his authenticating clause suggests that this might have been the case.[2]

Although the production of this final document might seem routine, it is nevertheless revealing. For one thing, it shows how carefully William continued to follow legal formalities, even after the trials were over. So far as is known, William did not keep a grand book of all his sentences (the way Bernard Gui did, for instance). William was not questioning and sentencing large numbers of people, who might need to be confronted at a later date with their earlier testimony. This kind of record keeping was an important part of the way inquisitors enforced conformity,[3] but in this case William's careful creation of documents made sense primarily as a precaution against the possibility of some future question arising about the proceedings. These documents, in other words, protected the inquisitor more than they threatened the two "heretics" (one of whom was already dead, and the other incarcerated for life).

More interesting still is William's choice to combine these two texts. Why preface the sentences with the theologians' decision about Marguerite's book? Not only was this decision altogether irrelevant to Guiard of Cressonessart's sentence, but it did not even mention Marguerite by name. If William had wanted to include a preliminary text justifying the final sentence, why not, for instance, use the 9 May decision by the canonists that actually placed Marguerite in the category of a relapsed heretic and authorized her relaxation to the secular arm?

In fact, the juxtaposition of the two discrete documents in J428 no. 15 created a link where William had previously fostered separation— between the condemnation of Marguerite's book and her personal guilt as a relapsed heretic. William had been careful to include only a minimum of relevant information in each consultation with his two sets of experts. His consultations with the canonists had not discussed the content of Marguerite's book, and his consultation with the theologians had not even recorded her name. He now toppled the very wall that he had so deliberately constructed. A reader of the new two-part document would receive the implicit message that the condemnation of Marguerite's ideas by an illustrious body of theologians had led inevitably to her burning. J428 no. 15 thus suggests a narrative that shelters the entire proceedings under the authority of the masters of theology. Indeed, the opening of the second text makes this link in a subtle fashion, by referring to the "same year 1310," with the word *same* referring the reader back to the first document and implying continuity. Thus, by a sort of sleight of hand (it is in fact necessary to read backwards from the sentence to the theologians' judgment to even deduce that Marguerite Porete was the author of the book they condemned), the composite document in its final form conflates the separate judgments against a burned text and its soon-to-be-burned author. Because the opinion of the nearly complete faculty of theology, far more than that of the smaller group of canonists, could provide unassailable public validation for the inquisitor's actions, William (and his notary) now thrust forward the theologians' findings as cover for the sentences as a whole.[4] The success of this strategy may be reflected in the wording of the contemporary *Grandes chroniques de France,* which simply says, "Certain masters, experts in theology, had condemned her." This was not literally true, but it was exactly the impression William wished to create.

The last known stage in the post-trial production of documents was the copying of AN J428 no. 16, which relates the original March meeting and subsequent 3 April decision by the canonists concerning Guiard. As detailed in chapter 4, the extant document is composed of three layers. But only two of these layers existed at the time of Guiard's imprisonment: the canonists' 3 April decision, embedded in an account of the calling of the March meeting. This bilevel document had been prepared and notarized by Evens Phili on or shortly after 3 April. But the text as we now have it adds one more layer, since it is a newly notarized copy prepared by Jacques of Vertus on 4 October 1310. Along with two other Parisian clerics (Jacques of Actrio and William Coffini), he transcribed Evens Phili's earlier document, collated the copy with the original for accuracy, and notarized it with his sign. Thus a new copy was commissioned five months after the trial's completion. Why? Perhaps William of Paris was responsible. Certainly Jacques of Vertus's close and continuing association with the inquisitor means that William was at least aware of this copy's production. But since William already had ample opportunity to have all his documents in order well before October, it seems more likely that some other interested party requested this new notarized instrument.

Most likely this was someone close to the royal court, because we know that all of the trial documents that survive were in the possession of William of Nogaret and William of Plaisians at the time of their deaths in 1313.[5] According to an inventory drawn up shortly afterward, the two notarized documents (nos. 15 and 16) were probably in Nogaret's possession when he died around April.[6] Other documents concerning Marguerite and Guiard were being kept by Plaisians, perhaps including a now lost additional copy of Guiard's notarized testimony.[7] Thus the trial documents were preserved down to the present by the lucky chance that the papers of these two men found their way into the royal archives (the Trésor des Chartes).[8]

In fact, it is likely that the new notarized copy (no. 16) produced on 4 October was commissioned by William of Nogaret (directly or through Plaisians). The timing of his travels suggests this strong possibility: from spring 1310 through August he was in the South of France leading the royal cause in the posthumous trial of Boniface VIII, attending to his own lands, and conducting other royal business. In September he was back in the Île-de-France, and he probably remained nearby through October before returning to Avignon for the resumption of the Boniface trial by 10 November.[9] Given this chronology and the fact that the documents ended up in his possession, it seems probable that he took an immediate interest in compiling the trial records for his own use, perhaps as indirect ammunition in the continuing attack on the memory of Boniface VIII or as preparation for the showdown over the fate of the order of the Temple looming at the Council of Vienne.

The implications of this parchment trail have been pointed out before but bear repeating. William of Nogaret was a ruthless royal bulldog who could be counted on to attack perceived religious enemies of the crown with unmatched vigor, and William of Plaisians was his right-hand man (labeled his "alter ego" by one historian and his "shadow" by another).[10] Indeed, Nogaret's "hand can be seen in every one of the legal assaults Philip made against his enemies."[11] With Plaisians, he was the leader of the verbal and physical attack on Boniface VIII in 1303; he played a role in confiscating the goods of expelled Jews in 1306; on 22 September 1308 he was made keeper of the seals, just in time for the arrest of the Templars; and he intervened personally in the prosecution of Guichard of Troyes.[12] The posthumous inventory of Nogaret's papers reflects these roles, with, for instance, a section on Boniface VIII (items 250–93) and one on the Templars (294–309). The fact that Marguerite and Guiard's trial documents ended up in his hands can only mean that the royal court had taken a keen interest in the proceedings and intended to use the results to its advantage.[13] For Nogaret and Plaisians, the archiving of such records provided both a future rebuttal of any charge that the court was not protecting the realm against heresy and an offensive weapon that could be used as further ammunition in the never-ending drive to portray the Most Christian King as the ever-vigilant sentinel watching over his chosen people.

The Last Years of William of Paris

If William of Nogaret continued to think about the potential uses of this trial, what about William of Paris? Did his handling of the cases of Marguerite and Guiard restore his reputation as an effective agent of papal authority? Perhaps so, since on 1 May 1311 Clement V issued three privileges in his favor.[14] They are all, however, addressed to him as "beloved son, brother William of Paris of the order of Preachers, confessor to our dearest son in Christ Philip the illustrious king of the Franks," with no mention of his inquisitorial title. In this sense, Clement's favor reflects William's services as a confessor, not an inquisitor, and was indeed being shown as much to Philip as to William. Nevertheless, these three privileges from Clement do suggest that William had regained a certain amount of papal confidence in the last years of his life.

The first request, specifically granted at Philip's urging, demonstrates that William maintained his chamber at the Dominican house of Saint-Jacques. Clement now conceded that William could take his meals in this chamber, sharing the ordinary rations for healthy brothers there with other brothers he might ask to join him. Should he fall ill, he could have the rations accorded to sick brothers served in his chamber as well.[15] The second privilege assured William that he could not be compelled by anyone to take up the office of prior against his will.[16] The third conceded that he might bequeath whatever books he wished to the Dominican convent in Paris, whether he had received them as royal gifts or as pious donations from other faithful.[17]

These privileges highlight the balancing act between royal duty and Dominican identity that continued to the end of William's life. He kept his room at Saint-Jacques and shared the common food of the brothers, yet in his last years (there is perhaps a hint here that he felt himself to be growing ill) he preferred to dine apart. The papal reassurance that he could not be made a prior suggests that his order wished him to take on more administrative duties. There may have been a move to appoint him prior in Paris or (nightmare of all Parisians!) somewhere else, but his royal responsibilities probably made him reluctant to take up this charge. The final privilege is particularly intriguing—what books had Philip IV given him? The text does not say, but it does give the impression that William was proud to specify that his bibliographic bequest to Saint-Jacques (again his own mortality was on his mind) would stem at least in part from royal favor.

Philip's continuing trust is further underlined by the fact that later this same month, on 17 May, William was again named as one of the executors of the king's testament. The newly revised version, in fact, now granted him a legacy of fifty livres tournois per year.[18] The royal accounts afford a few last glimpses of William in the first half of 1313: on 22 January he was paid for travel to Troyes on the king's business; on 2 February he was with the king in Arzilliéres; on 20 March he was reimbursed for considerable expenses involved in receiving Dominican masters at court in Paris;[19] and on 24 April he was sent from the king's side in Poissy to Paris.[20] This short trip, back to the city where he may well have been born, seems to be the last documentary trace of the career of William of Paris.[21]

If William demonstrably remained the royal confessor to the end of his days, is it equally certain that he continued to act as an inquisitor? No dated record of inquisitorial activities or reference to him with the title of inquisitor survives after 31 May 1310. One undated document, however, hints that he may have been less engaged by inquisitorial duties in his last years, even as he retained the formal title of inquisitor. This document, copied into an inquisitorial manual in Bohemia later in the fourteenth century (but based on compilations probably made in the second quarter of the century), is labeled a "commission concerning certain articles and against Jews." In this handbook it serves as a template, to be used by any later inquisitor who might wish or need to delegate authority. It begins:

> Brother William of Paris, etc., inquisitor against the perverse Jews and those who violate ecclesiastical sacraments, deputed by apostolic authority in the Kingdom of France, to a venerable and discrete man, beloved in Christ, greetings.

It has lately been made known to us, by relation from men worth of faith, that a certain person vomited forth words which right away tasted contrary to the faith insofar as it is preached through church doctrine: specifically, that no copulation with any woman whatsoever is illicit. And what is even crazier, he stubbornly asserted that he wanted to induce others to believe this same thing, just as the ones who were present were able to judge from his way of speaking.

Therefore, since we—entangled by many and arduous duties—are frequently unable to prosecute as we would like the office of inquisition of heretical depravity committed to us by apostolic authority, [and] since we desire the extirpation of this heresy and the augmentation of the Catholic faith above all the desires of our mind . . . we are able to commit our duties concerning citation and examination of witnesses, and those other things which are fully contained in papal writings, to certain persons, of whatever order, condition, or grade.[22]

This document has been cited earlier in regard to the unexpected title William here seems to give himself—"inquisitor against the perverse Jews and those who violate ecclesiastical sacraments." If there is any shadow of William's true self-conception here, such a title might suggest that the document dates from after 1 June 1310, since it seems to combine the lessons from the two executions of that date: the relapsed Jew had been accused of spitting on images of the Virgin, and Marguerite Porete had been remembered in the *Grandes chroniques de France* as saying "contrary and prejudicial things about the sacrament of the altar."[23] If this hypothesis is correct, it may be significant that William refers to the "many and arduous duties" that "frequently" have kept him from his inquisitorial role. Notably, he does not say that he is already overwhelmed with inquisitorial work; rather, he seems to suggest that other duties, not related to this office, prevent his taking up this inquiry.

In any case, William of Paris did not have long to continue any inquisitorial activities, since he died sometime between 24 April 1313 (the last reference to him in the royal accounts) and 28 November 1314, on which date the codicil to Philip IV's testament referred to him as the king's "onetime" confessor.[24] He was not present, then, at Philip's death 29 November, or at the cathedral of Notre-Dame-de-Paris on 2 December, where the royal funeral mass was presided over by Philip of Marigny (the latter survived his brother Enguerran's disgrace and execution to live until 1316).[25]

Thus, although William had been listed as one of the executors to Philip's testament since 1297, he was ultimately never called upon to act in this capacity. Those with a taste for historical irony might regret this fact, for if William had lived long enough to execute the king's testament it might have fallen to him to distribute the twenty pounds Philip left to the poor beguines of Paris and the hundred destined for beguines elsewhere in the kingdom.[26]

The Angel and the Doctor

While William of Paris and William of Nogaret were concerning themselves with the documentary record of the trial, other men were react-
ing to these events in different ways. Among the most interesting is
Arnau of Vilanova, a controversial doctor, professor, theologian, reformer, and advisor to kings and popes. He enters into the concluding
moments of this story because one of the last works in his prolific career
was a brief treatise intended for Guiard of Cressonessart's followers entitled (in one manuscript) the *Epistola ad gerentes zonam pelliceam*, or
"Letter to Those Wearing the Leather Belt" (Appendix C gives an English translation).[1] This text has only recently been identified by scholarship and now stands as an exciting demonstration of how reports of
Guiard's group were circulating in the South of France.[2]

Arnau of Vilanova and His Career

Arnau was born around 1238 and grew up in Valencia.[3] He arrived at
the University of Montpellier around 1255, where he studied the lib-
eral arts and then earned the title master of medicine by 1270. He was
by this time proficient in both Arabic and Latin, as well as married
with a daughter. He never obtained a university degree in theology or
trained as a priest (though he later claimed to have studied theology
with the Dominicans for six months), but his status as a member of the
university meant that he was in fact a cleric in minor orders. By 1281

Arnau was court physician to King Peter III of Aragon and studying Hebrew with the Dominican Raimon Martí. After 1290 he was professor of medicine at Montpellier, while still serving James II of Aragon (r. 1291–1327) and authoring numerous medical treatises.[4]

But by the 1290s Arnau was also developing his interests in eschatology and theology. Like Guiard of Cressonessart, he was influenced by the ideas of Joachim of Fiore, as shown most readily by the fact that one of his earliest theological works (1292) was the "Introduction to Joachim's Book *On the Seed of Scripture*" (though, in fact, the *De semine Scripturam* was falsely attributed to Joachim).[5] His eschatological treatises, however, built upon a loosely Joachite framework to develop their own unique predictions of when and how the time of Antichrist would arrive.

As early as 1287 Arnau had started working on the treatise that would eventually land him in trouble, "On the Time of Antichrist's Advent" *(De tempore adventus Antichristi)* in which he calculated that Antichrist would arrive in 1366 (or at least by 1376). When he found himself in Paris in late summer 1300 on diplomatic business for James II, he spoke with Parisian theologians about his book and gave a copy to the chancellor of the university (Peter of Saint-Omer), perhaps in September.[6] A few masters of theology, incensed at his audacity and novel interpretive principles, denounced him.[7] Arnau later claimed that he had offered to make changes if the theologians would explain what offended them; instead he was arrested by the official of Paris around the first week of October. He was released the next day when several figures close to Philip IV, including William of Nogaret and Gilles Aycelin, intervened and posted a bond.[8] A few days later, however, the theologians cited him before the bishop of Paris, who condemned a list of propositions that the hostile theologians had extracted from his book. Arnau was forced to recant these statements, and although they were labeled "rash" rather than explicitly heretical, his book was nevertheless burned.[9]

Arnau, however, was not the man to take such a rebuke lying down. Before leaving Paris he renounced his recantation, formally appealed to Pope Boniface VIII, and wrote a letter to Philip IV protesting his treatment.[10] But when he arrived in Rome in 1301, Arnau was again detained and his book again burned. At this point one would have expected either that Arnau would have had to abjure his errors more sincerely or that he would have faced punishment as a relapsed heretic. Instead, Boniface VIII made him his personal physician in the hope that he could cure him of his painful kidney stones! Arnau took advantage of this situation to submit a second treatise, "On the Mystery of the Bells of the Church" *(De mysterio cymbalorum ecclesiae),* to Boniface in 1301. Although this work reached essentially the same conclusions as its predecessor, Boniface granted it his approval.[11] An effective doctor, apparently, was worth a little questionable theology, and Arnau was for the moment free to circulate his ideas. Thus in November 1301 he sent a copy of this treatise to Philip IV of France along with other secular and ecclesiastical leaders. Philip, or at least his advisors, had supported Arnau during his run-in with the bishop and theologians, and Arnau seems to have assumed he could rely on the king. Yet shortly thereafter, when Philip IV's men charged Boniface VIII with a host of heretical errors, among them was the accusation that the pope had approved of Arnau's rewritten work, even though it contained the same faults as his earlier, twice-condemned text.[12]

Over the next few years, Arnau continued to embroil himself in controversy. He debated Dominicans in Girona in 1302 and defended himself at the synod of Lerida and the bishop's court in Marseille in 1303 and 1304.[13] Since Dominicans in particular had taken the lead in attacking Arnau's ideas, it was unfortunate for him that the new pope, Benedict XI (elected October 1303), was from this order. As always, however, Arnau was confident in his ability to defend himself, and he arrived at the curia in Perugia in early 1304. Benedict had him arrested but died shortly thereafter (7 July 1304), and Arnau's enemies now had the satisfaction of accusing him of conspiring to poison the pope.[14] He was apparently held by the college of cardinals for several months, but—for reasons not entirely clear—in September he was allowed to depart for the Sicilian court of Frederick III (brother of James II of Aragon).[15]

After the election of Clement V (5 June 1305), Arnau traveled to Bordeaux in order to state his case and present the new pope with a large compilation of his Latin writings. Clement neither affirmed nor condemned his ideas, but after 1305 Arnau enjoyed a greater sense of security while continuing to write on both medicine and religion. As Arnau no longer had to defend himself quite so vociferously, much of his energy over the last six years of his life shifted to exhorting the laity to spiritual reform as the time of Antichrist approached. Accordingly, many of his later works are in the Catalan vernacular appropriate to this audience. His greatest influence from 1306 to 1311 was with the court of Frederick III in Sicily, but he continued to travel back and forth between Catalonia, the papal court, and southern Italy before his death in September 1311 in a shipwreck off the coast of Genoa. The *Epistola ad gerentes zonam pelliceam* certainly dates from these last years of Arnau's life, around 1309–10. If (as I will argue below) it was written after Guiard's actual testimony of April 1310, then it can be situated even more precisely.[16]

Arnau's Message in the "Letter"

The "Letter" is divided into four sections, clearly marked and announced at the outset, dealing with the importance of poverty, humility, charity, and chastity for those wanting to cultivate apostolic poverty. The four sections, however, are of unequal importance and length. Arnau says only a few succinct words on poverty: possessions should be restricted to the bare spiritual and physical minimum and should not be worried about until absolute necessity intervenes. He expands only a bit more upon humility, arguing that it is necessary to be humbly obedient, like Christ, even when reviled or falsely accused. Arnau does insert here a striking counsel to be respectful even in response to a misguided accusation of heresy:

> If someone were to say that I was a heretic, I would not say to him "You lie," but "Brother," or "Lord, with all due respect owed to you—I am not." Especially because it is not clear to me that he would say this more as an assertion than as a doubt or a temptation. For although I may know that he says something false, still I do not know whether he is lying. Therefore . . . I should not say to such a person who is falsely accusing me that he is lying, but that, with all due respect, what he says is not true.[17]

Arnau had long personal experience on which to base this counsel!

By far the longest section is that on charity (lines 50–188, out of 195, in the modern edition). It is here that Arnau arrives at his practical point—wearing the *zona pellicea* in imitation of John the Baptist may arise from a pious impulse, but once it has been forbidden by church authority, it cannot be maintained by anyone in a true state of charity. For those seeking evangelical perfection, the only true model must be Christ and the apostles. Since these men did not adopt the *zona pellicea,* neither should "cultivators of evangelical truth." It is fine to imitate John, but not to confuse him with Christ, and it is essential to remember that John wore the belt only in the desert. Wearing it in public could give offense, especially if a bishop or church official has prohibited it. It would be failing in charity and humility to persist and thus would give rise to the suspicion that the wearers might be "schismatics or heretics." He concedes that "it is possible that the church authorities who prohibit the wearing of the leather belt might do this not out of malice but from the voice of conscience which is caused by ignorance or weakness of complexion, because they fear by reason of the Decretals to incur a sentence of excommunication, because it seems that such a sign of specific religious usage would be the beginning of a new state *[status]* in the Catholic Church, which is allowed to no one without the consent of the Apostolic See."[18] Here Arnau subtly tries to insinuate himself with his reader, suggesting that those prohibiting the belt may be misguided or fearful, and hinting that his sympathies may lie with those clinging to the belt.

Ultimately, however, Arnau cannot countenance disobedience to the church, for those pursuing evangelical perfection must be obedient. Anyone who refuses is either "melancholic" or too reliant on blunt arguments such as "No church authority is able to forbid what Christ concedes." Arnau explains how this statement, while certainly true, must be understood correctly, giving several examples of how evangelical men must imitate John in what he stands for, not in every aspect of his literal action and appearance. The church cannot forbid the faithful to imitate John's spiritual example, but it certainly can legislate against physical elements such as specific items of dress. And if it does so for legitimate reasons, then evangelical men must submit out of humility and obedience. Finally, Arnau concludes with only a few brief words on chastity.

The "Letter's" Composition

These contents leave little doubt that Arnau was really and truly writing in response to Guiard of Cressonessart and his followers. The *zona pellicea* becomes the primary subject of exhortation for Arnau, taking up most of the longest section (on charity) of the work; the plea to abandon the belt is really the underlying purpose of this epistle. It is hard to see how it could have been inspired by anyone other than the Angel of Philadelphia and his supposed associates.

So how did Arnau become aware of "those wearing the leather belt"? One possibility is that Guiard really did have a coherent group of followers and that after his arrest they sought guidance on how to proceed. Should they battle on or conform to the church's demands? Arnau was a known advisor to southern beguins and a famous advocate of apostolic poverty, so he might have been a logical source of advice. Perhaps this group made contact with him either by letter or through representatives who traveled south. In that case, Arnau's tract would truly be a letter responding directly to a specific group. There are problems, however, with this hypothesis. For one thing, it is not at all clear that Guiard really did possess the flock of loyal adherents he seems to suggest in his testimony. He may well have associated with a group of like-minded beghards, but no other evidence for a real circle of followers has come to light (and William of Paris would probably have tried to make arrests among any such group had he been convinced of their existence). For another, Arnau's treatise reads more like an "open letter" than a personal missive. There is no greeting to specific intended recipients, and no reference to having been contacted or to having had his advice solicited. The letter feels more as though it was written, uninvited, for the benefit of a loosely imagined group on a wayward path. Alternatively, perhaps travelers from the North brought Arnau word of this group after Guiard's arrest but before his testimony, and he took it upon himself to offer these northerners an open letter. But this scenario requires us to imagine either that a group of Guiard's followers was well known enough to generate these reports and yet able to avoid inquisitorial arrest and trial or that Guiard had somehow made his claims about followers wearing the belt known even as he was refusing to testify.[19] Neither option is easy to envision.

I am therefore inclined to believe that it was Guiard's testimony itself that alerted to Arnau the existence of this northern group wearing the *zona pellicea*. In this case, he would have written his open letter after April 1310.[20] Could Arnau in fact have received some report of Guiard's April testimony? Conduits for this kind of information from Paris certainly existed. Arnau maintained a wide correspondence with numerous contacts that kept him abreast of political and religious developments in France, Spain, and Italy (his longtime associate Ramon Lull, for instance, was in Paris from 1309 to 1311). Most immediately, Philip IV had recently informed Arnau of stirring events in his kingdom, apparently because he saw value in consulting this physician who seemed so certain of his ability to predict God's future plan. The king had personally written to Arnau concerning the Templar affair to express his own shock and ask for Arnau's reaction to these developments.[21] Philip's letter does not survive, but Arnau reported the correspondence and the gist of his response in a letter to James II. According to this account, Arnau had pointed out how the Christian world was falling into vanity and vice and had urged Philip and other kings to reverse this trend with reforms and their own moral example. But at the same time, Arnau was hardly astonished at the fall of the Templars, for he firmly expected this kind of apostasy as the advent of Antichrist loomed. Indeed, worse was to come, for "if there was great thunder, which you heard in the striking of the Templars, an incomparably greater one will be heard in the near future!"[22] The date of Philip's letter is not known, but Arnau's description of his response is contained in a letter written in Marseille and dated 19 February, probably in the year 1310.[23] Thus Arnau had been in communication with the court of Philip IV shortly before William of Paris moved against Guiard. Since Philip had shown an interest in keeping Arnau up to date on startling developments at Paris, and particularly since Arnau was known to be warning of worsening developments as the end of time drew near, someone at court might have solicited his thoughts on the group supposed to be following the self-proclaimed Angel of Philadelphia.

Arnau's movements offer possible corroboration for the scenario by which he could have heard news from Paris and responded with the "Letter to Those Wearing the Leather Belt" in the summer of 1310. Early in that year Arnau was in Almeria by the side of James II.[24] James dispatched him to Sicily on 25 January, and (as we have just seen) he was found in Marseille on 17 February. He was in Avignon around 8 June and was still in Marseille on 17 June before departing for the Sicilian court of Frederick III.[25] It would not have been difficult to receive news from Paris in Provence in early summer 1310, since William of Nogaret and William of Plaisians were hovering about the papal court at Avignon waiting for the posthumous trial of Boniface VIII to reconvene.[26] Their presence would have ensured a steady flow of information between Paris and the South. Direct contact between Arnau and Nogaret at this point would not be impossible. They had certainly been acquainted since at least the 1300 episode when Nogaret helped liberate Arnau from his night in the bishop's jail,[27] and they may even have met much earlier when both were professors in Montpellier around 1290. Furthermore, Nogaret's keen interest in Marguerite and Guiard's trials is shown by the fact that the trial documents ended up in his hands.[28] Even if there is no specific evidence for contact between these men at this moment, certainly Arnau was perfectly placed to inform himself about the associates of the Angel of Philadelphia in June 1310, when the trial was still breaking news that would have been carried south to Nogaret and Plaisians and circulated from there. It was probably around this time that Arnau composed his message to those wearing the leather belt and sent (or carried) a copy to the papal curia at Avignon, where it was then copied into the back of the volume containing his "collected works."[29]

If Arnau did indeed hear about Guiard and his followers in this manner, how specific was his information? Did he hear only general rumors, or did he somehow manage to see a copy of Guiard's testimony or at least receive an accurate oral summary of its contents? It seems that Arnau must have had more than just a vague idea of what Guiard's claims had been because of the way his letter focuses on the importance of the leather belt. The most specific evidence, however, that Arnau had some access to Guiard's testimony is his attempt to answer the claim that Jesus "gave the freedom" (*libertatem dedit*) to imitate John, which seems to respond explicitly to Guiard's reference to the "reminder of the Savior giving and authorizing freedom" (*monitione salvatoris libertatem dantis et auctorizantis*). Arnau phrases many of his counsels in this letter as answers to hypothetical defenses, such as "if someone should wear that said belt after the aforementioned prohibition . . ." In this case, however, he uses the indicative mood, stating, "*When* they say that Christ gives the freedom of imitating John the Baptist to any of the faithful . . ."[30] There is a clear sense that Arnau has actually seen or heard this statement, rather than imagined it as a response to his counsels. This in turn suggests that Arnau had actual knowledge of Guiard's testimony (though this need not imply that he literally read a word-for-word copy). If so, the treatise can be dated to after 9 April 1310, and very likely to (or shortly after) June 1310, when Arnau would be most likely to have had personal contact with royal agents in the South of France.[31]

Arnau's Motivations

Although Arnau's decision to formulate an epistolary response to an ill-defined, perhaps half-imagined group of angelically led northern French beghards might seem idiosyncratic, it actually fits well with the main objectives of his later years. The manuscript evidence demonstrates that a copy was sent to the papal court at this point; very likely the letter was intended in the first instance for the papal and perhaps French courts, from where it could be distributed as it seemed best— or, at the very least, where pope and king could appreciate Arnau's attempt to reason this renegade group into obedience.[32]

In the last years of his life, Arnau was working for a reform of Christian society and for a new crusade, to be led by Frederick III of Sicily and James II of Aragon (perhaps with the aid of a new, more pure, military order rising from the ashes of the Templars),[33] which would conquer Jerusalem, begin the conversion of the Muslim world, bring all erring Catholics back into the fold, and convert pagans and schismatic Christians.[34] Arnau's relationship with James grew strained between October 1309 and fall 1310,[35] so by the end of this year it was primarily Frederick whom he saw as the king divinely appointed to join with an angelic pope to reform the world in anticipation of the final battles with Antichrist.[36] Indeed, the negotiations that had him in Provence in 1309 and 1310 were with Robert of Anjou, king of Naples, concerning the possibility of transferring Robert's (decidedly empty) title of "king of Jerusalem" to Frederick. Arnau had earlier written the *Allocutio Christiani* for Frederick, and now in 1310 he composed the *Informació espiritual al Rei Frederic de Sicilia*, urging Frederick to reform his household and his kingdom in order to more effectively convert Muslims and Jews and prepare for his divine mission.[37] Thus Arnau was seeking concrete, practical reforms of Christian behavior in the name of his larger apocalyptic vision.

These cosmic concerns intersected with the other driving passion of Arnau's late career, guiding the piety of beguin communities of Catalonia and southern France. In this geographic context, the terms *béguin* and *béguine* tended to adhere to laypeople, generally associated with the Franciscan third order, who were inspired by the writings of Peter of John Olivi to think of their radical poverty as an important element in the coming battles with Antichrist.[38] Arnau might have met Peter of John when both were resident in Montpellier around 1289, and in any case he certainly did know his work.[39] Although Arnau was too much the individual thinker to truly be cast as anyone's disciple or as an adherent of any single party, he found his greatest lay audience with these beguin groups, on the basis of their shared stress on evangelical poverty in the face of the looming time of Antichrist.[40]

On a practical level, Arnau used his connections to defend beguins to secular and ecclesiastical authorities,[41] most concretely by convincing Frederick III to offer some of them a haven. But he also wrote at least two vernacular treatises for the beguins of Narbonne and Barcelona after 1305: The *Informatio beguinorum seu lectio Narbone (Llicó de Narbona)* and the *Alia informatio beguinorum*.[42] These works called for the embrace of poverty in the face of Antichrist's imminent arrival. The faithful could fully expect church corruption to characterize the time of Antichrist's approach, but in the meantime *béguins* and *béguines* should remain humble in simplicity and charity as they endured these events.[43] Ever a man of feverish action, Arnau even set up what might be termed a distribution center for his works in Barcelona, where scribes copied out books for beguins and their communities.[44]

In addition, Arnau continued to develop his understanding of the Apocalypse. By 1306 he had published his own very specific ideas on the Church of Philadelphia in the form of a commentary on the Book of Revelation.[45] Working in an overtly Joachite and Olivian vein, Arnau here understood the Church of Philadelphia to represent the sixth age of the church, characterized by the rise of the Mendicant orders with their embrace of apostolic poverty. He interpreted Philadelphia as meaning "saving the adhesion to the Lord" *(haerentem Domino salvans)* much as Guiard had, because "this status of evangelical perfection (in the way of a synecdoche) saves the adherents to the Lord."[46] But along with the rise of religious poverty, the sixth age—the present—could expect three principal events: the subversion of evangelical religion or extermination of Catholic sanctity; a period of reform associated with the first of five angelic popes; and the destruction of evangelical truth by Antichrist.[47]

In such circumstances, the few true "lovers of evangelical truth" would indeed need saving. Arnau, however glossed "I saw another Angel ascending from the rising of the sun, having the sign of the living God" (Apoc. 7:2) as referring equally to the two Mendicant orders, with Francis and Dominic representing the evangelical force whose "sanctity of life and actions" would counter the four kings who would team with Antichrist in the sixth age. This "joining" of the heralds of evangelical truth would be fulfilled near the end of the sixth age, when an angelic pope would "initiate the final reform of evangelical truth . . . and all will bear the aforementioned sign of the living God."[48] Although Arnau acknowledged that Francis's stigmata could in some sense be said to represent this sign of the living God, he departed from Bonaventure, Olivi, and their Franciscan tradition by not specifically limiting the identification of this angel to Francis but rather leaving it open to all true followers of Francis and Dominic, working together with a sequence of angelic popes.[49] If there was one figure above all to whom Arnau looked, it was the first of these five predicted angelic popes.[50] Quite possibly he hoped Clement V would play this role as the "vicar of Christ" who would be "holy in life and true in doctrine" and would have the key of David and open the door by his example of evangelical perfection.[51] He and his four successors would pave the way for the final battle where Antichrist would be defeated and the third *status* would begin. This interpretation, obviously, left little room for an angel in Paris. Arnau was not expecting a new Francis-like figure, certainly not one who might seem to challenge papal authority. Guiard, in short, did not fit into Arnau's confidently predicted scenario.

The main point of Arnau's "Letter," however, was not to counter Guiard's claims directly. The trial in Paris had effectively already accomplished this task, and Arnau may have been aware that Guiard was now silenced by imprisonment. In any case, the "Letter" does not address either Guiard's own fervently held ideas or the perspective of the canonists who condemned them. Rather, it was those adherents who might still be at large in northern France that were on Arnau's mind.[52] Guiard himself had suggested that there were indeed others "of his society," wearing a tunic and the leather belt. Might these wearers of the zona pellicea be waiting for Guiard's release, or perhaps appointing a successor? Arnau's goal was to explain to them how to channel their evangelical impulses in the proper direction. Elements of the hierarchy might be corrupt—that was to be expected as Antichrist approached. Perhaps indeed it was overly carnal churchmen who were unfairly labeling the "wearers of the leather belt" as heretics—but all the more reason for the latter to display evangelical humility. In the big picture, it was most important for all lovers of evangelical truth to work to reform society without needlessly attacking the church hierarchy.

This larger scenario explains how a man who had fended off attacks from theologians, bishops, and friars for a decade could insist—with all sincerity—on humble submission to the authority of the church. Arnau's counsel here is part of his "consistent, and generally unrecognized, championing of the Church's hierarchy as the sole possessor of authority to judge religious debates."[53] Indeed, this imperative may have reached its culmination right at this moment, when Clement V's bull Dudum ad apostolatus (14 April 1310) had just ordered a new investigation into persecution of Franciscan "spirituals" in their convents—a move that Arnau himself may have helped to inspire.[54] If in the summer of 1310 it was beginning to look as though church authority was going to stand behind Spiritual Franciscans, beguins, and other "cultivators" of evangelical poverty, then perhaps Clement V might yet prove to be the longed-for angelic pope. From this perspective, any northern beguini who thought their apostolic ideals necessitated opposing the pope would simply have misunderstood their place in the rapidly unfolding events of the sixth age. Arnau was eager to set them straight.

The Significance of Arnau's Interest

Comparing Guiard and Arnau's competing interpretations of the meaning of "Philadelphia" and the sixth age further highlights the extent to which Guiard was part of a larger intellectual and theological movement. Rather than a strange and lone voice, he was one figure in a passionately fought-out debate about exactly how to apply the words of Revelation to a world that seemed to be rushing toward the Apocalypse. Just as importantly, Arnau's interest shows that news of "those wearing the leather belt" was circulating far beyond Paris. If Arnau saw or received reports of Guiard's testimony while passing through Marseille and Avignon in summer 1310, then accounts of Guiard's fate were sufficiently important to move rapidly between Paris and Provence. Indeed, since Arnau—never exactly taciturn—considered "those wearing the leather belt" to be worthy of further attention, then some of his powerful patrons in Sicily and Catalonia probably received the news as well. Certainly later copies of the "Letter" circulated between Catalonia and Italy, while another was kept at the papal curia.[55] Just as news of Guiard's trial was important enough to be recorded by the "Continuer of William of Nangis," echoes of his ideas reverberated by means of Arnau's treatise and contributed to developing perceptions of apocalyptic agitation in the first quarter of the fourteenth century.

Indeed, Arnau's perspective on events in Paris in spring 1310 suggests the extent to which Guiard, perhaps even more than Marguerite Porete, intrigued or frightened some contemporaries. If Arnau heard anything about Marguerite's fate, he did not feel the need to comment. A *beguina* writing about a solitary path to spiritual annihilation might or might not have interested him;[56] a *beguinus* and his followers attempting to place themselves in a central apocalyptic role, however, needed to be explained in the context of urgent necessities brought on by the imminent arrival of Antichrist. For Arnau, the trial of Marguerite might have been only an adjunct to the more important testimony of Guiard of Cressonessart. In this perspective, Arnau might well have been in agreement with the circle around Philip IV. Nogaret, Plaisians, and their associates time and again attacked the crown's adversaries, using virulent language that portrayed them as not only heretical, but as demonically inspired, immoral, and anti-Christian threats to the French kingdom.[57] Particularly to the extent that connections to Antichrist were raised, these attacks carried an eschatological component. It has recently been suggested, for example, that the move to destroy the Templars carried overtones of apocalyptic prophecy because Jerusalem and the Temple were necessarily central to anticipated scenarios in the coming battles against Antichrist.[58] The royal list of accusations portrayed the Templars as attackers of the body of Christ and (implicitly) of the mystical body of the church and the chosen people of France. This rhetoric capped the larger move to present the Most Christian King as the defender of his people against Antichristian enemies—whether a "false" pope such as Boniface VIII, a disloyal ecclesiastic such as Bernard Saisset, or the Jews of France.[59]

Considering the three "heretics" involved in the sentencing and executions of 31 May and 1 June 1310, Marguerite Porete fits least well into the mold in which Philip's court liked to cast its enemies. The extracts from her book suggested she might be a dangerously immoral antinomian, and the trial records hinted at a wider ring of associates. But to a certain degree her "crimes" floated outside the usual target range of Philip IV's heresy hunters. She was, in the final analysis, merely (if immovably) obstinate in her refusal to bow to ecclesiastical demands. The "relapsed" Jew burned by her side fit somewhat better into the role of a threatening heretic, since he was accused of attacking the mother of Christ, and, through her image, the larger Christian community. Moreover, his trial fed into a wider pattern of fear about a continuing Jewish menace after the expulsions of 1306—those Jews who converted and stayed behind might represent a threat from within, perhaps biding their time until Antichrist's arrival. But it was in fact Guiard who overtly announced a threatening rival eschatology—even going so far as to insist that his central revelation had been granted him in the Sainte-Chapelle, the very seat of Capetian sanctity. Moreover, he alone had finally repented, thus symbolizing the crown's ability to foster contrition. From this perspective, the more widely Guiard's failed challenge was known, the better.[60]

Finally, if Arnau of Vilanova showed no apparent interest in Marguerite Porete, his battles with the faculty of theology at Paris should nevertheless be set alongside Marguerite's own confrontation with this same group. Arnau and Marguerite were in fact the first two lay theologians to have their ideas seriously examined—and censored—by the faculty of theology at the University of Paris. Both claimed a valid authority to proclaim God's truth and asserted that their knowledge could be more useful (for personal salvation or knowledge of the coming millennium) than that produced by academically trained theologians; both nevertheless actively sought out the approval of Parisian theologians, only to have the university faculty turn against them. Both had a book burned in Paris as a result. Although Arnau later increasingly claimed a visionary justification for his writings, at heart both authors spoke out of confidence in their philosophical or scientific certainty.[61] Moreover, both Arnau and Marguerite fought back against condemnation with additional writings and a tenacious belief in their own rectitude. Arnau and Marguerite were, in short, among the earliest intellectuals from outside university circles to attempt to break into the closed world of scholastic theology at Paris.[62] The great difference, of course, was that Arnau's status as famous physician and associate of kings ultimately allowed him to dodge the accusations of heresy that so frequently flew his way. Marguerite was not so fortunate.

The Council of Vienne and Beyond

By a bull of 12 August 1308 *(Regnans in excelsis),* Clement V had called for a universal church council to convene on 1 November 1310 in order to deal with the Templar question, the general reform of the church, and the organization of a new crusade.[1] But with the Templar inquiries dragging on and the posthumous trial of Boniface VIII still pending, on 4 April 1310—just as the trials of Marguerite and Guiard were in full swing—Clement postponed the opening of the council until October 1311. In the meantime (on 27 April 1311) the pope effectively brought the process against Boniface VIII to a close by suppressing specific acts that had been prejudicial to Philip IV, recognizing that Philip had acted through righteous zeal in confronting Boniface, and absolving William of Nogaret for his role in the attack at Anagni.[2]

When the Council of Vienne opened on 16 October 1311, it was lightly attended compared to the Fourth Lateran Council (1215) and the two Councils of Lyon (1245 and 1274). Still, close to 170 cardinals, archbishops, bishops, abbots, and assorted church dignitaries gathered at Vienne.[3] This modest town just south of Lyon lay on the imperial side of the Rhône, but French influence at the council was nevertheless dominant. At least half the abbots and a third of the bishops were from France, including men such as Philip of Marigny and John of Château-villain who had played a role in determining Marguerite Porete's fate.[4] Indeed, among the twenty-one theologians who had the year before condemned extracts from Marguerite's book, at least six—Jacques of

Thérines, Gerard of Bologna, John of Pouilly, Henry of Friemar, Berenger of Landora, and Jacob of Ascoli—now made the trip to Vienne. Other close royal advisors such as Enguerran of Marigny, William of Nogaret, and William of Plaisians appeared by February 1312 to pressure Clement V on the Templar issue, and Philip IV arrived in person on 20 March.[5] There is no direct evidence as to whether William of Paris—still the royal confessor—was also in Vienne for the conclusion of the council, but it is certainly possible. In short, a substantial number of men with direct knowledge of the trials of Marguerite Porete and Guiard of Cressonessart took part in the Council of Vienne.

The council, however, did not speak with one voice in either its deliberations or its eventual legislation. For one thing, it did its work through commissions, such as those assigned to deal with the large issues of the Templars, the crusade, and general reform, as well as with more specific questions such as the Franciscan conflict over poverty. Moreover, the canons of the council were not published immediately in May 1312. Rather, Clement and his advisors subjected them to further revision before they were finally read in consistory on 21 March 1314. Even then, however, they had not yet been "published" by being sent out to universities at the time of Clement's death a month later on 20 April. It was only after John XXII's election (on 7 August 1316) that a corrected version of the "Clementine" decrees was issued in 1317. Thus some canons must reflect Clement's personal revisions, and others may have been influenced by the corrections of John XXII (who had himself been present at Vienne as bishop of Avignon).[6]

These complicating factors notwithstanding, this final section will assess the links between events in Paris in 1310 and actions taken in Vienne in 1311–12 and will then conclude with a brief reflection on the resulting repressions (and their limits) that characterized the next several decades.

Vienne and the End of the Templars

The most pressing matter before the pope and council was resolving the Templar question. Most of the participants of the council favored allowing the Templars to offer a defense (as indeed Clement had previously promised would be the case). Even the French prelates leaned this way, with the unsurprising exception of a few who had been intimately involved in the earlier investigations, such as Philip of Marigny and Gilles Aycelin.[7] Philip IV, however, convoked a meeting of the Estates in Lyon for February 1312 to whip up public outcry just as his ambassadors were negotiating with Clement and the French cardinals (including Nicholas of Fréauville) in secret. Once Philip arrived in person, opposition quickly crumbled. The decision to suppress the order was reached behind closed doors and announced on 3 April, in the bull *Vox in excelso* (actually dated 22 March).[8] Clement did not condemn the order or even rule on the truth or falsity of the crimes ascribed to it. Instead, the pope simply suppressed the order of the Temple, citing its infamy, suspicious actions, and the scandals that had resulted. The Templars' goods were transferred to the Hospitallers (less a substantial sum to Philip IV for his time and expenses), and to a new crusading order created in Aragon.

The common brothers were pensioned off or allowed to join other orders if they had been found innocent or penitent. Most had no desire to risk their lives further for a lost cause. Matthew of Cressonessart, for example, who had helped lead the defense of the order in spring 1310 before capitulating after the summary executions of May, had finally given a full deposition on 12 February 1311 and confessed that at his reception into the order he had renounced Christ "with his mouth but not in his heart" (though he denied knowledge of other charges).[9] He was primarily insistent on not wishing to say anything that would endanger his earlier reconciliation with the church. In all likelihood, then, he was allowed to retire quietly to some monastery of another order. For men like Matthew (if not for modern conspiracy theorists), the history of the order of the Temple ended with the Council of Vienne.

The leadership of the order, however, had always been reserved for papal judgment. In December 1313 a papal commission of three cardinals, including Nicholas of Fréauville, was appointed to deal with them. The cardinals met in Paris, along with Archbishop Philip of Marigny and various experts on canon law, in March 1314. It is not known exactly which masters took part in these deliberations, but it seems likely that some of the men who had offered consultation during the trials of Marguerite and Guiard would have been involved.[10] The four senior leaders of the order apparently agreed to confess and repent and were to be sentenced to perpetual imprisonment on 18 March in a public gathering in front of the cathedral of Notre Dame. But after one of the cardinals preached a "sermon" (presumably including the terms of the sentence), the grand master Jacques of Molay and the preceptor of Normandy Geoffrey of Charney dramatically reversed themselves and proclaimed their innocence. The cardinals, doubtless taken aback by this deviation from what should have been a tightly scripted event, handed the two Templars over to the provost of Paris, just as had been done with Marguerite Porete. This time royal justice was even more swift. The grand master and preceptor were burned at the stake that same evening, on a small island in the Seine just off the east end of the Île-de-la-Cité (known as the Île-aux-Juifs, more or less where the Pont Neuf stands today). As with Marguerite Porete, the "Continuer of William of Nangis" reported that their resolve "brought from all those who saw them much admiration and surprise for the constancy of their death and final denial."[11]

Vienne and the Attack on Beguines and Beghards

The burnings of 18 March 1314 are linked to those of 1 June 1310 by the common involvement of men such as Philip of Marigny and by the wider royal claim to act as God's sentinel against the threat of heresy. But the Council of Vienne's two canons concerning beguines bear an even more direct relationship to Marguerite Porete's recent trial.

The first, *Cum de quibusdam mulieribus,* launched a broad attack.[12] Certain women "known in common speech as beguines" were here described as wearing a special habit "called that of the beguines," but as not promising obedience or renouncing possessions or professing a rule. Clement and the council had heard that some, "as though led by insanity of the mind," were said to dispute and preach on the Trinity and to express contrary opinions on articles of the faith and the sacraments, leading many simple people into error, under the "veil of sanctity." Therefore the new canon ordered "that their status be prohibited and completely abolished from the Church of God." Women were forbidden from following this way of life, and male religious were ordered not to give them "counsel, aid, or favor." But the decree ended with a seemingly contradictory saving clause, averring that "of course, by the aforesaid decree we in no way intend to prohibit certain faithful women, who want to do penance and serve the Lord of Hosts in a spirit of humility, whether they promise chastity or even if they do not, from living honestly in their dwelling places *(hospitiis)*. This is conceded to them, as long as the Lord will inspire them."[13]

This canon obviously makes no direct mention of Marguerite Porete and does not say anything that absolutely must have resulted from her case. Yet given the number of participants in the council who had just come from Paris with some level of involvement in her trial, it is reasonable to assume that one of the ways that the pope had "frequently heard sinister rumor" of beguines and had come to "hold them suspect" was through reports of the recent execution in Paris.[14] William of Paris himself had not used the *beguina* label in sentencing Marguerite, but chroniclers in Paris certainly were applying it, and churchmen involved in the case were aware of the way it had been employed in preparing the groundwork for her eventual execution. In the terse summaries of a theologian such as John Baconthorpe or a chronicle such as the *Grandes chroniques de France,* Marguerite was simply a beguine who had been condemned and executed as a result of her challenge to the church and its doctrines. She must, at the very least, have served as a prime example of the sort of "insanity" *Cum de quibusdam* was intended to suppress.

The second canon, *Ad nostrum,* announced the pope's deep desire that heretical depravity be extirpated from Christian lands.[15] For this reason he was greatly displeased to hear about the "abominable sect of malignant men called *beguardi* and unfaithful women called *beguinae*" that had damnably sprung up "in the kingdom of Germany" and was asserting sacrilegious doctrines and perverse errors. Eight of these are given in the canon:

1. That a person can attain such a degree of perfection in this life that he will be sinless.
2. That a man in such a state of perfection need not fast or pray and "can freely grant to the body whatever it pleases."
3. That those in such a degree of perfection are not bound to precepts of the church.

4. That man can be as blessed in this life as in the next.
5. That such men do not need the light of glory to see God.
6. That only imperfect men exercise the virtues, while the perfect do not need them.
7. That a woman's kiss is a sin but that the carnal act, since nature inclines to it, is not.
8. That it would be imperfection to rise at the elevation of the Body of Christ, since this would be a descent from the heights of contemplation.

The pope and council damned all these errors and those who held, approved, or defended them. Inquisitors of heretical depravity in areas where *beguardi* and *beguinae* lived were urged to investigate their lives and behaviors. Those found culpable, unless they abjured the aforesaid errors, were to be punished.

The clearest specific source that has been identified for some of these "errors" is the list of articles extracted from Marguerite Porete's book. Article 6 above (*perfecta anima licentiat a se virtutes*) is evidently related to the first article that was presented to the Paris theologians from Marguerite's book (*anima adnichilata dat licentiam virtutibus*). Article 8 echoes the fifteenth extract, which asserted that the annihilated soul did not worry about the consolations of God because this would impede the soul's focus on God. The article in Marguerite's dossier related by the "Continuer of William of Nangis," that the soul should give to nature all that it demands without remorse, may lie behind articles 2 and (less directly) 7 above.[16] This is not to say that Marguerite's condemned extracts were in fact the only (perhaps not even the prime) source for the articles in *Ad nostrum*. The decree refers to beguines of "Germany," and very likely other reports about beguines expressing daring theological propositions had reached the council. Authors such as Hadewijch and Mechthild of Magdeburg had earlier expressed related ideas, and claims about beguines disputing and translating without respect for orthodoxy went back at least as far as Gilbert of Tournai's shrill denunciation of 1274. Still, Marguerite's was the most recent and high-profile example of theological audacity by a woman labeled a *beguina* (and the reference to Germany would actually not be incompatible with her labeling as "from Hainaut"—an imperial territory).[17]

Thus it is very likely that Marguerite's process, and specifically the portion of it that involved the Parisian theologians (six of whom were now present at Vienne), did affect the creation of this canon.[18] More broadly, the inclusion of both sexes in this condemnation reminds us that the twin processes in Paris in 1310 had been against a *beguina* and a *beguinus*. Though the "depravities" of Marguerite and Guiard might have belonged to two different strands of heresy, the shared name suggested their commonality in a "sect" of beguines and beghards.

Through the sometimes contradictory constellation of accusations associated with *Cum de quibusdam* and *Ad nostrum,* canon law now defined *beguinae* as possessing no legitimate status in Christian society, on the basis of their dangerous disputing and preaching, and further asserted that their sect could be assumed to adhere to a coherent antinomian heresy. Thus the council and Pope Clement asserted the existence of a unified danger where before only disparate individuals and ideas had existed. In the minds of fearful churchmen, the newly imagined "beguine/beghard antinomian heretics" quickly took shape as the so-called "Heresy of the Free Spirit," fostering the idea that somewhere on the margins of European society lurked a sect whose secret doctrines justified gross immorality with the claim to be perfect and therefore free of all moral constraint.

If, in Robert E. Lerner's felicitous formulation, "*Ad nostrum* is the birth certificate of the Free Spirit . . . but without it being fully clear whether there was any child," then Marguerite Porete and her book were the poster children for the heresy, without it being fully clear whether anyone actually remembered seeing them pictured together before the poster had been torn down. Marguerite had been labeled a *beguina* in documents that accused her of patent disobedience, her book had then been convicted of espousing heretical doctrines involving taking leave of the virtues, and the influential *Grandes chroniques* asserted that she had "said contrary and prejudicial things about the sacrament of the altar." Put together, her trial dossier showed that beguines not only flouted church authority and attacked church teachings but also adhered to a dangerous set of amoral doctrines. Marguerite Porete was a crucial (and yet textually invisible) figure who linked the misbehaving beguines of *Cum de quibusdam* to the antinomians of *Ad nostrum.*

Vienne, Peter of John Olivi, and the Franciscan Controversy

Finally, there is the council's attempt to heal division within the Franciscan order, where the "Spiritual" wing, with its radical view of absolute poverty, had over recent decades increasingly come into conflict with the "Community" or "Conventuals." The Spirituals inclined toward Joachite prophecy, particularly insofar as Peter of John Olivi had tied absolute poverty to the coming battles with Antichrist and his henchmen in the "carnal" church. This dispute set in motion events that over the next two decades would lead to persecution of men and women whose ideas emerged from the same tradition as those of Guiard of Cressonessart.

After soliciting advance position papers from both sides and empowering a commission to work on the issue, at the council's closing session on 6 May 1312 Clement V read out the bull *Exivi de paradiso*. This decree was an attempt at compromise on explosive issues concerning what a truly "poor use" of goods meant, what the Franciscan vows really entailed, and what the obligation of obedience was for a friar who believed that a superior was asking him to break those vows.[19] Clement's decree tried to recall the whole order to moderate standards of poverty while forbidding further discussion.[20] The same day, the pope also issued *Fidei catholicae fundamento*, which dealt with the question of Peter of John Olivi's orthodoxy, though only in oblique fashion, since it never mentioned him by name.[21] Olivi had been censured in his lifetime but died peacefully in 1298. Since then confiscations and burning of his work had several times been ordered, first by his own order in 1299. Three articles from Olivi's works were now explicitly singled out for consideration (on the divine nature, on the rational soul, and on the timing of the wound Christ received in his side on the cross). *Fidei catholicae fundamento* offered somewhat ambiguous corrections of Olivi on these subjects, but without attaching any specific heretical stigma to his name.

These decisions relate to our larger story because the committees dealing with the question of Franciscan poverty and the ideas of Peter of John Olivi included the Parisian theologians Gerard of Bologna, Berenger of Landora, Jacques of Thérines, and John of Pouilly (Gerard had even been part of a three-man panel charged by Clement V with a preliminary inquiry on the subject of Olivi in July 1311).[22] Although the theologians had never issued an opinion on Guaird, these men must all have had some knowledge of his case: John of Pouilly, for instance, had been present at the Dominican house in March 1310 when Guiard and Marguerite were first discussed, and Berenger of Landora would have had ample opportunity to learn further details from his Dominican brother William of Paris. This is not to suggest that there was a direct link in the minds of these men between the testimony of the Angel of Philadelphia and the specific ideas of Peter of John Olivi under consideration at Vienne. But particularly given new evidence that Guiard was an educated cleric and that a man such as Arnau of Vilanova was fretting over Guiard's followers, his case can be seen as part of the background against which these theologians would have formulated their responses to the developing Spiritual challenges to the "carnal" church.

Repression after the Council of Vienne

The decrees of Vienne and their formal propagation in 1317 initiated a period of sustained persecution. During the 1320s, bishops in the Low Countries, including Marguerite's home diocese of Cambrai, launched thorough inquiries into beguine life.[23] Established court beguinages survived this scrutiny, though under tighter regulation concerning dress and travel. Some smaller houses disappeared, however, and "unregulated" beguines, those living alone or in little groups, were particularly targeted.[24] Inquisitors in German-speaking lands similarly carried out multiple waves of persecution across the fourteenth century and into the fifteenth, looking for immorally heretical beghards and beguines.[25] In Paris, the grand beguinage was investigated by the provost of Paris in 1317 but was put back on a stable footing under king Charles IV (r. 1322–28) after its statutes were revised by a team led by two Dominicans; one was the master of theology Peter de la Palu (the old adversary of John of Pouilly), while the other was Brother Imbert—William of Paris's successor as inquisitor and royal confessor.[26]

Moreover, the most celebrated victim of the new fear of "Free Spirit" thinking was surely the Dominican Meister Eckhart, who had been regent master in Paris in 1302–3 and 1311–12, had known many of the masters of theology involved in Marguerite's case, and had lived, in 1311–12, with William of Paris in the Dominican house where any confiscated copies of Marguerite's book would have been held. Eckhart was forced to defend himself from charges of heresy from 1326 to his death in 1328, first in the court of the bishop of Cologne (Henry of Virneburg), and then (after February 1327) at the papal court in Avignon. In 1329 John XXII's bull *In agro dominico* condemned twenty-six articles taken from Eckhart's writings,[27] some of which bear strong resemblance to those propagated by Marguerite. It has never quite been proven that Eckhart read the *Mirror* directly,[28] but certainly his teachings were related to Marguerite's.[29] The condemnation of this Dominican master's ideas in 1329 thus capped the growing fear of the kind of daringly paradoxical negative theological thought that had been highlighted by the burning of Marguerite's book in 1310.

John XXII's moves to crush Joachite-inspired apocalyptic thinking within and on the margins of the Franciscan order followed a similar chronology. A long list of writings by Arnau of Vilanova was condemned at the Synod of Tarragona in November 1316 by an inquisitor and a commission of theologians (made up of local Franciscan, Dominican, and Cistercian lectors), with the finding that some contained heresies and others errors, rash opinions, or false and dubious assertions about the faith (the *Epistola ad gerentes zonam pelliceam*, however, was not among the named titles).[30] Then, in several bulls, the pope ordered Spirituals to return to obedience and began summoning their leaders to defend themselves at the curia. When sixty-four brothers from southern France arrived in Avignon, they were asked if they would obey the pope's commands and whether they believed the pope had the power to regulate the order. Twenty-six friars who answered negatively were turned over to the Franciscan inquisitor for Provence, Michel Lemoine; four of these men were eventually relaxed to the secular authorities and burned at the stake in Marseille on 7 May 1318.[31] This was one of the most dramatic moments in the entire history of the medieval church, as members of an approved order were executed for seeking to follow their founder's precepts too ardently.

Michel Lemoine's sentence asserted that these heresies stemmed from the poisoned fountain of doctrine that was the thought of Peter of John Olivi.[32] Accordingly, John XXII convened a panel to investigate the orthodoxy of Peter of John's Apocalypse Commentary in 1318. At about the same time, papal agents dug up Olivi's body and removed it in order to end pilgrimages to his tomb.[33] In the meantime, after again consulting with a new panel, John issued a series of bulls stating in very clear language that Christ and the apostles had owned private goods and that to disagree with this was heretical. This shocked virtually all Franciscans (who had based the identity of their order on the imitation of Christ in the belief that he had lived in perfect poverty) and led to the defection of more of the order's leaders. In this atmosphere of renewed controversy, John XXII reopened the question of Olivi's writings in 1324 and formally condemned his Commentary in 1326.[34] For those true believers who continued to see themselves as opposed to the persecuting "carnal" church, this action demonstrated that the pope himself was in league with Antichrist—a sure sign of the imminent Apocalypse.[35] In this test of wills, between 1318 and 1330 at least 102 people were burned in southern France as adherents to "the heresy of the burned beguins."[36]

Guiard of Cressonessart's case was only one early step toward the larger crackdown on Olivi, the Spirituals, and Joachite apocalypticism. By the 1320s he may have been largely forgotten. Yet the way Guiard's claims were confronted and refuted in 1310 had set a precedent. Guiard, after all his fascinating testimony, had been convicted only of challenging papal authority by dividing the church and claiming jurisdiction (through the "key of excellence") over one church himself. In short, the regent masters in canon law at Paris preferred to make Guiard's case uniquely about obedience. This, in essence, was just what John XXII would do with the Spirituals a few years later by reducing the whole affair to the question of papal authority and specifically accusing Franciscan "heretics" of saying there were "two churches."[37] Moreover, Michel Lemoine's sentence of the four executed friars in 1318 stressed their assertion that no one could force them to remove their "short, narrow habits,"[38] echoing the statement of the "Continuer of William of Nangis" that Guiard claimed not even the pope could order him to remove his leather belt.

Thus the Council of Vienne set the stage for the condemnations and executions of the 1320s.[39] The posthumous condemnations of the writings of Olivi and Eckhart in 1326 and 1329 show how fears of heresy stretched upwards to the highest level of academic theology, as men who had been respected (if controversial) masters during their lifetimes had their ideas rejected as dangerous or heretical after their deaths. In turn, the separate condemnations of Marguerite Porete, her book, and Guiard of Cressonessart by canonists and theologians in Paris in 1310 had foreshadowed the direction taken by the decrees of Vienne. When a *beguina* and a *beguinus* were sentenced together in Paris in 1310, it presaged the twin strands of persecution that were unleashed against groups bearing both labels over the next two decades.[40]

Some of the men involved must have preserved memories of the trials well into these decades of repression. Although William of Paris himself was dead by 1314, one of the canonists he had consulted, John of Thélus, lived until about 1346, and the notary Jacques of Vertus did quite well out of royal service until his death around 1335.[41] The two bishops of Paris from 1326 to 1342 would have recalled the sentences of 31 May 1310 as a point of reference, since they were Hugh of Besançon (one of the canonists who had condemned both Guiard and Marguerite) and William of Chanac (one of the witnesses at their sentencing). And one of the theologians who condemned extracts from Marguerite's book, the Augustinian friar Henry of Friemar, also lived until at least 1340. In 1334 he wrote the first history of his order and commented there on his brethren's adoption of the *zona pellicea,* noting its association with both Elijah and John the Baptist.[42] He even linked his order and its characteristic *zona* to Joachim of Fiore's reference to an order of hermits that would help usher in the third *status,* "in the spirit of Elijah."[43] Though he certainly never mentioned Guiard of Cressonessart, perhaps in explaining his own order's legitimate claim to the leather belt he might have thought back to the Angel of Philadelphia, whose competing interpretations had caused such a stir in 1310.

Reflecting the Limits of Repression

Yet at least in their textual aspect John XXII's attempts at censorship were doomed to failure. Medieval people continued to read the works of Arnau, Peter of John, and the Meister. The story of Marguerite

Porete's text, however, is perhaps the most dramatic, for William of Paris's effort to "exterminate" it failed miserably. Readers in France, England, Italy, Germany, and the Low Countries were familiar with the *Mirror of Simple Souls* up into the seventeenth century, if not beyond.

Abundant evidence shows that the *Mirror* continued to be read and copied in northern France and the Francophone Low Countries. An exciting example is a recently discovered manuscript in the Bibliothèque municipale of Valenciennes that contains several chapters of the *Mirror*.[44] This fragment is based on a version from the first half of the fourteenth century (as its discoverer, Geneviève Hasenohr, has shown) and thus brings us closer to the work's fourteenth-century form in some respects. It further shows how teachings from the *Mirror* could be integrated into vernacular compilations of unimpeachably orthodox authors.[45] But since this manuscript was actually made in the last quarter of the fifteenth century, it also demonstrates the *Mirror*'s continuing interest to readers of that era. Farther south, in Dijon, the apothecary Amyot Salmonnet left a French copy at his death in 1482,[46] and the text enjoyed a certain vogue in the Loire valley region at just this time. A work for an aristocratic woman from this area seems to cite it in the first half of the fifteenth century, and a copy was for sale from a bookseller in Tours in the second half.[47] In 1470 a Celestinian monk at Notre-Dame of Ambert (near Orléans) crafted a book for female religious intended to counteract the dangers of the *Mirror*; at least four editions of this corrective work were published over the next seventy years.[48] The only surviving complete Middle French version of the *Mirror* (the Chantilly manuscript) was made at about this time at the nearby abbey of La Madeleine-lès-Orléans.[49] It was almost certainly this copy that was then read by Queen Marguerite of Navarre (sister of François I of France), who referred approvingly to the text and its author in her poem *Les prisons* in 1547.[50] The seventeenth-century copy of the *Mirror* once found in the Bibliothèque municipale of nearby Bourges was presumably made in this region as well (incredibly, this copy was lost in 1961 while being shipped to the Bibliothèque nationale).[51]

The work was well known in Carthusian circles in England, thanks to a fourteenth-century Middle English translation. The English translator, who gives his initials as "M. N.," may have been Michael Northburgh, bishop of London and co-founder of the Charterhouse outside that city.[52] The introduction provided by M. N. reveals a long and close engagement with the text; he had earlier made a first translation, but after receiving complaints about its potential dangers (a fact that he partly blamed on the defective nature of his exemplar), he produced a new version and provided glosses (labeled with his initials) for difficult passages. Much like Godfrey of Fontaines before him, M. N. admitted that the work could be spiritually dangerous if misunderstood, but he believed that the value of the *Mirror* could outweigh its danger.[53]

The origins of the first Latin version of the *Mirror,* which may be as old as (or even older than) the Middle English, are mysterious. It was unusual (though not unheard of) for a vernacular work to be translated into Latin in this era, and no one has yet ventured a plausible hypothesis for how, when, or why this translation was made.[54] Several of the earliest extant manuscripts of this translation are later fourteenth-century and seem to be of Italian provenance, raising the further question of how the work got to Italy and whether that was where the first Latin translation was made.[55] It has sometimes been claimed that the Latin translation stems from William of Paris's own inquiry and thus existed by 1310,[56] but this hypothesis has little to recommend it. Indeed, there is no hint that the Latin translation originally sought to portray this as a dangerous text. For a later Latin translation we do at least have the luxury of a name, since the Middle English was translated into a new Latin version by the English Carthusian Richard Methley in 1491.[57]

The original Latin version then served as the basis for two closely related Italian versions translated in the later fourteenth or early fifteenth century (in one the work passed under the name of the blessed Marguerite of Hungary, a princess who died in 1271).[58] If it is again not clear who made these translations, it is certain that the *Mirror* became the subject of spectacular new controversy on the Italian peninsula. For example, in the 1430s the Franciscan reformer Bernardino of Siena attacked it, a congregation of Benedictine houses in central Italy condemned it anew, and Cecilia Gonzaga was warned against "the little book by I-don't-know-what little woman, which is called the *Mirror of Simple Souls.*" Pope Eugenius IV (r. 1431–47) was even accused of favoring the spread of the text, and the bishop of Florence cautioned against it around 1450. Yet even this scandal failed to stamp out enthusiasm in Italy, since the bishop of Ferrara defended the reading of the book by upright men, a manuscript of the Latin version prepared at Subiaco in 1521 seems to have been intended for printing by a sympathetic editor (but then abandoned out of fear that such a printing would not be approved),[59] and the Franciscan Bartolomeo Cordoni (1471–ca. 1535) drew on the *Mirror* when writing his *Dialogo dell'unione dell'anima con Dio.*[60]

It has never been proven that the *Mirror* was translated into German, but the Latin version did circulate in German lands, and it is not impossible that evidence for such a translation will turn up.[61] The likelihood of a Dutch or Flemish translation is somewhat greater, given the bilingual nature of the Low Countries. Certainly the text was available in Flemish-speaking regions. For instance, the theologian and mystic Jan of Ruysbroeck (d. 1381) apparently was aware of the *Mirror* in some version, a copy known to have been donated by a patrician woman named Elisabeth of Grutere to a beguinage of Ghent around 1500 may perhaps have been in Flemish,[62] and the *Mirror* may have been known to the sixteenth-century female author of "The Evangelical Pearl."[63] Thus the *Mirror of Simple Souls* enjoyed a wide readership in at least four languages for centuries, with manuscripts "bobbing up continually in the seas of late-medieval western Europe like unsinkable corks."[64]

Not only did Marguerite Porete's book survive William of Paris's condemnation, but its rediscovery by modern scholarship has made Marguerite a best-selling author (at least by the standards of academic sales). If William's demand of 1310—never formally rescinded by the Catholic Church—were somehow to be enforced today, and those possessing copies of the book were compelled to turn them in to the Dominicans of Paris, the stacks of the modern Dominican library there would be buried under tens of thousands of well-thumbed copies of the *Mirror of Simple Souls.*

APPENDIX A

Translations of the Trial Documents

This appendix offers English translations of the documents in Paris, Archives nationales de France, carton J428, nos. 15 to 19bis. They are presented in chronological order according to the dates on which the documents were originally issued. All of these Latin documents have been previously edited, most more than once. Paul Verdeyen's edition is the most recent and complete, so my translation takes his work as a starting point. Because Verdeyen's edition is not without problems, however, I have consulted the original documents and noted places where they differ from Verdeyen's readings. The only other recent edition is Robert E. Lerner's presentation of all the documents relevant to Guiard of Cressonessart. In the notes I indicate errors in Verdeyen's edition (though excluding most cases that are simply misspellings, since these do not affect translation), and where there are meaningful discrepancies between Verdeyen's and Lerner's readings of these documents I give the correct manuscript reading. For the documents concerning Marguerite Porete, Verdeyen corrected many of the errors in the earlier transcriptions published by Henry Charles Lea and Charles-Victor Langlois (the latter also partially edited one document concerning Guiard). I do not note those earlier errors, except in several instances where misreadings by Lea and Langlois have caused lasting confusion.

Just before this book went to press, Elizabeth A. R. Brown generously shared with me her own transcription of these documents and critiqued my translations, which are much stronger as a result.

The canon lawyers and theologians who appear in the documents that follow are not identified in the notes because they have been treated elsewhere in this book. The men listed at the beginning of document VII, however, are briefly noted. Words within square brackets are editorial insertions, generally intended to clarify the referent of a pronoun or to more clearly identify a person.

Nos. 15 and 16 are in the hand of Jacques of Vertus. Nos. 17 and 18 are in a second hand, similar to and contemporary with that of nos. 15 and 16. Nos. 19 and 19bis are then in a third similar and contemporary hand.

I

AN J428 no. 16.   Masters of theology and canon law meet in the Dominican house in Paris in March 1310. Five canonists then issue their decision, dated 3 April, that Guiard of Cressonessart is a contumacious heretic.

Three earlier documents must once have existed: (1) a record of the March meeting prepared by Evens Phili; (2) the canonists' sealed decision of 3 April (referred to by Evens Phili); (3) the original document, notarized by Evens Phili, that integrated the decision of 3 April into an account of the March meeting (presumably prepared shortly after 3 April). The text of this third document is preserved within the notarized copy as we now have it, which was prepared 4 October 1310 by Jacques of Vertus and bears his notarial sign.

In the translation below, the later text added by Jacques of Vertus in October is given in small capitals; the description of the March meeting is indented; and the embedded decision of April 3 is further indented and in reduced type.

Editions: Verdeyen, "Procès d'inquisition," 56–58, and Lerner, "Angel of Philadelphia," 361–62.

Parchment. Pencil rulings. 480 x 366 mm. Folded in 8.

On dorse (bottom right): *Instrumentum factum super examinatione Margarete Porete culpabili de heresi* (Instrument prepared concerning the examination of Marguerite Porete, guilty of heresy). Reverse: *1309 16.*

IN THE NAME OF CHRIST AMEN. THIS IS THE COPY OR TRANSCRIPT OF A CERTAIN PUBLIC INSTRUMENT, THE CONTENTS OF WHICH FOLLOW WORD FOR WORD IN THIS FORM:

In the name of the Lord, amen. Whereas a certain *beguinus* named Guiard of Cressonessart, of the Diocese of Beauvais, came forth publicly and notoriously in defense and aid of Marguerite, called "Porete," of Hainaut—who was suspected for various and probable causes of the stain of heretical depravity, and because of this was arrested[1] by the religious man Brother William of Paris of the order of Preachers, appointed by apostolic authority as inquisitor of this same depravity in the Kingdom of France—for this and other reasons [Guiard] was suspected of the crime of heresy. The said inquisitor, not wanting to proceed impetuously or without deliberation against the said Guiard for this said crime, but rather in good time with the counsel of men expert in law, had masters in the faculties of theology and canon law brought together personally in his presence to offer him counsel on this matter with respect to [Guiard].

In the year of our Lord 1309, in the eighth indiction, in the month of March, in the fifth year of the pontificate of our most holy father and lord by divine providence Pope Clement V [i.e., March 1310], with me present as notary and the witnesses noted below called and especially asked for this purpose, these same masters of the said faculties gathered in the presence of the aforementioned inquisitor: namely, the venerable and distinguished men Masters Simon of Guiberville the dean, Thomas [of Bailly] the penitentiary, and John of Ghent, canons of the Church of Paris; Peter of Saint-Denis of the order of Saint Benedict; Gerard of Saint-Victor; Henry [of Friemar] of Germany; John of Pouilly; [Lawrence] the prior of Val-des-Écoliers; John of Mont-Saint-Éloi, canon regular of the order of Saint Augustine; Brother Berenger [of Landora] of the order of Preachers; Brother Jacob of Ascoli of the order of Minors, [all] masters of theology; and Masters W[illiam] called "Brother," archdeacon of Lothian in the Church of St. Andrew in Scotland, professor of both laws; John of Thélus; Hugh of Besançon, canon of Paris; Henry of Béthune; Peter of Vaux, [all] masters of canon law. The lord inquisitor asked the said masters to give him sound counsel on the said matter. These same masters of theology and canon law, having deliberated among themselves, by way of advising this same inquisitor more fully, decided to stand by the consultation or counsel of the masters of canon law. And [the masters of canon law] gave such advice as is contained in this same letter sealed with their seals, as they said, which is this:

> To all who will see the present letter, William called "Brother" archdeacon of Lothian in the Church of St. Andrew in Scotland, Hugh of Besançon canon of Paris, John of Thélus canon of Saint-Quentin in the Vermandois, Henry of Béthune, Peter of Vaux curate of the Church of Saint-Germain-l'Auxerrois in Paris, regents in canon law at Paris, send greetings[2] in the author of salvation.
>
> Whereas a certain *beguinus* named Guiard of Cressonessart, of the Diocese of Beauvais, came forth publicly, demonstrably, and notoriously in defense and aid of Marguerite, called "Porete," of Hainaut—who was suspected for various probable causes of the stain of heretical depravity, and because of this was arrested by the religious man Brother William of Paris of the order of Preachers, appointed by apostolic authority as inquisitor of this same depravity in the Kingdom of France—for this and other reasons Guiard was suspected of the crime of heresy. The said inquisitor, as he made known to us, proceeded in the following manner:
>
> After legitimate, canonically formulated warnings[3] from the said inquisitor about not impeding him in the exercise of his office of inquisition[4] and not offering defense, help, or favor to the aforesaid Marguerite—in which respects [Guiard] was found contumacious and rebellious—at last [William] had this same Guiard personally brought into his presence. [William] offered an oath to [Guiard], required by his office, concerning speaking truly about the aforesaid things and other matters pertaining to his office of inquisition.[5] The same obstinate and stubborn man contumaciously refused to offer or undergo [this oath], although thereafter, sufficiently informed, he recognized and admitted that this same Brother William was an inquisitor. And therefore, since [Guiard] was persisting in his contumacious behavior, after offering him many

sound exhortations this same inquisitor bound him with the chain of major excommunication. [Guiard] withstood this excommunication with a hardened spirit, at the expense of his salvation, for almost a year and a half. Before and after this, the same inquisitor frequently in legitimate form requested him to swear and respond, often offering him the benefit of granting him absolution in due form. [But Guiard], contumaciously refusing to swear and respond just as before, fleeing his salvation, did not care to seek or receive the absolution offered to him.

After these things had occurred, this same inquisitor, nearly despairing of correcting the aforesaid Guiard, took care to seek counsel on this point from us—although he undoubtedly sufficed to complete this matter himself—as to what further legal steps were to be taken in this matter. As obedient sons and zealots of the Catholic faith,[6] assenting to the just petition of this same inquisitor, as we should and ought to do according to our limited abilities, counseling sensibly, we said and we say:

Given the foregoing action and process, the demands of law require that further proceedings[7] be taken against the said Guiard. Specifically, since the aforementioned defense and aid passed over first into vehement and then into violent presumption of heresy, giving due consideration to his contumacies,[8] rebellions, and stubborn behaviors, things which require this result according to the law, the aforementioned unfortunate Guiard must be considered a heretic and definitively condemned as a heretic and relinquished to secular authority to receive due punishment for the nature of the crime, unless he will quickly repent, before or after the sentence, and return willingly to the unity of the Catholic faith and consent to abjure his error publicly to the satisfaction of the inquisitor himself. In which case, in satisfaction to be undergone for his great offense, and so that he not by chance infect other infirm people with his pestiferous doctrine, he will be deservedly confined to perpetual imprisonment. In testimony of which, at the request of the same inquisitor, we have caused our seals to be appended to the present letter. Given[9] at Paris, in the year of our Lord 1309, on the Friday after the Sunday on which is sung "Letare Jerusalem" [i.e., 3 April 1310].

Done at the house of the Brothers Preacher of Paris, in the year, indiction, month, day and pontificate aforementioned. Present were the religious men Brothers Alexander of Marcia; Ralph of Hotot; Jacques of Dijon of the Cistercian order; and Gregory of Lucca of the order of Saint Augustine, masters in theology, who also consented and expressly acquiesced in the counsel of the said masters, as witnesses specially called and invited for this purpose.

And I, Evens Phili of Saint-Nicaise, cleric of the Diocese of Quimper, public notary by apostolic authority, was present at the aforesaid events. And I have caused the letter of the aforesaid[10] consultation, sealed with the seals of the said masters, as they said, to be faithfully incorporated here, and having diligently collated it with the present instrument and found them to agree with each other, subscribed myself here and added my customary sign for greater certainty concerning the things set forth, having been requested to do so.

AND I, JACQUES OF VERTUS, OF THE DIOCESE OF CHÂLONS-SUR-MARNE, PUBLIC NOTARY BY APOSTOLIC AUTHORITY, HAVE SEEN THE AFORESAID ORIGINAL INSTRUMENT SIGNED WITH THE SIGN OF THE SAID MASTER EVENS PHILI NOTARY PUBLIC, AND HAVE MADE A COLLATION FROM IT WITH THE PRESENT TRANSCRIPTION, WITH JACQUES OF ACTRIO AND WILLIAM COFFINI,[11] CLERICS IN THE NEW STREET OF THE BLESSED MARY IN PARIS[12] ON THE FOURTH[13] DAY OF OCTOBER, IN THE YEAR OF THE LORD 1310, NINTH INDICTION, IN THE FIFTH YEAR OF THE PONTIFICATE OF THE MOST HOLY FATHER LORD CLEMENT V, BY DIVINE PROVIDENCE POPE. AND BECAUSE I HAVE FOUND THEM TO AGREE, I HERE SUBSCRIBE MYSELF AND ADD MY CUSTOMARY SIGN, HAVING BEEN REQUESTED TO DO SO.

II

3 April 1310. *AN J428 no. 17.*   An unnotarized copy of the canonists' decision of 3 April concerning Guiard of Cressonessart. It is nearly identical to the one integrated into document I, but with small differ-

ences that show it to be more faithful to the lost, sealed original issued by the canonists themselves.

Editions: Verdeyen, "Procès d'inquisition," 62–63.

(Variations from document I are noted in the apparatus to Lerner, "Angel of Philadelphia," but without separate edition.)

Parchment. 260 x 237 mm. Folded in 6.

Dorse (in more modern hand, vertically along left side): *1309 17.*

To all who will see the present letter, William called "Brother" archdeacon of Lothian in the Church of St. Andrew in Scotland, Hugh of Besançon canon of Paris, John of Thélus canon of Saint-Quentin in the Vermandois, Henry of Béthune, Peter of Vaux curate of Saint-Germain-l'Auxerrois in Paris, regents in canon law at Paris, send greetings in the author of salvation.

Whereas a certain *beguinus* named Guiard of Cressonessart, of the Diocese of Beauvais, came forth publicly, demonstrably, and notoriously in defense and aid of Marguerite, called "Porete," of Hainaut—who was suspected for various probable causes of the stain of heretical depravity, and because of this was arrested by the religious man Brother William of Paris of the order of Preachers, appointed by apostolic authority as inquisitor of this same depravity in the Kingdom of France—for this and other reasons Guiard was suspected of the crime of heresy. The said inquisitor, as he made known to us, proceeded in the following manner:

After legitimate, canonically formulated warnings from the said inquisitor about not impeding him in the exercise of his inquisitorial office and not offering defense, help, or favor to the aforesaid Marguerite—in which respects [Guiard] was found contumacious and rebellious—at last [William] had this same Guiard personally brought into his presence. [William] offered an oath to [Guiard], required by his office, concerning speaking truly about the aforesaid things and other matters pertaining to his office of inquisitor. The same obstinate and stubborn man contumaciously refused to offer or undergo [this oath], although thereafter, sufficiently informed, he recognized and admitted that this same Brother William was an inquisitor. And therefore, since [Guiard] was persisting in his contumacious behavior, after offering him many sound exhortations this same inquisitor bound him with the chain of major excommunication. [Guiard] withstood this excommunication with a hardened spirit, at the expense of his salvation, for almost a year and a half. Before and after this, the same inquisitor frequently in legitimate form requested him to swear and respond, often offering him the benefit of granting him absolution in due form. [But Guiard], contumaciously refusing to swear and respond just as before, fleeing from his salvation, did not care to seek or receive the absolution offered to him.

After these things had occurred, this same inquisitor, nearly despairing of correcting the aforesaid Guiard, took care to seek counsel on this point from us—although he undoubtedly sufficed to complete this matter himself—as to what further legal steps were to be taken in this matter. As obedient sons and zealots of the Catholic faith, assenting to the just petition of this same inquisitor, as we should and ought to do according to our limited abilities, counseling him sensibly, we said and we say:

Given the foregoing action and process, the demands of law require that further proceedings be taken against the said Guiard. Specifically, since the aforementioned defense and aid passed over first into vehement and then into violent presumption of heresy, giving due consideration to his contumacies,[14] rebellions, and stubborn behaviors, things which require this result according to the law, the aforementioned unfortunate Guiard must be considered a heretic and definitively condemned as a heretic and relinquished to secular authority to receive due punishment for the nature of the crime, unless he will quickly repent, before or after the sentence, and return willingly to the unity of the Catholic faith and consent to abjure his error publicly to the satisfaction of the inquisitor himself. In which case, in satisfaction to be undergone for his great offense, and so that he not by chance infect other infirm people with his pestiferous doctrine, he will be properly confined in perpetual imprisonment.

In testimony of which, at the request of the same inquisitor, we have caused our seals to be appended to the present letter. Given at Paris, in the year of our Lord 1309, on the Friday after the Sunday on which is sung "Letare Jerusalem" [i.e., 3 April 1310].

III

3 April 1310. *AN J428 no. 19.* Unnotarized copy of the decision by the same five canonists in the case of Marguerite Porete. Its wording is practically identical to that of document II.

Editions: Verdeyen, "Procès d'inquisition," 60–61.
Parchment. 210 x 210. Folded in half.
Dorse (in more modern hand, vertically on left side): *1309 19.*

To all who will see the present letter, William called "Brother" archdeacon of Lothian of the Church of St. Andrew in Scotland, Hugh of Besançon canon of Paris, John of Thélus canon of Saint-Quentin in the Vermandois, Henry of Béthune, Peter of Vaux curate of Saint-Germain-l'Auxerrois in Paris, regents in canon law at Paris, send greetings in the author of salvation.

Whereas a certain *beguina* named Marguerite Porete of Hainaut was suspected for various probable causes of the stain of heretical depravity, the religious man Brother William of Paris of the order of Preachers, appointed by apostolic authority as inquisitor of the aforementioned depravity[15] in the Kingdom of France, proceeded against the aforementioned suspected woman, as he made known to us, in the following manner:

After she many times contumaciously refused to appear, he caused this same woman to be personally brought into his presence. He offered an oath to her, required by his office, concerning speaking truly about those things which had been reported and revealed about her. This same obstinate and stubborn woman contumaciously refused to undergo this [oath] or to explain, although thereafter, sufficiently informed, she recognized and admitted that this same Brother William was an inquisitor. And therefore, since she was persisting in her contumacious behavior, after offering her many sound exhortations, this same inquisitor bound her with the chain of major excommunication. She withstood this excommunication with a hardened spirit, at the expense of her salvation, for almost a year and a half. Before and after this, the same inquisitor frequently in legitimate form requested her to swear and respond, often offering her the benefit of granting her absolution in due form. [But she], contumaciously refusing to swear and respond just as before, fleeing her salvation, did not care to seek or receive the absolution offered to her.

After these things had occurred, this same inquisitor, nearly despairing of correcting the aforesaid woman, took care to seek counsel on this point from us—although he undoubtedly sufficed to complete this matter himself—as to what further legal steps were to be taken in this matter. As obedient sons and zealots of the Catholic faith, assenting to the just petition of this same inquisitor, as we should and ought to do according to our limited abilities, counseling him sensibly, we said and we say:

Given the foregoing action and process, the demands of law require that further proceedings be taken against the said woman. Specifically, since the aforementioned suspicion passed over first into vehement and then into violent presumption of heresy, giving due consideration to her contumacies, rebellions, and stubborn behaviors—things which require this result in legal interpretation—the aforementioned unfortunate woman must be considered a heretic and definitively condemned as a heretic and relinquished to secular authority to receive due punishment for the nature of the crime, unless she will quickly repent, before or after the sentence, and return willingly to the unity of the Catholic faith and consent to abjure her error publicly to the satisfaction of the inquisitor himself. In which case, in satisfaction to be undergone for her great offense, and so that she not by chance infect other infirm people with her pestiferous doctrine, she will be properly confined in perpetual imprisonment.

In testimony of which, at the request of the same inquisitor, we have caused our seals to be appended to the present letter. Given at Paris, in the year of our Lord 1309, on the Friday after the Sunday on which is sung "Letare Jerusalem" [i.e., 3 April 1310].

IV

9 April 1310, *AN J428 no. 18.* Unnotarized copy of the canonists' further opinion concerning Guiard of Cressonessart's actual testimony. The canonists are given a summary of this testimony, and they find

Guiard's claims to be heretical. Note that only four of the five canonists from earlier documents are listed, with Henry of Béthune being absent. The present translation uses two distinct typefaces to distinguish the copy of the testimony from the canonists' preliminaries and opinion.

Editions: Verdeyen, "Procès d'inquisition," 65–67; Lerner, "Angel of Philadelphia," 363–54; Langlois, "Marguerite Porete," 297–98 (testimony only, without canonists' preliminaries and opinion).

Parchment. 390 x 238 mm. Folded in 4.

On dorse (more modern hand, vertically on left edge): *1309 18* (bottom right): *Actum anno M CC IX* (then in different hand) *Processus contra M. Porete culpabilem de heresi* (Done in the year 1309. Process against M. Porete, guilty of heresy).

To all who will see the present letter, William called "Brother" archdeacon of Lothian of the Church of St. Andrew in Scotland, Hugh of Besançon canon of Paris, John of Thélus canon of Saint-Quentin in the Vermandois, Peter of Vaux curate of the Church of Saint-Germain-l'Auxerrois in Paris, regents in canon law at Paris, send greetings in the author of salvation.

Whereas a certain pseudoreligious *(pseudo-religiosus)* named Guiard, arising from himself and perishing within,[16] for various probable causes was suspected of heretical depravity, notably[17] infamous for the stain of this depravity, the venerable and devout Brother William of Paris of the order of Preachers, inquisitor of heretical depravity appointed by the apostolic see in the Kingdom of France, caused the aforesaid Guiard thus suspect to be summoned to his presence. And finally, after many contumacies and various evasions, this same Guiard personally appeared in the presence of the aforementioned inquisitor [and was] judicially requested by the same inquisitor to tell the truth concerning those things which had been reported and revealed about him in this matter concerning the articles written below. [He] testified and confessed in this manner, just as the said inquisitor informed us:

Saying, namely, that he is the *Angel of Philadelphia,*[18] and explaining this term, he says that "Angel" is the name of an office, not of a nature. And he interprets "Philadelphia" as "saving the adhesion of the Lord or one adhering to the Lord." And thus "I consider myself sent to save the adhesion of the Lord or one adhering to the Lord in the Church of God."

And then, asked by whom he had been sent, he responds that it was by him who has the *key of David*,[19] explaining that by this he understands Christ, who has the key of excellence, and that his vicar the lord pope has the key of ministry. And he adds that four years earlier and more he perceived that this office had been given to him—but he reckons that it had [actually] been given to him twenty years earlier, when he first perceived it those four years ago, or less—and this was at Paris in the lower chapel of the lord king;[20] and that the mode of perception and reception of this office and of the opening of the door[21] was in a flash through the opening of the understanding of Scripture.

Next, asked if he knows that another has been sent in the same way, he responds no, and that only one can be sent, uniquely, unless he fails and then another can be sent.

Next, asked what he understands concerning the seven churches designated in the Book of the Apocalypse, he responds that there is always one church, but indeed there are and can be different *status* within it, and during various times the church shines forth more in one *status* than in another,[22] according to the divine mission, and takes its name more from that *status* in which it more esteems itself.

Asked "Since there is one church, what is the Church of Philadelphia?," he responds that among the different *status* of the church is a certain *status* of runners, who have cast away all things, wanting to hold to evangelical rigor, and to shine forth their light through outward conduct, [thereby] showing interior ardor. And [they do this] licitly without injury to the church[23] or to divine dispensation. And in those [runners] the Church of Philadelphia has its origin. Although anyone adhering to Christ in all things can be saved, nonetheless, especially among these. And among those, he who is the Angel of Philadelphia has a certain prerogative according to the gift given him by the Lord in his special mission and the opening of the door.

And he said that, just as at the end of his life he [i.e., Christ] was struck down for the misdeeds of the people and limited in his bodily strength,[24] so that he was not able to carry the cross, thus it is, or can be, that the angel would be sent and struck down by the Lord for the misdeeds of the people in a state of innocence, that is, before he had mortally sinned. And he reckons that such[25] an angel [was] sent and struck down for the misdeed of the people.

And he adds that he had been prepared to set himself forth, even unto death, to support and defend certain people adhering [to the Lord], until he had determined whether or not he had the right to do so—that is, whether this person was adhering to the Lord or not. And that he had come forward at Reims for such people against the Preachers and Minors, which Minors were preaching against these people directly. And at Paris he had also come forth for Marguerite called "Porete."

And the one who is speaking also says that the authority of his office, which[26] is specially [given] to him, is to rise up against all men attacking an adherent to the Lord or adhesion of the Lord, when those who had the office in the church of doing this were remaining silent.

And then, asked whether this pertained to him more than another, he responds that it pertains to others through zeal and it seems that it pertains to him more through his office.

Next, asked if any know that he has this gift, he responds yes, because he has declared the opening of the door to others receiving the habit of Christ—understanding by this a habit such as he himself wore. To whom he said that they should beware, because they ought not to receive [it] with the intention of receiving the habit of a new religion on their own authority, but rather a habit having[27] authority from Christ.

And the one who is speaking adds that, because he cannot have a patron in the New Testament because of the prohibition of the church, he takes one in the Old, according to the admonition of the Savior giving and authorizing freedom.[28]

Next, asked if those who wear tabards are of his society, he responds no, not with regard to all things, except those who have and wear a long tunic and *leather belt*,[29] which belt is essential to the habit. However, he believes that they are adherents to the Lord even if they have a secular form in their habit.

With these things having been diligently inquired[30] into, heard, and understood, the same inquisitor, not presuming to proceed further in this matter without counsel of those learned in the law, sought our counsel in the matters laid out above. We, therefore, obedient sons and zealots of the Catholic faith, more devoutly inclining to the just petition of this same inquisitor since it is both due and fitting, counseling him sensibly according to our limited abilities, have said and say that:

Given the foregoing act, confessions, and process, he ought to consider, judge, and even condemn the said Guiard as a true heretic, with[31] this reservation based on mercy, that he not be handed over to secular authority if he will have repented either before or soon after his sentence, just as the laws teach. For it is manifestly evident from his foregoing words and confessions that he establishes a division in the church militant, indeed really establishes two churches militant—he himself wielding the keys of excellence of one, and the pope holding the keys of ministry of the other. And this same pope is not altogether the unique head of this church militant and is not able altogether to order it through himself and his ministers and his sacred canons and his statutes, all of which is heretical. See *Decretum*, distinction 19, ch. 1;[32] cause 15, question 1, *Violatores*;[33] cause 25, question 2, *Si quis dogmata*;[34] and *Decretales*, book 1, title 1, ch. 1, *Una vero*.[35]

In testimony of which, at the request of the same inquisitor, we have affixed our seals to the present letter. Given at Paris, the Thursday after the Sunday on which is sung "Iudica me," in the year of our Lord 1309 [i.e., 9 April 1310].

V

11 April 1310. *AN J428 no. 15 (first section).*   Twenty-one masters of theology gather at Saint-Mathurin in Paris to consider extracts from a book, the title and author of which are not mentioned. No independent copy of their decision survives, and they do not seem to have issued a separate decision authenticated with their seals. Rather the notary Jacques of Vertus, mentioning the presence of Evens Phili, prepared a

memorandum of their decision and recorded it as a public document. The document was then presumably recopied—as we now have it— so as to form the first part of a single large sheet of parchment, on which follows document VII below. Both portions of this document are notarized individually by Jacques of Vertus sometime on or after 31 May (the date of the final sentence).

Editions: Langlois, "Marguerite Porete," 296–97; Verdeyen, "Procès d'inquisition," 50–51.

Parchment, 586 x 400 mm. Pencil rulings. Folded in 12.

Dorse: (more modern hand, vertically, on right-hand side): *1309 15* (bottom center): *XIII Instrumenta facta super examinacione M. Porete culpabili heresi* (different hand): *M CCC IX.*

In the name of Christ, amen. May it be known to all by means of the present public instrument that, in the presence of us, the no- taries public[36] designated below, assembled at Saint-Mathurin in Paris at the command or request of the religious man Brother [Wil- liam][37] of Paris, appointed by apostolic authority as inquisitor of heretical depravity in the Kingdom of France, [who was] present there, the [following] venerable and discreet men were gathered at the same place: Simon [of Guiberville] the dean, Thomas of Bailly, William Alexandri, and John of Ghent, canons of Paris; Peter of Saint-Denis; Gerard of Saint-Victor; Jacques [of Thérines] abbot of Chaalis; Gerard [of Bologna] the Carmelite; John of Pouilly; Lawrence, prior of Val-des-Écoliers; Alexander [of Marcia or of Saint'Elpido], Henry [of Friemar] the German, and Gregory of Lucca, of the order of Hermits of Saint Augustine; John of Mont- Saint-Éloi; Ralph of Hotot; Berenger [of Landora] of the order of Preachers; John of Clairmarais, Nicholas of Lyra, and Jacob of As- coli of the order of Minors; Jacques [of Dijon] the Cistercian; and Roger of Roseto, [all] masters of theology.

The same inquisitor asked for counsel from these masters, as to what should be done about a certain book which he showed them, from which the several articles exhibited there had been ex- tracted, which he had pointed out to them, as he said. The first of these articles is this: "That the annihilated soul gives license to the virtues and is no longer in servitude to them because it does not

have use for them; but rather the virtues obey [its] command."
Likewise the fifteenth article is this: "That such a soul does not care
about the consolations of God or his gifts, and ought not to care
and cannot, because [such a soul] has been completely focused on
God, and its focus on God would then be impeded."

After prior deliberation held among those same masters, the
above-mentioned Simon the dean,[38] at the will and with the harmonious assent and in the name of all of these masters, said, responding to the consultation requested from them,[39] that the counsel of all was and is: that such a book, in which the said articles are
contained, should be exterminated as heretical and erroneous and
containing heresy and errors.

Done in the aforesaid place in the year of the Lord 1309, the
eleventh day of April, in the eighth indiction, in the fifth[40] year of
the pontificate of Lord Clement V by divine providence pope [i.e.,
11 April 1310], in the presence[41] of those [mentioned] above who
were specially called forth for this purpose.

AND I, JACQUES OF VERTUS, CLERIC OF THE DIOCESE OF CHÂLONS-
SUR-MARNE, PUBLIC NOTARY BY APOSTOLIC AUTHORITY, WAS
PRESENT IN PERSON WHEN ALL THE FOREGOING THINGS WERE
DONE, SAID, AND ACCOMPLISHED, IN THE SAID MEETING, WITH
MASTER EVENS PHILI NOTARY PUBLIC,[42] [AND] HAVE RECORDED
THESE THINGS IN PUBLIC FORM, WRITTEN WITH MY OWN HAND,
AND SIGNED WITH MY CUSTOMARY SIGN, HAVING BEEN ASKED TO
DO SO.

VI

9 May 1310, *AN J428 no. 19bis.*   Unnotarized copy of the document
in which the canon lawyers summarize the information William of
Paris has given them about his inquiries into the case of Marguerite
Porete and render a judgment as to whether she can be judged a relapsed heretic.

Editions: Lea, *History of the Inquisition,* 577–78 (reprinted in Fredericq, *Corpus documentorum inquisitionis,* 155–57); Verdeyen, "Procès
d'inquisition," 78–79.

Parchment. 180 x 209 mm. Folded in half.

Dorse (vertically on right edge, in more modern hand): *1310 19*
(top center, lightly effaced): *J. 3.*[1]

To all who will see the present letter, William called "Brother"
archdeacon of Lothian of the Church of St. Andrew in Scotland,
Hugh of Besançon canon of Paris, John of Thélus canon of Saint-
Quentin in the Vermandois, Henry of Béthune canon of Furnes,
and Peter of Vaux curate of Saint-Germain-l'Auxerrois in Paris, regents in canon law at Paris, send greetings in the author of salvation.

Be it known that the venerable, devout, and distinguished
brother William of Paris of the order of Preachers, appointed by
apostolic authority as inquisitor of heretical depravity in the Kingdom of France, recently[43] has made known to us the case that follows and has requested the consultation with us that is noted below.

This, in fact, is the case: Whereas Marguerite, called "Porete,"
was suspected of heresy, [and] in rebellion and disobedience[44] not
wanting to respond or swear in the inquisitor's presence concerning those things pertaining to the office of inquisition committed
to him, this same inquisitor nevertheless conducted an inquiry
against her. From the depositions of many witnesses, he found that
the said Marguerite had composed a certain book containing heresies and errors, which had been[45] publicly and solemnly condemned
and burned by order of the reverend father Lord Guido, former
bishop of Cambrai. And by a letter of the aforesaid bishop it was
ordered that if she should again attempt by word or in writing any
things like those contained in the book, he was condemning her
and relinquishing her to be judged by secular justice. And this same
inquisitor also found that she acknowledged in court—once in
the presence of the inquisitor of Lorraine and once in the presence
of the reverend father lord Philip, then bishop of Cambrai—that
after the aforesaid condemnation she had possessed the said book
and others. This same[46] inquisitor also found that the said Marguerite, after the condemnation of this book, had communicated the
said book, one similar to it containing the same errors, to the reverend father Lord John, by the grace of God bishop of Châlons-
sur-Marne, and not only to the said lord but to many other simple
people—*begardis* and others—as a good book.

Therefore, the request for consultation resulting from the aforesaid things, made to us by the aforementioned inquisitor, as mentioned above, is the following: that is, whether from such things the said *beguina* ought to be judged relapsed? We, moreover, zealots of the Catholic faith and professors of canonical truth, responding to the said request for consultation, say that this same *beguina*—assuming the truth of the preceding facts—is to be judged relapsed and deservedly relinquished to the secular court.

In witness whereof we have attached our seals to the present letter. Given in the year of the Lord 1310, on the Saturday after the festival of the blessed John at the Lateran Gate [i.e., 9 May 1310].

VII

31 May 1310. *AN J428 no. 15b.*   William of Paris sentences Marguerite Porete to relinquishment to the secular arm, orders her book burned, and sentences Guiard of Cressonessart to perpetual imprisonment. This text as we now have it follows document V on a single sheet of parchment, but the upper and lower segments of no. 15 (a and b) are presented as two separately notarized documents, which must have been prepared by the notary Jacques of Vertus on or after 31 May.

Editions: Lea, *History of the Inquisition,* 575–76 (only section on Marguerite; reprinted Fredericq, *Corpus documentorum inquisitionis,* 157–60); Lerner, "Angel of Philadelphia," 359–60 (only section on Guiard); Verdeyen, "Procès d'inquisition," 81–83.

Dorse: See document V above.

In the name of Christ, amen. In this same year 1310, in the eighth indiction, on the Sunday after the Ascension of the Lord, in the fifth year of the pontificate of the most blessed father lord Clement V, by divine providence pope [i.e., 31 May 1310], at the Place de Grève in Paris, were present in a solemn congregation there the reverend in Christ father lord bishop of Paris;[47] Master John of Forgetis, official of Paris;[48] William of Chanac;[49] John of Dammartin;[50] Sanche of Charmoie;[51] Stephen of Brétencourt;[52] Brother Martin of Abbeville, bachelor in theology;[53] Brother Nicolas of Ennezat of the order of Preachers;[54] John Ploiebach, provost of Paris;[55] William of Choques,[56] and many others called together specially for this occasion. And also present [were] many processions of the city of Paris, a great multitude of people, and I, the public notary signed below.

The religious and honest brother William of Paris of the order of Preachers, appointed by apostolic authority as inquisitor of heretical depravity in the Kingdom of France, presented in writing the sentences here below in this form:

In the name of the Father and of the Son and of the Holy Spirit, amen. Since it is established and has been established by evident proofs to us, Brother William of Paris of the order of Preachers, appointed by apostolic authority as inquisitor of heretical depravity in the Kingdom of France, that you, Marguerite of Hainaut, called "Porete," were vehemently suspected of the stain of heretical depravity, because of this, we caused you to be summoned so that you might appear before us in judgment. When you appeared in person, having been warned[57] by us many times canonically and legitimately that you should offer an oath in our presence to tell the full, pure, and whole truth about yourself and others, regarding those things which are known to pertain to the office of inquisition committed to us—which you disdained to do, although you were requested by us many times about this in several places—in these ways you were proved contumacious and rebellious.

For these evident and notorious contumacies and rebellions which require this, with the counsel of many learned men, we imposed the sentence of major excommunication against you, rebellious and contumacious as you were, and put it in writing. Although you had been notified [of this], you stubbornly endured for nearly a year and a half after the said notification, at the expense of your salvation, although we offered to you many times the benefit of absolution to be administered according to the form of the church, if you would humbly ask for it. Up to now you have disdained[58] to seek it, nor have you wanted to swear or respond to us concerning the aforementioned things. Because of which, according to canonical sanction, we consider and must consider you as convicted and confessed and as lapsed into heresy or as a heretic.

But, while you, Marguerite, were remaining obstinate in these rebellions, we—led by conscience, wanting to carry out the responsibility of our office committed to us—conducted an inquiry against you, and we carried out the process concerning the aforesaid things as the law demands. By this inquiry and process it appeared evident to us that you composed a certain[59] pestiferous book containing heresy and error. For this cause the said book was condemned by Guido of blessed memory, then bishop of Cambrai, and by his order burned at Valenciennes, in your presence, publicly and openly. You were expressly prohibited by this bishop, under pain of excommunication, from composing or having again such a book, or using it or one like it. The same bishop added and expressly stated in a certain letter sealed with his seal that if you should again use the aforesaid book, or if you should attempt again by word or in writing those things that were contained in it, he was condemning you as heretical and relinquishing you to be judged by secular justice. After all these things, against the said prohibition, you several times had and[60] several times used the said book, as is evident from your acknowledgments, made not only in the presence of the inquisitor of Lorraine, but also in the presence of the reverend father and lord, Lord Philip[61] then bishop of Cambrai and now archbishop of Sens. After the aforesaid condemnation and burning, you even communicated the said book, as though good and licit, to the reverend father Lord John, bishop of Châlons-sur-Marne, and to certain other people, as is clear to us from the evident testimonies of many witnesses worthy of faith who have sworn concerning these matters in our presence.

Therefore, after diligent deliberation concerning all the aforestated matters and having received the counsel of many persons expert in both laws, having God and the sacred Gospels before our eyes, with the assent and counsel of the reverend father and lord, Lord William by the grace of God bishop of Paris, we condemn you by sentence,[62] Marguerite, not only as one lapsed into heresy but as one relapsed, and we relinquish you to secular justice, asking it that short of death and mutilation of the body it act mercifully with you, as far as canonical sanctions permit.

And we condemn, by sentence,[63] the said book as heretical and erroneous, as containing errors and heresies by the judgment and counsel of the masters of theology residing in Paris, and now we want it to be exterminated and burned,[64] and strictly order that every and each person having the said book, under pain of excommunication, is required to turn it over without fraud to us or to the prior of the Preaching Brothers of Paris,[65] our commissioner, before the next feast of the apostles Peter and Paul [i.e., 29 June].

Done in Paris in the Place de Grève, with the aforesaid reverend father the bishop of Paris and the clergy and people of the said city solemnly gathered there, on Sunday within the Octave of the Ascension, in the year of the Lord 1310 [i.e., 31 May 1310].

Next, in the name of the Father and of the Son and of the Holy Spirit, amen. Because it is lawfully evident to us, Brother William of Paris appointed by apostolic authority as inquisitor of heretical depravity in the Kingdom of France, that you, Guiard of Cressonessart of the Diocese of Beauvais, notoriously fell into aid and defense of Marguerite[66] of Hainaut, called "Porete"—who for various probable causes was vehemently suspected of the stain of the aforesaid heretical depravity and for this reason was arrested by us at Paris[67]—for this reason and others you were suspected by us of the crime of heresy. And you were properly and canonically warned by us, that you should not present[68] any impediment to us in the proceedings of our office of inquisition, nor provide defense, aid, counsel, or favor to the said[69] Marguerite, who was infected, as stated above, with the stain [of heresy]. In these respects we find you rebellious and contumacious, since,[70] appearing in our presence in judgment, many times exhorted[71] and required by us, and moreover sufficiently and canonically warned that you should swear in our presence on the holy Gospels of God to respond and tell[72] the full, pure, and whole truth concerning those things which pertain to our aforesaid office, about both yourself and others—in this you proved contumacious and rebellious, disdaining to respond and swear. For such contumacious behaviors which require this, with the counsel of many learned men, as justice requires, we published a sentence of excommunication against you—stubborn, contumacious, and rebellious—and put it in writing. After you were notified[73] of this, you endured this sentence of excommunication with a hardened spirit for nearly a year and a half, at the expense of your salvation, although we offered[74] repeatedly to grant you the benefit of absolution in the form approved by the church, if you humbly asked for this, which up to now you have disdained to seek. Because of this, according to canonical sanctions, we can and must condemn you as confessed and convicted of heresy and as a heretic.

But, after all the aforesaid events, you were not content with these things and appeared in court in our presence. And at last taking the oath, you raised yourself to such a point of madness that you were persistently asserting[75] that you were the Angel of Philadelphia, and indeed sent directly by Christ, who has the key of excellence, not by the lord pope, who only has the key of ministry, as you said. You added that another besides you cannot be sent, unless you fail, for the salvation of the adhesion of the Lord or those adhering to the Lord, because, even if[76] this pertains to others because of zeal, it pertains more to you because of [your] office, and [you added] other things derogatory to the power of the highest pontiff. From which it is manifestly clear that you propose division in the church militant. Indeed, you rather propose two churches militant, and that the same lord pope is not the one head of the church militant, which truly must be considered heretical and also condemned[77] as heretical.

Having received on all these things the deliberate counsel and agreement of many men expert in both theology and in canon and civil law, [and] with the counsel and assent of the reverend father and lord, Lord William by the grace of God bishop of Paris, having God and the holy Gospels before our eyes, unable in good conscience to further overlook things so pernicious, so erroneous, so disparaging to the truth[78] of the Catholic faith, we condemn you, by sentence,[79] the aforesaid Guiard, as a heretic, declaring you deprived of all clerical privileges, [and] asking the aforesaid reverend father that he remove clerical insignia from you immediately. When these steps have been carried out,[80] we condemn you, by sentence,[81] to perpetual imprisonment, reserving to ourselves and our successors in the aforementioned office of inquisitor the power of mitigating, diminishing,[82] changing, increasing, or completely absolving, as far as your merits will require and it shall seem proper to us and our successors in the aforesaid office.

Done at Paris at the Place de Grève, with the aforesaid reverend father, clergy and people of the said city solemnly gathered there, on the Sunday within the Octave of the Ascension, in the year of the Lord 1310 [i.e., 31 May 1310]. Done[83] as above.

AND I, JACQUES OF VERTUS, CLERIC OF THE DIOCESE OF CHÂLONS-SUR-MARNE, PUBLIC NOTARY BY APOSTOLIC AUTHORITY, WAS PRESENT AT THE PRONOUNCEMENT OF THE SAID SENTENCES WITH THE ABOVE-NAMED WITNESSES, AND THEN I MADE AND PUBLISHED THIS PUBLIC INSTRUMENT AND SIGNED IT WITH MY SIGN IN TESTIMONY OF THE FOREGOING EVENTS, HAVING BEEN REQUESTED TO DO SO.

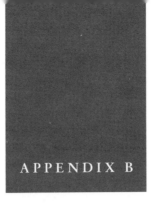

Translations of
Other Contemporary Sources

This appendix presents English translations of the relevant passages from the four contemporary chronicles that relate direct information about the trials of Marguerite Porete and Guiard of Cressonessart, plus one brief mention in the writings of a contemporary master of theology. Not all of these sources are of equal importance, but all are worth taking into account. I regret that I have had to rely entirely on published editions, specified below.

I

Continuer of William of Nangis.   William of Nangis was the most important historical writer in the later thirteenth century at the abbey of Saint-Denis, which was in turn the most important center of historical writing about the French crown. His Latin *Chronicon* "furnishes the single most important extant text for the last two decades of the thirteenth century,"[1] and after his death in 1300 other monks continued the year-by-year chronicle. Though we do not know the name of the monk who entered the continuation for 1310, he was obviously a well-informed observer. For instance, he must have known Peter of Saint-Denis, one of the masters of theology who condemned the extracts from Marguerite's book. My translation is based on Hercule Géraud, ed., *Chronique latine de Guillaume de Nangis, de 1113 à 1300, avec les continuations de cette chronique, de 1300 à 1368,* new ed. (Paris: Renouard, 1843), 1:379–80.

Around the feast of Pentecost[2] it happened at Paris that a certain pseudowoman *[pseudo-mulier]* from Hainaut, named Marguerite called "Porete," had published a certain book in which, according to the judgment of all the theologians who diligently examined it, many errors and heresies were contained—among others, "that the soul annihilated in love of the Creator, without blame of conscience or remorse, can and ought to concede to nature whatever it seeks and desires," which manifestly rings of heresy.

While she did not want to abjure this little book *[libellum]* or the errors contained in it, but rather for a year or more stubbornly had endured the sentence of excommunication that the inquisitor of heretical depravity set upon her—because she did not want to appear in his presence [although] she had been sufficiently warned—finally, hardened in her wickedness, at the Place de Grève in the presence of the clergy and people specially assembled for this purpose, with the counsel of learned men, she was brought forth and handed over to the secular court. The provost of Paris, taking her into his power immediately, in the same place caused her to be destroyed by fire the next day. She showed, however, many signs of penitence at her end, both noble and devout, by which the hearts of many were piously and tearfully turned to compassion, as revealed by the eyes of the witnesses who beheld this scene.

On the same day, in the same place, a man some time ago converted to the faith from Judaism was cremated in the temporal fire, passing over to eternity, when again, like a dog returning to his vomit, in contempt of the blessed Virgin, he was trying to spit on images of her.

Then, in addition, [there was] a pseudoperson *[pseudo-quidam]* by the name of Guiard of Cressonessart, who—calling himself the Angel of Philadelphia, sent directly by God to comfort those adhering to Christ—was saying that he was not required by the order of the pope to take off the leather belt with which he was girded, nor the habit in which he was dressed; indeed he would sin by [following] the papal command. At last, in fear of the fire, taking off his habit and belt and finally recognizing his error, he was sentenced to be belted with perpetual imprisonment.

II

Continuer of Gerard of Frachet. Gerard was a Dominican, whose Latin chronicle from the beginning of the world up to 1268 is not noted for its originality. After his death, however, his chronicle was continued by monks of Saint-Denis. Gabrielle Spiegel writes of the continuation from 1300 to 1340 that it "functions as an intermediary between the continuations of Guillaume de Nangis's *Chronicon,* which it revises, abridges, and develops, and the *Grandes Chroniques,* for which it serves in part as the Latin base."[3] Thus the text below is obviously heavily dependent on the "Continuer of William of Nangis," but the small differences are nevertheless of interest. My translation is based on Gérard de Frachet, *Chronicon Gerardi de Fracheto et anonyma ejusdem operis continuatio,* in *Recueil des historiens des Gaules et de la France,* vol. 21 (Paris: Imprimerie impériale, 1855), 34.

Around the feast of Pentecost it happened at Paris that [there was] a certain pseudowoman from Hainaut, Marguerite called "Porete," who had published a certain book, in which many errors were contained, especially that "the soul annihilated in love of the Creator, without remorse of conscience ought and can give to nature whatever it seeks," which manifestly rings of heresy. While she did not want to abjure this little book, and she had for a year stubbornly sustained a sentence of excommunication, finally in the Place de Grève she was cremated by a conflagration of fire. She demonstrated many signs of penitence, however, in her death.

On the same day in the same place a certain Jew expired in the fire. Having a while ago converted, he then reverted. [He] was of such great perversity that, in contempt of the Blessed Mary, he was trying to spit on an image of her.

A pseudoperson, Guiard of Cressonessart, who, calling himself the Angel of Philadelphia, sent directly by God to comfort those adhering to Christ, was saying that he was not required by the order of the pope to take off the leather belt with which he was girded, nor the habit in which he was dressed—indeed that he would sin by [following] the papal command—at last, in fear of the fire, taking off his belt with his habit and finally recognizing his error, was sentenced to be belted with perpetual imprisonment.

III

The *Grandes chroniques de France.*   This was the vernacular history undertaken by the monks of Saint-Denis. The first installment was published by the monk Primat in (or around) 1274. For the early fourteenth century, the *Grandes chroniques* are heavily, but not entirely, dependent on the continuations of William of Nangis. It is readily apparent, however, that the brief passage below is not overtly a translation of the "Continuer of William of Nangis," or of any other known source. The passage is followed by discussion of the accusations against the Templars and several other brief entries. The notice of the "relapsed Jew" then follows. Given the textual similarities, the latter passage seems to depend on the "Continuer of William of Nangis" (because it is separated from the account of Marguerite's death, however, it has often been missed by scholars interested in the trials). My translation is based on Jules Viard, *Les grandes chroniques de France,* vol. 8 (Paris: Champion, 1934), 273 and 277–78.

And the following Monday[4] was burned in the aforementioned place[5] a learned beguine *[beguine clergesse],* who was called Marguerite Poree. She had transgressed and overstepped Divine Scripture and had erred in the articles of the faith, and had said contrary and prejudicial things about the sacrament of the altar. And for this reason certain masters, experts in theology, had condemned her . . .

. . . And in this same year, a Jew had not long before converted to the faith but a little later renounced the faith and was worse than he had been before, because to spite Our Lady he was spitting on her images wherever he found them. He was sentenced to be burned and was burned the day that the above-mentioned Marguerite la Porete was burned.

IV

Ly Myreur des Histors of John of Outremeuse (d. 1400). This is a later, vernacular source from the end of the fourteenth century that is primarily dependent on the *Grandes chroniques de France* but that also seems to show knowledge of the Latin chronicles above. It is not always factually correct (for instance, it goes on to say that Templars were burned on the same day as Marguerite). It is therefore most useful as a reflection of how textual accounts of Marguerite's death were combined and transformed over time. My translation is based on the edition by S. Bormans, *Ly Myreur des Histors, chronique de Jean des Preis dit d'Outremeuse* (Brussels: Hayez, 1880), 4:141–42.

> And the Monday soon [after] was burned a beguine, very sufficient in learning *[en clergrie mult suffissant]*, in that same place, whom they call Marguerite Porete, who had translated the Divine Scriptures,[6] in which translation she erred greatly in the articles of the faith. And of the sacrament of the altar she said many words prejudicial to the Holy Scriptures, for which many very expert masters of theology condemned her, and she was burned. But God, by his great mercy, saw to it that she died in the true Catholic faith.

V

John Baconthorpe's Sentence Commentary. The English Carmelite John Baconthorpe was a student in Paris by 1312, became master of theology by 1324, and died around 1348. He wrote his Sentence Commentary around 1320 and revised it several years later. Brief as it is, this should therefore be an intriguing contemporary notice. The difficulty, however, is that the remark is known only as it is cited in John Bale's *Scriptorum illustrium maioris Brytannie catalogus* (Basel: Apud Ioannem Oporinum, 1557), 367. Its context in the original work has never been established, nor has the means by which Baconthorpe heard of these events (the "as they say" *[ut dicunt]* may indicate reliance on a written source). Nevertheless, this single sentence is a unique witness by a contemporary master of theology.

> A certain *beguuina,* who had published a little book against the clergy, was burned near Paris, with a certain Jewish convert who—as they say—apostatized.

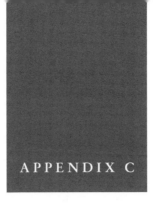

APPENDIX C

Translation of Arnau of Vilanova's
Epistola ad gerentes zonam pelliceam

This "Letter" was long known in only one incomplete manuscript copy, with some grounds for caution as to whether it was really the work of Arnau of Vilanova. Recent study of a second manuscript, however, has removed all doubt and has shown not only that this text was composed by Arnau but also that it must have been written toward the very end of his life.

The work was first known to scholarship in the now-incomplete version found at the end of BAV lat. 3824,[1] the grand compilation of Arnau's Latin theological and apologetic works that he had prepared for Clement V by August 1305. An incomplete copy of the "Letter" is found on the last extant folios of this book (fols. 262–63), in a separate hand from that of the rest of the volume. This change of hand demonstrates that it was added on after 1305 but might seem to leave open the possibility that the "Letter" could have had nothing to do with Arnau; a later scribe could have copied it at the end of this manuscript simply to use up available blank folios. A more plausible hypothesis, however, would be that Arnau wrote his *Epistola* after 1305 and sent or gave a copy to the curia, where it was copied into the back of the manuscript that represented Arnau's "collected works" (the manuscript surely did once contain the whole text; the last section has been lost because of a later removal of a concluding quire). Moreover, it seems highly likely that this copying probably did not occur until after the papal curia's

239

move to Avignon in 1309, where Arnau spent time in 1309 and 1310, just at the time of Guiard of Cressonessart's incarceration, testimony, and sentencing.[2]

Recent work by Josep Perarnau on the second known manuscript, Genoa, Biblioteca Universitària, Gaslini, ms. A IX 27, confirms the work's "Arnaldian" origins.[3] The second section of this manuscript (fols. 99–132) was once an independent booklet, and Perarnau has shown that all the texts that make up this section either were very likely written by Arnau or were connected to him.[4] The texts that made up this booklet must first have been copied together toward the very end of Arnau's life (after 1310), and further copies may have been disseminated from Arnau's "scriptorium" in Catalonia. Not only does the manuscript section in question show Catalan orthographical traits, but it was later owned and annotated by the "Renaissance magus" Pierleone of Spoleto (d. 1492), who is known to have acquired other manuscripts from Valencia.[5] Thus this text was transmitted to the papal court but also prepared for circulation along with several of Arnau's other late tracts.

Internal evidence strengthens our certainty of Arnau's authorship. For one thing, the author seems to have long personal experience with accusations of heresy—few authors were more habituated to defending themselves from such charges than Arnau. More conclusive is the extent to which this treatise develops language and ideas found in Arnau's authentic writings. The opening words, for example *(Cunctis viuere volentibus in euuangelica paupertate),* are nearly identical with the beginnings of both of his main vernacular works of spiritual guidance for beguins.[6] Just as strikingly, the fourfold division of the work (poverty, humility, charity, chastity) appears repeatedly in Arnau's works, for example as the four "building blocks of the faith" laid out in the dedicatory letter to Clement V of 1305,[7] or as the four "horns" of the true religion of Christ described in his commentary on the Book of Revelation in 1306.[8] More generally, the main ideas put forth here return to Christo-centric and evangelical themes favored by Arnau, both in vernacular works such as the *Informatio beguinorum* (*Lliço de Narbona*) and Latin works such as the *Philosophia catholica et divina.* Parallels are particularly pronounced with two of Arnau's late treatises (surviving in Italian translations), a *Tractatus de caritate* (written for a female religious) and a brief tract with the incipit "Per ciò che molti desiderano di sapero."[9] The notes provided by the work's modern editors (Cartaregia and Perarnau) detail these congruencies in convincing detail and need not be repeated here. Taken together, these multiple indications allow us to conclude that the identification of Arnau as the author of the *Epistola* is warranted and that the late date indicated by the manuscript evidence fits with a treatise written around 1310.

My translation is based on the Latin edition of Oriana Cartaregia and Josep Perarnau in "El text Sencer de l'*Epistola ad gerentes zonam pelliceam* d'Arnau de Vilanova," which uses Genoa, Biblioteca Universitaria, G. Gaslini, ms. A IX 27, fols. 99a-101a, as its base, with variant readings given from BAV lat. 3824, fols. 262–63 (in the notes below I refer to these manuscripts as G and V respectively). I have indicated the four main section breaks with Roman numerals within square brackets. Biblical quotations are based on the Douai-Reims translation but are slightly modernized. Where the manuscript readings differ from the Vulgate, however, I have reflected this in my translation.

I, the servant of all, advise all those wanting to live in evangelical poverty that they should follow in the footsteps of the head—that is Jesus Christ—and of his disciples, by living and acting with other faithful people in such a way that they themselves will always advance with regard to the spiritual life of evangelical perfection and always provide an example of advancing in it and never an opportunity of failure.

And therefore, just like disciples of Christ, they ought always and everywhere to cultivate and observe four virtues, as much in the heart as in actions: that is, the highest poverty, the fullest humility, the most perfect charity, the most sincere modesty or chastity.

[I] Concerning the first [virtue], one ought to observe [poverty] in two ways: the first is that they ought to have or wish to have nothing, except what is absolutely necessary either to the cultivation of spiritual life, such as writings necessary for the Office or for prayer, or to the everyday sustenance of bodily life, such as clothing and nourishment, which should just suffice for such sustenance. The second [is that] they should totally rid themselves of the worry of procuring these necessities for the future. Rather, only when necessity arises should they be worried about this, without prejudice to the other three virtues.

[II] Concerning humility, they ought to abase themselves in the condition not only of the body but also of the mind. In the condition of the body, let each one wholly—or at least as far as he is able—avoid everything that would be costly or curious. In the condition of the mind, let [each one] in no way esteem himself to be more deserving than any other of spiritual or bodily excellence, or worthy of any honor. Because of this, each one will always be obedient in church teachings, agreeable to honest counsel, long suffering in injuries, so that he will neither murmur nor chide nor litigate, with the result that he will reveal himself as a true cultivator of evangelical perfection through imitation of Christ, *Who, when he was reviled, did not revile, but delivered himself to him that judged him unjustly* (1 Pet. 2:23). Similarly, through the imitation of the apostles and disciples of Christ, of whom the apostle says, *We are reviled, and we bless* (1 Cor. 4:12). Similarly, in implementing the teaching of Christ, who says, *If someone strikes you on one cheek, turn to him also the other. And whoever will force you one mile, go with him two* (Matt. 5:39, 41). Similarly, in implementing the teaching of the apostle, who says that *The servant of the Lord must not litigate, but be mild towards all, teachable, patient,*[10] *and with modesty admonishing those who resist the truth* (2 Tim. 2:24–25). And that which he says, *In all things let us exhibit ourselves as the ministers of God, in much patience, in tribulation, etc.* (2 Cor. 6:4).

Because of this, if someone were to say that I was a heretic, I would not say to him, "You lie," but "Brother," or "Lord, with all due respect owed to you—I am not." Especially because it is not clear to me that he would say this more as an assertion than as a doubt or a temptation. For although I may know that he says something false, still I do not know whether he is lying. Therefore, because in true evangelical poverty *modesty* ought to always be manifest *to all people,* as the apostle says to the Philippians (Phil. 4:5), I should not say to such a person who is falsely accusing me that he is lying, but that, with all due respect, what he says is not true.

[III] Concerning charity, each one ought to be zealous for the salvation of other men, believers as well as infidels. And so that

they might attract them to eternal salvation, they ought to conform
to others in their habits, as much as they can without prejudice to
evangelical truth, especially when dealing with the weak and the
ignorant,[11] so that they may please them in order to effectively lure
them. Because of this the apostle says, *I became all things to all
men, that I might save all* (1 Cor. 9:22). That is, converse with Jews
like a Jew, with Gentiles like a Gentile, with the weak like a weak
person. Similarly, he says, *We that are stronger ought to bear the
infirmities of the weak and not to please ourselves; but let everyone
please his neighbor in good, for edification* (Rom 15:1). Because
of this he even says, *Let no one seek his own, but that which is
another's* (1 Cor. 10:24). Similarly, because of charitable zeal they
ought to beware lest through something that pleases them they
might give occasion for offense to others. Rather, they ought to
fulfill what the apostle says, *Be without offense to the Jews and
to the Gentiles and to the church of God, just as I am also* (1 Cor.
10:32–33). Similarly he says to each one of us: *If your brother is
scandalized because of your meat, now you are not walking according to charity* (Cf. Rom. 14:15). Similarly he says, *If meat scandal-
izes my brother, I will never eat flesh* (1 Cor. 8:13).

Thus if men of evangelical perfection, for the sake of avoid-
ing scandal or offense especially to the weak or ignorant, ought to
avoid what is more necessary for the body—that is, food—how
much more ought they to avoid that which is not necessary—such
as the leather belt, which is neither necessary for the sustenance of
the body nor for the perfection of spiritual life or evangelical poverty. For if it were necessary for this, it is certain that the apostles
or Christ would have worn it at some time. Nor would anyone of
sound mind dare to say that any evangelical men have cultivated
or observed evangelical poverty more perfectly than the apostles.
For the cultivator of evangelical truth ought not to take as a model
for himself anyone except Christ. Or if he might take the example
of others, he should not do this except in so far as they conform
to or have conformed to Christ and his truth.

Thus, if anyone might say that he wears the leather belt in imitation of John the Baptist, who was the first herald of the Gospel
and whom the Lord highly commended, he ought to understand

that what is proper to imitate in John out of devotion may in no way prejudice the truth of Christ. The Gospel expresses this in two places: once when it says that John *was not the light, but witness to the light* (Cf. John 1:8), and similarly when it says that *he that is the lesser in the kingdom of heaven is greater than John* (Cf. Matt. 11:11; Luke 7:28). Thus, whoever will have humbled himself more than John will be a greater cultivator of evangelical truth. Similarly, such a man devoted to John the Baptist ought to understand that John never wore the belt or would have worn it in a way that would have given offense, especially to the weak or ignorant. As a sign of this, the Gospel does not portray him wearing it except in the desert of Judea; but the Gospel does not hold that he wore it beyond the desert.[12] Wherefore, according to the Gospel, it is licit for all those devoted to [John] himself to wear it in the solitude of the desert. But if they are living in populated places, then, if it is prohibited to them by a bishop or official or any church authority, they would fall from the truth of spiritual life and from evangelical perfection if they wore it openly or publicly, by forsaking charity and evangelical humility.

[They would forsake] charity in so far as they would offend those near them and the church of God through their disobedience and contempt; because they would give an example to the weak and ignorant of despising and not obeying the church; and because they would give to them the occasion of judging and supposing that they were schismatics or heretics. And insofar as they would give an example of pleasing themselves and not others, and they would neglect to consider the weakness or ignorance of others. For it is possible that the church authorities who prohibit the wearing of the leather belt might do this not out of malice but from the voice of conscience that is caused by ignorance or weakness of complexion, because they fear by reason of the *Decretals* to incur a sentence of excommunication, because it seems that such a sign of specific religious usage would be the beginning of a new state *[status]* in the Catholic Church, which is allowed to no one without the consent of the Apostolic See; indeed, the ones doing this or agreeing with this incur a sentence of excommunication.

Therefore, even if it were known that the church authorities were prohibiting this out of malice, nevertheless those despising and disobeying publicly would fall from the truth of evangelical perfection, because the blessed Peter says that we ought to obey *not only the good and gentle but also the bad tempered* (1 Pet. 2:18)—always understanding that this refers to those matters not inconsistent with the Gospel. Because of this, it is clear that they would depart from the humility of evangelical perfection, which teaches to all its cultivators that they be *simple like doves* (Matt. 10:16) and *not aspiring to the highest things but rather being content with the humble* (Rom. 12:16). For anyone who would rely upon his judgment to this extent and despise the judgment of all others certainly is either damaged in the mind or has been seduced by the devil through some kind of heresy.

Therefore, if someone after the aforementioned prohibition should wear the said belt, then such stubbornness would show that he did not possess evangelical humility but rather the pride of individuality and presumption, because he would believe that he judged better than others, and undoubtedly would be either melancholic or seduced by the illusion of a sophistic explanation, as are they who say[13] that no church authority is able to forbid what Christ concedes, and that is true.

Similarly, when they say that Christ gives the freedom of imitating John the Baptist to any of the faithful, they ought to understand that this is true as far as it pertains to those things that are signified by John's actions, and not to the significant signs themselves. Which is shown in two ways: first, through those to whom the Lord spoke, when, commending John, he gave this freedom [of imitating him]. For he was speaking to crowds and gatherings, in which there were many married people and many who were in adolescence and even youth. John truly preserved virginity, and for all of his adolescence and much of his youth he inhabited the desert, *until* he was revealed *to Israel,* as Luke says (Luke 1:80). But it would be stupid to say that Christ would persuade married people to preserve virginity, or would persuade old people that in their adolescence or youth they should dwell in the desert. Rather, he persuaded married people that they should imitate John in observing chastity according to their station, and old people that they should imitate him in perfectly despising the world and worldly things, according to what justice requires of evangelical perfection.

And this is what the Lord was expressing to the Pharisees when he said, *John came to you in the way of justice, etc.* (Matt. 21:32). With these words he expressly declared that John should be imitated by those who might wish to follow him, with respect to the execution of perfect justice, which he cultivated, and not with respect to the signs of justice that he observed in exterior things. Otherwise neither the apostles nor all the disciples of the Savior would have been perfect evangelical men, unless they had preserved all the things that John observed materially; and no one would be able to be a true imitator of John unless from his boyhood or adolescence he had conformed to him in all things in exterior signs, which certainly is not only impious but absurd.

It is clear, therefore, from the aforementioned things, that when the Lord granted a concession to those wanting to imitate John, he urged them to imitate him in cultivating perfect justice, which he signified by the signs that John employed. Since [John] himself wore the leather belt around his loins to signify that whoever wanted to cultivate the justice of perfect chastity ought to always gird his flesh with the memory of death, then whoever will have done this will be a true imitator of John, even if he will not physically be wearing this belt. And no one can prohibit this spiritual belt to anyone; but any vicar of Christ can prohibit the physical belt according to the truth of the Gospels, that is, as long as evangelical justice requires this.

These aforesaid things are confirmed by sacred Scripture, which clearly teaches that those things that have been set forth by God as a representation of some spiritual truth God does not always want to be observed physically, but rather according to their spiritual significance. Whence, although God gave Jacob two sisters as wives (Gen. 29:16–30), nevertheless he does not now want this to be observed carnally, but rather [he wants] that every prelate should spiritually join himself to both lives—that is, the active and the contemplative. Because of which the apostle says that *all things happened in figure* (1 Cor. 10:11) at that time, because of our understanding of spiritual things.

Similarly, God once commanded the fathers that they pray on the mountain (Deut. 27:4,12) and then later in the Temple that he ordered to be built in Jerusalem, in which he promised audience to all those who would pray (3 Kings 8:29–30). However, he expressly said to the Samaritan that neither in one place nor the other should God be worshipped, but true worshippers would worship him *in spirit and truth* (John 4:23–24); wanting to indicate that after the appearance of the mountain—that is Christ who was figured by this mountain—and the appearance[14] of the figurative temple—that is, this same Christ and his church—in these things and not in figures God would be worshipped.

[IV] Because chastity indeed should be perfectly cultivated, the true imitators of John ought to avoid all occasions or opportunities of carnal uncleanness, as much in the mind as the body, as much as he himself did this. Thus those imitating him will truly announce Christ *in the spirit of Elijah* (Luke 1:17).

The end. Blessed be our Lord Jesus Christ. Amen.

NOTES

Introduction

1. This was the original title of the work. The longer, self-contradictory title given in the unique late fifteenth-century French manuscript (Chantilly, Condé, F xiv 26), "Le mirouer des simples ames qui en vouloir et en desire demourent," was based on medieval misunderstanding and modern mispunctuation of a passage in the *Mirror*. See Luisa Muraro, "*Le mirour des simples ames* de Marguerite Porete: Les avatars d'un titre," *Ons geestelijk erf* 70 (1996): 3–9, and further evidence in Robert E. Lerner, "New Light on the *Mirror of Simple Souls*," *Speculum* 85 (2010): 101–2.

2. The work was known in its Middle English version as early as 1911, published in a modernized English translation in 1927, and also discussed by several Hungarian scholars (as early as 1871) in the context of a mistaken attribution to the blessed Marguerite of Hungary. Not until Romana Guarnieri's announcement in 1946, however, was the condemned "heretic" Marguerite Porete identified as the author of the *Mirror of Simple Souls*. For a survey of early work on Marguerite and the *Mirror* before 1946, see Romana Guarnieri's "Prefazia storica" to *Lo specchio della anime semplici,* by Marguerite Porete, trans. Giovanna Fozzer (Milan: Edizioni San Paolo, 1994), 8–11. For a recounting of her discovery, see Romana Guarnieri, "Quando si dice, il caso!" *Bailamme: Rivista di spiritualità e politica* 8 (1990): 45–55. For a detailed description of scholarly activity on Marguerite and her book from 1946 through the 1960s, see Michael G. Sargent, "Medieval and Modern Readership of Marguerite Porete's *Mirouer des simples âmes*: The Old French and English Traditions," in *Middle English Religious Writing in Practice: Texts, Readers and Transformations,* ed. Nicole Rice (Turnhout: Brepols, forthcoming). In a provocative article, Lydia Wegener has recently wondered whether the text condemned in Paris in 1310 was really the *Mirror of Simple Souls* and whether (in turn) Marguerite Porete was really the author of the *Mirror*. See Lydia Wegener, "Freiheitsdiskurs und Beginenverfolgung um 1308: Der Fall der Marguerite Porete,"

in *1308: Eine Topographie historischer Gleichzeitigkeit,* ed. Andreas Speer and David Wirmer (Berlin: Walter de Gruyter, 2010), 199–236. To my mind, however, neither attribution is in serious doubt.

    3. For the French edition by Romana Guarnieri and the Latin edition by Paul Verdeyen, see *Margaretae Porete Speculum simplicium animarum / Marguerite Porete, Le mirouer des simples ames,* CCCM 69 (Turnhout: Brepols, 1986). Guarnieri's earlier edition is in "Il movimento del Libero Spirito," in *Archivio italiano per la storia della pietà,* vol. 4 (Rome: Edizioni di Storia et Letteratura, 1965), 501–636. Generally on modern translations, see Lerner, "New Light," 91. Bernard McGinn and a generation of his doctoral students from the Divinity School of the University of Chicago have been responsible for much of the best English-language intellectual work on Marguerite's thought; see, for example, Bernard McGinn, *The Flowering of Mysticism: Men and Women in the New Mysticism, 1200–1350* (New York: Crossroad, 1998); Bernard McGinn, ed., *Meister Eckhart and the Beguine Mystics: Hadewijch of Brabant, Mechthild of Magdeburg, and Marguerite Porete* (New York: Continuum, 1994); Amy Hollywood, *The Soul as Virgin Wife: Mechthild of Magdeburg, Marguerite Porete, and Meister Eckhart* (Notre Dame: University of Notre Dame Press, 1995); Joanne Maguire Robinson, *Nobility and Annihilation in Marguerite Porete's Mirror of Simple Souls* (Albany: SUNY Press, 2001); and Robin Anne O'Sullivan, "The School of Love: Marguerite Porete's Mirror of Simple Souls," *Journal of Medieval History* 32 (2006): 143–62. Essential works from a literary perspective include (but are certainly not limited to) Barbara Newman, "*La mystique courtoise*: Thirteenth-Century Beguines and the Art of Love," in *From Virile Woman to WomanChrist: Studies in Medieval Religion and Literature* (Philadelphia: University of Pennsylvania Press, 1995), 137–67, and "The Mirror and the Rose: Marguerite Porete's Encounter with the *Dieu d'amours,*" in *The Vernacular Spirit: Essays on Medieval Religious Literature,* ed. Renate Blumenfeld-Kosinski, Duncan Robertson, and Nancy Bradley Warren (New York: Palgrave, 2002), 105–23; Nicholas Watson, "Melting into God the English Way: Deification in the Middle English Version of Marguerite Porete's *Mirouer des simples âmes anienties,*" in *Prophets Abroad: The Reception of Continental Holy Women in Late-Medieval England,* ed. Rosalynn Voaden (Woodbridge: D. S. Brewer, 1996), 19–49; Kathryn Kerby-Fulton, *Books under Suspicion: Censorship and Tolerance of Revelatory Writing in Late Medieval England* (Notre Dame: University of Notre Dame Press, 2006), ch. 7; Suzanne Kocher, *Allegories of Love in Marguerite Porete's "Mirror of Simple Souls"* (Turnhout: Brepols, 2008); and most recently Wendy Rachele Terry, *Seeing Marguerite in the "Mirror": A Linguistic Analysis of Porete's "Mirror of Simple Souls"* (Leuven: Peeters, 2011). For an analysis of work on Marguerite from the

perspectives of women's studies and philosophy, see Michela Pereira, "Margherita Porete nello specchio degli studi recenti," *Mediaevistik* 11 (1998): 71–96. A full bibliography of work on Marguerite and her *Mirror* is now being maintained by Prof. Zan Kocher at http://margueriteporete.net.

4. Robert E. Lerner, "An 'Angel of Philadelphia' in the Reign of Philip the Fair: The Case of Guiard of Cressonessart," in *Order and Innovation in the Middle Ages: Essays in Honor of Joseph R. Strayer,* ed. William C. Jordan, Bruce McNab, and Teofilo F. Ruiz (Princeton: Princeton University Press, 1976), 343–64.

5. For instance, at this writing the reader can, if she wishes, become a "fan" of Marguerite Porete on Facebook; Marguerite makes a cameo appearance in Ken Follett's recent best seller *World without End*; and see the remarks by Lerner, "New Light," 91–92.

6. Henry Charles Lea, *A History of the Inquisition of the Middle Ages* (1887; repr., New York: Russell, 1955), 2:122–23.

7. Thomas Werner, *Den Irrtum liquidieren: Bücherverbrennungen im Mittelalter* (Göttingen: Vandenhoeck und Ruprecht, 2007), 119.

8. Barbara Newman, *God and the Goddesses: Vision, Poetry, and Belief in the Middle Ages* (Philadelphia: University of Pennsylvania Press, 2003), 306. Although I will argue that Marguerite's execution was technically for obstinate behavior, not for intellectual error, this judgment still rings true in a larger sense.

9. Robert E. Lerner, *The Heresy of the Free Spirit in the Later Middle Ages* (1972; repr., Notre Dame: University of Notre Dame Press, 1991). The Council of Vienne will be addressed briefly in Epilogue III.

10. Walter Simons, *Cities of Ladies: Beguine Communities in the Medieval Low Countries, 1200–1565* (Philadelphia: University of Pennsylvania Press, 2001); Dyan Elliot, *Proving Woman: Female Spirituality and Inquisitorial Culture in the Later Middle Ages* (Princeton: Princeton University Press, 2004).

11. See David Burr, *The Spiritual Franciscans: From Protest to Persecution in the Century after Saint Francis* (University Park: Pennsylvania State University Press, 2001), and Louisa A. Burnham, *So Great a Light, So Great a Smoke: The Beguin Heretics of Languedoc* (Ithaca: Cornell University Press, 2008).

12. See Alain Demurger, *The Last Templar: The Tragedy of Jacques de Molay,* updated ed., trans. Antonia Nevill (London: Profile Books, 2009); 201; Malcolm Barber, *The Trial of the Templars,* 2nd ed. (Cambridge: Cambridge University Press, 2006), 282.

13. Although my suggestion of a curse is entirely in jest, I am not the first to feel that there is something odd about the way scholarship on Marguerite has progressed. In 1996 Nicholas Watson observed that "the world of Porete

scholarship over the last six decades has looked all too like something out of Umberto Eco's novel about conspiracy theories, *Foucault's Pendulum*" ("Melting into God," 21).

14. Lea, *History of the Inquisition,* 2:123 and 577–78, where AN J428 no. 19bis is edited and misdated.

15. Lea hired others to copy archival documents while he remained in the United States. For a description of his working methods and the characterization of them as by "remote control," see Lerner, "Angel of Philadelphia," 343–44.

16. Paul Fredericq, *Corpus documentorum inquisitionis haereticae pravitatis Neerlandicae,* vol. 1 (Ghent: Vuylsteke, 1889), 155–57. The translation, by Richard E. Barton, can be found under the title "The Trial of Marguerite Porete (1310)" at www.uncg.edu/~rebarton/margporete.htm. Because this translation used Lea's occasionally flawed edition, it also perpetuated several other unfortunate errors, most notably giving the impression that William of Paris's sentence of 31 May directly ordered that Marguerite Porete be burned (he was in fact ordering that her book be burned). To judge from Francesca Caroline Bussey, "The World on the End of a Reed: Marguerite Porete and the Annihilation of an Identity in Medieval and Modern Representations—a Reassessment" (PhD diss., University of Sydney, 2007), Prof. John O. Ward appears to have circulated his own English translation of some or all of the trial documents to his students, but I have not myself seen this translation. See further the undergraduate essays in John O. Ward and Francesca C. Bussey, eds., *Worshipping Women: Misogyny and Mysticism in the Middle Ages* (Sydney: Department of History, University of Sydney, 1997).

17. Charles-Victor Langlois, "Marguerite Porete," *Revue historique* 54 (1894): 295, 296. Langlois may again have been following Lea here, who referred to "the first formal *auto de fé* of which we have cognizance at Paris, on May 31, 1310" (*History of the Inquisition,* 122–23). But if Lea meant to refer only to the sentencing as the "auto de fé," then it was Langlois who misinterpreted the evidence.

18. The first three are pointed out in Lerner, "Angel of Philadelphia," 343 n. 12, citing Herbert Grundmann, "Ketzerverhöre des Spätmittelalters als quellenkritisches Problem," *Deutsches Archiv für Erforschung des Mittelalters* 21 (1965): 526; Guarnieri, "Movimento del Libero Spirito," 413; and Lerner, *Heresy,* 71. Lerner was able to correct his error in the subsequent University of Notre Dame Press reprint of his book (72). See also Kurt Ruh, "*Le miroir des simples âmes* der Marguerite Porete," *Verbum et Signum* 2 (1975): 371; and Miri Rubin, "Choosing Death? Experiences of Martyrdom in Late Medieval Europe," in *Martyrs and Martyrologies,* ed. Diana Wood, Studies in Church History 30 (Oxford: Blackwell, 1993), 173. In this and the several following notes

I cite the work of excellent scholars only to underline how easily errors can be repeated once they are in print.

19. For the 1311 date, see Gordon Leff, *Heresy in the Later Middle Ages* (Manchester: University of Manchester Press, 1967); for the 1 May 1310 date, see Simons's otherwise invaluable *Cities of Ladies*, 133.

20. Lerner, "Angel of Philadelphia," 345–46. A notable example of accuracy earlier in the twentieth century is Ag. de Guimaräes, "Hervé Noël (d. 1323): Étude biographique," *Archivum fratrum praedicatorum* 8 (1938): 55 n. 124, where correct dates are given.

21. Paul Verdeyen, "Le procès d'inquisition contre Marguerite Porete et Guiard de Cressonessart (1309–1310)," *Revue d'histoire ecclésiastique* 81 (1986): 47–94.

22. Verdeyen's "Procès d'inquisition" dates AN J428 no. 15a incorrectly on page 50 and elsewhere. Verdeyen simply read "quarto" for the pontifical year, whereas the manuscript clearly reads "quinto." Among the studies that follow Verdeyen's mistaken dating to 1309 are Winfried Trusen, *Der Prozess gegen Meister Eckhart: Vorgeschichte, Verlauf und Folgen* (Paderborn: Ferdinand Schöningh, 1988), 37; Marie Bertho, *Le miroir des ames simples et anéanties de Marguerite Porete: Une vie blessée d'amour* (Paris: Découvrir, 1993), 131–43; Luisa Muraro, *Lingua materna, scienza divina: Scritti sulla filosofia mistica di Margherita Porete* (Naples: M. D'Auria Editore, 1995), 21; Guarnieri, "Prefazia storica," 14–16; Camille Bérubé, *L'amour de dieu selon Jean Duns Scot, Porète, Eckhart, Benoît Canfield et les Capucins* (Rome: Istituto Storico dei Cappuccini, 1997), 15; Irene Leicht, *Marguerite Porete: Eine fromme Intellektuelle und die Inquisition* (Freiburg: Herder, 1999), 337 ff.; Luc Richir, *Marguerite Porete, une âme au travail de l'Un* (Brussels: Éditions OUSIA, 2002), 10; Claire Le Brun-Gouanvic, "Le *Mirouer des simples ames aneanties* de Marguerite Porete (vers 1300) et le *Speculum simplicium animarum* (vers 1310): Procès d'inquisition et traduction," in *D'une écriture à l'autre: Les femmes et la traduction sous l'Ancien Régime*, ed. Jean-Philippe Beaulieu (Ottawa: Presses de l'Université d'Ottawa, 2004), 84; O'Sullivan, "School of Love," 147; and Werner, *Irrtum liquidieren*, 50. These are all nevertheless excellent studies from which I have benefited. Verdeyen repeats his error in Verdeyen and Guarnieri, *Margaretae Porete Speculum*, v.

23. Confusion over this date has led to mistakes in chronological accounts of the careers of some of the masters of theology involved. In his essential *Répertoire des maîtres en théologie de Paris au XIIIe siècle* (Paris: Vrin, 1933), Palémon Glorieux routinely gave the date of 11 April 1309 for the theologians' consultation, presumably out of confusion over new-style versus old-style dating. This was of course well before Verdeyen's work and may have indirectly influenced the latter's thinking. An example of a first-rate scholar of the Univer-

sity of Paris lured into this misdating is William J. Courtenay, "The Parisian Faculty of Theology in the Late Thirteenth and Early Fourteenth Centuries," in *Nach der Verurteilung von 1277: Philosophie und Theologie an der Universität von Paris im letzten Viertel des 13. Jahrhunderts,* ed. Jan A. Aertsen, Kent Emery Jr., and Andreas Speer (Berlin: Walter de Gruyter, 2001), 243.

24. Edmund Colledge, J. C. Marler, and Judith Grant, ed. and trans., *The Mirror of Simple Souls,* by Margaret Porette *[sic]* (Notre Dame: University of Notre Dame Press, 1999), xxxvi–xxxvii. The understanding here that this document dates from 30 May is confirmed when the sentence (31 May) is referred to as "on the next day" (xxxviii). It should be noted that the other recent English translation of the *Mirror* gets the dates of the documents and process exactly correct. See Ellen L. Babinsky, ed. and trans., *The Mirror of Simple Souls,* by Marguerite Porete (New York: Paulist Press, 1993), 20–24. Another brief but accurate account (following Babinsky and Lerner) is Michael G. Sargent, "The Annihilation of Marguerite Porete," *Viator* 28 (1997): 256–57.

25. For example, Bertho, *Miroir des âmes simples,* 6; Newman, "Mirror and the Rose," 120 nn. 19 and 21; Le Brun-Gouanvic, "*Mirouer,*" 84; most recently Francesca Caroline Bussey's interesting 2007 doctoral thesis ("World on the End") makes this mistake more than once (see, e.g., 151). Robinson has "by 1306" (*Nobility,* 27), while William Chester Jordan, in *Unceasing Strife, Unending Fear: Jacques de Thérines and the Freedom of the Church in the Age of the Last Capetians* (Princeton: Princeton University Press, 2004), says "1306 or a little before" but then asserts that Bishop Guido burned Marguerite's book in 1305 (33). The preface to Claude Louis-Combet's translation *Le miroir des simples âmes anéanties et qui seulement demeurent en vouloir et désire d'amour* (Grenoble: Millon, 1991), 5, has "en 1305 ou 1306." By contrast, the other modern French translation, by Max Huot de Longchamp, *Le miroir des âmes simples et anéanties et qui seulement demeurent en vouloir et désire d'amour* (Paris: Albin Michel, 1984), 25, has "en 1300," as does Richir, *Marguerite Porete,* 17. Terry, *Seeing Marguerite,* 46, says "1305/6." O'Sullivan, "School of Love," correctly gives the 1296–1306 range (146) but then refers to Marguerite's "condemnation by Bishop Guy de Colmieu in 1306" (159). For a final example of the range of assumptions, see Rubin, "Choosing Death?," which says, "around 1295" (173).

26. The classic work is Herbert Grundmann, *Religious Movements in the Middle Ages,* trans. Steven Rowan (Notre Dame: University of Notre Dame Press, 1996).

27. See, for instance, the recent analysis in Juan Marín, "Annihilation and Deification in Beguine Theology and Marguerite Porete's *Mirror of Simple Souls,*" *Harvard Theological Review* 103 (2010): 89–109.

28. For introductions to these women and their writings, see McGinn, *Flowering of Mysticism,* and Sean L. Field, "Agnes of Harcourt, Felipa of Porcelet, and Marguerite of Oingt: Women Writing about Women at the End of the Thirteenth Century," *Church History* 76 (2007): 298–328.

29. To use categories employed by Bernard McGinn *(Meister Eckhart)* and Barbara Newman (*"Mystique courtoise"*), respectively.

30. See ch. 131 of the *Mirror.*

31. The classic work here is Caroline Walker Bynum, *Holy Feast and Holy Fast: The Religious Significance of Food to Medieval Women* (Berkeley: University of California Press, 1987).

32. Those needing a fuller but still concise recent analysis might consult Michael Sargent, "Marguerite Porete," in *Medieval Holy Women in the Christian Tradition, c. 1100–1500,* ed. Alistair Minnis and Rosalynn Voaden (Turnhout: Brepols, 2010), 291–312.

33. My translation here takes Colledge, Marler, and Grant, *Mirror of Simple Souls,* as its starting point but modifies it after comparison with the Middle French and Middle English, as well as the modern English translation by Babinsky. I have removed the "character" labels, since they are not found in the Middle English and seem likely to have been added (or at least altered) after Marguerite's lifetime. The chapter numbers and divisions are likewise surely a later addition.

34. Among the most important works here are Catherine M. Mooney, ed., *Gendered Voices: Saints and Their Interpreters* (Philadelphia: University of Pennsylvania Press, 1999), and John W. Coakley, *Women, Men, and Spiritual Power: Female Saints and Their Male Collaborators* (New York: Columbia University Press, 2005).

35. Bertho is an exception in suggesting that she must have had a confessor (*Miroir des âmes simples,* 38–40).

36. Newman, *God and the Goddesses,* 305–6, where the remark is made in the context of Marguerite's death.

37. For a coherent introduction to Joachim's life and thought, see Robert E. Lerner, *The Feast of Saint Abraham: Medieval Millenarians and the Jews* (Philadelphia: University of Pennsylvania Press, 2001), 5–22. Other essential works include Bernard McGinn, *The Calabrian Abbot: Joachim of Fiore in the History of Western Thought* (New York: Macmillan, 1985), and Marjorie Reeves, *Joachim of Fiore and the Prophetic Future: A Medieval Study in Historical Thinking,* rev. ed (Phoenix Mill: Sutton, 1999).

38. Robert E. Lerner, "The Medieval Return to the Thousand Year Sabbath," in *The Apocalypse in the Middle Ages,* ed. Richard K. Emmerson and Bernard McGinn (Ithaca: Cornell University Press, 1992), 51–71. For a wider

survey, see Robert E. Lerner, "Millennialism," in *The Encyclopedia of Apoca-lypticism,* ed. Bernard McGinn, John Joseph Collins, and Stephen J. Stein (New York: Continuum, 1998), 2:326–60.

39. Joachim himself thought this time would be short, but those who de-veloped his ideas moved toward the possibility of a longer "Sabbath," culmi-nating in John of Rupescissa's pronouncement in 1349 that it would last for a literal thousand years. See Lerner, "Medieval Return."

40. I am following Lerner, *Feast of Saint Abraham,* who lays out Joachim's "three big ideas," 12–19.

41. Kurt-Victor Selge has argued that this supposedly lost treatise was re-ally the *Psalterium decem cordarum.* See David Burr's review of *Joachim von Fiore, Psalterium decem cordarum,* ed. Kurt-Victor Selge, *Speculum* 85 (2010): 978–80.

42. On Gerardino, see Lerner, *Feast of Saint Abraham,* 43–48.

43. For a succinct summary, see Joseph R. Strayer, "France: The Holy Land, the Chosen People, and the Most Christian King," in *Action and Con-viction in Early Modern Europe: Essays in Memory of E. H. Harbison,* ed. Theodore K. Rabb and Jerrold E. Seigel (Princeton: Princeton University Press, 1969), 3–16.

44. Sean L. Field, *Isabelle of France: Capetian Sanctity and Franciscan Identity in the Thirteenth Century* (Notre Dame: University of Notre Dame Press, 2006), and most recently Anne-Hélène Allirot, "Une *beata stirps* au féminin? Autour de quelques saintes reines et princesses royales," in *Une his-toire pour un royaume (XIIe–XVe siècle): Actes du colloque Corpus Regni or-ganisé en hommage à Colette Beaune,* ed. Anne-Hélène Allirot et al. (Paris: Perrin, 2010), 142–51.

45. See the classic work of Joseph R. Strayer, *On the Medieval Origins of the Modern State* (1970; repr., Princeton: Princeton University Press, 2005).

46. Elizabeth A. R. Brown, "The Religion of Royalty: From Saint Louis to Henry IV," in *Creating French Culture: Treasures from the Bibliothèque nationale de France,* ed. Marie-Hélène Tesnière and Prosser Gifford (New Haven: Yale University Press, 1995), 131–48.

47. On the development of Louis's sanctity, see M. Cecilia Gaposch-kin, *The Making of Saint Louis: Kingship, Sanctity, and Crusade in the Later Middle Ages* (Ithaca: Cornell University Press, 2008). The fundamental studies on Philip IV are Jean Favier, *Philippe le Bel,* rev. ed. (1998), reprinted in *Un roi de marbre: Philippe le Bel, Enguerran de Marigny* (Paris: Fayard, 2005) and cited from that latter source for convenience throughout this book; Joseph R. Strayer, *The Reign of Philip IV* (Princeton: Princeton University Press, 1980); and multiple articles by Elizabeth A. R. Brown, especially "The Prince Is Father

of the King: The Character and Childhood of Philip the Fair of France," *Mediaeval Studies* 49 (1987): 282–334, and "Persona et Gesta: The Image and Deeds of the Thirteenth-Century Capetians: The Case of Philip the Fair," *Viator* 19 (1988): 219–46.

48. Brown, "Prince," 315.

49. See Malcolm Barber, "The World Picture of Philip the Fair," *Journal of Medieval History* 8 (1982): 13–27.

50. Strayer, *Reign of Philip IV,* 13, for quotation and general idea of "two religions."

51. Joseph R. Strayer, "Philip the Fair: A 'Constitutional' King," *American Historical Review* 62 (1956): 18–32. The succeeding two quotations are from James Given, "Chasing Phantoms: Philip IV and the Fantastic," in *Heresy and the Persecuting Society in the Middle Ages: Essays on the Work of R.I. Moore,* ed. Michael Frassetto (Leiden: Brill, 2006), 271–89, and the third alludes to the title of Jordan's book *Unceasing Strife.* See also Geoffrey Koziol, "Imagined Enemies and the Later Medieval State: The Failure of France under Philip the Fair," in *Identities and National Formation: Chinese and Western Experiences in the Modern World* (Taipei: Institute of Modern History, 1994), 407–33.

52. For recent interpretations (with earlier bibliography), see Julien Théry, "Allo scoppio del conflitto tra Filippo il Bello di Francia e Bonifacio VIII: L'affare Saisset (1301)," in *I poteri universali e la fondazione dello Studium Urbis: Bonifacio VIII dalla "Unam sanctam" allo "schiaffo" di Anagni,* ed. Giovanni Minnucci (Rome: Monduzzi, 2008), 21–68; and Jeffrey H. Denton, "Bernard Saisset and the Franco-Papal Rift of December 1301," *Revue d'histoire ecclésiastique* 102 (2007): 399–427. Shorter recent accounts include Jordan, *Unceasing Strife,* 5–7, and Favier, *Roi de marbre,* 290–99, 314–15. The larger narrative of the string of "affairs" discussed here has long been shaped by the classic account in Charles-Victor Langlois, *Saint Louis, Philippe le Bel, les derniers Capétiens directs (1226–1328)* (Paris: Tallandier, 1901).

53. Denton, "Bernard Saisset," 408.

54. On Nogaret, see most recently Sébastien Nadiras, "Guillaume de Nogaret et la pratique du pouvoir," in *École nationale des Chartes, Positions des thèses* (Paris, 2003), 161–68; and Favier, *Roi de marbre,* 39–43, 262–64, 335 ff.

55. Jeffrey H. Denton, "The Attempted Trial of Boniface VIII for Heresy," in *Judicial Trials in England and Europe, 1200–1700,* ed. Maureen Mulholland and Brian Pullan with Anne Pullan (Manchester: Manchester University Press, 2003), 117–28.

56. Langlois, *Saint Louis,* 163.

57. William J. Courtenay, "Between Pope and King: The Parisian Letters of Adhesion of 1303," *Speculum* 71 (1996): 577–605.

58. On the evidence for two separate missions given to Nogaret (with his original marching orders in March being more pacific than generally acknowledged), see Jean Coste, "Les deux missions de Guillaume de Nogaret en 1303," *Mélanges de l'École française de Rome, Moyen Âge* 105 (1993): 299–326.

59. A stirring version of these events is found in Favier, *Roi de marbre,* 335–57. See also the classic account by Langlois, *Saint Louis,* 133–71, and Agostino Paravicini Bagliani, *Boniface VIII: Un pape heretique?* (Paris: Payot, 2003), 373–91, 393–98 for Boniface's last days and death.

60. See Céline Balasse, *1306: L'expulsion des juifs du royaume de France* (Brussels: De Boeck, 2008); William Chester Jordan, *The French Monarchy and the Jews: From Philip Augustus to the Last Capetians* (Philadelphia: University of Pennsylvania Press, 1989), 200–213; Jordan, *Unceasing Strife,* 12–13; Langlois, *Saint Louis,* 228–32.

61. As a starting point on the Templars, see Malcolm Barber, *The New Knighthood: A History of the Order of the Temple* (Cambridge: Cambridge University Press, 1994), and for orientation on recent work, Helen J. Nicholson, "The Changing Face of the Templars: Current Trends in Historiography," *History Compass* 8/7 (2010): 653–67.

62. Langlois, *Saint Louis,* 236–43; Strayer, *Reign of Philip IV,* 109, 396; concise account in Marion Melville, *La vie des Templiers,* 2nd ed. (Paris: Gallimard, 1974), 280.

63. See the historiographic survey in Barber, *Trial of the Templars,* 294–311.

64. Indeed, in 1311 Philip would expel from France all the "Lombards" (Italian merchants and moneylenders), just as he had the Jews, continuing this pattern. For a sketch of Philip's difficult financial position in this period, see Elizabeth A. R. Brown, *Customary Aids and Royal Finance in Capetian France: The Marriage Aid of Philip the Fair* (Cambridge, MA: Medieval Academy of America, 1992), 26–33.

65. Most historians reject the charges as fundamentally untrue. This position has been argued convincingly by Malcolm Barber in particular. See also Julien Théry, "Contre-enquête sur un procès," *Histoire* 323 (2007): 40–47, "Le procès des Templiers," in *Prier et combattre: Dictionnaire européen des ordres militaires,* ed. N. Bériou and Ph. Josserand (Paris: Fayard, 2009), 743–50, and "Philippe le Bel, la persécution des 'perfides Templiers' et la pontificalisation de la royauté capétienne," in *L'età dei processi: Inchieste e condanne tra politica e ideologia nel '300. Atti del convegno di studio svoltosi in occasione della XIX edizione del Premio internazionale Ascoli Piceno,* ed. Antonio Rigon and Francesco Veronese (Rome: Istituto Storico Italiano per il Medio Evo, 2009), 65–80, now expanded as "Une heresie d'état: Philippe le Bel, le procès des 'perfides Templiers' et la pontificalisation de la royauté française," *Médiévales* 60 (2011):

157–86; as well as Alan Forey, "Could Alleged Templar Malpractices Have Remained Undetected for Decades?" and Thomas Krämer, "Terror, Torture and the Truth: The Testimonies of the Templars Revisited," both in *The Debate on the Trial of the Templars (1307–1314)*, ed. Jochen Burgtorf, Paul F. Crawford, and Helen J. Nicholson (Farnham: Ashgate, 2010), 11–19 and 71–85 respectively. Some fine historians, however, have argued that while the charges of organized heresy were trumped up, some of the "immoral" practices around a supposedly secret portion of the Templar initiation rite really did take place. See, for example, Jonathan Riley-Smith, "Were the Templars Guilty?" in *The Medieval Crusade*, ed. Susan J. Ridyard (Woodbridge: Boydell, 2004), 107–24; Barbara Frale, "The Chinon Chart: Papal Absolution to the Last Templar, Master Jacques de Molay," *Journal of Medieval History* 30 (2004): 109–34; Favier, *Roi de marbre*, 402 ff.; and Demurger, *Last Templar*, 218. I am unconvinced, however, by this perspective.

66. Barber's *Trial of the Templars* is the standard survey in English, but see now also the essays in Burgtorf, Crawford, and Nicholson, *Debate on the Trial*, and important recent work by Théry, including "Contre-enquête," "Procès des Templiers," "Philippe le Bel, la persécution," and "Hérésie d'état." I thank Prof. Théry for sharing some of his work with me before its publication.

67. See Alain Provost, *Domus diaboli: Un évêque en procès au temps de Philippe le Bel* (Paris: Belin, 2010), as well as "On the Margins of the Templars' Trial: The Case of Bishop Guichard of Troyes," in Burgtorf, Crawford, and Nicholson, *Debate on the Trial*, 117–27. Other classic accounts are Strayer, *Reign of Philip IV*, 300–313; Favier, *Roi de marbre*, 413–18; Langlois, *Saint Louis*, 212–16.

68. Jean Coste, *Boniface VIII en procès: Articles d'accusation et deposition des témoins* (Rome: L'Erma di Bretschneider, 1995).

69. Extending this scope a few years would add Philip's attack on his (supposedly) adulterous daughters-in-law and their lovers in 1314, and even the trials of Enguerran of Marigny and other advisors to the king after Philip's death. See Langlois, *Saint Louis*, 217–24.

70. Jeffrey H. Denton, "Heresy and Sanctity at the Time of Boniface VIII," in *Toleration and Repression in the Middle Ages: In Memory of Lenos Mavrommatis* (Athens: Institute for Byzantine Research, 2002), 141–48.

71. Julien Théry, "Philippe le Bel, pape en son royaume," *L'histoire* 289 (2004): 14–17, "Philippe le Bel, la persécution," and "Hérésie d'état."

72. Théry, "Philippe le Bel, pape," 16.

73. See Hercule Géraud, ed., *Chronique latine de Guillaume de Nangis de 1113 à 1300, avec les continuationes de cette chronique de 1300 à 1368*, new ed. (Paris: Renouard, 1843), 1:340–41; Jules Viard, ed., *Les grandes chroniques*

de France, vol. 8 (Paris: Champion, 1934), 235–36; Gérard de Frachet, *Chron-icon Gerardi de Fracheto et anonyma ejusdem operis continuatio,* in *Recueil des historiens des Gaules et de la France,* vol. 21 (Paris: Imprimerie impériale, 1855), For an analysis, see Lerner, *Heresy,* 70; and Nancy Cacciola, *Discerning Spirits: Divine and Demonic Possession in the Middle Ages* (Ithaca: Cornell University Press, 2003), 124 n. 92.

74. Provost, *Domus diaboli,* 36. The possibility of constructing a compos-ite "Marguerite/Perrote" out of the latter two women is a striking coincidence.

75. This is the convincing argument of Edward Peters's influential work, *Inquisition* (Berkeley: University of California Press, 1989).

76. Richard Kieckhefer, "The Office of Inquisition and Medieval Heresy: The Transition from Personal to Institutional Jurisdiction," *Journal of Eccle-siastical History* 46 (1995): 38.

77. Grundmann, *Religious Movements.* On the popular heresies of the period, see Malcolm Lambert, *Medieval Heresy: Popular Movements from the Gregorian Reform to the Reformation,* 3rd ed. (Oxford: Wiley-Blackwell, 2002), and now Jennifer Kolpacoff Deane, *A History of Medieval Heresy and Inquisition* (Lanham, MD: Rowman and Littlefield, 2011).

78. For an introduction, see C. H. Lawrence, *The Friars: The Impact of the Early Mendicant Movement on Western Society* (London: Longman, 1994).

79. A sober introduction is Henry Ansgar Kelly, "Inquisition and the Prosecution of Heresy: Misconceptions and Abuses," *Church History* 58 (1989): 439–51.

80. Julien Théry, "Fama: L'opinion publique comme preuve judiciaire. Aperçu sur la révolution médiévale inquisitoire (XIIe–XIVe siècle)," in *La preuve en justice de l'antiquité à nos jours,* ed. Bruno Lemesle (Rennes: Presses universitaires de Rennes, 2003), 119–47; Thelma Fenster and Daniel Lord Smail, eds., *Fama: The Politics of Talk and Reputation in Medieval Europe* (Ithaca: Cornell University Press, 2003).

81. William Chester Jordan, *Louis IX and the Challenge of the Crusade* (Princeton: Princeton University Press, 1979), 51–64.

82. See Élisabeth Lalou et al., eds., *Enquêtes menées sous les derniers capé-tiens* (Paris: Centre de resources numériques TELMA, 2007), www.cn-telma .fr/enquetes/.

83. Théry, *"Fama,"* 127 and passim.

84. On the Albigensian Crusade, see most recently Mark Gregory Pegg, *A Most Holy War: The Albigensian Crusade and the Battle for Christendom* (Ox-ford: Oxford University Press, 2008); and the classic study by Joseph R. Strayer, *The Albigensian Crusades* (1972; repr., Ann Arbor: University of Michigan Press, 1992).

85. See Christine Caldwell Ames's analysis of how Dominicans over time reimagined their founder as the first inquisitor, in *Righteous Persecution: Inquisition, Dominicans, and Christianity in the Middle Ages* (Philadelphia: University of Pennsylvania Press, 2009), 94–134; and, for a survey of the relation of Dominicans to the office of inquisitor, Grado Giovanni Merlo, "Il senso delle opere dei frati predicatori in quanto *inquisitores haereticae pravitatis,*" in *Le scritture e le opere degli inquisitori,* Quaderni di stori religiosa 9 (Verona: Cierre, 2002), 9–30. An important new published source is Peter Biller, Caterina Bruschi, and Shelagh Sneddon, eds., *Inquisitors and Heretics in Thirteenth-Century Languedoc: Edition and Translation of Toulouse Inquisition Depositions, 1273–1282* (Leiden: Brill, 2011).

86. See Richard Kieckhefer, *Repression of Heresy in Medieval Germany* (Philadelphia: University of Pennsylvania Press, 1979) and "Office of Inquisition."

87. See, for example, J.-M. Vidal, *Bullaire de l'Inquisition française au XIVe siècle et jusque à la fin du Grand Schisme* (Paris: Letouzey et Ané, 1913), and Lea, *History of the Inquisition,* 2:120–21, 575, for evidence of the Dominican inquisitor Simon Duval operating in Normandy and Orleans in 1276–78, and William of Auxerre in 1285–86 in Champagne. Simon was involved in heresy charges against Siger of Brabant in 1276, but not in Paris itself (Siger was cited to appear in Saint-Quentin). On Simon Duval, see further M. Daunou, "Simon Duval," *Histoire littéraire de la France* 19 (1838): 385–87, and Antoine Dondaine, "Le manuel de l'inquisiteur (1230–1330)," *Archivum fratrum praedicatorum* 17 (1947): 186–92.

88. See Jean-Marie Carbasse, "Les origines de la torture judiciaire en France du XIIe au début du XIVe siècle," in *La torture judiciaire: Approches historiques et juridiques,* ed. Bernard Durand (Lille: Centre d'histoire judiciaire, 2002), 1:381–419; Walter Ullmann, "Reflections on Medieval Torture," in *Law and Jurisdiction in the Middle Ages,* ed. George Garnett (London: Variorum Reprints, 1988), 17:124–37.

89. Walter Ullmann, "The Defence of the Accused in the Medieval Inquisition," in Garnett, *Law and Jurisdiction,* 15:481–89.

90. Dondaine, "Manuel de l'inquisiteur." For a practical example, see the analysis of the earliest known inquisitor's manual, from 1248–49, in Peters, *Inquisition,* 58–60; and Walter L. Wakefield, *Heresy, Crusade and Inquisition in Southern France, 1100–1250* (Berkeley: University of California Press, 1974), 250–58 for English translation of the document (more clearly laid out than the translation of the same document in Edward Peters, ed., *Heresy and Authority in Medieval Europe: Documents in Translation* [Philadelphia: University of Pennsylvania Press, 1980]).

91. See, for example, Mark Gregory Pegg, *The Corruption of Angels: The Great Inquisition of 1245–1246* (Princeton: Princeton University Press, 2001), and Lerner, *Heresy.*

92. Henry Ansgar Kelly, "Inquisitorial Due Process and the Status of Secret Crimes," in *Proceedings of the Eighth International Congress of Medieval Canon Law,* ed. Stanley Chodorow (Vatican City: Biblioteca Apostolica Vaticana, 1992), 407–27.

93. James B. Given, *Inquisition and Medieval Society: Power, Discipline and Resistance in Languedoc* (Ithaca: Cornell University Press, 1997), 71–76.

94. Ames, *Righteous Persecution.* On inquisitors' own perceptions of their task, see now Karen Sullivan, *The Inner Lives of Medieval Inquisitors* (Chicago: University of Chicago Press, 2011).

95. Pegg, *Corruption of Angels,* 126. On the other hand, we do not know how many people they truly interviewed in total, because the two registers that survive (copied by two other Dominican inquisitors between 1258 and 1263, now Toulouse, Bibliothèque municipale, ms. 609) were part of an original set of ten (22).

96. Given, *Inquisition and Medieval Society,* 69–70.

97. A central point of Given's *Inquisition and Medieval Society.*

98. See Gaposchkin, *Making of Saint Louis,* 81–82, 119–23.

99. Courtenay, "Between Pope and King."

100. See J. A. Watt, trans., *On Royal and Papal Power,* by John of Paris (Toronto: Pontifical Institute of Mediaeval Studies, 1971). "Ablest" description on page 11. For a perspective that questions the influence of John's treatise, see Chris Jones, *Eclipse of Empire? Perceptions of the Western Empire and Its Rulers in Late-Medieval France* (Turnhout: Brepols, 2007), 238–46. For another aspect of John's career, and his engagement with Arnau of Vilanova, see Robert E. Lerner, *The Powers of Prophecy: The Cedar of Lebanon Vision from the Mongol Onslaught to the Dawn of the Enlightenment* (Berkeley: University of California Press, 1983), 63–66.

101. A concise introduction is John W. Baldwin, *The Scholastic Culture of the Middle Ages, 1000–1300* (1971; repr., Prospect Heights, IL: Waveland Press, 1997).

102. Sophia Menache, "La naissance d'une nouvelle source d'autorité: L'université de Paris," *Revue historique* 268 (1982): 305–27. See more recently William J. Courtenay, "Learned Opinion and Royal Justice: The Role of Paris Masters of Theology during the Reign of Philip the Fair," in *Law and the Illicit in Medieval Europe,* ed. Ruth Mazo Karras, Joel Kaye, and E. Ann Matter (Philadelphia: University of Philadelphia Press, 2008), 149–63; and Jürgen Miethke, "Philippe le Bel von Frankreich und die Universität von Paris: Zur

Rolle der Intellektuellen am Beginn des 14. Jahrhunderts," in Speer and Wirmer, *1308*, 182–98.

103. Gabrielle M. Spiegel, *The Chronicle Tradition of Saint-Denis: A Survey* (Brookline, MA: Classical Folia Editions, 1978), 7. On Saint-Denis in the later thirteenth century, see William Chester Jordan, *A Tale of Two Monasteries: Westminster and Saint-Denis in the Thirteenth Century* (Princeton: Princeton University Press, 2009).

104. See Spiegel, *Chronicle Tradition*, 98–108.

105. Previously described in Lerner, "Angel of Philadelphia," and in Verdeyen, "Le procès," 49–50.

106. Elizabeth A. R. Brown is also preparing a new study of these documents, which will no doubt greatly advance our understanding of their production.

Chapter 1. Background to a Beguine, Becoming an Angel

1. For a recent reconstruction of Marguerite's life, see Kocher, *Allegories of Love*, 21–44.

2. For instance at the end of ch. 131, where the *Mirror* speaks of emerging "out of the days of my childhood" *(hors de mon enffance yssir)*. This passage is intended more in a spiritual than a literal sense but still conveys the idea of maturing over time. See Guarnieri, "Prefazia storica," 29, for a reasonable argument that puts Marguerite's birth between 1250 and 1260.

3. On John of "Querayn" and the identification of this place name with modern Quérénaing (which I owe to Walter Simons and Zan Kocher), see chapter 2.

4. Lerner, "New Light"; Geneviève Hasenohr, "La tradition du *Miroir des simples âmes* au XVe siècle: De Marguerite Porete (†1310) à Marguerite de Navarre," *Comptes rendus des séances de l'Académie des inscriptions et belles-lettres* 4 (1999): 1347–66.

5. Jean Gerson, "De distinctione verarum revelationum a falsis," in *Oeuvres complètes,* vol. 3, ed. Palémon Glorieux (Paris: Desclée et Cie, 1962), 51, refers to mistaken ideas of beguines and beghards such as those found "in quodam libello incredibili pene subtilitate ab una foemina composito, quae Maria de Valenciennes dicebatur."

6. Leicht, *Marguerite Porete,* provides a survey of some of the relevant facts about Valenciennes in Marguerite's time and relates them to concepts expressed in the *Mirror,* 69–79. For a survey of Valenciennes's economy, see Gérard Sivery, "Commerce et marchands à Valenciennes à la fin du Moyen

Âge," in *Valenciennes et les anciens Pay-Bas: Mélanges offerts à Paul Lefrancq* (Valenciennes: Cercle archéologique et historique de Valenciennes, 1976), 71–80. Estimates of Valenciennes's medieval population vary, but Simons includes it in a list of towns that reached populations of between twenty thousand and forty thousand by the early fourteenth century (*Cities of Ladies,* 4). For an important new study considering Marguerite in her native context, see John Van Engen, "Marguerite (Porete) of Hainaut and the Medieval Low Countries," in *Marguerite Porete et le "Miroir des simples âmes": Perspectives historiques, philosophiques et littéraires,* ed. Sylvain Piron, Robert E. Lerner, and Sean L. Field (Paris: Vrin, forthcoming).

7. Bernadette Carpentier, "Le béguinage Sainte-Élisabeth de Valenciennes, de sa fondation au XVIème siècle," *Mémoires du Cercle archéologique et historique de Valenciennes* 4 (1959): 104.

8. On the relationship between Philip IV, the counts of Hainaut, and the city of Valenciennes, see most recently Jean-Marie Moeglin, "La frontière introuvable: L'Ostrevant," in Allirot et al., *Histoire pour un royaume,* 381–92, as well as Étienne Delcambre, *Les relations de la France avec le Hainaut, depuis l'avènement de Jean II d'Avesnes, comte de Hainaut, jusqu'à la conclusion de l'alliance franco-hennuyère (1280–1297)* (Mons: Union des Imprimeries, 1930); Favier, *Roi de marbre,* 270–72; Jones, *Eclipse of Empire?,* 279–83; Jules Viard, "L'Ostrevant, enquête au sujet de la frontière française sous Philippe VI de Valois," *Bibliothèque de l'École des Chartes* 82 (1921): 316–29; Georges Lizerand, "Philippe le Bel et l'Empire au temps de Rodolphe de Habsbourg (1285–1291)," *Revue historique* 142 (1923): 161–91; and Simon Le Boucq's seventeenth-century history (which preserves and transcribes several relevant sources) as edited in A. La Croix, *Annales du Hainaut: Guerre de Jean d'Avesnes contre la ville de Valenciennes, 1290–1297; et Mémoires sur l'histoire, la juridiction civile et le droit public, XI.me-XVIII.e siècle* (Brussels: A. Vandale, 1846).

9. See the informative discussion in Kocher, *Allegories of Love,* 23–26.

10. In Paris, Remont Porete lived in the Parish of Saint-Merri, on the rue de Blans-Mantiaus. (It is perhaps worth noting that Ysabieau d'Olovier "beguine" lived a few houses down from him.) Jehan Poret, a mercer, lived on the rue de Quiquenpoist, in the same parish. See Karl Michaëlsson, *Le livre de la taille de Paris l'an de grace 1313* (Göteborg: Wettergren och Kerbers Förlag, 1951), 115, 125.

11. See Alan Hindley, Frederick W. Langley, and Brian J. Levy, *Old French-English Dictionary* (Cambridge: Cambridge University Press, 2000), 490.

12. Ch. 96, though it is not entirely certain that the reference is autobiographical. On the question of whether Marguerite was really ever a beggar, see Leicht, *Marguerite Porete,* 112.

13. Social links between the two may in any case have been fairly close. Juliet Vale says that "the upper echelons of Valenciennois society" at this time were characterized by an "easy intercourse between patrician families and the rurally based nobility." See *Edward III and Chivalry: Chivalric Society and Its Context, 1270–1350* (Woodbridge: Boydell, 1982), 42.

14. See Robinson, *Nobility and Annihilation*, xii and passim; Leicht, *Marguerite Porete*, 77, also sees evidence in Marguerite's book for a mentality reflecting the experiences of Valenciennes's patrician class. On the theme of spiritual nobility, see also Mario Meliadò, "La dottrina mistica della nobilità: Margherita Porete e Meister Eckhart," *Rivista di ascetica e mistica* 33 (2008): 417–61.

15. Lerner, "New Light," 108. Tanya Stabler has pointed to an example of a Parisian beguine bequeathing a book of hours to a fellow beguine in 1408. See "Now She Is Martha, Now She Is Mary: Beguine Communities in Medieval Paris (1250–1470)" (PhD diss., University of California, Santa Barbara, 2007), 91, 201. Cheaper, plain *primers* or books of hours were surely available in the later Middle Ages, but ownership of such a book would still indicate access to a certain level of material support. See Marjorie Curry Woods, "Shared Books: Primers, Psalters, and the Adult Acquisition of Literacy among Devout Laywomen and Women in Orders in Late Medieval England," in *New Trends in Feminine Spirituality: The Holy Women of Liège and Their Impact,* ed. Juliette Dor, Lesley Johnson, and Jocelyn Wogan-Browne (Turnhout: Brepols, 1999), 177–93. Moreover, Walter Simons points out that devotional books could be passed around by beguines or left to them by pious testators. See "Staining the Speech of Things Divine: The Uses of Literacy in Medieval Beguine Communities," in *The Voice of Silence: Women's Literacy in a Men's Church,* ed. Thérèse de Hemptinne and María Eugenia Góngora (Turnhout: Brepols, 2004), 85–110.

16. Newman, "*Mystique courtoise*" and "Mirror and the Rose."

17. Vale notes that "knowledge of chivalric and romance themes had permeated bourgeois society at Valenciennes." See *Edward III and Chivalry*, 43.

18. For arguments about the possibilities for beguine learning, see Simons, "Staining the Speech"; Penelope Galloway, "Life, Learning, and Wisdom: The Forms and Functions of Beguine Education," in *Medieval Monastic Education,* ed. George Ferzoco and Carolyn Muessig (London: Leicester University Press, 2000), 153–65; and Stabler, "Now She Is Martha," 196–203.

19. Newman, "Mirror and the Rose." See also the evidence for bourgeois familiarity with the Alexander legend at Valenciennes given by Vale, *Edward III and Chivalry*, 42–43. Kocher, *Allegories of Love*, 56–79, shows Marguerite's familiarity with trouvère lyrics and suggests Chrétien. Terry, *Seeing Marguerite*, 80–95, surveys this issue as well.

20. Possible borrowings from Augustine, Bernard of Clairvaux, Bonaventure, Richard of Saint-Victor, and William of Saint-Thierry are noted in Simons, "Staining the Speech," 94, as taken from the "index auctorum" at the end of the CCCM critical edition of *The Mirror of Simple Souls* (Guarnieri and Verdeyen, *Margaretae Porete Speculum,* 412). Regarding pseudo-Dionysius, see Colledge, Marler, and Grant, *Mirror of Simple Souls,* 94 n. 3, 99 n. 4; on Augustine and Bonaventure, see Terry, *Seeing Marguerite,* 57–76; also Sylvain Piron's tracing of the thirteenth-century theological invention of terminology around the Latin word *adnichilatio* in his "Adnichilatio," in *Mots médiévaux offerts à Ruedi Imbach,* ed. I. Atucha et al. (Porto: Fédération internationale des instituts d'études médiévales, 2011), 23–31.

21. A point made by Bertho, *Miroir des âmes simples,* 35, since *clericus* and *litteratus* both had the meaning of "literate in Latin."

22. See the "Index biblicus" in the Guarnieri and Verdeyen, *Margaretae Porete Speculum* (411); more generally, Jonathan Juilfs, "Reading the Bible Differently: Appropriations of Biblical Authority in an Heretical Mystical Text, Marguerite Porete's *The Mirror of Simple Souls,*" *Religion and Literature* 42 (2010): 77–100.

23. Simons, *Cities of Ladies,* 80–85; O'Sullivan, "School of Love," 147–49. Kocher, *Allegories of Love,* suggests that Marguerite may have known the writings of Hadewijch and Beatrice of Nazareth, though without addressing the question of whether Marguerite could have read Middle Dutch.

24. Carpentier, "Béguinage Sainte-Élisabeth," 146; Simons, *Cities of Ladies,* 81; Bertho, *Miroir des âmes simples,* 38.

25. Carpentier, "Béguinage Sainte-Élisabeth," 147–48. An inventory from 1485 reveals that the beguinage did possess books, mentioning "trois livres en roman dont l'un est le livre Saint Bernard et les deux autres de sermon" (157). Simons, "Staining the Speech," 98–100, points out that because beguines could own their own books and did not usually compile corporate libraries (or catalogs) it is hard to identify surviving books that could have belonged to beguinages.

26. Sources calling Marguerite a beguine include AN J428 no. 19 and 19bis (twice); the *Grandes chroniques de France* (where she is labeled a *beguine clergesse*); John of Outremeuse's chronicle (which depends on the *Grandes chroniques*); and John Baconthorp's Sentence Commentary. See Appendices A and B for these texts.

27. Simons, *Cities of Ladies,* 48–60.

28. Ibid., ix. Jennifer Deane, "Beguines Reconsidered: Historiographical Problems and New Directions," *Monastic Matrix* (2008), Commentaria 3461, http://monasticmatrix.org/commentaria/article.php?textId=3461, remarks on

how difficult scholars have found it to describe beguines in terms of what they were, rather than what they were not.

29. Classic examples of early thirteenth-century attitudes are Jacques of Vitry's reverence for Marie of Oignies and the textual promotion provided by the Dominican Thomas of Cantimpré's lives of other beguines and like-minded holy women from the Low Countries. See Simons, *Cities of Ladies,* 38–39, and on the wider ideological reasons why churchmen "sponsored" beguines and their particular brand of piety, Elliot, *Proving Woman,* 47–84. For primary sources, see Anneke B. Mulder-Bakker, ed., *Mary of Oignies: Mother of Salvation* (Turnhout: Brepols, 2006), and Barbara Newman, ed., *The Collected Saints' Lives,* by Thomas of Cantimpré (Turnhout: Brepols, 2008). On later thirteenth-century suspicion, see Simons, *Cities of Ladies,* 118–37.

30. For this famous passage, see Autbert Stroick, ed., "*Collectio de scandalis ecclesiae.* Nova editio," *Archivum Franciscanum historicum* 24 (1931): 61–62.

31. See the discussion in Leicht, *Marguerite Porete,* 111–17, focusing largely on material found in the *Mirror,* chs. 96 and 97.

32. See Tanya Stabler's remark that there is little reason to assume that Marguerite could not have lived in a beguinage, in "What's in a Name? Clerical Representations of Parisian Beguines (1200–1328)," *Journal of Medieval History* 33 (2007): 62 n. 11. It should be noted that beguines in larger court beguinages were not necessarily more wealthy or even more secure than those in smaller residences, a point made by Bertho, *Miroir des âmes simples,* 28. Indeed, Stabler has shown that in Paris the beguines living in small groups outside the grand beguinage were often more prosperous because of their integration into the economy of silk production. See "Now She Is Martha," ch. 3.

33. Most famously in Ernest W. McDonnell, *The Beguines and Beghards in Medieval Culture: With Special Emphasis on the Belgian Scene* (New York: Octagon, 1969), 367, 90–92.

34. For example, Robinson, *Nobility and Annihilation,* 28–29, veers in this direction even as she justifiably criticizes McDonnell. Wegener, "Freiheitsdiskurs und Beginenverfolgung," offers a recent, sophisticated version of this argument.

35. Colledge, Marler, and Grant, *Mirror of Simple Souls,* xlviii (introduction), echoed in the same volume by Kent Emery Jr.'s preface (xi).

36. Ch. 122: "Amis, que diront beguines / et gens de religion / Quant ilz orront l'excellence de vostre divine chançon? / Beguines dient que je erre / presteres, clers et prescheurs / Augustins, et carmes / et les freres mineurs / Pource que j'escri de l'estre de l'affinee Amour." But refuting this logic, see Leicht's judicious comments in *Marguerite Porete,* 92, with which I would agree. See also her review of the whole question of whether Marguerite was a

beguine (107–11). As further proof of this point, one could note that Hadewijch's writings clearly reveal tensions between beguines and criticism by some beguines of others. See, for example, "Letter 29" in the translation by Mother Columba Hart, *Hadewijch: The Complete Works* (New York: Paulist Press, 1980), 114–15. I thank Walter Simons for this observation.

37. See the sensible assessments of Kocher, *Allegories of Love*, 37–38; Leicht, *Marguerite Porete*, 107–8; Bertho, *Miroir des âmes simples*, 27–29; and Gwendolyn Bryant, "The French Heretic: Marguerite Porete," in *Medieval Women Writers*, ed. Katharina M. Wilson (Athens: University of Georgia Press, 1984), 206–7.

38. Stabler, "What's in a Name?"

39. On royal support, see Stabler, "Now She Is Martha," ch. 1; McDonnell, *Beguines and Beghards*, 224–40, and Babinsky's brief survey in the introduction to her translation of the *Mirror*, 13–17, which is based on Léon le Grand's still useful study "Les béguines de Paris," *Mémoire de la société de l'histoire de Paris et de l'Ile-de-France* 20 (1893): 295–357 (305 for royal support through the 1280s).

40. Stabler, "Now She Is Martha," 22, 46–49.

41. Nicole Bériou, "La prédication au béguinage de Paris pendant l'année liturgique 1272–1273," *Recherches augustiniennes* 13 (1978): 105–29; see also Stabler, "What's in a Name?" For early evidence of Dominican involvement with the Parisian beguines, see Stabler, "Now She Is Martha," 52.

42. Stabler, "What's in a Name?" 68, and "Now She Is Martha," ch. 3.

43. A modern specialist in a technical field, for example, might reach out to a wider audience while acknowledging that her fellow specialists would not welcome her ideas. This would hardly provide evidence that she was not in fact a specialist in that field.

44. Nicole Bériou, "Robert de Sorbon, le prud'homme et le béguin," *Comptes-rendus des séances de l'année de l'Académie des inscriptions et belles-lettres* 2 (1994): 469.

45. On the larger question of names adopted by and assigned to lay religious women in this period, see the essays in *Labels, Libels, and Lay Religious Women in Northern Medieval Europe*, ed. Jennifer Kolpakoff Deane, Hildo von Engen, and Letha Boehringer (Turnhout: Brepols, forthcoming). For my own more detailed argument supporting the assertions given here, see my contribution to that volume, "Being a Beguine in France, ca. 1300."

46. For more detail, see Carpentier, "Béguinage Sainte-Élisabeth." The key facts are summarized in Simons, *Cities of Ladies*, 299–300, and Bernard Delmaire, "Les béguines dans le Nord de la France au premier siècle de leur histoire (vers 1230–vers 1350)," in *Les religieuses en France au XIIIe siècle*, ed.

Michel Parisse (Nancy: Presses universitaires de Nancy, 1989), 161–62; an insightful assessment is in Bertho, *Miroir des âmes simples,* 22–26. See also documents preserved in Simon Le Boucq, *Histoire ecclésiastique de la ville et comté de Valentienne (1650)* (1844; repr., Marseille: Lafitte Reprints, 1978), 72–79.

47. An early period in which beguines in most cities were largely (though not exclusively) drawn from the upper classes gave way by the later thirteenth century to a world where beguinages could house both the well off and the impoverished. Simons, *Cities of Ladies,* 91–104. See also Penelope Galloway, "Beguine Communities in Northern France, 1200–1500," in *Medieval Women in Their Communities,* ed. Diane Watt (Toronto: University of Toronto Press, 1997), 108, who reaches similar conclusions for a region near Valenciennes. Stabler likewise shows that elite, middling, and poor women all became beguines in Paris ("Now She Is Martha," 75).

48. Carpentier, "Béguinage Sainte-Élisabeth," 130; Simons, *Cities of Ladies,* 97.

49. See the example of Marie d'Avesnes, discussed in Delmaire, "Béguines dans le Nord," 138, and Carpentier, "Béguinage Sainte-Élisabeth," 158. In 1329 this beguine left lands to St. Elisabeth's. I know of no evidence clarifying her possible relationship to the ruling Avesnes family of Hainaut, but the elaborate and atypical provisions made for her burial discussed in Carpentier's article indicate her high status.

50. Delmaire, "Béguines dans le Nord," 145 n. 33. There is absolutely no reason to think that the Marguerite referred to in this document was the woman later tried in Paris, yet it serves as a reminder that since we do not know when or how our Marguerite acquired the nickname "Porete" it is possible that references to her could be hidden in plain sight, as it were, in the archives of this beguinage.

51. The rule, written in French and dated May 1262 (the surviving version is slightly later), is edited in Carpentier, "Béguinage Sainte-Élisabeth," 176–77, and in Le Boucq, *Histoire ecclésiastique,* 75–76.

52. Delmaire, "Béguines dans le Nord," 127.

53. Ibid., 128.

54. This situation certainly did exist in other towns. Evidence for Paris has already been cited above, showing that beguines lived outside the grand beguinage. For evidence for a similar situation in Reims from the 1270s through the 1350s, see Gaston Robert, *Les béguines de Reims et la maison de Sainte-Agnès* (Reims: Monce et Cie, 1923), 6–12. Oft-cited (e.g., in Bertho, *Miroir des âmes simples,* 28 n. 4) statutes issued by the bishop of Liège in 1246 distinguished between women living within the formal beguinage (who were given his protection) and those living outside (who were not). Mons, quite near to

Valenciennes, had many small beguine convents besides the larger community of Cantimpré. See Walter de Keyser, "Aspects de la vie béguinale à Mons aux XIIIe et XIVe siècles," in *Autour de la ville en Hainaut,* ed. Jean Dugnoille and René Sansen (Ath: Cercle royal d'histoire et d'archéologie d'Ath et de la région et musées Athois, 1986), 205–26. Finally, for comparison on the various kinds of living arrangements and economic background of beguines, see Bernard Delmaire, *Le diocèse d'Arras de 1093 au milieu du XIV siècle,* 2 vols. (Arras: Commission départementale d'histoire et d'archéologie du Pas-de-Calais, 1994), 1:318–33.

55. I base this remark on communication with Walter Simons and thank him for consultation on this point. For patterns in neighboring towns, see Robert, *Béguines de Reims*; de Keyser, "Aspects de la vie"; and Delmaire, *Diocèse d'Arras.*

56. See Bertho, *Miroir des âmes simples,* 27–29, and Leicht, *Marguerite Porete.* Lerner ("New Light," 107) raises the possibility that Marguerite could have had ties to the beguinage in the neighboring town of Masny. Unfortunately, no records from this community seem to survive; at any rate none are listed in Simons, *Cities of Ladies,* 289, #70.

57. See McDonnell, *Beguines and Beghards,* 246–65, for a separate treatment of beghards. Beghards and beguines are treated together in Lerner, *Heresy,* ch. 2, and "Beguines and Beghards," in *Dictionary of the Middle Ages,* ed. Joseph R. Strayer (New York: Scribner, 1983), 2:157–62; Kieckhefer, *Repression of Heresy,* ch. 2; and Michel Lauwers and Walter Simons, *Béguins et Béguines à Tournai au Bas Moyen Âge: Les communautés béguinales à Tournai du XIIIe au XVe siècle* (Tournai: Archives du Chapitre Cathédral de Tournai et Association des Diplômes en archéologie et histoire de l'art de l'UCL, 1988), esp. 18.

58. See, for the example of a beghard community at Bruges, Walter Simons, "The Lives of Beghards," in *Medieval Christianity in Practice,* ed. Miri Rubin (Princeton: Princeton University Press, 2009), 238–45.

59. Burnham, *So Great a Light,* 33.

60. See the discussion of the overlapping meanings of *béguine/béguin* in Kerby-Fulton, *Books under Suspicion,* 404–6.

61. Lerner, "Angel of Philadelphia," 350, speculated that "perhaps this clause was just a precaution taken against someone who had been assuming some clerical functions in the ignorance of whether he was truly in orders or not." It now seems more likely, however, that Guiard was perceived as a renegade or apostate cleric of some sort, and Lerner has adopted this position in "Addenda on an Angel," in *Marguerite Porete et le "Miroir des simples âmes": Perspectives historiques, philosophiques et littéraires* (Paris: Vrin, forthcoming).

62. An "essart" was forest land cleared for cultivation, so the settlement's original name was surely Cresson-essart, perhaps named after an original cultivator of the area.

63. The 1303 population figure is given by E. de Lépinois, *Recherches historiques et critiques sur l'ancien comté et les comtes de Clermont en Beauvoisis du XIe au XIIIe siècle* (Beauvais: D. Pere, 1877), 203. For an introduction to the modern village, see the attractive website maintained at www.cressonsacq .com, or Daniel Delattre and Emmanuel Delattre, *Le canton de Saint-Just-en-Chaussée* (Grandvilliers: Éditions Delattre, 2000), 24–30. These sources rely in large measure on Louis Graves's 1835 study, "Précis statistique sur le canton de St.-Just-en-Chaussée, arrondissement de Clermont (Oise)," reprinted in *Cantons de Mouys et de Saint-Just-en-Chaussée*, vol. 9 (Paris: Res Universis, 1991), 51–54.

64. For hostile evidence, see McDonnell, *Beguines and Beghards*; for a more sympathetic treatment, see Lerner, *Heresy*, 36–44.

65. Beguines in Reims were overseen in part by Dominicans, according to Robert, *Béguines de Reims*, 16.

66. Meredith Cohen, "An Indulgence for the Visitor: The Public at the Sainte-Chapelle of Paris," *Speculum* 83 (2008): 873–74, quotation on 874.

67. The Feast of the Reception of the Relics (30 September) and its octave, the Feast of the Crown of Thorns (11 August), Good Friday (and indeed any Friday in the year), the Feast of the Dedication (26 April) and its octave, and the Feast of the Exaltation of the Cross (14 September).

68. M. Cohen, "Indulgence for the Visitor," 866–67. For the papal bulls of 1298, 1300, and 1306, see A. Vidier, "Le Trésor de la Sainte-Chapelle (suite)," *Mémoires de la Société de l'histoire de Paris et de l'Ile-de-France* 36 (1909): 268–69, 282–84.

69. M. Cohen, "Indulgence for the Visitor," 872–73.

70. I am following Lerner, "Angel of Philadelphia," 349–50.

71. See in general de Lépinois, *Recherches historiques*, 203–6. This family can be traced through their patronage of the Cistercian monasteries of Saint-Antoine (just outside the eastern walls of medieval Paris) and Ourscamps (near Noyon). The following notes, however, are by no means an attempt at an exhaustive survey of all monastic (or other) documents relating to the Cressonessart family. The cartulary of Ourscamps (BnF ms. lat. 5473; actually a seventeenth-century book containing copies and summaries of medieval documents) mentions "Heresindis domina de Cressonessart" as early as 1145 (fol. 106v; she is identified as the mother of Dreux I on fol. 107v) and then Dreux I of Cressonessart in 1165 and 1177 (fols. 107r and 107v, the latter with his wife Emmelina). Dreux II appears in documents from 1199, 1201, and 1202 (fols. 107r

and 105v), which also refer to his father Dreux, his sisters Hersendis (and her sons Bernard and John) and Mathilda, his wife Agnes, and their children Dreux, Robert, Thibault, Adelina (or Emmelina), and Beatrix. Thibault I is then mentioned as lord of Cressonessart in documents of 1226 and 1231 (fols. 109v and 110r) along with his wife Elisabeth/Isabelle and children Dreux, Robert, Thibault, Mathilda, and Marie.

72. Thibault II appears (with a reference to his father Thibault) in a document from 1247 in BnF ms. lat. 5473, fol. 137r, and from 1254 on fol. 106r. Anselm is recorded in 1281 (February 1280 in old-style reckoning) on fol. 137r. A document from his widow Colai dated 1286 shows he was deceased by that date (fol. 80v), as does another document issued by Thibault lord of Cressonessart (mentioning his wife Peronelle) found on fol. 80r. In 1318 a Thibault de Cressonessart refers to the inheritance of his father of the same name in a document summarized fol. 80r. Presumably these last two could be labeled Thibault III and IV. The name "Anselm" seems odd in this list, but a summary in the cartulary of Ourscamps of a document of 1177 (BnF ms. lat. 5473, fol. 107r) says that Dreux I's daughter Hersendis married (or at least was betrothed to marry) an Anselm, so the name was in the family.

73. Konrad Eubel, *Hierarchia catholica medii aevi* (Regensberg: Monasterii Libr. Regensbergiana, 1898), 1:135; L'abbé Delettre, *Histoire du diocèse de Beauvais, depuis son établissement, au 3.me siècle, jusqu'au 2 septembre 1792,* vol. 2 (Beauvais: Imprimerie d'Ach. Desjardins, 1843), 284–308.

74. Eubel, *Hierarchia catholica medii aevi,* 1:475. On Robert, see Louis Carolus-Barré, *Le procès de canonisation de saint Louis (1272–1297): Essai de reconstitution,* ed. Henri Platelle (Rome: École française de Rome, 1994), 216–23.

75. On Saint-Antoine, see Constance H. Berman, "Cistercian Nuns and the Development of the Order: The Abbey at Saint-Antoine-des-Champs outside Paris," in *The Joy of Learning and the Love of God: Studies in Honor of J. Leclercq,* ed. E. Rozanne Elder (Kalamazoo, MI: Cistercian Publications, 1995), 121–56. See n. 13 for Agnes's gift of rents in 1206 (AN H5 3859–1) and n. 56 for 1208 (AN S*4386, no. 171, fol. 61v; I have not examined these two documents myself). According to the original document still bearing her seal found in AN S4373, dossier 2, no. 8, Agnes of Cressonessart, sister of Robert Mauvoisin, donated a rent of ten soldi to the sisters of Brolius in January 1214 (new style), with the consent of her sons Robert and Thibault. Then, in a document issued June 1228 (AN S4373, dossier 2, no. 11), Thibault of Cressonessart, knight, says that when his dearest mother, Sister Agnes of Cressonessart took the habit of the nuns of Saint Antoine, she gave ten soldi of rent to the *sororibus conversis de Brolio.* She must therefore have become a nun in 1214. The abbot of Brolius sold this rent for one hundred soldi to the sisters of

Saint-Antoine by 1228, and Thibault, with the assent of his wife Isabelle, confirms this gift [AN S4373, dossier 2, nos. 10 and 11). It is generally said that Agnes was abbess from 1233 to 1240, but Berman suggests (n. 56) that perhaps Agnes of Cressonessart was the "Agnes I" who was abbess from 1214 to 1221, or that she may never had been abbess at all. I am unable to offer any additional evidence bearing on this question.

76. In August 1231 Thibault I (described as knight and lord of Cressonessart), with the assent of his wife Isabelle, gave new lands to Saint-Antoine. Witnesses included Robert of Cressonessart his brother, as well as an otherwise unidentified "Martinus de Cressonessart," in AN S4373, dossier 2, no. 12. In July 1237 Thibault, knight and lord of Cressonessart, confirms a rent that the nuns of Saint-Antoine have recently purchased and mentions the land that the now-deceased Hersendis de Cressonessart (and others) have given them in alms, as well as the donation of vineyards by his brother Robert, here labeled "deacon of Beauvais," in dossier 2, no. 13. Finally no. 15 of this same dossier formerly contained a document issued in 1251 by Thibault II with his wife Agnes (I noted this document in 2000; when I returned to the carton in 2010, however, it seemed to have vanished). I thank Robert Lerner and Constance Berman for referring me to the archives of Saint-Antoine. I regret that I have been unable to consult Sandrine Delaforge-Marchand, "Edition du chartrier de l'abbaye de Saint-Antoine-des-Champs, 1191–1256" (Thèse pour le diplôme d'archiviste paléographe, École des Chartes, Paris, 1994).

77. Favier, *Roi de marbre,* 108.

78. Though a Latin training need not reflect noble status, it does indicate an elite education that would be compatible with such a hypothesis.

79. Delattre and Delattre, in *Canton de Saint-Just-en-Chaussée,* 26, follow Graves's "Précis statistique" in assuming that Guiard was part of the seigniorial family, though they refer to him as Gaspart and misdate his trial to 1210. See also the interesting observations in Caterina Bruschi, *The Wandering Heretics of Languedoc* (Cambridge: Cambridge University Press, 2009), 149, associating higher social background with a willingness to take the risk of expressing criticisms of the church.

Chapter 2. Seven Churchmen and a Beguine

1. Pascal Montaubin, "'Avec de l'Italie qui descendrait l'Escault': Guido da Collemezzo, èvêque de Cambrai (1296–1306)," in *Liber largitorius: Études d'histoire médiévale offertes à Pierre Toubert par ses élèves,* ed. Dominique Barthélemy and Jean-Marie Martin (Geneva: Droz, 2003), 477–502. In a note, the author indicates that he intends a further study of Guido's activities as

bishop (489 n. 56); Prof. Montaubin kindly informed me, however, that he has not yet been able to undertake this work and that to this point his researches have uncovered no further evidence pertaining to Marguerite Porete. I am most grateful to Prof. Montaubin for his communication on these points. Previously the best biographical summary on Guido was F. Lajard, "Gui de Colle di Mezzo," *Histoire littéraire de la France* 25 (1869): 280–83.

2. This and the following two paragraphs summarize the findings of Montaubin's thorough study.

3. Boniface had seen to it that the cathedral chapter of Cambrai was dominated by Italians at this moment, a number of whom were from the Collemezzo family. Montaubin, "Avec de l'Italie," 496–98.

4. Montaubin calls him "un proche d'Boniface VIII" (ibid., 478). One of Boniface's uncles had earlier been a chaplain in the household of Peter of Collemezzo (see Agostino Paravicini Bagliani, *Boniface VIII: Un pape heretique?* [Paris: Payot, 2003], 30), and in 1297 Guido had supported Boniface by arresting an agent of the Colonna family (Thomas of Montenero) at the pope's orders (191). Although Thomas was on a mission to Philip IV, in 1297 the king and the pope were temporarily on good terms, so Guido's action would not have constituted a direct provocation to the royal court.

5. Kochner, *Allegories of Love,* 30, citing Lille, Archives du Nord, 4 G 843 (no. 6). This paper cartulary from the end of the fourteenth century is briefly described (with reference to this case as entry #3) in Pierre Piétresson de Saint-Aubin, *Archives Departmentales du Nord, Répertoire numérique, Série G* (Lille: Douriez-Bataille, 1968), 2:469. I thank Prof. Kochner for sharing his notes with me, Elizabeth A. R. Brown for sending me a digital image of this document, and Walter Simons for pointing out that Marion and her father were probably part of the same family that produced the fifteenth-century composer Guillaume Dufay.

6. Saint-Omer, Bibliothèque municipale, ms. 283, fols. 22va–24vb, preserves an incomplete copy of the "Extractio facta per G. de Collemedio episcopum Cameracensem de dictis Bernardi et quibusdam aliis super Evangelio Missus est Angelus Gabriel." It contains common reflections on the opposition between Marie and Eve. Although it is heavily reliant on Bernard, a study of this short text might shed light on Guido's attitudes toward women. I hope to undertake such a study elsewhere.

7. This preface has been edited in Arturo Bernal Palacios, "La *Summa Innocenti abreviatti [sic]* de Guido de Collemedio," in *Cum Vobis et pro Vobis: Homenaje de la Facultad de Teología San Vicente Ferrer, de Valencia, al Excmo. y Rvdmo. Dr. D. Miguel Roca Cabanellas,* ed. Ramón Arnau-García and Roberto Ortuño Soriano (Valencia: Facultad de Teología San Vicente Ferrer, 1991), 465–71.

8. For a concise survey of decretal codification that situates Innocent IV's *Apparatus,* see Peter D. Clarke, *The Interdict in the Thirteenth Century: A Question of Collective Guilt* (Oxford: Oxford University Press, 2007), 4–12.

9. Arturo Bernal Palacios identifies eight manuscripts: one thirteenth-century (Bologna); six fourteenth-century (three in Paris, one each in Frankfurt, Todi, and Toledo); and one fifteenth-century (Valencia). See "*Summa Innocenti abreviatti,*" 466–67. The work sometimes follows Innocent's original text in a single manuscript, thereby acting as a sort of student's aid to comprehension, as in BnF ms. lat. 3987, and Valencia, Biblioteca universitaria, ms. 294. I have examined only the manuscripts in Paris myself.

10. Not all manuscripts agree on this place name, but this seems the most likely interpretation. The Toledo ms. calls him "archdeacon of Arras and doctor of canon law *[decretorum doctor]*."

11. Palacios, "*Summa Innocenti abreviatti,*" 468: "Ego Guido de Collemedio, thesaurarius [nionensis] sepe considerans Innocentii pape quarti apparatum in decretalibus editum peritis esse valde proficuum, ratione tamen triplici cunctis constare potest illum nonullis inutilem satis fore: Primo, quoniam ex thesauris tante sciente dampnosa superexcrescit tyronibus sepe materia; Secundo, quia opinionum in eo diversitas ignorare cogit plurimos in quo approbata Innocentii requiescat opinio; Tertio, quia peregrinas sub non suis titulis scribens materias in eo litus aravit propter iuvenes tenerem habentes memoriam qui illum per summas vigilias non noverint. Ac ideo illo ut potui diligenter inspecto presentem libellum condere studui in quo nulla alicubi superhabundet materia, vera semper Innocentii resecatis superfluis reperitur opinio, et sub debitis titulis hic recte omnia situata que per eundem sunt Innocentium sparsim tamen in maiori volumine comprobata." I have included some readings that Palacios relegates to his variants, when all other manuscripts agree against his base (Valencia, Biblioteca universitaria, ms. 294).

12. A point made by Montaubin, "Avec de l'Italie," 493.

13. Although this version of events was recorded in documents meant to serve specific legal purposes (discussed in chapter 7), I do not see any reason to believe that William of Paris would have fabricated the entire story of Marguerite's earlier encounters with authority. No matter how selective he may have been in recounting the facts, William had no incentive to invent this "back story" out of whole cloth. Thus my analysis assumes that these events really did take place, even if we have only a very partial and tendentious account of them.

14. "Quod dicta Margareta librum quemdam composuerat continentem hereses et errores, qui de mandato reverendi patris domini Guidonis, condam Cameracensis episcopi, publice et sollempniter tamquam talis fuerat condempnatus et combustus." Verdeyen, "Procès d'inquisition," 78 (Verdeyen incorrectly read "fuit" for "fuerat" and changed "Margareta" to "Margarita").

15. "Constitit evidenter quemdam composuisse te librum pestiferum contentivum heresum et errorum, ob quam causam fuit dictus liber per bone memorie Guidonem, olim Camaracensem episcopum, condempnatus et de mandato ipsius in Valencenis in tua combustus presentia publice et patenter." Ibid., 81–82 (Verdeyen incorrectly read "quondam" for "quemdam").

16. In general on practices around book burning, see Werner, *Irrtum liquidieren.*

17. "Et per litteram predicti episcopi fuit ordinatum quod, si talia sicut ea que continebantur in libro, de cetero attemptaret verbo vel scripto, eam condempnabat et relinquebat iustitiandam iustitie seculari." Verdeyen, "Procès d'inquisition," 78.

18. "A quo episcopo tibi fuit sub pena excommunicationis expresse inhibitum ne de cetero talem librum componeres vel haberes aut eo vel consimili utereris, addens et expresse ponens dictus episcopus in quadam littera suo sigillata sigillo, quod, si de cetero libro utereris predicto vel si ea que continebantur in eo, verbo vel scripto de cetero attemptares, te condempnabat tamquam hereticam et relinquebat iustitiandam iustitie seculari." Ibid., 82.

19. I thank Walter Simons for raising this distinction.

20. In AN J428 no. 15b, William seems to distinguish between his initial summary and the literal quotation that follows (from the "quod" clause). The use of the imperfect indicative in this clause (*condempnabat . . . relinquebat*) is awkward and may indicate transposition from an existing letter. I thank Larry F. Field for raising this point.

21. This point is briefly remarked by Trusen, *Prozess gegen Meister Eckhart,* 34, and is discussed in Leicht, *Marguerite Porete,* 334.

22. Again suggested by Trusen, *Prozess gegen Meister Eckhart,* 38.

23. "Invenit etiam idem inquisitor quod ipsa recognivit in iudicio semel coram inquisitore Lotharingie et semel coram reverendo patre domino Philippo, tunc Cameracensi episcopo, se post condempnationem predictam habuisse librum dictum et alios. Invenit etiam idem inquisitor quod dicta Margareta dictum librum in suo consimili eosdem continentem errores post ipsius libri condempnationem reverendo patri domino Johanni, Dei gratia Cathalaunensi episcopo, communicavit ac necdum dicto domino sed et pluribus aliis personis simplicibus, begardis et aliis, tamquam bonum." Verdeyen, "Procès d'inquisition," 78. (In the second sentence, Verdeyen omitted the word *idem.*)

24. "Post vero ista omnia dictum librum contra dictam prohibitionem pluries habuisti eo pluries usa es, sicut ex tuis patet recognitionibus, factis non solum coram inquisitore Lotharingie, sed et coram reverendo patre et domino domino Philippo, tunc Cameracensi episcopo, nunc archiepiscopo Senonensi. Dictum etiam librum post condempnationem et combustionem predictas sicut bonum et licitum communicasti reverendo patri domino Johanni, Cathalaunensi

episcopo, et quibusdam personis aliis, prout ex plurium fidedignorum iuratorum et super hiis coram nobis evidentibus testimoniis nobis liquet." Ibid., 82 (Verdeyen omitted the words "pluries habuisti eo" where the ms. reads "contra dictam prohibitionem pluries habuisti eo pluries usa es"). Verdeyen also read "Johanne" as the name of the new bishop of Cambrai. Knowing very well this had to be Philip of Marigny, bishop of Cambrai and then archbishop of Sens, Verdeyen made this emendation and explained it in a note. This explanation was entirely unnecessary, however, since the manuscript reads, "domino Ph."

25. Peter Dronke may have originated this idea; in 1984, he noted parenthetically that "seventeen further chapters were added later, after the 'Explicit'" (*Women Writers of the Middle Ages: A Critical Study of Texts from Perpetua [† 203] to Marguerite Porete [† 1310]* [Cambridge: Cambridge University Press, 1984], 218, referring to the "explicit" that follows ch. 122 in the Chantilly manuscript). Dronke gave no additional reasoning and did not himself say that "later" meant after the book's initial condemnation. Bertho, *Miroir des âmes simples,* 99, adopted this view, and by 1999 Edmund Colledge and his collaborators stated, "We conjecture that the book, as burned at Valenciennes, contained nothing beyond chapter 122, and that Margaret thereafter was prompted to add Chapters 123–139" (Colledge, Marler, and Grant, *Mirror of Simple Souls,* xli). Similarly, Barbara Newman in a 2002 footnote asserted that chapters 123–39 were "added as a kind of appendix after its initial condemnation" ("Mirror and the Rose," 120 n. 21). In 2004 Bernard McGinn's "likely supposition" was that Marguerite wrote the original 122 chapters in the 1290s; after the book's burning she "added chapters 123–139 to explain and defend her views." Bernard McGinn, "Evil-Sounding, Rash, and Suspect of Heresy: Tensions between Mysticism and Magisterium in the History of the Church," *Catholic Historical Review* 90 (2004): 196 n. 13. Kocher, *Allegories of Love,* 32, 54, seems persuaded by this view as well, as does Meliadò, "Dottrina mistica della nobilità," 424. Recently, however, Lerner, "New Light," 100, has contested this reading. In my view, however, his observations do not negate the possibility that Marguerite wrote the *Mirror* in several stages. At a minimum we can be certain that at least two versions existed during her lifetime, because one had to be available to show to her three recommenders, and then another with their recommendations attached.

26. Discussing this section of the *Mirror* is complicated by the fact that all three main versions have large holes. The Middle English is missing the end of ch. 122 through the opening of 126, but since the summary at the end of ch. 129 makes it clear that the whole section was originally present, the Middle English exemplar did include this material (except perhaps the end of ch. 122). Similarly the French omits some of ch. 134 and then all of chs. 135–36 and part

of 137, but these chapters are listed in the table of contents in the Chantilly manuscript so must have been present in the exemplar. The Latin version, in turn, omits the end of ch. 121 and all of 122 ("chapter" listings here refer to the way the Middle French manuscript is divided up).

27. The "Explicit" that follows ch. 121 in the Chantilly (Middle French) manuscript has often been assumed to be evidence for the initial stopping point of an early version of the *Mirror*. It is less often remarked, however, that the Chantilly manuscript also has an "Explicit" after the table of contents, and after the brief extra prologue—and both of these elements were almost certainly added by a later scribe or editor, not written by Marguerite. Therefore, just because an "Explicit" appears in Chantilly does not mean that Marguerite included such a notation in an original version of her work. Arguments about when, how, and why Marguerite may have revised her *Mirror*, should therefore be wary of relying too much on this single word. I thank Walter Simons for the intriguing suggestion that chs. 123–39 could originally have been part of another work written by Marguerite, a hypothesis that seems worthy of further consideration.

28. Rina Lahav, by contrast, reads this as the most provocative part of Marguerite's work. See "Marguerite Porete and the Predicament of Her Preaching in Fourteenth-Century France," in *Gender, Catholicism and Spirituality: Women and the Roman Catholic Church in Britain and Europe, 1200–1900,* ed. Laurence Lux-Sterritt and Carmen M. Magion (New York: Palgrave Macmillan, 2011), 38–50. I thank the author for sending me a prepublication version of this essay.

29. My translation here is based on Colledge, Marler, and Grant, compared with the Middle French and Babinksy. The Middle English has a different last clause: "And therefore divine will is always one same will in love."

30. It is also possible that Marguerite's English translator, the mysterious M. N., added this "gloss." This does not seem the most likely assumption, however, given the way he clearly identifies his own interventions throughout his translation.

31. There is debate about whether Marguerite sought and obtained these praises before or after her book was condemned by Guido of Collemezzo. Some excellent scholars have suggested that respected churchmen, particularly Godfrey of Fontaines, would never have risked praising a book that had already been condemned by a bishop. See, for example, Leicht, *Marguerite Porete,* who is noncommittal at 66 but categorical at 334 n. 126, where she follows Winfried Trusen, *Prozess gegen Meister Eckhart,* 35. Verdeyen, "Procès d'inquisition," 52, makes the same assumption, as does Babinsky in her introduction to *Mirror of Simple Souls,* 22–23. Lerner, "New Light," has now

taken this view as well. I side, however, with those who argue that Marguerite's interaction with her three recommenders probably took place after her book's condemnation and before her second clash with authority. McGinn lays this scenario out in his article "Evil-Sounding, Rash," 196 n. 133, though he calls it only a "likely supposition." Colledge, Marler, and Grant present the same series of events in their introduction to *Mirror of Simple Souls*, xli–xlii. Colledge advanced this position earlier in "The Latin *Mirror of Simple Souls*: Margaret Porette's Ultimate Accolade?," in *Langland, the Mystics and the Medieval English Tradition: Essays in Honour of S. S. Hussey,* ed. Helen Phillips (Cambridge: Boydell and Brewer, 1990), 177–78. Most recently Stabler, "What's in a Name?," 83, n. 113, and O'Sullivan, "School of Love," 146, both follow Colledge, and Kerby-Fulton, *Books under Suspicion*, 278, seems to adhere to this line as well. I have laid out my reasoning fully in Sean L. Field, "The Master and Marguerite: Godfrey of Fontaines' Praise of the *Mirror of Simple Souls,*" *Journal of Medieval History* 35 (2009): 136–49. Briefly: if other evidence shows that Marguerite was recirculating her book in this period, it is logical to deduce that she sought out these recommenders as part of this same campaign for rehabilitation. Second, the actions of the bishops of Cambrai make more sense in this light. If Godfrey of Fontaines really offered his praise of the book before it was burned, then Guido of Collemezzo's decision to consign it to the flames was strikingly bold, in effect attacking a master of theology as well as a beguine; moreover, we would have a good reason why the next bishop of Cambrai was hesitant to deal with Marguerite in a summary manner. Finally, in Godfrey's case, there is the evidence of his very public stance rejecting episcopal censures of intellectual freedom. In his academic writings he laid out the circumstances under which he believed that a theologian should register his dissent from an episcopal condemnation—basically if and when that condemnation preemptively closed off free debate on an opinion that had never been condemned by pope or council, or when the bishop was simply in error. Particularly since Godfrey was not subject to the direct authority of the bishop of Cambrai, I find it quite possible that he would have risked praising the *Mirror* as part of this larger campaign against unwarranted episcopal condemnations. It should also be noted that at least two of Marguerite's three recommenders seem to have given only oral encouragement, that each of them strongly counseled her not to show the book around, that none of them can be said to have "approved" the book in even a semiofficial sense, and that we have only Marguerite's attenuated version of their responses, which may have included even stronger warnings that she chose not to recopy.

32. "Querayn" has more often been equated with the modern town of Queregnon in Hainaut, approximately ten kilometers west of Mons and thirty

kilometers from Valenciennes. I made this error myself in Field, "Master and Marguerite." I owe what I take to be the correct identification to Walter Simons, who also noted the way this fact provides further proof that Marguerite must have been from Valenciennes or its immediate surroundings. Kocher, *Allegories of Love,* 22–23, raises the same possibility, followed by Lerner, "New Light," 98. This interpretation is more likely not only because of the proximity to Valenciennes but also because it explains the rendering of the Middle English as "Querayn."

33. Substantial records do survive for this community. Unfortunately, neither *Inventaire des archives de l'abbaye de Villers,* ed. Georges Despy (Brussels: Ministère de l'instruction publique, Archives générales du Royaume, 1959), nor Edouard de Moreau, *L'abbaye de Villers-en-Brabant aux XIIe et XIIIe siècles* (Brussels: Dewit, 1909), refers to a "Franco" or "Francon" who dates to the relevant decades. De Moreau in fact verified that no such documents were known to him. See Clare Kirchberger, ed., *The Mirror of Simple Souls, by an Unknown French Mystic of the Thirteenth Century, Translated into English by M.N.* (London: Burns, Oates, and Washbourne, 1927), xxxi–xxxii, and xxv (starred footnote), for de Moreau's personal assurances to the author on this question.

34. Simons, *Cities of Ladies,* 46–47; de Moreau, *L'abbaye de Villers-en-Brabant,* 105–14; For an example of a close personal friendship between a prior of Villers and a beguine visionary, see the summary of an exemplum by Caesarius of Heisterbach given in McGinn, *Flowering of Mysticism,* 162. If extended back to the twelfth century, the list of women associated with Villers would include Hildegard of Bingen.

35. On Goswin and the duties of the chanter, see Barbara Newman's preface to Martinus Crawley, trans., *Send Me God: The Lives of Ida the Compassionate of Nivelles, Nun of La Ramée; Arnulf, Lay Brother of Villers; and Abundus, Monk of Villers,* by Goswin of Bossut (Turnhout: Brepols, 2003), xxxiii, and Cawley's introduction, 7.

36. I address their relationship in more detail in Field, "Master and Marguerite." Anneke B. Mulder-Bakker suggests that Godfrey could have been the author of the extant vita of Juliana of Mont-Cornillon. See *Lives of the Anchoresses: The Rise of the Urban Recluse in Medieval Europe,* trans. Myra Heerspink Scholz (Philadelphia: University of Pennsylvania Press, 2005), 235 n. 18. Although I agree that Godfrey is a "possible candidate," there is little beyond circumstance to recommend him. I thank Barbara Newman for this reference.

37. On Godfrey's biography, see Maurice De Wulf, *Étude sur la vie, les oeuvres et l'influence de Godefroid de Fontaines* (Brussels: Hayez, 1904) (family background, 6–7, 10–11); updated in Robert J. Arway, "A Half Century of

Research on Godfrey of Fontaines," *New Scholasticism* 36 (1962): 192–218; and John F. Wippel, *The Metaphysical Thought of Godfrey of Fontaines: A Study in Late Thirteenth-Century Philosophy* (Washington, DC: Catholic University of America Press, 1981), xv–xxi. Godfrey does not seem to have been a canon of Tournai, as some secondary sources claim. See Jacques Pycke, *Répertoire biographique des chanoines de Notre-Dame de Tournai, 1080–1300* (Louvain-la-Neuve: Collège Erasme, 1988), 389, no. 402. Similarly, the story that Godfrey was actually chosen bishop of Tournai in 1300 only to renounce his claim is probably based on a misunderstanding of the evidence.

38. He is listed among those attending a meeting of the Sorbonne in February 1304 (new style). See Palémon Glorieux, *Aux origines de la Sorbonne,* 2 vols. (Paris: Vrin, 1965–66), 1:206.

39. A doubtful reference to his presence in Liège in 1305 (see Christine Renardy, *Les Maîtres universitaires du diocèse de Liège: Répertoire biographique, 1140–1350* [Paris: Les belles lettres, 1981], 258–59) depends on John of Outremeuse's *Ly Myreur des Histors.* John wrote in the later fourteenth century, and although he was well informed about events in his native region, his description here of the canons of Liège and their conflict with their bishop is not precise enough to trust a reference to an exact year. See Stanislas Bormans, ed., *Ly Myreur des Histors, chronique de Jean des Preis dit d'Outremeuse,* 7 vols. (Brussels: Hayez, 1859–87), 6:72. Another reference would place him again at a meeting of the Sorbonne in 1306. For this claim De Wulf relied on Paris, Bibliothèque de l'Arsenal, ms. 1022, which according to Glorieux (*Aux origines,* 1:72 n. 6) is an incomplete copy of Arsenal ms. 1021, itself a late seventeenth-century history of the Sorbonne by Mauduison, in turn building on the mid-seventeenth-century work of Claude Hémeré. This seems a less than secure source.

40. Godfrey can be shown to have visited the Low Countries periodically between 1284 and 1303. Evidence for stays in Liège is detailed in Jean Lejeune, "Contribution à l'histoire des idées politiques: De Godefroid de Fontaines à la paix de Fexhe (1316)," *Annuaire d'histoire liègeoise* 6 (1962): 1231–40. He was in Liège in 1284, 1289 and 1300, in Tournai that same year, then in Rome, in Paris at least briefly around February 1301 (see H. Denifle and A. Chatelain, eds., *Chartularium universitatis Parisiensis,* 4 vols. [Paris: Delalain, 1889–97], 2:90), and back in Liège in 1302–3 (chronicle evidence of his trip to Tournai and Rome, and a possible reference to his continuing presence in Liège in 1305, are noted above). It is likely, however, that Godfrey returned to his native region even more frequently than this, as Parisian scholars routinely returned home during academic vacations.

41. Kerby-Fulton, *Books under Suspicion,* 280, justifiably remarks that the Middle English version "is the fullest and most informative extant, main-

taining . . . much better than the Latin does, the distinctive styles of the different clerics."

42. For the Middle English, see Marilyn Doiron, ed., "Margaret Porete: *The Mirror of Simple Souls,* a Middle English Translation," *Archivio italiano per la storia della pietà,* vol. 5 (Rome: Edizioni di Storia e Letteratura, 1968), 249–50. I thank Prof. Jenny Sisk for consulting with me on this translation into modern English.

43. Colledge's translation purposely obscures this fact (as his note admits) by preferring the Latin, apparently under the belief that the *we* here can only refer to Marguerite. Colledge, Marler, and Grant, *Mirror of Simple Souls,* 180 n. 16.

44. On university masters and beguines in Paris, see Stabler, "Now She Is Martha." Godfrey's knowledge of such preaching is demonstrated by the fact that he owned a copy of a sermon preached by Robert of Sorbon at the grand beguinage (BnF ms. lat. 16507, fol. 421 ff.). See Bériou, "Robert de Sorbon." This sermon presented beguin(e)s in a highly positive light. (I thank Tanya Stabler for this reference.) Nor need these interactions have been all one-way, since beguines sometimes played active roles in these relationships by questioning or even presuming to teach male ecclesiastics. For an example of a beguine superior of Cambrai challenging a preacher, see McDonnell, *Beguines and Beghards,* 344. On beguines preaching, see Bériou, "Prédication au béguinage," and on claiming to teach theologians, at least in literature, see the exchange cited by Renate Blumenfeld-Kosinski in "Satirical Views of the Beguines in Northern French Literature," in *New Trends in Feminine Spirituality: The Holy Women of Liège and Their Impact,* ed. Juliette Dor, Lesley Johnson, and Jocelyn Wogan-Browne (Turnhout: Brepols, 1999), 237.

45. This again is Kerby-Fulton's insight, from *Books under Suspicion,* 279–80, and 24 more generally. See further Elliot, *Proving Woman,* 3 and passim, for the multivalent resonance of the verb *probare.*

46. The record of the three clerks' responses appears at the end of manuscripts in the Latin tradition but functions as an introduction to the Middle English. It seems logical to assume that it originally was tacked onto the end and that at some point either Marguerite or a later editor or translator moved it to the beginning. Marleen Cré, *Vernacular Mysticism in the Charterhouse: A Study of London, British Library, MS Additional 37790* (Turnhout: Brepols, 2006), 191, suggests the possibility "that M. N. moved the approval passage forward from the end of the text, even though he does not say so explicitly in his prologue, because the move of the passage reinforces M. N.'s guidance of his readers." This is a reasonable hypothesis, but this issue surely deserves further close study, as does the question of why the praises are not found in the unique Middle French manuscript. Note also Wegener's close reading of AN

J428 no. 19bis, which refers to Marguerite sending a book "in suo consimili eosdem continentem errores" to the bishop of Châlons-sur-Marne ("Freiheitsdiskurs und Beginenverfolgung," 217) and suggests a recognition of a new "edition" of the book.

47. This general dynamic holds even if some readers may disagree with my dating of Godfrey's intervention to after Guido's condemnation; since both events took place before Marguerite was again taken into custody, around 1306 she would have had both opinions in her mind, no matter which came first.

48. This observation should be credited to Wegener, "Freiheitsdiskurs und Beginenverfolgung," 216.

49. On this point, see Kocher, *Allegories of Love,* 32–33, and Bertho, *Miroir des âmes simples,* 29–32, who then further wonders (32–34) whether Marguerite might have been a professional *calligraphe*—though perhaps *scribe* would be the apt term in English for this speculation.

50. It is possible that she might have simply moved into the Diocese of Châlons-sur-Marne. But if indeed her interactions with her three recommenders occurred after her book's condemnation, then it would seem more likely that she had not changed her physical residence, given the way these recommenders centered on the area close to Valenciennes.

51. Guillaume Mollat, "Chateauvillain (Jean de)," in *Dictionnaire d'histoire et de géographie ecclésiastiques,* ed. Alfred Baudrillart et al. (Paris: Letouzey at Ané, 1953), 12:584; Eubel, *Hierarchia catholica medii aevi,* 1:175.

52. Élisabeth Lalou, *Itinéraire de Philippe IV le Bel (1285–1314),* 2 vols. (Paris: Boccard, 2007), 2:131; Courtenay, "Between Pope and King," 578 n. 5.

53. See Philip IV's letter to Clement V, in Étienne Baluze, *Vitae paparum avenionensium,* 2nd ed., ed. Guillaume Mollat, vol. 3 (Paris: Letouzey et Ané, 1921), 63–64; Sauveur-Jérôme Morand, *Histoire de la Sainte-Chapelle royale du palais* (Paris: Clousier, 1790), 87.

54. M. Pélicier, "Une émeute à Châlons-sur-Marne sous Philippe IV le Bel, 1306–1307," in *Bulletin historique et philologique du Comité des travaux historiques et scientifiques: Année 1889* (Paris: Ernest Leroux, 1890), 142–47. On the twists and turns of Philip's monetary policy, see Favier, *Roi de marbre,* 135–62.

55. I thank Walter Simons for suggesting these interpretations.

56. Although Robert le Bougre passed through the area in the 1230s, I am aware of no evidence that anyone was appointed inquisitor specifically for Cambrai before the fifteenth century. See Vidal, *Bullaire de l'Inquisition,* xxvi.

57. Thomas Ripoll, ed., *Bullarium ordinis fratrum praedicatorum,* vol. 2 (Rome: Hieronymus Mainardus, 1730), 29–30. See also Augustus Potthast, *Regesta pontificum romanorum,* vol. 2 (Graz: Akademische Druck- U. Verlagsanstalt, 1957), #23297 (22 June 1290) and #23298 (27 June); Ernest Langlois, ed., *Registres de Nicolas IV,* vol. 1 (Paris: Thorin, 1890), 461, #2776, p. 463

#2779. Useful though outdated analysis is in Vidal, *Bullaire de l'Inquisition*, xiv–xviii.

58. After our mention, which must refer to events around 1307–8, I know of no extant documents referring to an inquisitor of Lorraine for the next thirty years. This label reappears with Reginald of Rucesses (d. 1345), John of Fonte (removed from this office in 1356), and Martin of Amance (mentioned 1381). See Vidal, *Bullaire de l'Inquisition*, xiv–xviii, xxx.

59. Strayer, *Reign of Philip IV*, 316, 349–50; Favier, *Roi de marbre*, 272–74. Indeed, Thibault II, Duke of Upper Lorraine from 1303 to 1312, was a cousin of queen Jeanne of Navarre and a military ally of Philip IV. As Favier puts it, "No one doubted that Lorraine was part of the Empire, but the duke of Lorraine was in the habit of considering the king of France as his *seigneur.*" *Roi de marbre*, 274.

60. See Hans-Joachim Schmidt, *Kirche, Staat, Nation: Raumgliederung der Kirche im mittelalterlichen Europa* (Weimar: Hermann Böhlaus, 1999), 318. I thank Walter Simons for the reference.

61. AN J413 B no. 15. This document was edited in Hans Prutz, *Entwicklung und Untergang des Tempelherrenordens* (Berlin: Grote, 1888), 325. Prutz, however, did not fully publish the salutation to the letter, crucial here: "Excellentissimo principi ac domino Philippo Dei gratia Franc. regi, frater Radulphus de Lineyo inquisitor heretice pravitatis in Tullensi, Metensi et Virdunensi civitatibus et dyocesibus auctoritate appostolica deputatus, reverentiam et honorem."

62. There is no entry for him in Thomas Kaeppeli's *Scriptores ordinis praedicatorum medii aevi* (Rome: S. Sabinae, 1970–93). Because I made this identification only after this book had been sent to press, I have not been able to carry out a full search for data on Ralph of Ligny or a full analysis of J413 B no. 15 (I hope to publish elsewhere further observations on this document and its significance).

63. The episode is briefly analyzed in Barber, *Trial of the Templars*, 69–70.

64. Before the Council of Vienne papal policy did not formally require inquisitors to act in tandem with local bishops, but it was always wise, and in fact Philip IV had at least temporarily insisted on such cooperation in parts of his kingdom as early as 1301, in connection with the contest between Bernard Délicieux and southern Dominican inquisitors. See Alan Friedlander, *The Hammer of the Inquisitors: Brother Bernard Délicieux and the Struggle against the Inquisition in Fourteenth-Century France* (Leiden: Brill, 2000), 88–97.

65. Montaubin, "Avec de l'Italie," 494–95, makes this suggestion. Clement in fact named Philip of Marigny bishop elect of Cambrai as early as 12 January, ten days before Guido's formal transfer, which makes it particularly compelling to see the point of this move as getting the king's loyal henchman into

this important see. Moreover, when Philip IV subsequently asked Clement to transfer Philip of Marigny to the archbishopric of Sens in 1309, the king simultaneously put forward his candidate to replace him in Cambrai (William of Trie). Robert Fawtier, *Registres du Trésor des Chartes*, vol. 1, *Règne de Philippe le Bel: Inventaire analytique* (Paris: Imprimerie nationale, 1958), 144, #812. Evidently Philip IV felt able to manipulate the see of Cambrai. On Philip's successes and setbacks in getting his men appointed to bishoprics, see Strayer, *Reign of Philip IV,* 93–96.

66. Montaubin, "Avec de l'Italie," 495.

67. Philip's tenure as bishop of Cambrai lasted until he became archbishop of Sens, sometime between July and October 1309. He held the latter see until his death in December 1316. Eubel, *Hierarchia catholica medii aevi,* 1:160, 447.

68. The full study of Enguerran's career is Jean Favier, *Un conseiller de Philippe le Bel: Enguerran de Marigny* (Paris: PUF, 1963), reissued as part of Favier, *Roi de marbre,* from which edition page numbers are cited here. For a concise summary in English, see Dorothy Gillerman, *Enguerran de Marigny and the Church of Notre-Dame at Ecouis: Art and Patronage in the Reign of Philip the Fair* (University Park: Pennsylvania State University Press, 1994), 11–19.

69. See Favier, *Roi de marbre,* 619–21.

70. Favier makes this point in ibid., 539, 540.

71. Fawtier, *Registres,* 32, #189. He apparently carried out such tasks with a heavy hand, since Lalou, *Itinéraire,* 2:193, records that on 22 November 1307 Philip IV ordered Philip of Marigny to return to the abbots of Normandy possessions taken against their will. Generally on Philip of Marigny, see Favier, *Roi de marbre,* 425–28, 479, 539–40, 643, 715.

72. Favier, *Roi de marbre,* 573.

73. Ibid., 540–41. See also an intriguing document printed by the abbé Dancoisne in his "Mémoire sur les établissements religieux du clergé séculier et du clergé régulier qui ont existé à Douai avant la Révolution," *Mémoires de la Société d'agriculture de sciences et d'arts séant à Douai, centrale du Département du Nord,* 2nd ser., 14 (1876–78): 310–12, which describes a meeting at Douai in October 1309 "apud mag. Johannem de Marigny, Sti Amati praepositum, canonic. et cantor. ecclesiae Parisiensis, nunc belviacensem episcopum." The Templars of Douai had been arrested in October 1307, and now the bishop of Arras announced at this meeting his commission to carry out an inquiry against the brothers. The document seems to suggest that John himself helped in this inquiry, since the bishop informed those present that they had been selected for this purpose. There is reason to be cautious about the authenticity of the document, which claims to be a report by a Dominican inquisitor named Wauthier, one of the participants in the meeting, and was supposedly rediscov-

ered by the Dominicans of Douai in the eighteenth century (the abbé Dancoisne cited it from a handwritten *Mémoire* by one M. Guilmot). Yet the abbé's cautious arguments for its possible legitimacy (see Dancoisne, in an earlier portion of his "Mémoire," vol. 9 [1866–67], 602–7) are not without basis. I am most grateful to Walter Simons for bringing this document to my attention and for suggesting the relevance of John of Marigny to events near Valenciennes.

74. Favier, *Roi de marbre,* 541.

75. Information on Philip's prebends comes from the *Corpus Philippicum* (see Appendix A, note 48, for description of this database).

76. Perhaps formal testimony was recorded at this point, since William of Paris's later reference to her acknowledgments (the Latin is plural, *tuis recognitionibus*) may imply that transcripts from these hearings were available to him. If so, they are now lost.

77. Trusen's suggestion in *Prozess gegen Meister Eckhart,* 36 (echoed in Leicht, *Marguerite Porete,* 335), that Philip did not have enough evidence to go on, seems dubious.

78. A point made by Bertho, *Miroir des âmes simples,* 128. This reasoning supports my argument that the three recommenders read the *Mirror* after its condemnation, since it helps to explain the extreme care with which Marguerite's case was handled from this point on.

Chapter 3. The Inquisitor

1. The starting points for William's biography are Xavier de la Selle, *Le service des âmes à la cour: Confesseurs et aumôniers des rois de France du XIIIe au XVe siècle* (Paris: École des Chartes, 1995), 264–65; Kaeppeli, *Scriptores ordinis praedicatorum,* 2:130–32; F. Lajard, "Guillaume de Paris, dominicain," *Histoire littéraire de la France* 27 (1877): 140–52; Jacques Quétif and Jacques Echard, *Scriptores ordinis praedicatorum* (1719–21; repr., New York: Burt Franklin, 1959), vol. 1, pt. 2, 518–19; and R. Coulon, "Guillaume de Paris," in *Dictionnaire de théologie catholique,* ed. Alfred Vacant and E. Mangenot, vol. 6 (Paris: Letouzey et Ané, 1920), cols. 1977–80. It should be noted that the name "William Humbert" by which this inquisitor is sometimes known does not appear in the contemporary sources. Apparently he has been confused and combined with Brother Imbert (or Humbert), another Dominican who was an inquisitor and confessor to the king after our William. See de la Selle, *Service,* 266.

2. Élisabeth Lalou, *Les comptes sur tablettes de cire de la chambre au deniers, de Philippe III le Hardi et de Philippe IV le Bel (1282–1309)* (Paris:

Boccard, 1994), 777, #143 (comptes extraordinaires): "Guesots, nepos confessoris pro vadiis suis usque ad primam diem julii 10/10."

3. In the early fourteenth century the royal chaplains and confessor were assigned a "chambre" in the Hôtel du Roi; confessors did not receive wages but were provided meals in their chamber at royal expense. But Dominican confessors of this era seem to have retained their status as residents at Saint-Jacques as well, and William kept a chamber there. See de la Selle, *Service,* 58–61, and Epilogue I to the present book.

4. AN J403 no. 13 (Philip's Testament). I thank Elizabeth A. R. Brown for sharing her transcription of this document with me. On royal testaments of this era, see Elizabeth A. R. Brown, "Royal Testamentary Acts from Philip Augustus to Philip of Valois: Executorial Dilemmas and Premonitions of Absolutism in Medieval France," in *Herrscher- und Fürstentestamente im westeuropäischen Mittelalter,* ed. Brigitte Kasten (Cologne: Böhlau, 2008), 415–30.

5. I am grateful to Xavier Hélary for this information. William appears in the codicil to the testament of Philip of Artois (son of Robert II of Artois and brother of Mahaut of Artois), dated 18–19 August 1298 (Philip died 11 September). The first executor listed is Durand of Champagne, the second is brother William of Paris. Dr. Hélary is preparing an edition of this document, AN J1019 no. 2bis, to appear in his article "Les testaments de Philippe d'Artois (d. 1298) et la naissance du culte de Saint Louis dans la famille capétienne." I thank him for a prepublication copy of this study.

6. See M. Michèle Mulchahey, *"First the Bow Is Bent in Study . . .": Dominican Education before 1350* (Toronto: Pontifical Institute of Mediaeval Studies, 1998), chs. 3 and 4.

7. See William J. Courtenay, "The Instructional Programme of the Mendicant Convents at Paris in the Early Fourteenth Century," in *The Medieval Church: Universities, Heresy, and the Religious Life. Essays in Honour of Gordon Leff,* ed. Peter Biller and Barry Dobson (Woodbridge, Boydell, 1999), 77–92.

8. Kaeppeli, *Scriptores ordinis praedicatorum,* 3:165–68; André Duval, "Nicolas de Gorran," in *Dictionnaire de spiritualité, ascétique et mystique, doctrine et histoire,* vol. 11 (Paris: Beauchesne, 1981), 281–83; F. Lajard, "Nicholas de Gorran, dominicain," *Histoire littéraire de la France* 20 (1842): 324–56; Mulchahey, *First the Bow,* 500–501, 517. On the *Distinctiones,* see Silvia Serventi, "Did Giordano da Pisa Use the *Distinctiones* of Nicolas Gorran?" in *Constructing the Medieval Sermon,* ed. Roger Andersson (Turnhout: Brepols, 2007), 83–116.

9. De la Selle, *Service,* 263–64; Baluze, *Vitae paparum avenionensium,* 2:117–19; Quétif and Echard, *Scriptores ordinis praedicatorum,* vol. 1, pt. 2, 555–58.

10. It is sometimes said Nicholas of Fréauville taught at the University of Paris (cf. de la Selle, *Service,* 263) but he does not appear in Glorieux, *Répertoire.* On the education of Dominican confessors in this period generally, see de la Selle, *Service,* 125–28.

11. Indeed, William must have known both Nicholases well. For instance Nicholas of Fréauville and William of Paris were both added as executors of Philip's testament of March 1297 (J403 no. 13) and were listed together: "ac fratres Nicolaum de Freauilla Confessorem & Guillelmum de Paris[ius] Capellan[um] nostr[um] ordinis predicatorum." I rely here on Elizabeth A. R. Brown's transcription and thank her for sharing it with me.

12. Jules Viard, ed., *Les journaux du Trésor de Philippe IV le Bel* (Paris: Imprimerie nationale, 1940), no. 2200 (5 March 1299), "Frater Guillelmus de Parisius, ordinis Predicatorum, confessor liberorum Regis, pro quodam missali ad opus capelle eorum emendo, 20 l. p. cont. per Stephanotum, valletum suum, super Regem"; no. 3524 (5 November 1299), "Frater Guillelmus de Parisius, ordinis Predicatorum, pro quodam breviario et uno libro De eruditione principum emendis pro domino Ludovico primogenito Regis, 32 l. p. cont. per se, super Regem"; no. 4480 (4 March 1300), "Frater Guillelmus de Parisius, ordinis Predicatorum, pro duabus bibliis ad opus dominorum Ludovici et Philippi liberorum Regis, 80 l. t. cont per Stephanum de Matiscone, valletum suum, super Regem." This evidence incidentally reveals the name of William's valet. Two others are mentioned in the "tablettes de cire" (comptes ordinaires for 1303): "Havardus, valetus fratris Guillelmi de Parisius (8 d. per diem) pro 211 diebus cum 30 s. pro malis gistis et 5 s. 4 d. pro duplicibus festis usque tunc." Lalou, *Comptes sur tablettes,* 687, and, for 1307 (comptes extraordinaires), 785, #259: "[R]obinetus, valetus fratris Guillelmi confessoris, ibi tunc, pro infirmitate sua per [eundem confesso]rem 72 s."

13. The codicil is edited from AN J403 no. 18, in Edgar P. Boutaric, "Notices et extraits de documents inédits relatifs à l'histoire de France sous Philippe le Bel," *Notices et extraits des manuscrits de la Bibliothèque Impériale et autres bibliothèques* 20, no. 2 (1862): 229–35, quotation at 231: "Item librum vocatum Speculum hystoriale quem nobis dedit frater Guillelmus de Parisius quondam confessor noster, legamus ad usum fratrum apud Pissiacum commorantium; quem quidem librum habet penes se frater Reginauldus nunc confessor noster." I am grateful to Elizabeth A. R. Brown for sharing with me her own transcription of this document as well. See Epilogue I for a papal privilege from 1311 that suggests that Philip returned the favor by giving books to William. Unfortunately, no titles of such gifts are known.

14. Along the very top edge of fol. 195v of BMaz ms. 248, in a small hand, is written: "[li]ber est fratris Guillelmi de Parisius ordinis fratrum predicatorum, domini regis [Fran]cie confessoris" (the first lacuna has been trimmed

off, the second is the result of a hole in the parchment). Since he is styled confessor to the king, this note must have been written after December 1305. See Auguste Molinier, *Catalogue des manuscrits de la Bibliothèque Mazarine* (Paris: Plon, 1885), 1:89.

15. Two volumes were noted in the library of San Domenico in Bologna by the humanist Fabio Vigili in a list compiled between 1508 and 1512. He described the first as "Prima pars Biblie in hebraico, optimis characteribus, quam frater Guillelmus Parisiensis, ordinis Praedicatorum, confessor regis Francorum, donavit conventui anno 1310," and the second as "Secunda pars Biblie in hebraico, videlicet a Iosue usque ad Malachiam finitum, iisdem characteribus." The reference to "iisdem characteribus" makes it possible that this may have been the second half of a single gift from William; it also implies that the first volume may have included only Genesis to Deuteronomy. See M.-H. Laurent, *Fabio Vigili et les bibliothèques de Bologne* (Vatican City: Biblioteca Apostolica Vaticana, 1943), 12. In 1702 the erudite Benedictine Bernard de Montfaucon examined this book and described it (presumably the first volume mentioned by Vigili) as a "codex complectitur Biblia Hebraïca perantiqua in quorum frontispicio legitur *Istam Bibliam Hebraïcam dedit frater Guillelmus Parisiensis ordinis Fratrum Praedicatorum Confessor Illustrissimi Regis Franchorum (sic) conventui Bononiensi pro communi Libraria Fratrum, propter reverentia (sic) Beati Dominici anno MCCCX pridie idus Februarii. Quicunque legerit in ea, oret pro eo. amen.*" Bernard de Montfaucon, *Diarium italicum* (Paris: J. Anisson, 1702), 401.

16. The attribution is sufficiently proved by Amédée Teetaert, "Un compendium de théologie pastorale du XIIIe–XIVe siècle," *Revue d'histoire ecclésiastique* 26 (1930): 96–100. For the medieval evidence of attribution, see Gillis Meersseman, ed., *Laurentii Pignon catalogi et chronica* (Rome: Apud Institutum Historicum Fratrum Praedicatorum, 1936), 31, 66, 75.

17. Kaeppeli, *Scriptores ordinis praedicatorum*, #1619, lists fifteen manuscripts.

18. I have been able to consult only BnF lat.13667 (fourteenth-century, parchment, two columns, from the collection of Saint-Germain-des-Prés) and BAV, Borgh. 276 (fourteenth-century, parchment, two columns; the latter on microfilm at the Institut de recherche et d'histoire des textes in Paris). Both manuscripts contain first the *Tabula super decretales* and then the *Tabula super decreta* (the mistaken statement about lat. 13667 by Teetaert, "Compendium de théologie pastorale," 99, notwithstanding). Before the second work, a second preface is included in Borgh. 276 (but not in lat. 13667) that is nearly identical to the first but uses different examples to fit the different texts treated. The transcriptions in the following notes are taken from Borgh. 276, fol. 1r, but there are only superficial differences from lat. 13667.

19. "Quod totum opus per abecedarium procedit, ita quod primo po-
nuntur notabilia casus, questionis, et sententie quorum termini principales incipiunt per 'a'; deinde illa quorum termini principales incipiunt per 'b'; et sic
de aliis secundum ordinem abecedarii, quod faciliter apparere potest etiam su-
perficia littere intuenti."

20. "Postquam positum est notabile, casus, sive questio, sive sententia,
statim signatur titulus et principium decretalis ubi poterit inveniri. Dictio
autem que signatur principium decretalis inferius est virgata et ei supponitur
littera que indicat numerum glose in qua est illud quod queritur hoc modo.
Talem enim numerum facit glosa illa inter glosas decretalis qualem facit in al-
fabeto littera que supposita est dictioni illi. . . . Si littera illa supposita sit 'a,'
querenda est prima glosa; si 'b' secundum; si 'c' tercia; et sic de aliis . . . supponitur hoc sillabi 'fi' signatur quod querenda est ultima vel penultima glosa.
Quando vero supponitur hoc littera 't' aperte superiori percussa signatur
quod id quod queritur est in textu."

21. "Et idcirco in principio cuiuslibet vocabuli antequam tangatur aliquid
de pertinentibus ad ipsum premittuntur quedam dictiones inferius virgate
cum quibusdam litteris alfabeti quibus ostenditur ubi cetera que cadere possunt sub tali vocabulo nec ibi habentur poterunt inveniri."

22. Kaeppeli, *Scriptores ordinis praedicatorum*, #1619, lists fifty manuscripts (which I can correct by noting that BnF ms. lat. 14842 does not contain
the work under consideration) and fifteen early editions. Nine more manuscripts and at least ten editions are added by Carmen Cardelle de Hartmann,
Lateinische Dialoge, 1200–1400: Literaturhistorische Studie und Repertorium
(Leiden: Brill, 2007), 489–91.

23. I argue for the existence of at least two versions (based on a study of
only the Parisian manuscripts) and return to the question of authorship in my
article "The *Dialogus de septem sacramentis* Attributed to William of Paris,
O.P.: One Text in Two Versions," in *Archivum fratrum praedicatorum* 80,
forthcoming. The first version must have been written before 1298, because it
lacks references to Boniface VIII's *Liber sextus*. The longer, second version includes multiple citations from this new collection of decretals. It should be
noted that my division into two versions is surely too neat; closer study would
undoubtedly reveal further stages of development.

24. Following Teetaert's study of 1930 ("Compendium de théologie pas-
torale"), which agreed with Quétif and Echard, *Scriptores ordinis praedicato-
rum*, vol. 1, pt. 2, 518–19, standard sources on Dominican authors, such as
Kaeppeli, *Scriptores ordinis praedicatorum*, have adopted this attribution. P. C.
Boeren was among those unconvinced. See *La vie et les oeuvres de Guiard de
Laon, 1170 env.–1248* (The Hague: Nijhoff, 1956), 107–10. However, Leonard
Boyle credited it to our William of Paris without hesitation. See "The Summa

confessorum of John of Freiburg and the Popularization of the Moral Teaching of St. Thomas and Some of His Contemporaries," in *Pastoral Care, Clerical Education and Canon Law, 1200–1400* (London: Variorum Reprints, 1981), 3:246. If William of Paris was not the author, the most likely alternative possibility is William Baufet, the contemporary bishop of Paris. The most recent treatment, Cardelle de Hartmann, *Lateinische Dialoge*, 489–91, leaves the question open between these two men.

25. Teetaert has shown that indeed the *Dialogue* draws explicitly on both Thomas and Peter of Tarentaise (though he gives only one short and not entirely conclusive example for the latter). See "Compendium de théologie pastorale," 82–87. Thomas is also cited once by name in a comparison with Godefroy of Fontaines in a passage found in some manuscripts (e.g., BnF mss lat. 3209, fol. 37rb; 3210, fol. 43v; 14741, fol. 20v; 13451, fol. 28v) and in the concluding passage to all manuscripts I have seen ("propter maiora ad scripta fratris Thome et aliorum doctorum recurras"). The "Summa Raymondi" and its gloss are cited in all manuscripts as well (e.g. lat. 3208, fol. 28v; 3209, fol. 34rb; 3210, fol. 41r; 14741, fol. 18v; 14922, fol. 134r).

26. If William of Paris was indeed responsible for the longer, revised version, then a date ca. 1298–1301 seems most likely. Not only are there hints that the *Liber sextus* had only recently appeared, but it is hard to envision a close advisor to Philip IV urging "total adherence" to the opinion of Boniface VIII after about 1301. See Teetaert, "Compendium de théologie pastorale," 87–90, on the *Dialogue*'s reliance (beyond explicit quotations) on decrees of Boniface VIII (in fact, this evidence is only found in the longer, later version). Only a full study of the entire text in both versions and all manuscripts would definitely show the nature and probable date of the revisions. Such a study is obviously beyond the parameters of the present work.

27. Although the later post-1298 version inserts even more explicit references to various decretals, even the early version does contain a substantial number: examples include a citation of the famous decree of 1215 *Omnis utriusque sexus* (e.g., BnF ms lat. 14922, fol. 125v); "illa decretalis extra de usuris, *Cum tu sicut asseris*" (lat. 14922, fol. 137v); "illa decretalis extra de feriis, *Capellanus*" (lat. 14922, fol. 145v); "in decretis xxvii q. ii. *Si quis uxorem desponsaverit*" (lat. 14922, fol. 151v). Some of these references, however, may have come straight from the author's reliance on Thomas Aquinas.

28. BnF ms. lat. 3209, fol. 24r: "Hereticus. Id est falso contra Deum sentiendo contra articulos fidei predicando docendo aperte vel secrete et omnes factores et consentientes heretici reputantur."

29. I have consulted the printed edition, Vincent of Beauvais, *Bibliotheca mundi seu Speculi Maioris Vincentii Burgundi praesulis Bellovacensis, . . . tomus*

quartus, qui Speculum historiale inscribuntur (Douai: Baltazarus Bellerius, 1624). The best introduction is Monique Paulmier-Foucart, with Marie-Christine Duchenne, *Vincent de Beauvais et le Grand miroir du monde* (Turnhout: Brepols, 2004), with a summary of the contents of the *Speculum historiale,* 93–104.

30. Indeed, this copy was traded back and forth from royal to Dominican hands several times. In 1314, it was actually in the possession of William's Dominican successor as confessor, Reginald of Aubigny, and in his codicil Philip left it to the brothers resident at the female Dominican abbey of Poissy.

31. The fundamental work is Antoine Dondaine, "Guillaume Peyraut: Vie et oeuvres," *Archivum fratrum praedicatorum* 18 (1948): 162–236. For a useful recent summary of the *De eruditione principum,* see Michael Verweij, "Princely Virtues or Virtues for Princes? William Peraldus and His *De eruditione principum,*" in *Princely Virtues in the Middle Ages, 1200–1500,* ed. István P. Bejczy and Cary J. Nederman (Turnhout: Brepols, 2007), 51–72. The "certain prince" could have been a member of the French royal family, but there is no specific evidence for his identity.

32. William draws extensively on Vincent's *De eruditione filiorum nobilium.* See Arpad Steiner, "Guillaume Perrault and Vincent of Beauvais," *Speculum* 8 (1933): 51–58, and Arpad Steiner, ed., *De eruditione filiorum nobilium,* by Vincent of Beauvais (Cambridge, MA: Mediaeval Academy of America, 1938). The two are discussed together briefly in Jacques Krynen, *L'empire du roi: Idées et croyances politiques en France, XIIIe–XVe siècle* (Paris: Gallimard, 1993), 173–79. Vincent and William provide a good example of Dominican interdependence, since Vincent in his *De morali principis institutione* drew on William's earlier *Summa de vitiis.* William in turn extensively reused materials from his Summae on the virtues and vices in the *De eruditione principum.* See Robert J. Schneider, ed., *Vincentii Belvacensis, De morali principis institutiutione,* CCCM 137 (Turnhout: Brepols, 1995), xxxv. Indeed, it is possible that the notation in the royal records to the purchase of a "De eruditione principum" could be a reference to Vincent's work under a slightly different title, or even another work for the education of princes (of which there were no shortage circulating at the Capetian court). Nevertheless, the specific title given in the records makes Peraldus's book the most likely.

33. Verweij, "Princely Virtues," 70–71.

34. William Peraldus, *De eruditione principum* 2.3, quoted in Vermweij, "Princely Virtues," 63 n. 39: "Nec debet homo moveri, si aliquos haereticos videat vel abstinentes, vel misericordes, cum plures tales inveniantur qui sunt fidei Catholicae, vel si aliqui, qui sunt fidei Catholicae, inveniantur mali, multi enim magnae malitiae sunt inter haereticos, sed occulant eam quantum possunt, nec mirum cum et seipsos occultent."

35. See the essays in Louis-Jacques Bataillon, Gilbert Dahan, and Pierre-Marie Gy, eds., *Hugues de Saint-Cher (d. 1263): Bibliste et théologien* (Turnhout: Brepols, 2004); Mulchahey, *First the Bow,* 486–500; and Robert E. Lerner, "Poverty, Preaching, and Eschatology in the Revelation Commentaries of 'Hugh of St-Cher,'" in *The Bible in the Medieval World: Essays in Memory of Beryl Smalley,* ed. Katherine Walsh and Diana Wood (Oxford: Blackwell, 1985), 157–89. Nicholas, in fact, has been called "the only really prolific commentator on Scripture working in Paris towards the end of the thirteenth century." See Beryl Smalley, "Some Latin Commentaries on the Sapiential Books in the Late Thirteenth and Early Fourteenth Centuries," *Archives d'histoire doctrinale et littéraire du Moyen Âge* 18 (1950–51): 106–16, quotation at 106.

36. See the manuscript references in note 25 above.

37. Several of Thomas's opinions were widely attacked by Franciscans, seculars, and even other Dominicans. The most dramatic instance was the controversy at Paris over a challenge by the Dominican Durand of Saint-Pourçain, which broke out in 1307 and dragged on past Thomas's canonization in 1323. In the course of this dispute, the Dominican chapter general of 1313 decreed that all Dominican lectors would expound the Sentences after the opinions of Thomas. See Mulchahey, *First the Bow,* 142–66; and Josef Koch, "Die Magister-Jahre des Durandus de S. Porciano O.P. und der Konflikt mit seinem Orden," in *Kleine Schriften* (Rome: Edizioni di Storia e Letteratura, 1973), 2:7–118.

38. To my knowledge it has not previously been noted that the work cites Geoffrey of Trani's *Summa super titulis decretalium,* written in the early 1240s by this canonist and cardinal (d. 1245). See, e.g., BnF mss lat. 3208, fol. 11r, and 3210, fol. 8: "Gauffridus in summa sua de consecratione ecclesie."

39. In this mixture of legal and theological interests with a Dominican slant, William resembled Nicholas of Fréauville, who left works by Aquinas *(Summa contra gentiles, Secunda secundae)* and treatises on both canon law *(Summa decretalium)* and pastoral care (works by Gregory the Great and others) in his testament, where he notes specifically that he acquired the works by Thomas and on canon law before his elevation to the cardinalate. See Quétif and Echard, *Scriptores ordinis praedicatorum,* vol. 1, pt. 2, 557–58.

40. Augustine and Jerome are cited among other places in the section on marriage: for example, BnF mss. lat. 3209, fol. 52v; 3208, fol. 39r; 3210, fol. 57r;14922, fol. 144r.

41. See note 25 above.

42. *Pecia* simply means "piece" and shows that a manuscript was divided for quick copying in a university stationer's shop. Here see Giovanna Murano, "Postille perdute e problemi d'autenticità (Nicola di Gorran O.P. e Guglielmo

di Melitona Omin)," *Archivum Franciscanum historicum* 92 (1999): 302–4. The manuscript ends (fol. 195ra) with "Expliciunt postille super Lucam, scripte a Martino de Histria," indicating that Martin of Histria was the actual copyist.

43. See Friedlander, *Hammer of the Inquisitors,* 88–97; B. Hauréau, *Bernard Délicieux et l'inquisition albigeoise* (Paris: Hachette, 1877), 29–45; and, more broadly, Given, *Inquisition and Medieval Society,* 130–39.

44. Lalou, *Itinéraire de Philip IV,* 2:195, follows Hauréau, *Bernard Délicieux,* 41 n. 2, in suggesting that the true recipient of this letter was William of Peter Godin (for a short summary of the latter's career, see W. D. McCready, *The Theory of Papal Monarchy in the Fourteenth Century: Guillaume de Pierre Godin, Tractatus de causa immediata ecclesiastice potestatis* [Toronto: Pontifical Institute of Mediaeval Studies, 1982], 7–9). The document, however, is clearly addressed "religio viro fratri G. de Parisius, dilecto capellano nostro," and later in the text the "G" is expanded to "Guillhelmus." This can only be our William of Paris (Hauréau mistakenly assumed the letter would have read "Guillelmus de P." This was evidently just a guess).

45. The letter is found in AN J306 no. 90, a contemporary document on high-quality parchment that preserves copies of seven letters from Philip IV concerning Toulouse, four of which directly bear on the Foulques of Saint-George affair (the dorse reads, "littere pro archid. Algie"). This document is edited in Claude Devic and J. Vaissete, *Histoire générale de Languedoc,* vol. 10, *Preuves* (Toulouse: Privat, 1885), 383–84. The edition is sound, except that the order of the letters is not respected; though Devic and Vaissete print it fourth, the letter to William of Paris is actually the last of the seven and is in fact written on a separate piece of parchment that has been sewn onto the longer piece that contains the other six letters. All seven letters, however, are in the same hand: "Philippus, Dei gratia Francorum rex, religioso viro fratri G. de Parisius, dilecto capellano nostro, salutem et dilectionem. Super tractatu, nuper in conventu fratrum Predicatorum Parisius circa [ms. corrected from *super*] inquisitionis negocium et personam fratris Falconis habito, ejusdem conventus intentione reperta, plura ex intencione eadem concepimus, que plus ad nostri dedecus ac totius populi ignominiam, quam ad Ecclesie utilitatem et commissorum excessuum ultionem vergere dignoscuntur. Ex predicta etenim intentione concepimus, quod deliberato super premissis in conventu predicto, prioris et fratrum tunc ibidem existentium in hoc voluntas residet, quod dictus frater Falco, ajuncto sibi quodam fratre ejusdem ordinis, in inquisitionis negotio saltem usque ad instantem mediam XLam remaneat, ut interim per se inchoatos possit complere processus et super eisdem sentencialiter diffinire; circa hec dicti fratris et ordinis sui vehementer elationem querentes, nostrum dedecus ampliantes ac gravi periculo et generali scandalo, que ex comissis hujusmodi sequi possunt,

nullatenus obviantes. Quis enim, frater Guillelme, ausu quocumque crederet, quod regni nostri provincialis et alii ordinis vestri fratres, nostris temporibus, personam tam detestabilem et apud nos tantis opprobriis et discriminibus diffamatam, contra nostram et totius populi opinionem sustinere presumerent, quemadmodum faciunt hiis diebus? Quid plura? Brevi sermone, grandi tamen affectu vos requirimus, quatenus provincialem et fratres predictos ad hoc curetis efficaciter inducere, quod hujusmodi voluntatem suam sic in melius commutare studeant, quod per commutationem eamdem optimo provideatur remedio in premissis. Nos siquidem ob inmense et sincere dilectionis affectum, quem pro toto tempore vite nostre ad ordinem vestrum et ejusdem ordinis fratres habuimus, usque ad hec tempora pro firmo tenuimus, quod provincialis et priores predicti aliquem fratrem ordinis ejusdem, cujuscumque auctoritatis esset, status vel supereminencie, eciam majorem fratre Falcone predicto, contra voluntatem nostram non tenerent in officio, cujus hiis diebus dicti fratris Falconis persona contrarium manifestat. Datum apud Montemargi, sabbato post octabas yemalis festi sancti Nicholai." The Dominican provincial prior at this moment was William of Cayeux (1296–1302), who had earlier been prior of Paris and then would be elected as provincial a second time (1306–9), following Raymond Romain and just before Hervé Nédellec. See Meersseman, *Laurentii Pignon catalogi,* 18–19, 81–82, 85.

46. See Antoine Dondaine, "Documents pour servir à l'histoire de la province de France: L'appel au concile (1303)," *Archivum fratrum praedicatorum* 22 (1952): 405; Courtenay, "Between Pope and King."

47. Among the first signers were Reginald of Aubigny (first) who had taken the lead in Philip's cause, Nicholas of Fréauville (fourth), and the master of theology John of Paris (sixth). Reginald and Nicholas were William's successor and predecessor as royal confessor, respectively, and John was known as an ardent royal supporter. It is worth noting that William is given no title (such as chaplain or inquisitor) after his name in this document. I am following William Courtenay's analysis, which shows that a group of some thirty-seven Dominicans whose names appear two-thirds of the way down the document probably held out for some time before adhering, including Raymond Romain, provincial prior (1302–6), and Bernard of Auvergne, prior of Paris. Courtenay also estimates that perhaps forty to fifty non-French Dominicans, resident in Paris for studies, refused to adhere ("Between Pope and King," 599).

48. Kaeppeli *(Scriptores ordinis praedicatorum)* and de la Selle *(Service)* both give 1303 as the date of William inquisitorial appointment, but without evidentiary support. Vidal *(Bullaire de l'Inquisition)* suggests 1303, with a question mark. Coulon ("Guillaume de Paris") also says 1303, but he is demonstrably incorrect with a number of his dates. All of these authors would seem to

simply be following Quétif and Echard *(Scriptores ordinis praedicatorum),* but Lajard ("Guillaume de Paris") and Teetaert ("Compendium de théologie pastorale") both correctly note the lack of evidence for their claim. Nevertheless, the date of 1303 or early 1304 does seem likely to be substantially correct.

49. The reference is in a letter from John of Burgundy to James II of Aragon, reporting events at Poitiers on 30 May 1308, when Philip IV and Clement V were engaged in intense negotiations over the Templar affair. According to this source, Clement stated that "bene credit, quod inquisitor habebat litteras generales predecessorum suorum super inquisitionis negotio." Heinrich Finke, *Papsttum und Untergang des Templerordens* (Munster: Aschendorffschen Buchhandlung, 1907), 2:149. For English translation, see Malcolm Barber and Keith Bate, trans., *The Templars: Selected Sources* (Manchester: Manchester University Press, 2002), 263–72. For analysis, see Barber, *Trial of the Templars,* 107–12.

50. It should be noted that Clement used the plural to refer to letters of "our predecessors." Strictly construed, this should mean that Clement believed William to have been confirmed in his inquisitorial powers by more than one previous pope (unless this plural is a grammatically dubious use of the papal "we"). It should be recalled, however, that we do not have the pope's own precise words but rather a report of them, and that even if Clement did use the plural he had no need to worry about absolute precision in this context; Clement was merely making the point that although he himself had not appointed William inquisitor he knew that William did in fact hold this office legitimately. Moreover, it seems impossible to think that Boniface VIII could have approved the appointment of a royal chaplain as a new inquisitor after about 1301, and to push William's assumption of inquisitorial office back earlier than this seems unrealistic. I am therefore inclined to date William's investment with the office of inquisitor to 1303–4.

51. Favier, *Roi de marbre,* 307; Friedlander, *Hammer of the Inquisitors,* 151–77. See specifically the document of 14 January 1304, edited in Devic and Vaissete, *Histoire générale de Languedoc,* vol. 10, *Preuves,* cols. 428–31. Philip notes there that his reforms are not meant to encroach on papal authority ("ac summi pontificis auctoritate in omnibus semper salva") but otherwise does not refer to papal power and seems ready to legislate for inquisitors on his own, in consultation with local prelates, barons, "doctors," and Dominicans. The only one of the latter mentioned by name is William of Peter Godin. William of Paris is not mentioned, and I am unaware of any evidence that would prove whether he actually traveled south with Philip.

52. It is unlikely that Philip was already preparing the attack on the Templars as early as 1303–4 and therefore laying the groundwork through his

promotion of William's powers. By 1306, however, when the inquisitor was also named confessor, this possibility becomes more plausible. I thank Julien Théry for a stimulating discussion on this and related issues.

53. There is no surviving indication of the exact date on which Philip named a new confessor, but it must have been not long after December 1305. I have found no evidence for the claim that the Dominican brother Imbert (who was certainly later a confessor to King Louis X) occupied this office briefly before William.

54. Jean Favier wrote aptly (if not literally) that for Philip, "The inquisitor of France, this was well and truly the king." Favier, *Roi de marbre,* 302.

55. For Simon Duval, the Dominican prior of Provins and inquisitor active around 1276–78, see Dondaine, "Manuel de l'inquisiteur," 186–92 (also at 110, "Simon Duval OP" appears in a document; Dondaine seems to assume this is a different man, but the reason for this assumption is unclear). Since he was well known to Louis IX and an executor of Pierre d'Alençon's will, Simon must be counted as close to the royal family. See Daunou, "Simon Duval." Nevertheless, Simon is not known to have been confessor to the king or to have conducted any process in Paris. I thank Sylvain Piron for discussion on this point. On Philip IV's support of William of Auxerre, see Dondaine, "Manuel de l'inquisiteur," 138–39.

56. I thank Sylvain Piron for suggesting this neat formula. It is remarkable that scholars have paid so little attention to this moment when the offices of inquisitor and royal confessor were combined for the first time. Although Charles-Victor Langlois long ago noted that this was "une nouveauté," subsequent scholars of the reign of Philip IV have not emphasized this crucial step toward amalgamating secular and sacred power. For Langlois, see his "L'affaire des Templiers," *Journal des savants,* ser. 6 (1908): 433 n. 1.

57. See Annette Pales-Gobilliard, ed. and trans., *Le livre des sentences d'inquisiteur Bernard Gui, 1308–1321,* 2 vols. (Paris: CNRS Éditions, 2002), 1:326, "frater Bernardus Guidonis ordinis Predicatorum, inquisitor heretice pravitatis in regno Francie auctoritate apostolica deputatus," from a *sermo generalis* of 23 October 1309, and 1:333 similarly for 5 April 1310. The same styling appears in forms included in Bernard's *Practica inquisitionis heretice pravitatis,* ed. Célestin Douais (Paris: Picard, 1886): for example, the *Forma communis citationis,* 1. This same title and phrasing had been used by an earlier Dominican inquisitor in Toulouse, Pons of Parnac, in 1276. See Biller, Bruschi, and Sneddon, *Inquisitors and Heretics,* 652. At the very same time (1276) the same title was used in the North by Simon Duval. See Dondaine, "Manuel de l'inquisiteur," 191.

58. Lalou, *Comptes sur tablettes* (comptes extraordinaires), 770, #11 "[Guillel]mus, confessor missus de Longo Ponte veneris sequenti [20 January 1307] ad quedam [. . . . . . .]rum negocia. 20L" Also 771, #33.

59. BnF ms. lat. 10919, fols. 65rb–65vb. Partially transcribed in Finke, *Papsttum und Untergang,* 2:46 (with incorrect folio number).

60. See the analysis below of William's letter of 22 September. This title could be honorific (without real duties), which must be the case here, since William was certainly not in attendance at the papal curia.

61. On the early portion of the Templar affair, see Barber, *Trial of the Templars,* 59–87; and Georges Lizerand, *Clément V et Philippe IV le Bel* (Paris: Hachette, 1910), 94–131.

62. Georges Lizerand, ed., *Le dossier de l'affaire des Templiers,* 2nd ed. (Paris: Les belles lettres, 1964), 20–22 (based on AN J413 B n. 22): "Unde nos, qui ad defensionem fidei ecclesiastice libertatis sumus a Domino super regalis eminencie specula constituti, et pre cunctis desiderabilibus mentis nostre augmentum catholice fidei affectamus, per dilectum in Christo fratrem G. de Parisius, inquisitorem heretice pravitatis auctoritate apostolica deputatum, super premissis, infamia publica referente, diligenti informatione prehabita, et tam in informatione ipsa quam ex aliis diversis presumptionibus, argumentis legitimis et probabilibus conjecturis, contra prefatos Dei, fidei et nature hostes ac humani federis inimicos vehementi suspitione concepta, inquisitoris predicti, qui brachii nostri auxilium invocavit, justis in hac parte supplicationibus annuentes . . . decrivimus ut singulares persone predicti ordinis regni nostri sine exceptione aliqua capiantur." A full translation of this letter can be found in Barber and Bate, *Templars,* 244–47. It should be noted that J413 B n. 22 is an unsealed, unnotarized (though contemporary) copy of a *vidimus* by Peter of Hangest, bailli of Rouen. The *vidimus* is dated Saturday, 23 September 1307. A digitial image can now be viewed through the ARCHIM database at www.culture.gouv.fr/documentation/archim/proces -templiers.html.

63. A document from the Diocese of Bayeux attests that this letter really was received by Dominicans all over the kingdom. J413 B no. 17 is a copy, made by the public notary Henry "called le Gay" at Caen, on 28 October (two weeks after the arrest of the Templars), of several confessions by Templars. They were brought before the notary by four local Dominicans, who cited their authority as agents of William of Paris. The notarized document then quotes from the opening and closing of William's commissioning letter to specify the nature of this commission. For small variations between this version and that edited by Finke, see the following note. See also the analysis concerning the copy sent to Amiens in Filip Hooghe, "The Trial of the Templars in the County of Flanders (1307–1312)," in Burgtorf, Crawford, and Nicholson, *Debate on the Trial,* 291–92. Langlois, "Affaire des Templiers," 433 n. 2, further notes that another original of this directive can be found in ms. 1920 of the Bibliothèque d'Angers.

64. The most reliable edition of the document is Finke, *Papsttum und Untergang*, 2:44–46, here 44, from J413 B n. 22. This *vidimus* by Peter of Hangest, bailli of Rouen, includes first Philip IV's letter of September 14 and the vernacular instructions that accompanied it (as edited by Lizerand), and then William's letter. Since this *vidimus* is dated September 23, it seems that the bailli of Rouen received these three texts together, or at approximately the same time. Words included here within square brackets are variants from J413 B no. 17 (see previous note): "Religiosis et venerabilibus fratribus inquisitoribus heretice pravitatis Tholose et Carcassone auctoritate apostolica deputatis, prioribus conventualibus, supprioribus et lectoribus ordinis fratrum Predicatorum in regno Francie constitutis, eorum videlicet singulis, frater G[uillelmus] de Parisius, eiusdem ordinis, capellanus domini pape, serenissimi [excellentis] principis domini [Philippi dei gratia *add.*] regis Francie confessor et inquisitor heretice pravitatis in regno Francie [regni Francie] predicto [*om.*] auctoritate apostolica deputatus, salutem in actore et consummatore fidei Ihesu Christo." Earlier edition in Fredericq, *Corpus*, 52–59 (reprinted from Du Puy's seventeenth-century *Histoire de la condamnation des Templiers*); and portions in Edgar P. Boutaric, *Clément V, Philippe le Bel et les Templiers* (1874; repr., Whitefish, MT: Kessinger, 2010), 36–37. Discussion in Barber, *Trial of the Templars*, 67–68.

65. Finke, *Papsttum und Untergang*, 2:45: "Prefatus igitur dominus rex christianissimus premissis auditis, admiracionis stupore perterritus et fidei ardore succensus, ea non spernit sed nedum nobis suisque secretis consiliariis sed patri nostro sanctissimo domino summo pontifici apud Lugdunum primo et Pictavius secundo audita diligenter aperuit."

66. See Clement's letter of 24 August 1310, in Baluze, *Vitae paparum avenionensium*, 3:60, translated in Barber and Bate, *Templars*, 243–44.

67. Finke, *Papsttum und Untergang*, 2:45–46: "Et nobis postmodum adhibitis diligencius perquisivit pluresque testes fidedigni, omni excepcione maiores, maxime in causa fidei, sunt recepti per nos iudicialiter. Per quos omnes singulariter turpis recepcio predicta probatur in eorum personis facta fuisse. Ac vehemens inducitur presumpcio contra omnes . . . Ea propter per ipsum dominum regem reverendis patribus archi-episcopis, abbatibus et aliis eminentibus viris ecclesiasticis ad hoc specialiter congregatis eorum tam per ipsum dominum regem quam per nos requisito consilio, provida eorum et concordi deliberacione accedente, ipsum dominum regem duximus pro causa fidei requirendum, ut contra singulares personas dicti ordinis de premissis vehementer suspectas huius regni nobis dare favorem, opem et auxilium dignaretur, ut eas habere valeamus examinandas, ut decet, super hiis non intendentes negocium hoc contra dictum ordinem assumere seu contra fratres ipsius ordinis universaliter, sed solum contra singulares suspectas perquiri. Qui religiosus princeps

animo prompto requisicionem nostram exaudiens per diversas partes regni sui dictas singulares personas suspectas perquiri et ecclesie iudicio presentari precepit, ad hoc certas eminentes specialiter destinando."

68. Finke, *Papsttum und Untergang,* 2:45–46: "Nos igitur per diversas partes regni presencialiter accedere non valentes, pluribus negociis et infirmitate proprii corporis impediti, vos exhortamur in domino, vobis presencium tenore committentes ac vos singulariter deputantes, quatinus nobis in adiutorium cause fidei assurgentes non pigri sed vigiles, adhibitis duabus religiosis personis et discretis cum personis suspectis sic vobis per gentes domini regis predicti exhibendis inquiratis ex parte nostra immo pocius apostolica super premissis diligentius veritatem, deposicionibus eorumdem per pubicam personam, si comode poterit haberi, aut per duos viros idoneos conscribendis. Et si premissa scelera inveneritis esse vera, probis viris ordinis fratrum Minorum ac aliis religiosis viris negocium sic aperire curetis, quod apud eos vel populum non oriatur scandalum ex huiusmodi processibus sed odor pocius bone fame. Deposicionesque talium testium domino regi et nobis in Francia sub vestris et dicti domini regis gencium, que ad predicta specialiter destinantur, sigillis interclusas fideliter mittere non tardetis."

69. Barber, *Trial of the Templars,* 68. Lizerand, *Dossier,* 26: "par gehine, se mestier est."

70. Barber (*Trial of the Templars,* 324 n. 41) raises the possibility that William did not personally draft this letter and suggests Nogaret's involvement. While it is true that this letter repeats the accusations emanating from the court (and likely from Nogaret), the subtle way it seeks to place more responsibility on Philip and less on William in instigating the attacks suggests to me William's overall responsibility for the wording of at least these passages. Marion Melville, *La vie des Templiers,* 2nd ed. (Paris: Gallimard, 1974), 293, alertly noticed this "différence de ton" between the two letters. Moreover, Finke's edition omits a small portion of William's letter and simply states that it repeats "die Aufzählung der Anschuldigungen wie in dem Schreiben des Königs vom 14. Sept. 1307." This description is somewhat misleading. While it is true that the omitted passage repeats the charges about illicit kisses and other corrupt practices during the Templar reception ceremony, it does not follow the exact wording of Philip's letter, and Finke does not specify that only a few sentences are omitted here (only six lines out of a letter of thirty-six lines in J413 B n. 22).

71. On the use of torture at this juncture, see Barber, *Trial of the Templars,* 71.

72. Barber, *Trial of the Templars,* 79; Jules Michelet, *Le procès des Templiers,* new ed. (Paris: Éditions du C. T. H. S., 1987), 2:305–6. Translation in Barber and Bate, *Templars,* 252–53.

73. Michelet, *Procès des Templiers,* 2:275–420. The original copy of these depositions (a roll of some 22 meters) is AN J413 no. 18. Images of this entire document are now available through the ARCHIM database at www.culture .gouv.fr/documentation/archim/proces-templiers.html

74. Finke, *Papsttum und Untergang,* 2:307–13, #149 and #150. For insightful explanation of the difference between the two days' audiences, see Courtenay, "Learned Opinion," 156–58; and William J. Courtenay, "Marguerite's Judges: The University of Paris in 1310," in Piron, Lerner, and Field, *Marguerite Porete.* See also Barber, *Trial of the Templars,* 78–80; and Paul F. Crawford, "The University of Paris and the Trial of the Templars," in *The Military Orders,* vol. 3, *History and Heritage,* ed. Victor Mallia-Milanes (Aldershot: Ashgate, 2008), 115–23.

75. This is the last date on which he appears in the records as personally present at questioning. See Michelet, *Procès des Templiers,* 2:101. His Dominican deputy Nicholas of Ennezat, who had taken over much of the questioning in November, continued up through November 24 (408). Denifle and Chatelain, *Chartularium universitatis Parisiensis,* #666, has been the source of some confusion. Under the date of 25 May 1308, this collection gives the text of Jacques of Molay's confession, made in the presence of William of Paris. This was not, however, a new confession but merely a copy of the original confession that had been made in the presence of the university in October 1307. William's name is simply copied here, it does not indicate new activity on his part (*pace* Teetaert). See Finke, *Papsttum und Untergang,* 2:309, on this point.

76. Barber, *Trial of the Templars,* 86–87.

77. No actual papal letter to this effect survives. It must be deduced from the letters Clement issued in July lifting this suspension, discussed below. See ibid., 94–95.

78. On these three aspects of the royal campaign I am summarizing, see ibid., 95–105. These were among the first meetings of the "Estates," after those called in 1302–3 during the crisis with Boniface VIII. See the recent comments by Théry, "Philippe le Bel," 17.

79. Barber, *Trial of the Templars,* 106–24.

80. An original of this letter is AN J416 no. 3, with Clement V's lead seal still attached. A copy is also found in BnF ms. lat. 10919, fols. 135ra–136vb. The best printed version is the *vidimus* of 11 February 1309, in Célestin Port, ed., "Livre de Guillaume le Maire," in *Mélanges historiques: Choix de documents,* vol. 2, *Collection de documents inédits sur l'histoire de France* (Paris: Imprimerie nationale, 1877), 418–23. My transcriptions here are from J416 no. 3: "Clemens, episcopus servus servorum Dei, venerabilibus fratribus universis archiepiscopis et episcopis per regnum Francie constitutis, et dilectis filiis

Guillermo et aliis inquisitoribus heretice pravitatis in eodem regno auctoritate apostolica generaliter deputatis, salutem et apostolicam benedicionem. . . . Dudum siquidem Templariorum subitam capcionem, quam ad nostri apostolatus et fratrum nostrorum pertulit vulgatus rumor auditum, quia raciones et cause, que carissimum in Christo filium nostrum Philippum regem Francorum illustrem induxerant ad hujusmodi capcionem, tibique fili Guillermo suggesserant regem super hoc requirere memoratum, nostram et dictorum fratrum latebant noticiam, non immerito nos et fratres ipsi dolentes suscepimus, cum per te, Guillermum predictum, nobis, quibus quodam modo vicinus eras in januis, nichil intimatum fuisset, ac de precipiti festinacione processus per vos contra ipsos habiti et, ut timebatur, habendi, super quo inaudita publica referebat assercio, grandis suspicionis materia in nostra et fratrum ipsorum mentibus extitit suscitata, propter quod omnem quam habebatis in hujusmodi negocio potestatem, de predictorum fratrum consilio, suspendentes, ad nos negocium ipsum totaliter duximus revocandum."

81. J416 no. 3: "Demum vero processibus, per vos archiepiscopos et episcopos et Guillermum predictos ante tempus suspensionis et revocacionis predictarum vel saltim, priusquam ad vestram noticiam hujusmodi suspensio et revocacio pervenissent, habitis contra Templarios memoratos, exhibitis in nostra et fratrum presencia predictorum et diligenter inspectis, multa per eosdem processus contra ipsos apparent fuisse reperta, de quibus modicam habebamus verisimilem conjecturam, nec ad illa credenda nostre mentis oppinio poterat inclinari."

82. The original of this document is AN L291 no. 15. A printed version, with several errors of transcription, can be found in (M. le Comte) de Loisne, "Bulles de papes pour l'Ordre du Temple, conservées aux Archives nationales (1155–1312)," *Bulletin philosophique et historique (jusqu'à 1715) du Comité des travaux historiques et scientifiques* 5 (1917): 232. Better is the *vidimus* of 11 February 1309, in Port, "Livre," 424. The following transcription is from the original: "Clemens episcopus servus servorum Dei, dilecto filio fratri Guilhermo, ordinis Predicatorum, inquisitori heretice pravitatis in regno Francie generaliter auctoritate apostolica deputato, salutem et apostolicam benedictionem. Licet indignacionem nostram ex eo non inmerito incurrere debuisses, quod nobis existens tam evicino propinquus [*sic*], contra fratres ordinis milicie Templi, nobis inrequisitis, presumptuose processisti, volentes tamen uti clemencia potius quam severitate, erga te in hac parte, instancia carissimi in Christo filii nostri Philipi, regis Francie illustris inducti pluries repetita, tibi, quod contra singulares personas Templariorum ipsorum simul cum prelatis regni predicti et aliis per nos associandis eisdem, et non aliter, procedere valeas, de benignitate apostolica duximus concedendum, hoc idem aliis dicti regni inquisitoribus

tenore presentium concedentes. Datum Pictavis, v die Julii, pontificatus nostri anno tercio." It is worth stressing that the correct reading in the greeting is "generaliter," and not "generali," which would be an adjective implying that William was "inquisitor general," as de Loisne would have it. A comparison with J416 no. 3 (cited above) shows that Clement applied this adverb *generaliter* to all the inquisitors of the kingdom, not just to William.

83. Leicht, *Marguerite Porete*, 345, notes briefly that "sein Ruf als Inquisitor dürfte seit seiner Suspendierung 1308 angekratzt gewesen sein." Muraro, *Lingua materna*, 23, also alertly notes that "Guglielmo di Parigi era stato biasimato da papa Clemente V per la maniera irregolare con cui aveva proceduto verso i Templari." Melville, *Vie des Templiers*, 305, again has a brief but insightful analysis.

84. Barber, *Trial of the Templars*, 124; Port, "Livre," 423–24.

85. Barber, *Trial of the Templars*, 125–26.

86. Ibid., 138–39.

87. Philip IV, however, continued to find it useful to insist that he had acted only at William's request. In a document dated 27 July 1308 (just after William's reinstatement) he noted to Clement V that in arresting the Templars he had only wanted to bring the truth to light, "ad requisicionem inquisitoris heretice pravitatis." I thank Elizabeth A. R. Brown for providing me with this passage from AN J413 no. 6.

88. On the Jewish community of Paris and its contraction after 1290, see Gérard Nahon, "Les juifs de Paris à la veille de l'expulsion de 1306," in *Finances, pouvoirs et mémoire: Mélanges offerts à Jean Favier*, ed. Jean Kerhervé and Albert Rigaudière (Paris: Fayard, 1999), 27–40.

89. This opinion was formalized by Clement IV's bull *Turbato corde* of 1267. See Solomon Grayzel, "Popes, Jews, and Inquisition from *Sicut* to *Turbato*," in *Essays on the Occasion of the Seventieth Anniversary of the Dropsie University*, ed. Abraham Isaac Katsch and Leon Nemoy (Philadelphia: Dropsie University, 1979), 151–88. For evidence of Dominican inquisitorial attitudes, see Bernard Gui's section on Jews in his manual, which depicts them as treacherous attackers of the faith. Guillaume Mollat, ed., *Manuel de l'inquisiteur*, by Bernard Gui, vol. 2 (Paris: Champion, 1926), 6–18; and Janet Shirley, trans., *The Inquisitor's Guide: A Medieval Manual on Heretics*, by Bernard Gui (Welwyn Garden City: Ravenhall, 2006), 139–47. See also citations in Célestin Douais, ed., *Documents pour servir à l'histoire de l'inquisition dans le Languedoc* (Paris: Renouard, 1900), 1:xxviij–xxix.

90. This name of a Christian saint would have been taken upon conversion. Since his brother is referred to as "Moses" and was not apparently arrested or questioned, perhaps Samuel converted some time before 1306, while

his brother then departed as part of the mass expulsion (Samuel could place blame on his brother without fear if he knew that Moses was beyond the reach of French power after the expulsions of 1306). But in all likelihood this story was only a wild attempt, under pressure and perhaps torture, to explain away Samuel's return to Judaism and should not be taken at face value. For a list of all the Jews reported in the *taille* rolls at the end of the fourteenth century, see Isidore Loeb, "Le role des juifs de Paris en 1296 et 1297," *Revue des études juifs* 1 (1880): 60–71. The names Moses (Mousse) and Samuel do appear there several times, but I am unable to say whether any of the men in the tax rolls should be identified with the two figures here.

91. Géraud, *Chronique latine,* 1:363: "Quidam de judaismo ad fidem conversus Protus nomine, coram inquisitore pravitatis haereticae recognovit, quod, instinctu cujusdam fratris sui nomine Mousseti ad judaismum redierat.... Postmodum tamen tractu temporis examinatus super hoc, ac demum requisitus, dixit per omnia se mentitum, et solum in odium fratris sui praefati, qui aliqua sibi solvere debita nolebat, recognovisse praemissa: et quia vertebatur in dubium cui consilio standum esset, tandem de consilio peritorum, assensu Parisiensis episcopi, adjudicatum est confessioni primae standum potius quam secundae: ipsumque, tamquam lapsum a fide, perpetua poena carceris puniendum; quod et factum est. Verum postmodum cum recognovisset coram inquisitore praedicto, se dixisse in carcere quod christinus non erat, sed judeaus, Samoeque vocatus, quodque Christiani comedunt Deum suum, cum instantia requirens quod si mori eum contingeret, fieret de eo sicut de judaeo, de communi peritorum consilio adjudicatus est statim absque ulla audientia curiae saeculari tradendus."

92. "La fame Molot Corrat" appears in the *taille* rolls for 1296–97. See Loeb, "Role des juifs," 63.

93. Géraud, *Chronique latine,* 1:363–64: "Eodem vel circa concursu temporis, quidam alius ad fidem conversus, Johannes nomine, confessus fuit coram inquisitore praedicto, quod palam et publice coram Casteleto Parisius dixerat se christianum non esse, sed judaeum nomine Mutlotum, atque de peccato quod in aqua commiserat recipiendo baptismum, per ignem purgari se velle. Postmodum tamen cum hoc fecisse graviter poeniteret, instanterque requireret sibi super hoc misericorditer indulgeri, dicens se ex melancholia et levitate capitis in talia porupisse, juxta peritorum consilium imposita est ei poenitentia salutaris." Note that the difference in punishment between the two cases can be explained by the fact that the former could be treated as a case of "relapse" whereas the latter could not.

94. William certainly had Dominican assistants, most notably Nicholas of Ennezat, who took over some of the Templar interrogations and would

later be present at the sentencing of Marguerite and Guiard. Nicholas, however, never held a formal office as inquisitor (as far as is known) and is never referred to in this way in the Templar documents.

95. I thank Professors Shona Wray, Brian Carniello, Elizabeth A. R. Brown, Michele Mulchahey, and Guy Geltner for corresponding with me on the question of dating practices in Bologna, where the calendar year began on Christmas (see also Guy Geltner, *The Medieval Prison: A Social History* [Princeton: Princeton University Press, 2008], xiii). If the date of "1310" was recorded in Bologna, it might then be understood as indicating 1310 in modern reckoning as well. But the date is written in a style foreign to Bolognese practice, and the book may well have been inscribed in Paris or France (by William or someone acting at his direction), in which case the date would probably be 1311 in modern reckoning (since Parisians began the year with Easter).

96. According to the "Anonymum S. Martialis chronicon," in *Recueil des historiens des Gaules et de la France,* vol. 21 (Paris: Imprimerie impériale, 1855), 813: "Item, nota quod anno Domini M. CCC. nono tres plenae magnae quadrigae librorum Judaeorum fuerunt combusti Parisius ante festum nativitatis Domini, in crastinum festi sancti Nicolai hyemalis, quos Judeai compilaverunt et fecerant." I thank Deeana Klepper for this reference. It is likely that these were Talmudic and other writings, not Hebrew Bibles.

97. See, e.g., Deeana Copeland Klepper, *The Insight of Unbelievers: Nicholas of Lyra and Christian Reading of Jewish Text in the Later Middle Ages* (Philadelphia: University of Pennsylvania Press, 2007), 13–31, and the fundamental work of Beryl Smalley, *Study of the Bible in the Middle Ages,* 3rd ed. (Oxford: Blackwell, 1983).

98. B. M. Reichert, ed., *Monumenta ordinis fratrum praedicatorum historica, tomus IV: Acta capitulorum generalium,* vol. 2 (Rome: Ex Typographia Polyglotta S. C. de Propoganda Fide, 1899), 50.

Chapter 4. First Steps

1. For a spectacular contemporary example, see Burnham's study of Na Prous Boneta in *So Great a Light,* 140–61.

2. Barber, *Trial of the Templars,* 156.

3. Coste, *Boniface VIII en procès,* 445.

4. On resistance to inquisitors, see Given, *Inquisition and Medieval Society,* section II.

5. Lerner, in *Heresy*, 71, wrote that her first judges "apparently" sent her to Paris; but in "Angel of Philadelphia," 347, he stated that either "Marguerite had fled to Paris as a fugitive" or "she was escorted to Paris under inquisitorial custody." In "New Light," 94, he assumes that she had some ability to decline William's initial summons, which he therefore dates to "early" 1308, presumably to allow time for her then to be actually arrested later in the fall. See also Trusen, *Prozess gegen Meister Eckhart*, 36, and Leicht, *Marguerite Porete*, 339 n. 147. Wegener, "Freiheitsdiskurs und Beginenverfolgung," 211–13, has given this claim a new twist.

6. For example, the phrase "ut compareas in iudicio coram nobis" is echoed in standard documents that are included in Bernard Gui's *Practica inquisitionis heretice pravitatis* (finished by 1323), such as a "Forma communis ad citandum fugittivos et eos qui contumaciter se absentant" (Célestin Douais, ed., *Practica inquisitionis heretice pravitatis*, by Bernard Gui [Paris: Picard, 1886], 8): "personaliter et peremptorie compareant coram nobis, responsuri de fide et de his que contra fidem in facto heresis commiserunt plenariam veritatem." The same wording is given in the following two forms (9–11).

7. AN J428 no. 19 (3 April 1310): "Ipsam namque post multas contumacias in non comparendo commissas tandem coram se fecit personaliter presentari." Verdeyen, "Procès d'inquisition," 61.

8. AN J428 no. 17 (3 April 1310): "ex causis variis probabilibus super labe pravitatis heretice suspecte et propter hoc per religiosum virum fratrem Guillelmum de Parisiis . . . arrestate." Ibid., 62.

9. AN J428 no. 15b (31 May 1310): "te, Margaretam de Hannonia, dictam Porete, super labe pravitatis heretice vehementer esse suspectam, propter quod citari te fecimus, ut compare[a]s in iudicio coram nobis." Ibid., 81.

10. Peters, *Inquisition*, 64.

11. Géraud, *Chronique latine*, 379: "quia coram ipso sufficienter monita comparere nolebat, per annum vel amplius pertinaci sustinuisset animo."

12. Baluze, *Vitae paparum avenionensium*, 3:63–64; Morand, *Histoire de la Sainte-Chapelle*, 87.

13. On Mahaut, see Jules-Marie Richard, *Mahaut comtesse d'Artois et de Bourgogne (1302–1329)* (1886; repr., Monein: Editions Pyremonde, 2006), which does not mention this specific dispute with Philip of Marigny. For Mahaut's relationship with Enguerran and John of Marigny, see Favier, *Roi de marbre*, 625–32. It may be worth remembering here that William of Paris had been an executor to the testament of Mahaut's brother Philip in 1298 (see chapter 3).

14. Fawtier, *Registres*, 179, no. 990. In the simultaneous dispute between Mahaut and the provost and chapter of Cambrai, Evens Phili also notarized a document the same day, in the cloister of Notre-Dame, that accepted royal

arbitration on behalf of the provost and chapter. It is also worth noting that the other notary public involved in the trial proceedings, Jacques of Vertus, later prepared a collation of a document indemnifying Enguerran of Marigny for lands given to Thibault and Louis of Sancerre. The original document was dated September 1312, but Jacques's collation was probably carried out in 1314. See Fawtier, *Registres,* no. 1801. Thus it would seem that the Marigny brothers were at least known to the notaries involved in the trials of Marguerite and Guiard.

15. See Fawtier, *Registres,* 177–80, nos. 982, 983, 990–92. Philip in fact retained the jurisdiction in question but agreed to pay a lump sum and an annual amount to Mahaut. Note also that Philip's hôtel must have been very near his brother's building site, since Enguerran acquired a block of houses near the Louvre (in the *censive* of Saint-Germain-l'Auxerrois) starting in 1306. Favier, *Roi de marbre,* 557–58.

16. It is of course possible that this is an illusion, created by the loss of documents that might have revealed other ongoing activities. Moreover, a copy of at least one undated document from William survives (mentioned briefly in chapter 7 and analyzed in Epilogue I) that could conceivably be placed in this period.

17. AN J428 nos. 16 and 17 (3 April 1310): "in defensione et fautoria Margarete . . . publice, probabiliter et notorie se haberet." Verdeyen, "Procès d'inquisition," 62.

18. J428 no. 15b: "te, Guiardum . . . in fautoriam et defensionem Margarete . . . notorie incidisse, et ob hoc et alia quedam de crimine heresis nobis esses suspectus, necnon et ex parte nostra competenter et canonice monitus fueris, ne nobis in nostro inquisitionis officio procedentibus impedimentum presentares nec dicte Margarete sic predicta labe infecte preberes defensionem, auxilium, consilium seu favorem." Verdeyen, "Procès d'inquisition," 82. Verdeyen read "domine Margarite" where the ms. has "dicte Margarete." If she were truly addressed as "Domina" here, it would be striking evidence for social respect—it is odd that scholars have not picked up on this reference, mistaken though it was. The trial documents also consistently use the spelling "Margareta," which Verdeyen alters to "Margarita."

19. See Burnham, *So Great a Light,* 170; on inquisitorial prisons in Toulouse in the 1270s, see Biller, Bruschi, and Sneddon, *Inquisitors and Heretics,* 57–59. On medieval prisons generally (though particularly in Italy), Geltner, *Medieval Prison.*

20. Barber, *Trial of the Templars,* 152–54.

21. Minor excommunication would have entailed only loss of the sacraments, whereas major excommunication had the wider implication of being cut off from all social relations with other Christians, attendance or benefit

from any church services, or any other rights or benefits of the church, including ecclesiastical burial.

22. Spelled out in J428 nos. 19, 17, 16. "Absolution" in this context does not imply that they would have been freed, only that their excommunication would have been lifted.

23. J428 no. 15b: "de plena, pura et integra veritate dicenda de te et de aliis super hiis que ad nobis commissum inquisitionis officium pertinere noscuntur." For model sentences of excommunication imposed under similar circumstances, see Mollat, *Manuel de l'inquisiteur*, 1:182–88. Translation in Shirley, *Inquisitor's Guide*, 131–34.

24. From the decretal *Ad Abolendam* issued by Lucius III in 1184. Translation from Edward Peters, ed., *Heresy and Authority in Medieval Europe: Documents in Translation* (Philadelphia: University of Pennsylvania Press, 1980), 172.

25. Mollat, *Manuel de l'inquisiteur*, 1:178–82. My translation is based on, but modified from, Shirley, *Inquisitor's Guide*, 129–31.

26. J428 no. 15b. Verdeyen, "Procès d'inquisition," 81 and 83. Verdeyen notes how closely William seems to follow the procedures laid down by Bernard Gui (64).

27. To be strictly correct according to canon law, William should have informed Marguerite and Guiard of the specific charges against them before asking them to take an oath to respond truthfully to those charges. See Henry Ansgar Kelly, "The Right to Remain Silent: Before and after Joan of Arc," *Speculum* 68 (1993): 992–1026. The wording of William's reports allows the possibility that he did do this when Marguerite was asked to swear the full, whole, and pure truth "de te et de aliis super hiis que ad nobis commissum inquisitionis officium pertinere noscuntur." The question would be whether "those things" *(hiis)* were ever spelled out. The rather vague wording in this phrase may have been intentional. Kelly's work, however, even as it insists that inquisitors legally should have followed this procedure, tends to show that they did not consider themselves to have committed a legal infraction when they did not. See Kelly, "Inquisition," 449.

28. Kelly, "Right to Remain Silent," 1004.

29. See Daniel Hobbins, trans., *The Trial of Joan of Arc* (Cambridge, MA: Harvard University Press, 2005).

30. Edward Peters, *Torture*, expanded ed. (Philadelphia: University of Pennsylvania Press, 1985), 54–58, and *Inquisition*, 65.

31. Given, *Inquisition and Medieval Society*, 54 and n. 8; Ames, *Righteous Persecution*, 166, esp. references in n. 95, and Douais, *Documents*, ccxxxviij–ccxlij. The best evidence for inquisitorial use of torture in the early

fourteenth century comes from contemporaries such as Bernard Délicieux and Angelo Clareno (both Franciscans), who accused inquisitors of torturing to extract false confessions. See Friedlander, *Hammer of the Inquisitors,* 87, and David Burr and E. Randolph Daniel's translation of *A Chronicle or History of the Seven Tribulations of the Order of Brothers Minor,* by Angelo Clareno (St. Bonaventure, NY: Franciscan Institute Publications, 2005), 171 (an example that also shows the medieval recognition that confessions under torture could not be trusted). For a later inquisitor's explicit rationalization of torture (Nicholas of Eymerich, d. 1399), see Sullivan, *Inner Lives,* 180–90.

32. David Nirenberg, *Communities of Violence: Persecution of Minorities in the Middle Ages* (Princeton: Princeton University Press, 1996), 109–11.

33. For a very clear example, see the testimony of the Templar Ponsard of Gizy, in Barber, *Trial of the Templars,* 146; full translation in Barber and Bate, *Templars,* 289–92.

34. See Ames, *Righteous Persecution,* 167–68.

35. Hobbins, *Trial of Joan of Arc,* 178–80.

36. Mollat, *Manuel de l'inquisiteur,* 1:182. My translation is modified from Shirley, *Inquisitor's Guide,* 131. Angelo Clareno again provides vivid descriptions of such harsh conditions of inquisitorial imprisonment. See Burr and Daniel, *Chronicle or History,* 146. I thank Robert E. Lerner for this reference.

37. Peters, *Torture,* 55.

38. The mere fact that the records do not say Guiard was tortured into talking cannot be conclusive. The best evidence that he was not subjected to torture, however, is that he did not name his associates. Had he been asked to do so under torture, he surely would have divulged names.

39. J428 no. 15b: "Porro dum tu, Margareta, in istis rebellionibus obstinata maneres, ducti conscientia, volentes officii nobis commissi debitum exercere, inquisitionem contra te." Verdeyen, "Procès d'inquisition," 81.

40. Trusen, *Prozess gegen Meister Eckhart,* 38, is quite right to remind us that there is no concrete proof that these two men formally gave evidence. Nevertheless, because they were so well known to royal circles it seems virtually certain that they communicated with William on some level.

41. It might also explain how he came to have Bishop Guido's letter, but presumably this could have been retrieved by Philip of Marigny or one of his officers as well.

42. Wegener, "Freiheitsdiskurs und Beginenverfolgung," 211–15, reads the documents as suggesting that William only himself learned of (or invented) this story after April 1310, when he interviewed his "witnesses." According to this reconstruction, Marguerite would have been arrested in Paris for some kind of unidentified conspicuous conduct, without William even knowing of her

book's existence. I do not believe that this interpretation can be sustained. If any part of the account contained in the trial documents is true, then it is inconceivable that Marguerite was freed after being questioned by Philip of Marigny and the inquisitor of Lorraine (Ralph of Ligny); in turn, these men could not have turned Marguerite over to William in fall 1308 without imparting some version of this history, which Marguerite had already confessed twice. And to completely dismiss the inquisitor's narrative as made up out of whole cloth would require us to imagine a vast conspiracy, without apparent point, intended to construct an entirely fictional history for Marguerite before her arrest. William must in fact have been in possession of these facts during the entire time of Marguerite's incarceration, and the pertinent question concerns how and why he gave out or held back information as the trial unfolded.

43. I have considered the possibility that William did not take further steps at this time simply because of extended travels away from Paris, which might be suggested by the possibility that his donation of a Hebrew Bible to the Dominicans of Bologna took place in February 1310. But the year may also have been 1311, and in any case there is no supporting evidence to suggest an Italian trip for William, and no plausible reason why either royal or Dominican business would have taken him there at this moment. The Dominican general chapter met in Piacenza in 1310 (some 225 kilometers from Bologna), but since meetings began on Pentecost, which was not until 7 June 1310, William could hardly have spent February to June in Italy while also conducting the trial of Marguerite and Guiard in Paris.

44. On Gilles, see Jo Ann McNamara, *Gilles Aycelin: The Servant of Two Masters* (Syracuse: Syracuse University Press, 1973), esp. 160–86, as well as Franklin J. Pegues, *The Lawyers of the Last Capetians* (Princeton: Princeton University Press, 1962), 90–98.

45. On the makeup of the commission, see Barber, *Trial of the Templars,* 138–39.

46. Ibid., 150.

47. In McNamara, *Gilles Aycelin,* 166, Gilles is portrayed as efficiently carrying out the royal will. If this were the case, William of Paris would have had little cause to worry (note, however, that McNamara's rapid survey is occasionally inaccurate, as when she confuses William of Paris with William Baufet, bishop of Paris [174]). But compare Pegues, *Lawyers,* 96, who sees Gilles as more independent of Philip IV. Barber may be closest to the truth, describing Gilles as retreating from the affair as it became clear that his role as royal counselor was incompatible with a fair hearing for the Templars. *Trial of the Templars,* 177.

48. Coste, *Boniface VIII en procès,* 441–544; Lizerand, *Clément V,* 191 ff.

49. Coste, *Boniface VIII en procès,* 441 n. 4, 547, 550. Lizerand, *Clément V,* 200, believed that Nogaret and Plaisians returned to Philip IV's side after May 21, but Coste has shown that Nogaret, et least, remained close to the papal court in the region of Avignon.

50. Regarding the king's presence in Paris in March and April, see Favier, *Roi de marbre,* 650. Enguerran of Marigny was also in Paris April 1–10 according to the itinerary in Favier, *Roi de marbre,* 794. Regarding the king's subsequent travels, see Lalou, *Itinéraire de Philip IV,* 2:348–53.

51. Notaries public were a relatively new import into northern France. The two universally recognized sources of notarial authority were the emperor and the pope; thus the designation "apostolic notary" by which Jacques and Evens style themselves in these documents does not mean that they were employed by the pope, merely that they held commissions from him. See James M. Murray, *Notarial Instruments in Flanders between 1280 and 1452* (Brussels: Académie royale de Belgique, 1995), 13, and more broadly James A. Brundage, *The Medieval Origins of the Legal Profession: Canonists, Civilians, and Courts* (Chicago: University of Chicago Press, 2008), 213, 394–406. I thank Elizabeth A. R. Brown for pointing out that "Evens" must have been the true, Breton name of "Evenus Phili," since it appears that way in his notarial sign manual. For the rather different context of notaries employed more directly by inquisitors in Toulouse, see Biller, Bruschi, and Sneddon, *Inquisitors and Heretics,* 83–106.

52. Verdeyen assumed that no action at this point was necessary against Marguerite because he mistakenly believed that the formal theological condemnation of extracts from her book had taken place in April 1309 and had served an analogous purpose.

53. I owe this observation to Courtenay, "Marguerite's Judges." The faculty of canon law at Paris is not well studied. See generally Brundage, *Medieval Origins,* 230–37. John of Thélus appears in one additional university document from 1302 and must have lived into the 1340s (perhaps to 1346), to judge from a testamentary bequest recently studied and dated in William J. Courtenay, "Une correction au Chartularium universitatis Parisiensis: Le legs de Jean de Thélus et la chapellenie de l'université à Saint-André-des-Arts," *Paris et Ile-de-France: Mémoires* 52 (2001): 7–18.

54. Courtenay, "Marguerite's Judges."

55. The evidence for the career of Hugh of Besançon was compiled by Lerner in "Angel of Philadelphia," 356–57, drawing on Auguste Castan, "L'évêque de Paris, Hughes de Besançon," *Mémoires de la Société d'émulation du Doubs,* 4th ser., 1 (1865): 250–70.

56. Castan, "Évêque de Paris," 257.

57. Finke, *Papsttum und Untergang,* 2: 307–8, 310. "Doctor of both laws" at 308; also on his tombstone at Notre Dame, cited by Castan, "Évêque de Paris," 264 n. 2.

58. *Regestrum Clementis Papae V,* 3:318, #3522.

59. Stated by Castan, "Évêque de Paris," 258, but without evidence. Favor shown to Hugh by Jeanne and Philip is well attested, however. In 1319 he also appears as a counselor to Mahaut of Artois, mother of Queen Jeanne. Richard lists Henry of Béthune as a counselor to Mahaut as well. See *Mahaut comtesse d'Artois,* 35–36, for these two references. Moreover, John "of Thélus" must have come from a town very near Béthune and Artois (and Valenciennes). Courtenay, "Marguerite's Judges," remarks on these ties to the Diocese of Arras, and it might be recalled that the Marigny family's influence stretched in this direction as well.

60. J428 no. 16: "cum prefata defensio et fautoria heresis primo in vehementem et postmodum in violentam presumptionem transierit, suis contumaciis, rebellionibus et pertinaciis pensatis et hoc exigentibus, iuris interpretatione prefatus Guiardus infelix pro heretico est habendus et diffinitive tamquam hereticus condempnandus relinquendusque curie seculari. " Verdeyen, "Procès d'inquisition," 57.

61. On this group, see William Courtenay, "Marguerite's Judges." Courtenay suggests that Ralph may have been a member of a religious order (possibly the Franciscans), rather than the secular he is usually assumed to be, in "Radulphus Brito, Master of Arts and Theology," *Cahiers de l'Institut du Moyen-Âge grec et latin* 76 (2005): 134–39. For analysis of witnesses to inquisitorial documents, see Biller, Bruschi, and Sneddon, *Inquisitors and Heretics,* 106–16.

62. On Jacques, see Robert E. Lerner, "A Note on the University Career of Jacques Fournier, O. Cist., Later Pope Benedict XII," *Analecta cisterciana* 30 (1974): 66–69, correcting the earlier misidentification of Jacques of Dijon as Jacques Fournier.

63. See Courtenay, "Radulphus Brito," for a disentangling of Ralph Hotot's career from that of Ralph Brito.

64. My reading of this document assumes that the "Actum" clause that begins the authenticating passage by the notary Evens Phili is part of a memorandum drawn up at the time of the March meeting. It would therefore show that the four theologians acting as witnesses were present at that meeting and that its location was the Dominican house. Against this reading is the specific fact that whereas the clause refers to the "anno, indictione, mense, die et pontificatu predictis," only the dating clause of the 3 April opinion has a specific "die." (If, instead, the "Actum" clause were taken to refer to the 3 April decision, it would

show that these four theologians were present for a later meeting where the canonists drew up their opinion and that this meeting took place at the Dominican house.) My reading also raises the question of why four theologians are singled out to act as witnesses (rather than listed with the eleven others who were listed as potential consultants) and insists on the somewhat awkward fact of a document dated 3 April being collated into a larger document recording a meeting in March. I am nevertheless convinced that this is the correct reading, for several reasons. First, the dating passage in the "Actum" clause, in spite of its reference to a day, seems clearly to refer to the earlier section recorded by Evens Phili that describes the March meeting and gives a year, indiction, month, and pontificate (the 3 April opinion gives only a year and day). Second, the same opening clause refers to masters of theology and canon law called in to consult, but also to "testibus infrascriptis ad hoc vocatis specialiter et rogatis" and then in the "Actum" clause calls the four masters of theology "testibus ad hoc vocatis specialiter et rogatis." Finally, it should be noted that the unnotarized copy found in J428 no. 17 ends with the "Datum" clause and does not proceed to include the list of witnesses, indicating that this list was not appended to the sealed original itself. These men were therefore the witnesses present in March; they are simply listed by name separately from the other theologians, since Evens Phili knew in retrospect that they were the ones who had been asked to formally witness the opinion given by the canonists at the meeting. If we were to imagine these four men as being present only at a later meeting on 3 April, we would then have the equally vexing question of why there was absolutely no overlap between the first group of eleven and the later group of four. Instead, my reading shows that all fifteen were present at the Dominican house in March; they are simply listed by name in two different parts of the document, to reflect the fact that only four of them acted as witnesses. This fact, in turn, does not prove that the other eleven refused to certify the results of the meeting (though that is possible), only that they did not append their names as witnesses. Because it was the canonists who took responsibility for this decision, it was necessary only to have a token witnessing by a contingent of theologians. My deep gratitude to William Courtenay for a stimulating debate on this point. For his own somewhat different reading of this evidence, see "Marguerite's Judges."

65. Judges in ecclesiastical courts (not just inquisitors) normally consulted with legal experts in rendering their decisions. Brundage, *Medieval Origins*, 350–51, 456.

66. Sargent, "Marguerite Porete," 292, asserts that at the March meeting "it was decided that, since she could not be examined on her actual beliefs by the normal inquisitorial process, a separate judgment on the orthodoxy or heterodoxy of her book could be rendered by a committee of the theological faculty of the university, and corroborating evidence that she had in fact cir-

culated the book would suffice to prove that she had relapsed." This reasoning may or may not have been already present in the mind of William of Paris, but nothing shows that any of this information was presented at the March meeting or that anything like this was "decided" at this time.

67. See Michelet, *Procès des Templiers,* 2:301, 316, 335, 347, 348, 377, 401. The latest of these is dated 15 November 1307. Also Finke, *Papsttum und Untergang,* 2:309, where Evens Phili and Jacques of Vertus notarize the confession of Jacques of Molay before the university masters on 25 October 1307.

Chapter 5. *Philadelphia Story*

1. Evens Phili and Jacques of Vertus, the notaries who prepared the trial documents of Marguerite and Guiard, were not among these men, nor do they appear in any of the documents produced by the papal commission.

2. Barber, *Trial of the Templars,* 159.

3. See his deposition in Michelet, *Procès des Templiers,* 1:535. I intend to tell Matthew's story more fully elsewhere.

4. Ibid., 1:74, 109.

5. Ibid., 1:130: "cum eum bonum et sanctum reputent et legalem."

6. Ibid., 1:145–46.

7. Ibid., 1:164–72; analysis in Barber, *Trial of the Templars,* 159–62.

8. In his later deposition, he is labeled "frater Matheus de Cresson Essart serviens, Belvacensis diocesis, preceptor domus de Belleyvial Ambianensis diocesis." Michelet, *Procès des Templiers,* 1:535. The Latin term *serviens* here shows that he was at the rank of sergeant, or fighting man beneath the level of knight. *Serviens* or sergeant did not necessarily imply a low-status birth. See Barber, *New Knighthood,* 190–92, and the more detailed investigation of Jochen Schenk, "Aspects of Non-Noble Family Involvement in the Order of the Temple," in *The Military Orders,* vol. 4, *By Land and by Sea,* ed. Judi Upton-Ward (Aldershot: Ashgate, 2008), 155–61, who states that sergeants either were non-noble or were the sons of knights but had not yet been knighted and that some sergeants were indeed related to knights in the order. Jonathan Riley-Smith, *Templars and Hospitalers as Professed Religious in the Holy Land* (Notre Dame: University of Notre Dame Press, 2010), 38–40, offers a similar assessment. According to his deposition, Matthew also "intelligebat Latinum," which would be further evidence of high status. Michelet, *Procès des Templiers,* 1:538.

9. Barber, *Trial of the Templars,* 163.

10. There is some possibility that a notarized copy of Guiard's testimony once existed in the papers of William of Plaisians in 1313 (see Epilogue I). No such freestanding copy of his testimony, however, is now extant.

11. For recent discussions of the methodological problems involved in reading inquisitorial records, see the differing perspectives of Caterina Bruschi, *The Wandering Heretics of Languedoc* (Cambridge: Cambridge University Press, 2009), who generally stresses the deponent's ability to shape the written record and who discusses the idea of "filters" in ch. 1; John H. Arnold, *Inquisition and Power: Catharism and the Confessing Subject in Medieval Languedoc* (Philadelphia: University of Pennsylvania Press, 2001), esp. 1–15; and, more briefly, Burnham, *So Great a Light,* 55–59.

12. Perhaps for this reason Verdeyen does not insert a paragraph break before this sentence (as Lerner does), implying that it is not yet part of Guiard's actual testimony. This editorial decision seems misguided, however, given the way the wording almost immediately slips into the first person.

13. AN J428 no. 18: "deposuit et confessus est in hunc modum prout nobis dictus inquisitor intimavit: Dicens videlicet se esse angelum Philadelphie, et, exponens verbum, dicit quod angelus est nomen officii, non nature, et Philadelphia interpretatur salvans adhesionem Domini vel adherentem Domino; et sic reputo me missum ad salvandum adhesionem Domini vel adherentem Domino in ecclesia Dei." Verdeyen, "Procès d'inquisition," 65. I have provided punctuation closer to that employed in Lerner, "Angel of Philadelphia," 363.

14. The biblical "key of David" comes ultimately from Isa. 22:22.

15. Here and elsewhere I give a slightly modernized version of the Douai-Reims English translation of the Bible.

16. J428 no. 18: "Et tunc, requisitus a quo missus erat, respondit quod ab illo qui habet clavem David, exponens quod per hec intelligit Christum qui habet clavem excellentie et quod vicarius eius dominus papa habet clavem ministerii." Verdeyen, "Procès d'inquisition," 65 (in the manuscript, the word *hec* is added in above the line).

17. See, for example, Karlfried Froehlich, "St. Peter, Papal Primacy, and the Exegetical Tradition, 1150–1300," and Walter H. Principe, "The School Theologians' Views of the Papacy, 1150–1250," both in *The Religious Roles of the Papacy: Ideals and Realities, 1150–1300,* ed. Christopher Ryan (Toronto: Pontifical Institute of Mediaeval Studies, 1989), 3–44 and 45–116.

18. And thus hardly a "distinction inouïe," as Verdeyen would have it in "Procès d'inquisition," 72.

19. *In IV Sententiarum,* distinctio 18, quaestio 1, art. 1, quaestiuncula 1, corpus: "quod in corporalibus dicitur clavis instrumentum quo ostium aperitur. Regni autem ostium nobis clauditur per peccatum et quantum ad maculam, et quantum ad reatum poenae; et ideo potestas qua tale obstaculum regni removetur, dicitur clavis. Haec autem potestas est quidem in sanctissima Trinitate per auctoritatem; et ideo dicitur a quibusdam quod habet clavem auctori-

tatis; sed in Christo homine fuit haec potestas ad removendum praedictum obstaculum per meritum passionis, quae etiam dicitur januam aperire; et ideo dicitur habere secundum quosdam claves excellentiae. Sed quia ex latere dormientis in cruce sacramenta fluxerunt, quibus Ecclesia fabricatur; ideo in sacramentis Ecclesiae efficacia passionis manet; et propter hoc etiam in ministris Ecclesiae, qui sunt dispensatores sacramentorum, potestas aliqua manet ad praedictum obstaculum removendum, non propria virtute, sed virtute divina, et passionis Christi; et haec potestas metaphorice clavis Ecclesiae dictur; quae est clavis ministerii." For Thomas's views on the keys more broadly, see Christopher Ryan, "The Theology of Papal Primacy in Thomas Aquinas," in Ryan, *Religious Roles*, 193–225.

20. The Latin grammar of this passage is ambiguous, but I have taken his meaning to be twenty years before 1306 (rather than twenty years before 1310). J428 no. 18: "Et addit quod, quattuor annis elapsis et ultra, percepit illud officium sibi datum fuisse, sed reputat sibi datum fuisse viginti annis elapsis, cum primo percepit a dictis quattuor annis, vel citra, et hoc Parisius in capella domini regis inferiori." Verdeyen, "Procès d'inquisition," 66. It might even be possible to read this passage as indicating that it was actually the event of twenty years earlier that took place in the Sainte-Chapelle.

21. J428 no. 18: "et quod modus perceptionis et receptionis illius officii et apertionis ostii fuit in momento per aperturam intellectus scripturarum." Ibid., 66.

22. J428 no. 18: "Et addit qui loquitur quod, quia non posset habere patronum in novo testamento propter prohibitionem ecclesie, resumit in veteri, monitione salvatoris libertatem dantis et auctorizantis." Ibid., 67.

23. J428 no. 18: "Item requisitus si illi qui deferunt tabardos sunt de societate sua, respondit quod non quantum ad omnia, nisi illi qui tenent et portant tunicam longam et zonam pelliceam; que zona est de essentia habitus, tamen reputat illos adherentes Domino, licet habeant formam secularem in suo habitu." Ibid.

24. Ibid., 76, suggests the relevance of this passage as well, but somewhat puzzlingly calls John the Baptist an Old Testament figure and makes no mention of Elijah.

25. Lerner, "Angel of Philadelphia," 349–50.

26. Ibid., 350; developed more fully in Lerner, "Addenda on an Angel."

27. Géraud, *Chronique latine*, 380: "Tunc etiam pseudo-quidam, Guiardus nomine de Cressonessart, qui Angelum Philadelphiae a Deo immediate missum ad confortandum adhaerentes Christo se nominans, dicebat quod nec cingulum pelliceum quo erat praecinctus, nec habitum quo erat indutus ad mandatum Papae deponere tenebatur, imo Papa praecipiendo peccaret."

28. This was the suggestion of both Lea and Langlois (See Lerner, "Angel of Philadelphia," 344).

29. The main lines of my discussion in this section rely explicitly on Lerner, "Angel of Philadelphia." See also Leicht, *Marguerite Porete,* 384–95.

30. Lerner, "Angel of Philadelphia," 351–52.

31. Ibid., 352–53, and "Addenda on an Angel." For more detail on how and why Franciscans began to adopt a Joachite perspective in the late 1240s, see Robert E. Lerner, "Frederick II, Alive, Aloft, and Allayed, in Franciscan-Joachite Eschatology," in *The Use and Abuse of Eschatology in the Middle Ages,* ed. Werner Verbeke, Daniel Verhelst, and Andries Welkenhuysen (Leuven: Leuven University Press, 1988), 359–84.

32. See Reeves, *Joachim of Fiore,* 29–31.

33. See Ewert Cousins, trans., *The Soul's Journey into God, the Tree of Life, the Life of St. Francis,* by Bonaventure (New York: Paulist Press, 1978), 181.

34. See Lerner, "Angel of Philadelphia," 353, and "Ecstatic Dissent," *Speculum* 67 (1992): 52–53.

35. Lerner, "Angel of Philadelphia," 354, referring again to the Prologue to Bonaventure's *Legenda maior.*

36. Franciscans in particular might be expected to have taken offense at Guiard's replacement of Francis with himself. We have no explicitly Franciscan reactions, however, since we have no record of theologians commenting on his ideas. Guiard may have considered himself a successor to Francis in this "office," since even if only one "Angel" could be sent at a time, Francis had been dead for eight decades.

37. Lerner, "Angel of Philadelphia," 355, and further "Addenda on an Angel," with reference to Sylvain Piron, "Le métier de théologien selon Olivi: Philosophie, théologie, exégès et pauvreté," in *Pierre de Jean Olivi—Philosophe et théologien,* ed. Catherine König-Pralong, Olivier Ribordy, and Tiziana Suarez-Nani (Berlin: De Gruyter, 2010), 54. Verdeyen, "Procès d'inquisition," 71, thought he detected Olivi's influence on Guiard, but did little to substantiate the claim.

38. Friedlander, *Hammer of the Inquisitors,* 244–49 (with reference to Guiard 248–49).

39. Lerner, "Angel of Philadelphia," 355. For a sketch of Dolcino's career before his burning in 1307, see Lambert, *Medieval Heresy,* 222–23. By coincidence, one of Dolcino's main followers was named Marguerite, which has caused more than one historian to confuse documentary references to Dolcino and his Marguerite with those to Guiard and Marguerite Porete. For example, Sophia Menache, *Clement V* (Cambridge: Cambridge University Press, 1998), 301–2, makes this mistake in asserting that Bernard Gui referred to Marguerite

Porete. Although related less directly to Guiard's ideas on keys, in the 1320s the southern beguine "heresiarch" Na Prous Boneta would claim to wield the keys of the abyss. See Burnham, *So Great a Light,* 149–50, with an explicit comparison to Guiard and the assertion that the influence of Peter of John Olivi can be seen in his ideas (as it can in overwhelming fashion with Prous).

40. Robert E. Lerner deserves the credit for suggesting a possible link between Brother Columbinus and Guiard. See "Addenda on an Angel," where the possibility is given further discussion. On Columbinus, see Elizabeth A. R. Brown and Robert E. Lerner, "The Origins and Import of the Columbinus Prophecy," *Traditio* 45 (1989–90): 219–56 (221 for date of 1306/7); Kathryn Kerby-Fulton and E. Randolph Daniel, "English Joachimism, 1300–1500: The Columbinus Prophecy," in *Il profetismo gioachimita tra Quattrocento e Cinquecento* ed. Gian Luca Potestà (Genoa: Marietti, 1991), 313–50; and Friedlander, *Hammer of the Inquisitors,* 158–60.

41. Brown and Lerner conclude ("Origins and Import," 255–56) that the Columbinus prophecy may not have been directly inspired by Joachim but that "the author was surely a Joachite." Kerby-Fulton and Daniel, in "English Joachimism," treat the prophecy as unproblematically Joachite (see previous note).

42. I thank Robert E. Lerner for suggesting this as the logical explanation for the apparent use of Latin terms in Guiard's own expression of his ideas. Lerner develops this argument fully in "Addenda on an Angel."

43. For example, in Gilbert of Tournai's sermon for the feast of St. Francis, written in the 1250s, on the theme *Vidi alterum angelum.* Edited in Hal Friday, "I Saw Another Angel: An Edition of Two Sermons by Guibert of Tournai for the Feast of St. Francis of Assisi," (MA thesis, University of Vermont, 2008). Given Guiard's apparent echo of Thomas's Sentence Commentary, it is worth mentioning that the statement in its more general form (without reference to Francis) is also found there, citing Gregory (*In II Sententiarum,* distinctio 9, quaestio 1, art. 4, resp. ad argum. 2).

44. See Lerner, "Addenda on an Angel." The *Interpretationes* were sometimes attributed to Stephen Langton.

45. Verdeyen, "Procès d'inquisition," 71, 73, 74, for instance, attempts to make textual links and then explains away differences by asserting that Guiard did not properly understand Marguerite. To my mind, however, these links are not convincing. Verdeyen does admit that Guiard's spirituality seems more influenced by "certains commentaires sur l'Apocalypse que du *Mirouer* de Marguerite Porete" (77). My reading aligns with that of Lerner, "Angel of Philadelphia." See also the thoughtful discussion in Leicht, *Marguerite Porete,* 395–401, tending to support Lerner's position.

46. A less overt link between Marguerite and Guiard, proposed by several scholars, would be the influence of Peter of John Olivi on both of them. Peter of John likely did have some impact on Guiard's thinking (though perhaps not as directly as Verdeyen asserts), but it is less clear that his work was known, even indirectly, to Marguerite. For an exploration of the possibility, see Kerby-Fulton, *Books under Suspicion*, 273–74.

47. J428 no. 18: "Nos autem . . . diximus and dicimus . . . quod dictum Guiardum debet verum hereticum reputare, iudicare ac etiam condempnare, habita cum ratione sui ex misericordia, ut non tradatur curie seculari, si vel ante sententiam vel cito postea penituerit, sicut iura docent. Liquet namque manifeste ex dictis suis et confessionibus prelibatis quod ipse ponit divisionem in ecclesia militante, immo potius ponit duas ecclesias militantes, seipsum unius claves excellentes gerentem et alterius papam claves ministerii optinentem et ipsum papam non esse omnino unicum capud ipsius ecclesie militantis nec posse ipsam omnino ordinare per se et ministros suos sacrosque canones et statuta sua, quod totum est hereticum." Verdeyen, "Procès d'inquisition," 67. (Verdeyen reads "tamen ratione" for "cum ratione.")

48. The *Dialogue on the Seven Sacraments* (assuming it was truly authored by William) had explained a slightly different aspect of the doctrine of the two keys. See BnF ms. lat. 3209, fol. 25vb;14922, fol. 129r; 3209, fol. 24r; 3210, fol. 32: "Tua Petre questio potestatem clavium ecclesie requirit. Ut autem scias quod queris agnoscere, debes scire ecclesie clavem esse duplicem. Quarum una est iurisdictionis, et alia clavis ordinis." This passage relies on Thomas's Sentence Commentary for his further explanation, just as Guiard had done, particularly *IV Sententiarum* distinctio 18, quaestio 2, art. 2, quaestiuncula 1, resp. ad argum. 1, as well as distinctio 19, quaestio 1, art. 1, quaestiuncula 3, corpus, and distinctio 20, quaestio 1, art. 3, quaestiuncula 2, resp. ad argum. 1.

49. Of course they could not have read this passage (written after the fact) and no testimony in the record indicates it, but perhaps Guiard's behavior was communicated to them orally by William.

50. A point made by Verdeyen, "Procès d'inquisition," 76. The same author also makes the interesting observation that Fra Dolcino, burned in 1307, had given the title "Angel of Philadelphia" to the coming angelic pope (72). If the canonists were aware of this fact, it might have influenced their association between Guaird's claims and defiance of the legitimate pope.

51. AN J428 no. 15b: "Super quibus omnibus communicato peritorum multorum tam in theologia quam in iure canonico et civili deliberato consilio et concordi." Verdeyen, "Procès d'inquisition," 83. Against this interpretation would be the fact that William cites only the canonists' opinion in his final sentence.

52. Géraud, *Chronique latine,* 380: "tandem incendii [timore], habitum cingulumque deponens, et errorem suum finaliter recognoscens, adjudicatus est perpetua muri inclusione praecingi." Larry Field drew my attention to the Latin pun in this passage. Perhaps this attempt at dark humor explains why the Continuer chose to use "cingulum" rather than "zonam" here.

Chapter 6. Twenty-One Theologians and a Book

1. The present chapter was written before the appearance of two recent studies that consider this group of twenty-one theologians: William J. Courtenay, "Marguerite's Judges," and Paul F. Crawford, "The Involvement of the University of Paris in the Trials of Marguerite Porete and of the Templars, 1308–1310," in Burgtorf, Crawford, and Nicholson, *Debate on the Trial,* 129–43. I have benefited from both essays, however, while revising for publication, and from Wegener, "Freiheitsdiskurs und Beginenverfolgung." Although I disagree with the latter analysis in fundamental ways, the close attention there to the way the theologians' intervention relates to the rest of the trial is thought-provoking.

2. For the location of Saint-Mathurin, see Philippe Lorentz and Dany Sandron, *Atlas de Paris au Moyen Âge: Espace urbain, habitat, société, religion, lieux de pouvoir* (Paris: Parigramme, 2006), 157.

3. That fact that Jacques was from the Diocese of Châlons-sur-Marne, whose bishop had likely been instrumental in Marguerite's arrest, could suggest that he had particular knowledge about this affair, but there is no further evidence to substantiate such a possibility. Jacques is first attested as a notary public in 1307. In the documents generated by William of Paris's interrogations of Templars in fall of that year, Jacques always styled himself notary by imperial (rather than papal) authority. See Michelet, *Procès des Templiers,* 2:317, 325, 347, 361, 365, 370, 377, 386, 393, 401, 408. He had referred to the same authority in documents from July 1307 recording agreements of towns in Flanders to the peace treaty with France (these are found in AN J549 2); he is also associated with Evens Phili in most of these 1307 documents. In the 1310 documents concerning Marguerite and Guiard, however, he calls himself notary by papal authority (with no mention of an imperial commission), as he does in documents found in AN J551, 552, and 553 (dating back to May 1309). Though the acquisition of this second commission would not be unusual, more surprising is the fact that Jacques used a different sign manual when acting under papal authority than when signing as an imperial notary. This shift is clearly documented, however, so the difference between the sign used in the Templar documents

and that appearing in our trial documents does not raise suspicions of forgery or fraud (moreover, the hands from AN J413 no. 18 and AN J428 nos. 15 and 16 appear to be identical). I am deeply grateful to Elizabeth A. R. Brown for raising this issue, and to Olivier Canteaut for helping to clarify it. I also thank James M. Murray for a more general discussion of notarial practices.

4. AN J428 no. 15a: "idem inquisitor ab eisdem magistris consilium postulavit quid esset faciendum de quodam libro quem ibi ostendit, de quo extracti fuerant plures articuli ibidem exhibiti, quos eis demonstraverat, ut dicebat." Verdeyen, "Procès de l'inquisition," 50 (with incorrect date).

5. See ch. 4, n. 61, for William Courtenay's suggestion that Ralph could have been a Mendicant rather than a secular.

6. On the proper identification of Lawrence of Dreux, see William J. Courtenay, "Reflections on Vat. Lat. 1086 and Prosper of Reggio Emilia, O.E.S.A.," in *Theological Quodlibeta in the Middle Ages: The Fourteenth Century,* ed. Christopher Schabel (Leiden: Brill, 2007), 353.

7. William Courtenay points out that Clairmarais was a Cistercian monastery near Saint-Omer and raises the possibility that John (about whom little is known) was really a Cistercian. The assumption that he was a Franciscan depends on his grouping in this document with Nicholas and Jacob; a change in punctuation might call that assumption into question. Courtenay, "Parisian Faculty of Theology," 243 n. 23. Crawford likewise doubts that this man was a Franciscan and instead suggests that he was a secular master. See "Involvement of the University," 137.

8. Present on October 25 were Simon of Guiberville, Lawrence of Dreux, Henry of Friemar, Gerard of Saint-Victor, and Gerard of Bologna. These men, with the exception of Gerard of Saint-Victor, were again present on October 26, as were John of Ghent, William Alexandri, Nicholas of Lyra, and Jacques of Dijon—the latter two still as bachelors at this point. Signers to the March 1308 decision included Alexander of Marcia, Gerard of Bologna, Gerard of Saint-Victor, Henry of Friemar, Jacques of Thérines, John of Mount-Saint-Éloi, Lawrence of Dreux, Ralph of Hotot, and William Alexandri. On these lists, see in particular Courtenay, "Marguerite's Judges," and William J. Courtenay, "The Role of University Masters and Bachelors at Paris in the Templar Affair, 1307–1308," in Speer and Wirmer, *1308,* 171–81.

9. On Carracioli, see Glorieux, *Répertoire,* #227, and on his absence here see Courtenay, "Marguerite's Judges." The exact date of his assumption of the chancellorship is not known, but Simon of Guiberville must have stepped down from this role before 11 April 1310, since he is called only "decanus" in this document. On Hervé's absence, see de Guimaräes, "Hervé Noël" 55, and Glorieux, *Répertoire,* #64. Hervé was named vicar of the province of France on

17 May 1309 and was formally elected Dominican provincial prior for France on 17 September. He held this position until June 1318, when he became master general of the order (succeeding Berenger of Landora upon the latter's appointment as archbishop of Compostella). Hervé probably resigned his teaching chair by February 1310, but he could still have participated with other non-regent masters if he was in Paris (see note 11 for a probable explanation for his absence). As this example shows, it is not possible to fix an exact number of members for the faculty of theology at any one time because, in addition to regent masters (those currently holding a teaching chair), past masters still resident in Paris and those who had qualified but not yet assumed a chair might be called on to participate in panels such as this. Other masters of theology generally resident in Paris in 1310 who do not appear here include the secular Henry Amandi (Glorieux, *Répertoire*, #217), John of Blangi (#230), Alan Gontier (#226), and Deodatus (#375). To this list (kindly supplied to me by William Courtenay via Robert Lerner) might be added Hervé Nédellec's Dominican successor, Laurent of Nantes (see de Guimaräes, "Hervé Noël," 51). See also the brief discussion in Leicht, *Marguerite Porete*, 349 n. 192.

10. Courtenay, "Marguerite's Judges," deserves the credit for this observation.

11. For example, Hervé Nédellec was probably among the Dominican faction that attempted to maintain a certain distance from Philip IV (see Courtenay, "Between Pope and King," 599), but his absence is more plausibly explained by his new position as provincial prior of France. In this capacity he would have attended the Dominican general chapter meeting in Piacenza in June; probably he either had already departed by April or was fully occupied with preparations for the trip. See de Guimaräes, "Hervé Noël," 59.

12. The grammar of the passage "de quo extracti fuerant plures articuli ibidem exhibiti, quos eis demonstraverat" would seem to indicate that William had shown or pointed out *(demonstraverat)* the articles at an earlier time. This text does not, however, spell out exactly how or when William made these articles available. I thank Ian Wei for drawing my attention to the importance of this passage.

13. There is no indication, however, that he prepared a complete Latin translation at this time. While this possibility cannot be completely ruled out, no convincing evidence has ever been adduced in its favor.

14. The first and fifteenth articles as found in J428 no. 15a: "Quorum articulorum primus talis est; 'Quod anima adnichilata dat licentiam virtutibus nec est amplius in earum servitute, quia non habet eas quoad usum, sed virtutes obediunt ad nutum.' Item decimus quintus articulus est: 'Quod talis anima non curat de consolationibus Dei nec de donis eius, nec debet curare

nec potest, quia tota intenta est circa Deum, et sic impediretur eius intentio circa Deum.'" Verdeyen, "Procès de l'inquisition," 51. The additional article is given in Géraud, *Chronique latine,* 379, as "quod anima annihilata in amore conditoris sine reprehensione conscientiae vel remorsu potest et debet naturae quidquid appetit et desiderat [concedere]."

15. See J. M. M. H. Thijssen, *Censure and Heresy at the University of Paris, 1200–1400* (Philadelphia: University of Pennsylvania Press, 1998), with a description of procedures in cases of academic error (19–39). The formative work on this subject is Josef Koch, "Philosophische und theologische Irrtumslisten von 1270–1329: Ein Beitrag zur Entwicklung der theologischen Zensuren," in *Kleine Schriften* (Rome: Edizioni di Storia e Letteratura, 1973), 2:423–50.

16. These identifications were the means by which Guarnieri first attributed the *Mirror* to Marguerite. See more recently Verdeyen, "Procès de l'inquisition," 52; Colledge, Marler, and Grant, *Mirror of Simple Souls,* xlv; Bertho, *Miroir des âmes simples,* 109–10; Leicht, *Marguerite Porete,* 352–57.

17. *Le mirouer des simples ames,* in Guarnieri and Verdeyen, *Margaretae Porete Speculum,* 32: "laquelle Ame ne desire ne ne desprise pouvreté ne tribulation, ne messe ne sermon, ne jeune ne oraison, et donne a Nature tout ce qu'il ly fault, sans remors de conscience; mais telle nature est si bien ordonnee par transformacion de unité d'Amour, a laquelle la voulenté de ceste Ame est conjoincte, que la nature ne demande chose qui soit deffendue." Translation from Babinsky, *Mirror of Simple Souls,* 87. The Middle English (Doiron, "Margaret Porete," 18) has only "þis soule ne desireþ dispite ne pouert ne tribulacion ne diseese ne masses ne sermons ne fastynge ne orisons, and sche ȝiueþ to nature al þat he askiþ wiþoute grucchynge of conscience."

18. Lerner, "New Light," 113.

19. Kocher, *Allegories of Love,* 38. This is assuming that William did not somehow end up with a copy of the "first edition," a possibility that seems unlikely. Wegener, however, is quite right to point out that we cannot be certain exactly how the version of Marguerite's book possessed by William would have read. See "Freiheitsdiskurs und Beginenverfolgung."

20. Glorieux, *Répertoire,* #212.

21. J428 no. 15a: "Symon decanus, de voluntate et concordi assensu et ipsorum omnium magistrorum nomine, dixit respondendo consultationi ab eis petite, quod consilium omnium erat et est, quod talis liber, in quo continentur dicti articuli, tamquam hereticus et erroneus et heresum et errorum contentivus exterminetur." Verdeyen, "Procès de l'inquisition," 51 (Verdeyen read "eisdem" where the ms. has "eis").

22. The inquisitor may have intended to draw up a fuller condemnation later, or such a condemnation may indeed have been prepared but does not

survive. It is also possible, however, that the omission of at least thirteen articles was intended to obscure disagreement by the theologians, or it might have been meant to hide the fact that they had not formally and thoroughly considered every article. Wegener sees more "propagandistic" reasons for the selection of these two ("Freiheitsdiskurs und Beginenverfolgung," 230–31).

23. If one were to follow this line of speculation, the notary might have declined to copy such a document if it did not contain the kind of unambiguous condemnation the inquisitor sought.

24. This paragraph owes a great deal to Courtenay, "Marguerite's Judges."

25. A comparable example might be the apparent approval of Ramon Lull's *Ars brevis* by forty masters and bachelors in Arts and Medicine, in a document issued at Paris 10 February 1310. But though this episode is quite close in time and space, it did not involve the theologians, and in any case Ramon—however controversial a figure in his own right—had far more support and influence than Marguerite. See J. N. Hillgarth, *Ramon Lull and Lullism in Fourteenth-Century France* (Oxford: Clarendon Press, 1971), 135; Denifle and Chatelain, *Chartularium universitatis Parisiensis*, 2:140–42, #679.

26. We have seen, however, that William was also consulting with university masters on questions concerning "relapsed" Jews in this period. William may therefore have done more to establish this practice than has previously been recognized.

27. Courtenay, "Learned Opinion"; Ian P. Wei, "The Masters of Theology at the University of Paris in the Late Thirteenth and Early Fourteenth Centuries: An Authority beyond the Schools," *Bulletin of the John Rylands Library* 75 (1993): 37–63; Menache, "Naissance d'une nouvelle source."

28. Thijssen, *Censure and Heresy*, 10–11; William J. Courtney, "Inquiry and Inquisition: Academic Freedom in Medieval Universities," *Church History* 58 (1989): 173.

29. The case of Arnau of Villanova in 1300 (see Epilogue II) presents important parallels. It does seem that a group of hostile theologians extracted articles from his work and submitted them to the bishop. It is not clear though how many masters participated in this process. In any case, Arnau, as a doctor of medicine at Montpellier and a married cleric, was not quite as far removed from academic theological circles as a beguine from Hainaut.

30. Thijssen, *Censure and Heresy*, 3, 33.

31. See, for example, the case of John of Monzón, excommunicated twice for contumacy. Thijssen, *Censure and Heresy*, 27.

32. This point was made by Verdeyen, "Procès de l'inquisition," 52–53. See also Field, "Master and Marguerite."

33. Crawford also came to this conclusion, in "Involvement of the University," particularly showing how a comparison with Marguerite's trial

demonstrates the way the secular masters declined to sign off on the March 1308 consultation on the Templars. Courtenay makes a similar point in "Marguerite's Judges."

34. Ian P. Wei, "The Self-Image of the Masters of Theology at the University of Paris in the Late Thirteenth and Early Fourteenth Centuries," *Journal of Ecclesiastical History* 46, no. 3 (1995): 404–5.

35. Brief biography in Beryl Smalley, "John Baconthorpe's Postill on St. Matthew," in *Studies in Medieval Thought and Learning* (London: Hambledon Press, 1981), 289–344. See further B. Xiberta, "De magistro Iohanne Baconthorp, O. Carm.," *Analecta Ordinis Carmelitarum* 6 (1927): 3–128, and recently Alain Boureau, *La religion de l'état: La construction de la République étatique dans le discours théologique de l'Occident médiéval (1250–1350)* (Paris: Les belles lettres, 2006), 236–52.

36. "Beguuina quaedam, quae libellum quendam adversus clerum ediderat, prope Parisium combusta fuit, cum quodam converso, qui a fide (ut dicunt) apostatasset." Robert E. Lerner, in *Heresy*, 206, n. 20, drew attention to this passage and connected it to Marguerite (crediting Auguste Jundt, *Histoire du panthéisme populaire au Moyen Âge et au seizième siècle* [Paris, 1875], 109 n. 3). The reference to burning alongside a "conversus" makes the identification certain. Lerner relied on John Bale's quotation from Baconthorpe, printed in *Scriptorum illustrium maioris Brytannie catalogus* (Basel: Apud Ioannem Oporinum, 1557), 367, where it is included in an appendix labeled "Scala Chronicorum." (See also Bale's separate entry on Baconthorpe, 382–86.) Bale attributes the citation to "Ioannes Baconthorpius, in quarto Sententiarum," which should indicate that he found the passage in book 4 of the commentary. To my knowledge, however, no one since Bale has located the passage in any existing manuscript or printed edition of Baconthorpe's Sentence Commentary. On the basis of consultation with several experts (Stephen Dumont, Richard Copsey, James Carley, William Courtenay, Christopher Schabel) carried out by Elizabeth A. R. Brown and kindly shared with me, the problem seems to be that book 4 of Baconthorpe's commentary survives in two versions: one (known as the "quaestiones canonicae") is quite late (1340s) and forms the basis for all printed editions; the other ("quaestiones speculativae") is earlier (ca. 1325) but survives only partially in London, British Library, MS Royal 9. C. VII. Since neither Robert E. Lerner, Elizabeth A. R. Brown, nor I have been able to locate Bale's quotation in any printed edition (I myself searched the 1526 Venice edition as well as BMaz ms. 900), it seems that Bale must have taken the reference from the earlier version of book 4 and thus that it either is lost (since only parts of this version are extant) or may be preserved in MS Royal 9. C. VII. It is not found, unfortunately, in the portions of that manuscript edited in Ernst Bochert,

ed., *Die Quaestiones speculativae et canonicae des Johannes Baconthorp über den sakramentalen Charakter* (Munich: Ferdinand Schöningh, 1974). Richard Copsey further confirms that Bale's quotation is not found in Bale's own surviving notebooks. It is greatly to be desired that this reference be tracked down and contextualized, particularly because Baconthorpe's "ut dicunt" may indicate he was quoting another source. If, for example, he was merely paraphrasing the *Grandes chroniques de France* or the "Continuer of William of Nangis," this would diminish the importance of his reference (it is also possible, of course, that Bale made a mistake in his attribution). For tentative dates on Baconthorpe's career, see Christopher Schabel, "Carmelite Quodlibeta," in Schabel, *Theological Quodlibeta,* 527–37. See also James P. Etzwiler, "John of Baconthorpe, Prince of the Averroists?" *Franciscan Studies* 36 (1976): 151 n. 15; and Walter Ullmann, "John Baconthorpe as a Canonist," in *Church and Government in the Middle Ages: Essays Presented to C.R. Cheney on His 70th Birthday,* ed. C. N. L. Brooke et al. (Cambridge: Cambridge University Press, 1976), 223–47.

37. On expulsion of the Jews, see Jordan, *Unceasing Strife,* 9–17; on virtues, 11. As my notes indicate, my treatment of Jacques relies heavily on Jordan's recent work.

38. Ibid., 28–31.

39. Ibid., 50–54.

40. Ibid., 35.

41. Ibid., 41 and passim. See also William Chester Jordan, "The Anger of the Abbots in the Thirteenth Century," *Catholic Historical Review* 96 (2010): 219–33.

42. Jordan, *Unceasing Strife,* 49.

43. Ibid., 109 n. 77.

44. Klepper, *Insight of Unbelievers,* 110.

45. See the convenient biographical sketch in ibid., 6–10; the introduction to Philip D. W. Krey and Lesley Smith, eds., *Nicholas of Lyra: The Senses of Scripture* (Leiden: Brill, 2000); Charles-Victor Langlois, "Nicolas de Lyre, frère mineur," *Histoire littéraire de la France* 36 (1927): 355–401; and Henri Labrosse, "Biographie de Nicolas de Lyre," *Études franciscaines* 19 (1907): 489–505, 593–608.

46. It is usually said that he was provincial minister of France by 1319. Lerner, however, has recently argued that this was a mistaken assumption made by Labrosse (cf. "Biographie," 596–600) and repeated since. See Robert E. Lerner, "Antichrist Goes to the University: The *De victoria Christi contra Antichristum* of Hugo de Novocastro, OFM (1315/1319)," in *Crossing Boundaries at Medieval Universities,* ed. Spencer E. Young (Leiden: Brill, 2011), 283 n. 22.

47. Klepper, *Insight of Unbelievers*, 8. On Blanche's entry, see BnF ms. fr. 11662, in Auguste Molinier, ed., *Obituaires de la province de Sens*, vol. 1, pt. 2 (Paris: Imprimerie nationale, 1902), 669–70.

48. On Nicholas's quodlibets, see William O. Duba, "Continental Franciscan *Quodlibeta* after Scotus," in Schabel, *Theological Quodlibeta*, 582–91; also Deeana Copeland Klepper, "The Dating of Nicholas of Lyra's Quaestio de adventu Christi," *Archivum Franciscanum historicum* 86 (1993): 297–312.

49. Viard, *Grandes chroniques*, 273: "qui avoit trespassée et transcendée l'escripture devine."

50. Klepper, *Insight of Unbelievers*, 7, 106.

51. Ludwig Hödl, "The Quodlibeta of John of Pouilly (d. c. 1328) and the Philosophical and Theological Debates at Paris, 1307–1312," in Schabel, *Theological Quodlibeta*, 201–2. See also Ludwig Hödl, "Die Aulien des Magisters Johannes de Polliaco und der scholastische Streit über die Begründung der menschlichen Willensfreiheit," *Scholastik* 35 (1960): 57–75. On redating to 1306 (instead of 1307), see the important recent study by William J. Courtenay and Karl Ubl, *Gelehrte Gutachten und königliche Politik im Templerprozess* (Hannover: Hansche, 2010), 3–4.

52. Hödl, "Quodlibeta," 201.

53. Courtenay and Ubl, *Gelehrte Gutachten*, 13–14, speculate that he may have been present but not yet important enough to have been noted in the documents.

54. This is suggested by William Courtenay, "Marguerite's Judges" (noting that Simon of Guiberville and John of Ghent did not add their seals either).

55. Noel Valois, "Jean de Pouilli, théologien," *Histoire littéraire de la France* 34 (1914): 266 n. 1; and Courtenay and Ubl, *Gelehrte Gutachten*, 14–15, with an edition of John's quodlibet 2, q. 19, on pp. 73–82.

56. John says the debate started "in the year of the arrest of the Templars," but for the date of 1309 or perhaps early 1310, see Courtenay and Ubl, *Gelehrte Gutachten*, 45.

57. Valois, "Jean de Pouilli," 222; Courtenay and Ubl, *Gelehrte Gutachten*, 28–57. For an edition of his quodlibet 5, q. 15, see 85–146. See also Karl Ubl, "*Haeretici relapsi*: Jean de Pouilly und die juristischen Grundlagen für die Hinrichtung der Tempelritter," in Speer and Wirmer, *1308*, 161–70.

58. John has also been suggested as the author of a legal opinion, dated by Malcolm Barber to early 1310, that firmly supported the royal position. See Barber, *Trial of the Templars*, 171–74. But Courtenay and Ubl, *Gelehrte Gutachten*, 57–62, have raised doubts about both the date (they suggest a link to the Council of Vienne) and the author (they see William of Plaisians or a similar figure as more likely). See 149–57 for edition of the text.

59. Josef Koch, "Der Prozess gegen den Magister Johannes de Polliaco und seine Vorgeschichte (1312–1321)," *Recherche de théologie ancienne et médévale* 5 (1933): 391–422.

60. One recent summary of the beginnings of this controversy in the 1280s is found in Alain Boureau, *L'inconnu dans la maison: Richard de Mediavilla, les Franciscains et la Vierge Marie à la fin du XIIIe siècle* (Paris: Les belles lettres, 2010), 46–47.

61. See Jean Dunbabin, *A Hound of God: Pierre de la Palud and the Fourteenth-Century Church* (Oxford: Clarendon Press, 1991), esp. 58–68 and 113–19, as well as J. G. Sikes, "John de Pouilli and Peter de la Palu," *English Historical Review* 49 (1934): 219–40.

62. See Hödl, "Quodlibeta," 203, for date of 1328; Courtenay and Ubl, *Gelehrte Gutachten,* 8, however, say his date of death cannot be determined.

63. De Guimarães, "Hervé Noël," 52, on John's vehement opposition to Hervé.

64. It is of course not certain that John was aware of this fact. But given his ties to Cambrai, it seems quite possible that he would have known of Godfrey's involvement with the *Mirror.*

65. On John of Pouilly's conflicts with John of Ghent, see Hödl, "Quodlibeta," 205; with Ralph of Hotot, see Valois, "Jean de Pouilli," 270–73; with Jacques of Thérines, see Hödl, "Quodlibeta," 227.

66. Valois, "Jean de Pouilli," 268–69.

67. The formative study on Henry is Clemens Stroick, *Heinrich von Friemar: Leben, Werke, Philosophisch-Theologische Stellung in der Scholastik* (Freiburg: Herder, 1954). See 73 for the abbreviation of Godfrey's quodlibets. For an English-language introduction to Henry, see Jeremiah Hackett, "Augustinian Mysticism in Fourteenth-Century Germany: Henry of Freimar [*sic*] and Jordanus of Quedlinburg," in *Augustine: Mystic and Mystagogue,* ed. Frederick Van Fleteren, Joseph C. Schnaubelt, and Joseph Reimo (New York: Peter Lang, 1994), 439–56; see also Hackett's "The Reception of Meister Eckhart: Mysticism, Philosophy and Theology in Henry of Friemar (the Elder) and Jordanus of Quedlinburg," in *Meister Eckhart in Erfurt,* ed. Andreas Speer and Lydia Wegener (Berlin: Walter de Gruyter, 2005), 562–63. Stroick identified this Henry as the same man who was born around 1245 and became provincial of the Augustinians in Germany by 1279. There is some doubt, however, about whether a man of around sixty years of age could have been first promoted to the status of doctor, so there may be two separate Augustinian hermits under this name. I thank William Courtenay for raising this point.

68. Finke, *Papsttum und Untergang,* 2:309–10; Lizerand, *Dossier,* 70.

69. A fact briefly noted in Leicht, *Marguerite Porete,* 348.

70. On the work's date, see Adolar Zumkeller, ed., *Henri de Frimaria O.S.A, Tractatus ascetico-mystici,* vol. 1 (Würzburg: Augustinus Verlag, 1975), xi. I quote the translation in Hackett, "Augustinian Mysticism," 445, from Zumkeller's edition of the *Tractatus de adventu verbi,* pars 1, principale 2, 17–18.

71. My translation is expanded from the one in Hackett, "Augustinian Mysticism," 447, which is based on the edition of the *Tractatus de adventu verbi,* pars 2, principale 1, 48, in Zumkeller, *Henri de Frimaria,* vol. 1.

72. Adolar Zumkeller, ed., *Henrici de Frimaria O.S.A. Tractatus ascetico-mystici,* vol. 2 (Rome: Augustinianum, 1992), 52: "Primus amor appropriate dici poterit incisivus, quia animam a faece temporalium separat. Secundus amor dicitur incensivus, quia ipsam animam igne divini amoris inflammat. Tertius dici potest vulnerans, quia sua dulcedine cor amantis sauciat. Quartus dicitur ligans, quia amantem immobilitat. Quintus dicitur superfervens, quia affectum indesinenter et infatigabiliter sursum elevat, ut sibi solum donum divinum sapiat. Sextus dicitur languens, quia animam liquefacit et dissolvit. Septimus dicitur interficiens, quia animam in sui ipsius defectum et annihilationem inducit."

73. Ibid., 2:85: "qui ad dictum gradum amoris perfectionis profecerunt, nihil iam propria voluntate agunt, nihil proprio arbitrio relinquunt, sed omnia divinae dispensationi committunt."

74. *Le mirouer des simples ames,* ch. 118, in Guarnieri and Verdeyen, *Margaretae Porete Speculum,* 326.

75. Translation from Hackett, "Augustinian Mysticism," 446, based on Zumkeller's edition of the *Tractatus de adventu verbi* in *Henrici de Frimaria,* 1:42.

76. Robert G. Warnock and Adolar Zumkeller, eds., *Der Traktat Heinrichs von Friemar über die Unterscheidung der Geister* (Wurzburg: Augustinus-Verlag, 1977). See recent summaries in Elliot, *Proving Woman,* 257–59, and Cacciola, *Discerning Spirits,* 215–18.

77. This poem is actually very likely not the work of Marguerite herself but rather added by a later scribe to the Chantilly manuscript (Guarnieri and Verdeyen, *Margaretae Porete,* 8). Nevertheless its evocation here seems legitimate, since it encapsulates an idea Marguerite expresses less concisely elsewhere.

78. I thank William Jordan for this suggestion.

Chapter 7.   Toward the Stake

1. AN J428 no. 19bis: "nuper processum qui sequitur nobis intimasse." Verdeyen, "Procès de l'inquisition," 78 (Verdeyen incorrectly read "super"

instead of "nuper." The correct reading emphasizes the canonists' sense of only now being told a larger story).

2. This information was probably conveyed via a written text given to them by William, because of the way the wording here matches closely (though not exactly) William's own language in the final sentence of 31 May. This would not, however, preclude the oral communication of additional evidence.

3. J428 no. 19bis: "Nos autem . . . dicimus, quod ipsa beguina, supposita veritate facti precedentis, iudicanda est relapsa et merito relinquenda est curie seculari." Verdeyen, "Procès de l'inquisition," 78.

4. Hence there is no evidence for the assertion in Sargent, "Marguerite Porete," 292, that William submitted the theologians' judgment to the canon lawyers.

5. See the informative discussion in Courtenay and Ubl, *Gelehrte Gutachten,* 36–41, concluding, "Den Inquisitoren stand daher in dieser Frage ein erheblicher Spielraum für Interpretation offen."

6. Ibid., 42–57. See the discussion of John of Pouilly in chapter 6 above.

7. Barber, *Trial of the Templars,* 162–71.

8. On the date, see Jules Viard, "Le concile de Paris de mai 1310," *Revue des questions historiques* 115 (1931): 358–61.

9. Favier has argued that Philip of Marigny's purchase of land in December 1309 and donation of it to Enguerran in March 1310 must have been in recognition of this aid. Favier, *Roi de marbre,* 539, 644. More generally I am following 643–44. Favier, however, goes too far in saying that Philip of Marigny was a "man whom the king barely knew." As bishop of Cambrai, Philip had already had extended dealings with the king, as shown in chapter 4.

10. Barber, *Trial of the Templars,* 175.

11. Favier, *Roi de marbre,* 539.

12. Michelet, *Procès des Templiers,* 1:259–60.

13. Ibid., 1:262–63.

14. Ibid., 1:274: "pervenisset ad noticiam dictorum dominorum commissariorum, in dicta capella existencium, quod LIV ex Templariis qui coram eisdem dominis commissariis se obtulisse dicebantur ad defensionem dicti ordinis, erant dicta die comburendi."

15. See the account by the "Continuer of William of Nangis," in Géraud, *Chronique latine,* 377 (with incorrect date for the council).

16. Ibid.: "juxta consilium tam in jure divino quam canonico peritorum." Those executed are labeled "relapsos in haeresim."

17. Courtenay and Ubl, *Gelehrte Gutachten,* 64, emphasize the way the royal court could solicit determinations from the (relatively autonomous) faculty of theology and then ignore those it did not like while publicizing those

it did. This strategy in turn could create the appearance that the university supported the royal court more uniformly than it actually did.

18. Michelet, *Procès des Templiers,* 1:275–77, trans. in Barber and Bate, *Templars,* 301–3.

19. Michelet, *Procès des Templiers,* 1:279: "Qualiter bienium erat elapsum quod fuerat inchoata inquisicio contra dictum fratrem Reginaldum, tanquam contra fratrem singularem dicti ordinis, super criminibus que imponebantur eidem et aliis fratribus dicti ordinis, et quod ipsi erant Parisius in concilio congregati ut dictam inquisicionem et alias, factas contra singulares fratres Templi provincie eorumdem, juxta formam mandati apostolici racione previa terminarent, et quod idem dominus archiepiscopus non poterat quocumque volebat dictum concilium congregare; requirentes dicti magistri . . . ab eisdem dominis commissariis, ex parte ejusdem domini archiepiscopi Senonensis . . . ut declararent eis quid intendebant per significacionem quam dicta die hodierna eis fieri fecerant . . . asserentes quod non erat intentionis ejusdem domini archiepiscopi Senonensis . . . in aliquo impedire officium dominorum commissariorum predictorum."

20. Barber, *Trial of the Templars,* 181–82.

21. Viard, *Grandes chroniques,* 273. Various accounts differ about this date and number, but if Philip of Marigny's council ran until 26 May (as shown in Viard, "Concile de Paris") summary punishments carried out the next day might be expected.

22. Michelet, *Procès des Templiers,* 1:535.

23. In broad strokes, these parallels were sketched by Bertho, *Miroir des âmes simples,* 137–39. My interpretation of William of Paris's motives, however, differs somewhat from hers, and Bertho's analysis is hampered by following Verdeyen's incorrect dating of the theologians' condemnation and by her failure to realize that William was not involved in the Templar proceedings after fall 1307. See now the remarks of Courtenay and Ubl, *Gelehrte Gutachten,* 42.

24. Pointed out by Bertho, *Miroir des âmes simples,* 142. Courtenay and Ubl, *Gelehrte Gutachten,* 41–42, even go so far as to speculate that consultation on the question of Marguerite's relapse may have been intended to pave the way for the more controversial issue of whether Templars could similarly be treated as relapsed.

25. Favier, *Roi de marbre,* 700.

26. I thus agree with the suggestion raised by Leicht, *Marguerite Porete,* 380: "Vielleicht war Wilhelms Rolle im Prozeß gegen Marguerite durch persönliche Motive einer ihn rehabilitierenden Profilierung geprägt."

27. Lea, *History of the Inquisition,* 2:122–23.

28. See summary in Given, *Inquisition and Medieval Society,* 73–75.

29. See, for instance, the fifteenth-century view in Lorentz and Sandron, *Atlas de Paris,* 195.

30. Werner, *Irrtum liquidieren,* 560.

31. B. Hauréau, "Guillaume Baufet, évêque de Paris," *Histoire littéraire de la France* 32 (1898): 469–74, states that he had formerly been Philip IV's physician.

32. On these men, see the notes to Appendix A.

33. See Kaeppeli, *Scriptores ordinis praedicatorum,* 3:141–43; and P. Fournier, "Nicolas d'Ennezat, canoniste," *Histoire littéraire de la France* 35 (1921): 603–5. His *Tabulae super Decretum, Decretales, Sextum et Clementinas,* completed by 1319 and widely copied in manuscript but never printed, sounds very much like a self-conscious update of William of Paris's similar work.

34. Glorieux, *Répertoire,* #346. The other two men mentioned as prominent attendees were William of Choques, a Parisian townsman who witnessed documents in the Templar dossier, and Stephen of Brétencourt, whom I have not been able to identify.

35. Given, *Inquisition and Medieval Society,* 74, on this general practice.

36. AN J428 no. 15b: "Propter que secundum xanctiones canonicas pro convicta et confessa ac pro lapsa in heresim seu pro heretica te habemus et habere debemus." Verdeyen, "Procès de l'inquisition," 81.

37. Contrary to what has been suggested by (among others) Bertho, *Miroir des âmes simples,* 146.

38. J428 no. 15b: "Nos igitur super premissis omnibus deliberatione prehabita diligenti communicatoque multorum peritorum in utroque iure consilio. Deum et sacrosancta evangelia habentes pre oculis, de reverendi patris et domini domini Guillelmi, Dei gratia Parisiensis episcopi, consilio et assensu, te, Margaretam, non solum sicut lapsam in heresim, sed sicut relapsam sententialiter condempnamus et te relinquimus iusticie seculari, rogantes eam ut citra mortem et memborum mutilationem tecum agat misericorditer, quantum permittunt canonice xanctiones." Verdeyen, "Procès de l'inquisition," 82. (Verdeyen read "finaliter" where the ms. has "sententialiter." I thank Elizabeth A. R. Brown for pointing out the correct reading.)

39. J428 no. 15b: "Dictum etiam librum tanquam hereticum et erroneum utpote errorum et heresum contentivum iudicio magistrorum in theologia Parisius existentium et de eorundem consilio sententialer condempnamus ac nunc exterminari volumus et comburi, universis et singulis habentibus dictum librum precipientes districte et sub pena excommunicationis, quod infra instans festum apostolorum Petri et Pauli nobis vel priori fratrum predicatorum Parisius, nostro commissario, sine fraude reddere teneantur." Verdeyen, "Procès de l'inquisition," 82. (Verdeyen again read "finaliter" for "sententialiter," and omitted the word "Parisius.")

40. Werner, *Irrtum liquidieren*, 467, makes this argument convincingly. In particular, he draws attention to the word "now" *(nunc)* in the sentence, which implies an immediacy to the desired burning of the book. He also notes that an incorrect reading in Henry Charles Lea's older edition of the sentence could lead to confusion, where "nunc exterminari" was read as "demum excommunicari." I can verify that Verdeyen's reading of "nunc exterminari" is correct.

41. See Werner, *Irrtum liquidieren*, 474.

42. J428 no. 15b: "te esse angelum Filadelphie asseres et constanter necnon et missum immediate a Christo, qui habet clavem excellentie, non a domino papa, qui solum habet clavem ministerii." Verdeyen, "Procès de l'inquisition," 38.

43. J428 no. 15b: "Super quibus omnibus communicato peritorum multorum tam in theologia quam in iure canonico et civili deliberato consilio et concordi, de reverendi patris et domini domini Guillelmi, Dei gratia Parisiensis episcopi, consilio et assensu . . . te, Guiardum predictum, ut hereticum sententialiter condempnamus, denuntiantes te esse privatum omni privilegio clericali, supplicantes predicto patri reverendo, ut insignia clericalia tibi auferat et confestim. Quibus peractis et te ad murum perpetuum sententialiter condempnamus, nobis et successoribus nostris in predicto inquisitionis officio mitigandi, annuendi, mutandi, aggravandi vel penitus absolvendi, prout tua exigerint merita et nobis et successoribus in predicto officio expedire videbitur, potestate retenta. " Ibid., 38. (Verdeyen again here twice read "finaliter" for "sententialiter.")

44. See J. M. M. H. Thijssen, "Master Amalric and the Amalricians: Inquisitorial Procedure and the Suppression of Heresy at the University of Paris," *Speculum* 71 (1996): 60.

45. Pointed out by Lerner, *Heresy*, 75.

46. Géraud, *Chronique latine*, 379–80: "tandem in communi platea Graviae, coram clero et populo ad hoc specialiter evocatis, de peritorum consilio exposita est et tradita curiae saeculari. Quam Parisiensis praepositus in sua potestate statim accipiens, ibidem in crastino incendio fecit exstingui."

47. On the role of the provost, see Jordan, *Louis IX*, 171; Strayer, *Reign of Philip IV*, 122–23.

48. According to Jean Froissart, two men (the king of Navarre's treasurer, Josseran de Mâcon, and the Parisian alderman Charles Toussac) were executed as traitors in the Place de Grève in 1358. See Geoffrey Brereton, trans., *Chronicles*, by Jean Froissart (Harmondsworth: Penguin, 1978), 160. I owe this reference to Robert E. Lerner.

49. See Esther Cohen, "To Die a Criminal for the Public Good: The Execution Ritual in Late Medieval Paris," in *Law, Custom, and the Social Fabric*

in Medieval Europe: Essays in Honor of Bruce Lyon, ed. Bernard S. Bachrach and David Nicholas (Kalamazoo, MI: Medieval Institute Publications, 1990), 285–304. For a more colorful survey, see Jacques Hillairet [Auguste André Coussilon], *Gibets, piloris et cachots du vieux Paris* (Paris: Éditions de minuit, 1956), 15–29.

50. E. Cohen, "To Die a Criminal," 290.

51. See in general Thijssen, "Master Amalric," and in particular the passage from Rigord's *Gesta Philippi Augusti* reproduced in G. C. Capelle, *Autour du décret de 1210: III.—Amaury de Bène. Étude sur son panthéisme formel* (Paris: Vrin, 1932), 100: "et cremati sunt Parisius extra portam, in loco qui nuncupatur Campellus." This designation probably refers to the fields *(les champeaux)* outside the walls of the city, near the Louvre and Les Halles.

52. On Robert, see Jules Frederichs, *Robert le Bougre, premier inquisiteur général en France* (Ghent: Librairie Clemm, 1892); Charles Homer Haskins, "Robert le Bougre and the Beginnings of the Inquisition in Northern France," in *Studies in Mediaeval Culture* (New York: Frederick Ungar, 1929), 193–244; Georges Despy, "Les débuts de l'Inquisition dans les anciens Pays-Bas au XIIIe siècle," in *Problèmes d'histoire du Christianisme: Hommages à Jean Hadot,* ed. Guy Cambier (Brussels: Éditions de l'Université de Bruxelles, 1980), 71–104; and Simon Tugwell, "The Downfall of Robert le Bougre, OP," in *Praedicatores, inquisitores,* vol. 1 (Rome: Istituto Storico Domenicano, 2004), 753–56. The execution of a beguine by "master Robert" is mentioned by Hadewijch, presumably referring to Robert le Bougre's campaign through Cambrai, Doui, and Lille in early 1236. See Lerner, *Heresy,* 64.

53. Werner, *Irrtum liquidieren,* 468, argues that the passage in the "Continuer of William of Nangis" has been mispunctuated and hence misread; he argues that a comma should be applied after, not before, the word *ibidem* (see n. 46 above), to indicate that the provost of Paris took Marguerite into his power "in the same place" as the sentence had been read out. In this reading, the chronicler was saying nothing about the place of execution, which, Werner suggests, would more likely have taken place in the same spot where the Templars had recently met the same fate, outside the eastern walls of the city (although Werner does not spell this out, it is also possible that the *ibidem* could have that meaning overtly if it referred back to the previously mentioned burning—though this is a less likely reading, since several other items intervene between the two episodes in the chronicle). The problem, which Werner admits, is that when the Continuer goes on to say that a relapsed Jew was also "ibidem incendio concrematur," the wording directly parallels the description of Marguerite's execution, and here the *ibidem* must indeed indicate the place of burning. Reading the passage as a whole thus strongly suggests that in both

cases *ibidem* is meant to imply that the burning occurred "in the same place" as the sentencing. It should also be noted that Werner's suggested reading has a certain redundancy to it; there was no question but that the provost of Paris would have taken Marguerite into his custody in the Place de Grève, since he did it "statim." The additional information to be conveyed concerned the place of execution. Werner also considers the supporting evidence of two other contemporary chroniclers. Viard, *Grandes chroniques,* 273, says Marguerite was burned "ou lieu devant dit" in a more compressed context that grammatically must refer back to the immediately proceeding reference to the burning of the Templars (Werner rightly points out the way Verdeyen glosses over this problem). But on the other hand, the Continuer of the Dominican Gerard de Frachet, although clearly basing his description on that of the Continuer of William of Nangis, in his light reworking clarified that Marguerite "in platea Graviae ignis incendio concrematur" (*Chronicon Gerardi de Fracheto,* 33–34). Although this source cannot be considered an independent witness, it does show that this contemporary writer believed the execution had taken place in the Place de Grève. Both these sources were compiled at Saint-Denis, and it is not clear that one should be preferred over the other. Though Werner is right to point out that the *Grandes chroniques* show independent knowledge of these events, it is still true that they rely on the Continuers of William of Nangis and indeed at times on the Continuers of Gerard of Frachet for their framework (Spiegel, *Chronicle Tradition,* 112, 120). The "lieu devant dit" is obviously a translation of the "ibidem" found in the Continuer of William of Nangis; and since the intervening episodes between the burning of the Templars and the burning of Marguerite are deleted in the *Grandes chroniques,* the retention of this term may create the illusion of an explicit claim that Marguerite was burned in the same place as the Templars. Perhaps the best support for Werner's position is a passage he did not adduce, when the contemporary master of theology John Baconthorpe notes that Marguerite was burned "near Paris" *(prope Parisius).* But as noted in chapter 6, the context and source of this passage have yet to be clarified; Baconthorpe did not arrive in Paris until around 1312, and he may have been relying on an intermediary written source. In sum, the most straightforward reading of the main source—the Continuer of William of Nangis—seems warranted; and that reading identifies the Place de Grève as the place of execution.

54. E. Cohen, "To Die a Criminal," 288.

55. See Stabler, "Now She Is Martha," 250, for a convenient map showing beguine houses in this part of the city.

56. Géraud, *Chronique latine,* 380: "Eodem die quidam de judaismo dudum ad fidem conversus, dum iterum sicut canis ad vomitum reversus, in

contemptum beatae Virginis super ejus imagines conspuere niteretur, ibidem incendio concrematur temporali, transiens at sempiternum." Another version of this report (often overlooked) is given in Viard, *Grandes chroniques*, 8:277–78.

57. Alexander Patschovsky, *Die Anfänge einer ständigen Inquisition in Böhmen: Ein Prager Inquisitoren-Handbuch aus der ersten Hälfte des 14. Jahrhunderts* (Berlin: Walter de Gruyter, 1975), 200: "Frater Guillelmus de Paris etc. <inquisitor>contra perversos Iudeos ac eos, qui ecclesiastica violant sacramenta, in regno Francie auctoritate apostolica deputatus, venerabili viro et discreto ac in Christo sibi dilecto tali salutem etc." I thank Robert E. Lerner for making me aware of this document, discussed in more detail in Epilogue I.

58. See also the letter of the future Philip IV, dated 25 February 1285, that refers to William of Auxerre as inquisitor "haereticorum ac perfidorum Judaeorum in regno Franciae," according to the transcription (from Doat, XXXII, fol. 127) in Lea, *History of the Inquisition*, 2:575.

59. "Extraits d'une chronique anonyme française finissant en M. CCC. VIII," in *Recueil des historiens des Gaules et de la France*, vol. 21 (Paris: Imprimerie impériale, 1855), 132–33.

60. See Miri Rubin, *Gentile Tales: The Narrative Assault on Late Medieval Jews* (Philadelphia: University of Pennsylvania Press, 1999), 40–46; Jordan, *French Monarchy*, 192–94.

61. Nahon, "Juifs de Paris," 32. This evidence is from the *taille* roles of 1292 and 1296–97.

62. Géraud, *Chronique latine*, 380: "Multa tamen in suo exitu poenitentiae signa ostendit nobilia pariter ac devota, per quae multorum viscera ad compatiendum ei pie ac etiam lacrymabiliter fuisse commota testati sunt oculi qui viderunt."

63. Ibid., 378. On the inability of inquisitors to control the meanings crowds took from execution, see Given, *Inquisition and Medieval Society*, 76.

64. See Kocher, *Allegories of Love*, 42–44, for an assessment of Marguerite's "complicity."

65. Ames, *Righteous Persecution*, ch. 5.

66. Marcel Pagnol, *La gloire de mon père* (1957; repr., Paris: Éditions de Fallois, 2004), 16.

Epilogue I. An Inquisition's End, the End of an Inquisitor

1. This statement seems safe because it is difficult to imagine that a written record of the theologians' verdict of 11 April was not prepared at that time, and equally difficult to imagine that that original verdict was written

onto the top portion of a large sheet of parchment, the lower portion of which would then have been kept blank until 31 May.

2. It might be possible to imagine this notarized copy being prepared any time up until the death of William of Nogaret in 1313 (when the copy is known to have been among his papers; see below). But it seems far more likely that this instrument was prepared more or less immediately after the public sentencing, not only because William of Paris would have wanted such a public record immediately, but also because of the lack of a separate notarial dating by Jacques of Vertus.

3. This is a central argument of Given, *Inquisition and Medieval Society.*

4. See Appendix B.

5. Charles-Victor Langlois, "Les papiers de Guillaume de Nogaret et de Guillaume de Plaisians au Trésor des Chartes," *Notices et extraits des manuscrits de la Biliothèque nationale et autre bibliothèques* 39 (1909): 215–41. Analysis in Lerner, "Angel of Philadelphia," 357. The inventories are found in BnF, Dupuy ms. 635, fols. 99–108.

6. Item 129 (C.-V. Langlois, "Papiers de Guillaume de Nogaret," 226) in the "Littere reperte in domo defuncti domini Guillelmi de Nogareto" has the entry "Instrumenta facta super examinatione Margarite Porete, culpabilis de heresi." The plural "instrumenta" indicates multiple documents. On the dorse of AN J428 nos. 15 and 16 one can still read the labels "Instrumenta facta super examinatione M. Porete culpabili heresi" and "Instrumentum factum super examinatione Margarete Porete culpabili de heresi" (although no. 16 in fact concerns the canonists' judgment on Guiard from 3 April). Because no. 15 reads "instrumenta" (reflecting the fact that two documents are copied onto this single sheet) it is possible that the entry in the Nogaret inventory refers only to this document; but it is also possible that both 15 and 16 were indicated here. On the date of Nogaret's death, see Louis Thomas, "La vie privée de Guillaume de Nogaret," *Annales du Midi* 16 (1904): 195.

7. Item 395 (C.-V. Langlois, "Papiers de Guillaume de Nogaret," 238) in the "Littere reperte in domo defuncti domini Guillelmi de Plasiano," is labeled "Processus contra M. Porete, culpabilem de heresi." The label "Processus" is not specific in indicating single or multiple documents. The identical label is found on the dorse of AN J428 no. 18, which would seem to provide a clear identification, except that no. 18 is actually the unofficial copy of Guiard's testimony and the canonists' response. To complicate matters, however, #460 in the Plaisans inventory (241) is "Instrumentum de responsionibus illius heretici qui se dicebat angelum Filadelphie." This would seem most likely to refer to no. 18, except that then two separate entries would be referring to the same document. To my mind, the most likely solution is that the entry referring to

the "Process" must refer to no. 18, because that is how it is labeled (the person compiling the inventory surely would have gone by such superficial labels). Moreover, nos. 17, 19, and 19bis do not have these kinds of labels on the dorse. It seems likely that at one time there might have been a packet with no. 18 on top, including then 17, 19 and 19bis, with the label "Processes" intending to refer to all these unnotarized documents. The separate entry in the inventory referring to Guiard's testimony may very well indicate a no longer extant copy; such a document must once have existed, because a formal copy of his testimony must have been provided to the canonists. Moreover, the label "instrumentum" may refer to a formally notarized public instrument. My suggestions here for how to interpret the evidence differ slightly from those in Lerner, "Angel of Philadelphia," 357n56.

8. See, generally, Olivier Guyotjeannin and Yann Potin, "La fabrique de la perpétuité: Le Trésor des Chartes et les archives du royaume (XIIIe–XIX siècle)," *Revue de synthèse* (2004): 15–44; Olivier Guyotjeannin, "Les méthodes de travail des archivistes du roi de France (XIIIe–début XVIe siècle)," *Archiv für Diplomatik* 42 (1996): 295–373, and *"Super omnes thesauros rerum temporalium*: Les fonctions du Trésor des Chartes du roi de France (XIVe–XVe siècles)," in *Écrit et pouvoir dans les chancelleries médiévales: Espace français, espace anglais,* ed. Kouky Fianu and DeLloyd J. Guth (Louvain-la-Neuve: Fédération internationale des instituts d'études médiévales, 1997), 109–32.

9. Coste, *Boniface VIII en procès,* 547, 550, 600–601. He remained at the papal curia through 22 December 1310 and is found in Paris in February 1311 (755). A document issued in September 1310 (without day or place) by the royal court "per d. G. de Nogareto militem" shows his presence by the king in this month. Lalou, *Itinéraire de Philippe IV,* 2:357.

10. Lerner, "Angel of Philadelphia," 357; Pegues, *Lawyers,* 37.

11. Pegues, *Lawyers,* 39.

12. Provost, *Domus diaboli,* 303; Strayer, *Reign of Philip IV,* 307.

13. Perhaps William of Nogaret's possession of these documents shows a close working association with William of Paris. Melville, *Vie des Templiers,* portrayed them as close allies in 1307, though without evidence beyond their common work in the Templar arrest.

14. *Regestum Clementis papae V,* vol. 5 (Rome: Ex Typographia Vaticana, 1887), 114–15, nos. 6744–46.

15. Ibid., no. 6744. Remarked by De la Selle, *Service,* 58–59.

16. Ibid., no. 6745.

17. Ibid., no. 6746.

18. AN J403 nos. 17–17ter. I thank Elizabeth A. R. Brown for her transcription from no. 17ter. In Philip's 1297 Testament, William had been made

an executor while still royal chaplain (see chapter 3). Although in 1297 William would have received a yearly allowance as part of Philip's general wording providing for all the clerics of his household, only in 1311 is he granted an annual income for life: "Item, legamus fratri Guillelmo de Par. confessori nostro, aut illi qui obitus nostri tempore confessor noster extiterit, quinquaginta libr. tur. annis singulis eidem." It can be seen by this wording that the legacy was intended for the office of royal confessor and is thus perhaps not as personal a statement about William's worth as it might seem.

19. Lalou, *Comptes sur tablettes* (Comptes de l'Hôtel en rouleaux), Comptes de l'Hôtel du roi pour le terme de la pentecôte 1313: "—Expense fratris Guillelmi, confessoris regis pro diebus lune, 22 Januarii et martis sequenti, quibus fuit apud Trecas, missus per regem: 60 s" (878, #134); "—Frater Guillelmus, confessor regis, pro quadam die lune qua rex comedit carnes: 40 s., die Candelose, apud Argiliam . . .—Frater Guillelmus, confessor regis, pro curiali receptione magistri sui ordinis, sabbato ante Mediam Quadragesimam: 16 L, per elemosinarium" (880). See also Lalou, *Itinéraire de Philippe IV,* 2:400.

20. Lalou, *Itinéraire de Philippe IV,* 2:402.

21. De la Selle, *Service,* 264, gives the date of his death as between July 1313 and November 1314, but I cannot say what evidence would show that William was still alive in July.

22. Patschovsky, *Anfänge einer ständigen Inquisition,* 200: "Frater Guillelmus de Paris etc. <inquisitor>contra perversos Iudeos ac eos, qui ecclesiastica violant sacramenta, in regno Francie auctoritate apostolica deputatus, venerabili viro et discreto ac in Christo sibi dilecto tali salutem etc. ex fide dignorum relacione nuper nobis innotuit, quod talis quidem verba evomuit, que prima facie sapiunt contrarium fidei prout per doctrinam ecclesiasticam predicatur, videlicet quod nullus concubitus cum muliere quacumque est illicitus; et quod maioris demencie est, pertinaciter asseruit et alios ad hoc idem credendum volebat inducere, sicut ex modo suo loquendi qui presentes erant perpendere potuerunt. Cum igitur pluribus et arduis negociis prepediti frequenter commissum nobis auctoritate apostolica inquisicionis heretice pravitatis officium nequeamus prosequi ut vellemus, cum tamen exstirpacionem ipsius heresis et fidei katholice augmentum pre cunctis nostre mentis desiderabilibus cupiamus, nos, quibus apostolica concessit auctoritas et quantum ad citaciones testium examinaciones et quod alia, que in scriptis papalibus plenius continentur, personis quibuscumque, cuiuscumque ordinis condicionis aut gradus existant, possumus committere vices nostras."

23. Moreover, as we shall see in Epilogue III, the fear of "heretics" believing themselves empowered to act in wildly immoral ways increased after the decree *Ad nostrum* (which was certainly known before the Clementines issued in 1317), as inquisitors began to hunt for "Free Spirit" heretics.

24. Boutaric, "Notices et extraits," 23.

25. On the accusations and process that led to the execution of Enguerran of Marigny after the death of Philip IV, see Favier, *Roi de marbre*, 719–33.

26. These provisions are found in Philip's last testament of May 1311, unchanged from 1297.

Epilogue II. The Angel and the Doctor

1. The text was first partially edited from the incomplete copy at the end of BAV lat. 3824, fols. 262–63, by Heinrich Finke, *Aus den Tagen Bonifaz VIII: Funde und Forschungen* (Munster: Druck und Verlag der Aschendorffschen Buchhandlung, 1902), CCI–CCII; and then more fully from the same manuscript (with the suggestion of the title by which it is now known) by Josep Perarnau in "Troballa de tractats espirituals perduts d'Arnau de Vilanova," *Revista catalana de teologia* 1 (1976): 508–12; it was explicitly connected to Guiard of Cressonessart (after Lerner's 1976 publication of "Angel of Philadelphia") in Josep Perarnau, "Noves dades biogràfiques de Mestre Arnau de Vilanova," *Arxiu de textos catalans antics* 7–8 (1988–89): 279–80, and the whole text was edited from Genoa, Bib. Univ. ms. A IX 27, by Oriana Cartaregia and Josep Perarnau, "El text Sencer de l'*Epistola ad gerentes zonam pelliceam* d'Arnau de Vilanova," *Arxiu de textos catalans antics* 12 (1993): 7–42. For further analysis of that manuscript, see Perarnau, "L'*Allocutio christini* d'Arnau de Vilanova," *Arxiu de textos catalans antics* 11 (1992): 10–24, "Problemes i criteris d'autenticitat d'obres espirituals atribuides a Arnau de Vilanova," *Arxiu de textos catalans antics* 13 (1995): 78–94, and "Noves dades sobre manuscrits 'espirituals' d'Arnau de Vilanova," *Arxiu de textos catalans antics* 27 (2008): 415–24. See "Novas dades biogràfiques," 8–12, for the earlier history of misidentifications. This work was briefly analyzed (with no mention of the *zona pellicea*) while being confused with the *Informatio beguinorum* by Raoul Manselli in 1959. In consulting Manselli's work, I have used the French translation by Jean Duvernoy, *Spirituels et béguins du Midi* (Toulouse: Bibliothèque historique Privat, 1989), here 61–62.

2. See now the analysis in Lerner, "Addenda on an Angel." Though I owe my knowledge of this text and much of the bibliography in the preceding note to Professor Lerner, we have reached slightly different conclusions about some aspects of its likely date and context, noted below. Readers will certainly wish to be fully aware of his arguments as well as those presented here.

3. Convenient short biographies in English can be found in Joseph Ziegler, *Medicine and Religion c. 1300: The Case of Arnau de Vilanova* (Oxford: Clarendon Press, 1998), 21–34; and Harold Lee, Marjorie Reeves, and

Giulio Silano, *Western Mediterranean Prophecy: The School of Joachim of Fiore and the Fourteenth-Century Breviloquium* (Toronto: PIMS, 1989), 27–46. See also Francesco Santi, *Arnau de Vilanova: L'obra espiritual* (València: Diputació provincial de València, 1987); and Joaquim Carreras i Artau's prologue to Miquel Batllori, ed., *Obres catalanes,* by Arnau Vilanova, vol. 1, *Escrits religiosos* (Barcelona: Editorial Barcino, 1947), 11–49.

4. Ziegler, *Medicine and Religion,* 24.

5. See Harold Lee, "Scrutamini Scripturas: Joachimist Themes and Figurae in the Early Religious Writing of Arnold of Vilanova," *Journal of the Warburg and Courtauld Institutes* 37 (1974): 33–56, and the treatment of Arnau in Lee, Reeves, and Silano, *Western Mediterranean Prophecy.*

6. On the date, see Michael McVaugh, "Arnau de Vilanova and Paris: One Embassy or Two?" *Archives d'histoire doctrinale et littéraire du Moyen Âge* 73 (2006): 29–42. Perarnau has now answered with a restatement of his argument for two separate trips to Paris (December 1299, when Arnau would have been arrested but then released, and late summer 1300). See Josep Perarnau, "Sobre l'estada d'Arnau de Vilanova a París, 1299–1300: Les dues dates dels textos," *Arxiu de textos catalans antics* 28 (2009): 623–28 (I thank Robert E. Lerner for alerting me to this publication). For my part, however, I remain convinced by McVaugh's position, which is supported by significant contextual evidence drawn from the archives of the crown of Aragon.

7. At one point Arnau seems to assert that these masters were seculars. See Josep Perarnau, "Sobre la primera crisi entorn el *De adventu antichristi* d'Arnau de Vilanova: París 1299–1300," *Arxiu de textos catalans antics* 20 (2001): 355 n. 9. But elsewhere he insinuated that a Franciscan master took the lead against him (379).

8. It is true that Arnau's account identifies "domino C. de Nogareto" or "Nagorato" (as transcribed in Perarnau, "Sobre la primera crisi," 378 and 383) where one would expect "G" for "Guillaume." It seems nearly certain, however, that this "milito domini regis Francie" (William of Nogaret's usual styling) can be none other than William of Nogaret.

9. Following McVaugh's reconstruction, "Arnau de Vilanova," 38–39. On book burning, see the passage cited in Lerner, "Ecstatic Dissent," 43 (from Denifle and Chatelain, *Chartularium universitatis Parisiensis,* 2:90); and Werner, *Irrtum liquidieren,* 565. See also, more generally, Matthias Kaup and Robert E. Lerner, "Gentile of Foligno Interprets the Prophecy 'Woe to the World,' with an Edition and English Translation," *Traditio* 56 (2001): 154–58.

10. The "Instrumentum alterum appellationis magistri Arnaldi de Villanova a processu parisiensium ad apostolicam sedem" and the "Notificatio, protestatio ac requisitio ad regem Francorum" are edited most recently in

Perarnau, "Sobre la primera crisi," 377–88. The "Instrumentum" is translated in Lynn Thorndike, *University Records and Life in the Middle Ages* (New York: Columbia University Press, 1944), 128–32.

11. Perhaps, as Robert E. Lerner speculates in "The Pope and the Doctor," *Yale Review* 78 (1988): 73–74, because Boniface hoped Arnau could offer him the secret of physical rejuvenation.

12. Lerner, "Ecstatic Dissent," 43.

13. J. Carreras i Artau, "La polémica gerundense sobre el anticristo entre Arnau de Vilanova y los dominicos," *Anales de Instituto de estudios gerundenses* 5/6 (1950/51), 5–58; Ziegler, *Medicine and Religion*, 28.

14. See the account of Arnau's supposed conspiracy with Bernard Délicieux, in Friedlander, *Hammer of the Inquisitors*, 277–88.

15. Clifford R. Backman, "The Reception of Arnau de Vilanova's Religious Ideas," in *Christendom and Its Discontents: Exclusion, Persecution, and Rebellion, 1000–1500*, ed. Scott L. Waugh and Peter D. Diehl (Cambridge: Cambridge University Press, 1997), 115–17.

16. The work must have been written after August 1305 (because it was not included in BAV lat. 3824 at that date but was subsequently copied into the back of the volume) and before Arnau's death in September 1311. More precisely, it seems highly unlikely that it could have predated the arrest of Guiard in fall 1308, and I agree with Lerner, "Addenda on an Angel," that it is also unlikely to have been copied into BAV lat. 3824 before Clement V's move to Avignon in March 1309. The possible dates therefore seem to be summer 1309 to autumn 1311. Lerner has suggested July–September 1309 as most likely. Perarnau at one point argued that perhaps Arnau's letter had actually been sent directly to Guiard before April 1310 and helped convince him to testify. See "Noves dades biogràfiques," 280. I do not find this hypothesis likely, since the condemnation by the canonists of 3 April is sufficient to explain Guiard's decision to testify during the following week. This reasoning, however, seems to account for Perarnau's assertion in "L'*Allocutio christini*" that the date of copying in the Vatican manuscript was "around 1309." In "Text Sencer," however, Cartaregia and Perarnau link the letter to events around Clement V's issuance of the bull *Dudum ad apostolatus* (14 April 1310).

17. Cartaregia and Perarnau, "Text Sencer," 27–28: "si quis diceret me fore hereticum, non dicerem ey: 'Mentiris,' sed: 'Frater,' aut 'Domine, salua reuerencia tibi debita, non sum'; maxime, quia non constat michi quod hoc dicat magis asserendo quam dubitando uel temptando. Vnde, licet ego sciam eum dicere falsum, tamen nescio utrum menciatur. Proinde . . . non debeo taliter michi calumpniati dicere quod mentitur, sed quod non est verum id quod dicit, salua reuerentia."

18. Ibid., 30–31: "Nam possibile est quod rectores ecclesie qui prohibent non gerere zonam pelliceam faciant hoc non ex malicia, sed ex murmure consciencie uel ignorancia vel infirmitate complecionis causato, quia timent racione Decretalis incurrere sentenciam excomunicacionis, ideo quia uidetur quod tale signum determinate cerimonie sit inchoacio noui status in ecclesia catholica, quod nemini licet sine consensu apostolice sedis."

19. It is true that Guiard himself could have created a stir when he opposed Dominicans and Franciscans in Reims (as he testified). But he says nothing about others of his group taking similar actions.

20. Lerner, "Addenda on an Angel," argues that the letter was probably written without direct knowledge of Guiard's testimony. For my part I remain convinced that the simplest explanation for how Arnau came to hear of "those wearing the leather belt" was through Guiard's testimony, either in the direct sense of having seen a copy or, perhaps more likely, of having spoken with someone possessing a detailed knowledge of its contents.

21. See Arnau's letter to James II in Finke, *Papsttum und Untergang,* 2:94–98. For analysis, see Barber, *Trial of the Templars,* 85–86.

22. Finke, *Papsttum und Untergang,* 2:97: "si magnum fuit tonitruum, quod audivistis in percussione Templariorum, maius incomparabiliter audietur in proximo."

23. Finke believed that 1308 was the most likely year (just after the arrest of the Templars), but P. Martì de Barcelona, "Regesta de documents arnaldians coneguts," *Estudios franciscanos* 47 (1935): 290, put forth convincing arguments for 1310. I am grateful to John Bollweg for bringing this point to my attention.

24. J. Carreras i Artau, *Relaciones de Arnau de Vilanova con los reyes de la casa de Aragón* (Barcelona: Academia de buenas letras de Barcelona, 1955), 57; Paul Diepgen, *Arnald von Villanova als Politiker und Laientheologe* (Berlin: Rothschild, 1909), 81.

25. For 25 January, see Diepgen, *Arnald von Villanova,* 82; for 8 June, Barcelona, "Regesta de documents arnaldians," 291. The letter of 17 June is in connection with negotiations with Robert of Anjou and papal responses and shows his presence at Avignon earlier in the month. See Batllori, *Obres catalanes,* 1:248–50. It is true that the letter gives only the date of "xv kalendas iulii" with no year, but the contextual dating to 1310 is persuasive. See Carreras i Artau, prologue to Batllori, *Obres catalanes,* 81–84, and *L'epistolari d'Arnau de Vilanova* (Barcelona: Institut d'estudis catalans, 1950), 22–23. Arnau then wrote to James II from Messina in January 1311. See *Obres catalanes,* 1:32. He is likely to have reached Sicily much earlier, however, if he wrote the *Informació espiritual* there in 1310. On Arnau's connections with Marseille generally, see Donatella Nebbiai, "Un intellectuel catalan à Marseille: Arnaud de Vil-

leneuve," in *Marseille au Moyen Âge, entre Provence et Méditerranée: Les horizons d'une ville portuaire,* ed. Thierry Pécout (Méolans-Revel: Éditions Désiris, 2009), 340–43.

26. Coste, *Boniface VIII en procès,* 441 n. 4, 547, 550, 600, shows that "ils sont restés, durant le mois de juin au moins, en contact direct avec les affaires du procès" and that on 10 July Nogaret was at Nîmes (in the very near vicinity of Avignon), where he was probably found again on 31 July. Most of August was also spent in Provence (while Clement V was at his summer residence at Groseau) before Nogaret's brief return to Paris in September. Nogaret's principal landed holdings at this point were in the Diocese of Nîmes, especially at Marsillargues. See Thomas, "Vie privée." Another eyewitness to Marguerite and Guiard's sentencing, John of Forgetis, the official of Paris, traveled to Avignon in November 1310 as part of a delegation to Clement V. Though this is probably too late to bear on Arnau, it suggests the regular traffic of men and documents between Paris and Provence at this moment. See Coste, *Boniface VIII en procès,* 600.

27. It is true that Nogaret then used Boniface VIII's tolerance for Arnau's condemned book as a charge against the pope, but since Philip IV was writing to Arnau in 1310 there is no reason to suspect lingering antagonism over this charge.

28. It is of course uncertain exactly when Nogaret and Plaisians took possession of the trial documents, or what state they were in in summer 1310. It is not impossible, however, that unofficial copies (such as those that ended up in Nogaret and Plaisians' possession and survive in the Archives nationales today) could have circulated among royal advisors at this point.

29. That is, BAV lat. 3824, which must have traveled from Bordeaux to Avignon with the curia in 1309.

30. Cartaregia and Perarnau, "Text Sencer," 32: "Similiter, cum dicunt quod Christus libertatem dedit quibuscumque fidelibus ymitandi Johannem baptistam."

31. It can be objected that Guiard himself seems to make his reference to "giving freedom" in connection with the Old Testament, while Arnau assumes that the claim is for explicit license to follow the New Testament model of John the Baptist. This is a valid objection, but Guaird's mention of an Old Testament patron and his insistence on the importance of the leather belt are actually in response to two different questions; he does not ever quite say that he wears the *zona pellicea* in imitation of an Old Testament model. Even if this was what he meant, it might not have been clear to someone reading or hearing a summary of the testimony. Moreover, Guiard and Arnau would likely have agreed that imitating Elijah in the Old Testament was in any case fundamentally equivalent to imitating John in the New; and Guiard's testimony hints

that he would have preferred a New Testament patron but had been prevented, so that his shift to point to Elijah was a way around this prohibition. In that case, if Arnau heard a summary of Guiard's testimony, he still might have assumed, logically enough, that he and his followers actually sought to model themselves on John the Baptist. And indeed Arnau ended his treatise with the sentiment that those preserving chastity, like John the Baptist, would truly announce Christ "in the spirit of Elijah."

32. Thus it would have made sense for him to write in Latin. Although in recent years he had been composing in Catalan for audiences of southern beguins, this treatise was for a northern audience. And since it was intended, at least in part, to be presented to the papal court, Catalan would not have served for this purpose. On Arnau's relation to vernacular propaganda, see Robert E. Lerner, "Writing and Resistance among Beguins of Languedoc and Catalonia," in *Heresy and Literacy, 1000–1530,* ed. Peter Biller and Anne Hudson (Cambridge: Cambridge University Press, 1994), 191–96 (192 for the appeal to Arnau of writing in the more prestigious Latin). I thank John Bollweg for raising this question of Latin versus vernacular as a choice for the "Letter."

33. Santi, *Arnau de Vilanova,* 231–34.

34. He outlined these goals in the *Interpretatio in somniis Jacobi et Frederici* (1308), which particularly focuses on the worsening state of the carnal church and the need for reform, and especially in the *Raonament d'Avinyó* (written perhaps in early 1310), which describes a presentation given to the papal curia in late 1309. For the *Interpretatio,* see Marcelino Menéndez y Pelayo, ed., *Historia de los heterodoxos españoles,* 2nd ed. (Madrid: Librería general de Victoriano Suárez, 1911–32), 7:232–54, and for the *Raonament d'Avinyó,* see Batllori, *Obres catalanes,* 1:218. See also the discussion in Lee, Reeves, and Silano, *Western Mediterranean Prophecy,* 42–46; and the printing of these two works in parallel columns in Jose M. Pou y Marti, *Visionarios, beguinos y fraticelos catalanes (siglos XIII–XV),* rev. ed (Madrid: Colegio Cardenal Cisneros, 1991), 68–84. For Arnau's ideas on conversion, see John August Bollweg, "Sense of Mission: Arnau de Vilanova on the Conversion of Muslims and Jews," in *Iberia and the Mediterranean World of the Middle Ages: Studies in Honor of Robert I. Burns,* ed. Larry J. Simon (Leiden: Brill, 1995), 50–71.

35. James received reports that at the papal curia Arnau was attributing various dubious sentiments to him, connected to the *Interpretatio in somniis.* See Pou y Marti, *Visionarios, beguinos y fraticelos,* 90–93, particularly 91 n. 1; more generally, Clifford R. Backman, "Arnau de Vilanova and the Franciscan Spirituals in Sicily," *Franciscan Studies* 50 (1990): 12. However, Arnau's continuing correspondence with James shows that there was no immediate break in relations between the two men. See Batllori, *Obres catalanes,* 1:75.

36. Backman, "Arnau de Vilanova," 13; Lee, Reeves, and Silano, *Western Mediterranean Prophecy,* 44–45.

37. Edition in Batllori, *Obres catalanes,* 1:224–43.

38. For an evocation of the southern beguin mind-set, see Burnham, *So Great a Light,* 30–40.

39. Lerner, "Writing and Resistance," 192 n. 18.

40. Backman, "Arnau de Vilanova," 8.

41. See, for example, the *Raonament d'Avinyó,* where he lists ways that evangelical truth is coming under attack; the second way "és en les pressones seglars, les quals volen fer penitència en àbit seglar, e viure en pobrea e meynspreu de si metexs, axí com són beguins e beguines." Batllori, *Obres catalanes,* 1:206.

42. "Lliçó de Narbona," in Batllori, *Obres catalanes,* 1:141–66; Josep Perarnau, ed., *"L'Alia informatio beguinorum" d'Arnau de Vilanova* (Barcelona: Facultat de Teologia de Barcelona, 1978). It is generally assumed that the "Lliçó de Narbona" was composed first, and if a note in one manuscript can be believed (*Obres catalanes,* 1:n. 43) it was read before Clement V (presumably in a Latin version), placing it after August 1305. Batllori further argued for a dating before the end of 1308 (1:64–65).

43. See the characterization in Lerner, "Writing and Resistance," 193.

44. Ibid., 193–94.

45. Joachim Carreras i Artau, Olga Marinelli Mercacci, and Joseph M. Morató i Thomàs, eds., *Expositio super Apocalypsi,* by Arnau de Vilanova, vol. 1 of *Arnaldi de Villanova scripta spiritualia* (Barcelona: Institut d'estudis catalans, 1971). For analysis, see Santi, *Arnau de Vilanova,* 163–241; Lee, Reeves, and Silano, *Western Mediterranean Prophecy,* 40–42; and Lerner, "Ecstatic Dissent," 51. This work has long been attributed to Arnau. Recently, however, doubts have been raised by Perarnau, "Problemes i criteris," 48–70. While perhaps some caution is necessary, I am not convinced that this work was by someone other than Arnau.

46. Carreras i Artau, Mercacci, and Morató i Thomàs, *Expositio,* 56–57: "ECCLESIA PHILADELPHIAE: Sextum tempus universalis Ecclesiae primo respicit, in quo famosius claruit status regularium militantium spiritualiter cum abdicatione communis et proprii, deinde regulares eiusdem status in tempore vicarii supradictii . . . et recte tali statui convenit interpretatio Philadelphiae, scilicet 'haerentem Domino salvans,' quoniam status evangelicae perfectionis antonomastice salvat Domino adhaerentes."

47. Ibid., 135: "ET SEXTUS ANGELUS. Quia tempore sexto Ecclesiae, in quo sumus, tres erunt principales eventus qui sument ortum a tubicinio, id est a publica christianorum doctrina, quarum prima est subversio evangelicae

religionis vel exterminatio catholicae sanctitatis, secunda reformatio ipsius, tertia destructio veritatis evangelicae per Antichristum fienda." Generally on Arnau's vision of the sixth age, see Santi, *Arnau de Vilanova*, 211–36.

48. Carreras i Artau, Mercacci, and Morató i Thomàs, *Expositio*, 110–11: "Coetus autem istorum praeconum coepit venire tempore supradicto, quia tempore dicti Frederici [i.e. Emperor Frederick II] emerserunt in populo christiano beatus Franciscus et beatus Dominicus in praemissa perfectione, et eorum praedictatione commoniti tenuerunt praedicti reges et ipsorum complices populos a commotione. Idem etiam coetus veniet circa finem sexti temporis in imitatoribus praedictorum, et principaliter in pontifice memorato supra, qui erit initium finalis reformationis evangelicae veritatis; et omnes erunt uniformes in zelo promovendi hanc veritatem, et omnes habebunt signum Dei vivi praedictum. Stigmata namque quibus beatus Franciscus fuit a Deo corporaliter insignitus, licet per reductionem alicuius consequentiae possint dici signa Dei vivi, tamen proprie et per se non sunt signa nisi hominis vulnerati ad mortem; et sermo Dei absolutus est principaliter de re illa quae significatur per se et proprie per sermonem."

49. Ibid., and Santi, *Arnau de Vilanova*, 214

50. For an introduction to the theme of the angelic pope, see Bernard McGinn, "Pastor Angelicus: Apocalyptic Myth and Political Hope in the Fourteenth Century," in *Santi e Santità: Atti del XV Convegno Internazionale, Assisi, 15–16–17 ottobre 1987* (Perugia: Università degli studi di Perugia, 1989), 221–51.

51. Carreras i Artau, Mercacci, and Morató i Thomàs, *Expositio*, 59: "Vicarius autem Christi supradictus, qui erit *sanctus* in vita et *verus* in doctrina et qui habebit *clavem David* in potestate summi pontificatus ad ordinandum plene de templo Dei sicut David, *dabit ostium apertum* per exemplum clarum evangelicae perfectionis." See Santi, *Arnau de Vilanova*, 222.

52. The fact that he does not address Guiard directly does not prove that he did not know anything about Guiard; merely that in this letter his intention was to address his followers.

53. Backman, "Reception," 127.

54. Angelo Clareno, at least, credited Arnau. See Burr, *Spiritual Franciscans*, 111–13. This point is made by Cartaregia and Perarnau, "Text Sencer," 17–18, who suggest that this might have been the moment when someone at the papal curia might have wanted to copy the *Epistola* to note Arnau's intervention.

55. On the circulation of manuscripts, see Appendix C and references there.

56. As to whether Arnau might have had a potential interest in Marguerite and her book, it is relevant to note Donatella Nebbiai's argument that he may have possessed a copy of Angela of Foligno's *Liber* at the time of his

death. See "Angèle et les spirituels: À propos des livres d'Arnau de Villeneuve (†1311)," *Revue d'histoire des textes* 32 (2002): 265–83. I thank Juan Marín for this reference.

57. Given, "Chasing Phantoms"; Barber, "World Picture."

58. Théry, "Philippe le Bel," 78.

59. I am following Théry's line of argument here, now most fully expressed in "Hérésie d'état."

60. There are obvious limits to my attempt here to suggest Guiard's importance. Marguerite always appears first in the chronicle accounts, and the trial documents preserved in Nogaret's and Plaisians' papers seem to have thought of her name as covering both trials.

61. On Arnau's visionary justification, see Lerner, "Ecstatic Dissent."

62. Ian Wei will consider a similar idea in *Intellectual Culture in Medieval Paris* (Cambridge University Press, 2012). I thank him for corresponding with me about his work. My point is also related to Alain de Libera's argument for the "déprofessionnalisation de la philosophie," or "sortie de la philosophie *extra muros*" of the university, at just this time. See *Penser au Moyen Âge* (Paris: Seuil, 1991), 137 and passim.

Epilogue III. The Council of Vienne and Beyond

1. See Ewald Müller, *Das Konzil von Vienne (1311–1312): Seine Quellen und seine Geschichte* (Munster: Aschendorff, 1934), and Joseph Lecler, *Vienne* (Paris: Éditions de l'orante, 1964), 23–29, for analysis of the bull *Regnans in excelsis.* On French royal involvement, see Lizerand, *Clément V,* 250–340, and Favier, *Roi de marbre,* 655–663.

2. Coste, *Boniface VIII en procès,* 759. Clement did allow that further depositions on Boniface might be heard, so the affair was not formally concluded until the end of the council, on 6 May 1312.

3. Lercler, *Vienne,* 28–54; see Müller, *Konzil von Vienne,* 663–70, for list.

4. Müller, *Konzil von Vienne,* 76, 79. Philip of Marigny probably arrived sometime after the opening of the council, perhaps with William Baufet, bishop of Paris, in tow. Among those traveling from Paris to Vienne in fall 1311 was Ramon Lull, who had been in Paris in close contact with Philip IV since fall 1309. Unfortunately, no reaction to Marguerite or Guiard's trials has yet been demonstrated in Lull's writings.

5. Lecler, *Vienne,* 77–81.

6. See Jacqueline Tarrant, "The Clementine Decrees on the Beguines: Conciliar and Papal Versions," *Archivum historiae pontificiae* 12 (1974): 300–308.

7. Barber, *Trial of the Templars,* 264.

8. Translated in Barber and Bate, *Templars,* 309–18.

9. See Michelet, *Procès des Templiers,* 1:511, 535–38.

10. No records exist to identify the specific masters of theology or canon law who were involved. We have only the general account in the "Continuer of William of Nangis" (Géraud, *Chronique latine,* 402), who lists "Senonensi archiepiscopo, aliisque quibusdam praelatis necnon in jure divino et canonico peritis ob hoc specialiter Parisius convocatis." On these events, see generally Barber, *Trial of the Templars,* 281–82, and Demurger, *Last Templar,* 197–99.

11. This is Barber's translation in *Trial of the Templars,* 282, from Géraud, *Chronique latine,* 404.

12. Text in Emil Friedberg, *Corpus iuris canonici* (1879–81; repr., Graz: Akademische Druck– u. Verlagsanstalt, 1959), vol. 2, col. 1169. For analysis, see Lerner, *Heresy,* 47; Elizabeth Makowski, *"A Pernicious Sort of Woman": Quasi-Religious Women and Canon Lawyers in the Later Middle Ages* (Washington, DC: Catholic University of America Press, 2005), 23 ff., where a helpful, literal English translation can be found; and Tarrant, "Clementine Decrees."

13. Friedberg, *Corpus iuris canonici,* vol. 2, col. 1169: "Sane per praedicta prohibere nequaquam intendimus, quin, si fuerint fideles aliquae mulieres, quae promissa continentia vel etiam non promissa, honeste in suis conversantes hospitiis, poenitentiam agere voluerint et virtutum Domino in humilitatis spiritu deservire, hoc eisdem liceat, prout Dominus ipsis inspirabit."

14. Ibid., "nos, tam ex his quam ex aliis, de ipsarum opinione sinistra frequenter auditis."

15. Text in ibid., vol. 2, cols. 1183–84. Analysis in Lerner, *Heresy,* 81–84. I have also benefited from Robinson's translation in *Nobility and Annihilation,* 110.

16. Lerner, *Heresy,* 82–83: Edmund Colledge and Romana Guarnieri, "The Glosses by 'M. N.' and Richard Methley to 'The Mirror of Simple Souls,'" appendix to Doiron, "Margaret Porete," 359. Leicht, *Marguerite Porete,* 357–60, however, raises doubts about these identifications.

17. I thank Walter Simons for this observation.

18. Tarrant, "Clementine Decrees," showed that the council's original text of the legislation that became *Ad nostrum* referred only to beghards in Germany; Clement V's personal revisions extended the definition to include beguines and included the clause that ordered inquisitors to scrutinize them. Clement also made *Cum de quibusdam* much harsher in its apparent condemnation of the beguines and added the "escape clause" at the end to make clear that he referred only to those who meddled in matters beyond them and therefore led others astray. But the errors listed in *Ad nostrum* were indeed part of

the council's first text, and Clement's changes seem to reflect a wish to more accurately reflect the source of some of the known errors. If the text had originally mentioned only male beghards, but women were known to be the source of some errors, it made sense to extend the condemnation.

19. Analysis in Burr, *Spiritual Franciscans*, 144–50; Lecler, *Vienne*, 92–105.

20. Burr, *Spiritual Franciscans*, 111–44.

21. David Burr, *The Persecution of Peter Olivi* (Philadelphia: American Philosophical Society, 1976), 73–80, *Spiritual Franciscans*, 151–58, and *Olivi's Peaceable Kingdom: A Reading of the Apocalypse Commentary* (Philadelphia: University of Pennsylvania Press, 1993), 198–201; and Lecler, *Vienne*, 105–13. On Olivi generally, in addition to the works of Burr, see Piron, "Métier de théologien."

22. Lecler, *Vienne*, 99–100, 97, and Sylvain Piron, "Censures et condamnation de Pierre de Jean Olivi," *Mélanges de l'École française de Rome, Moyen Âge* 118, no. 2 (2006): 347–49.

23. Simons, *Cities of Ladies*, 133–35.

24. Ibid., 136–37.

25. Lerner, *Heresy*, 85–181; Alexander Patschovsky, "Strassburger Beginenverfolgungen im 14. Jahrhundert," *Deutsches Archiv für Erforschung des Mittelalters* 30 (1974): 56–198; and more broadly John Van Engen, *Sisters and Brothers of the Common Life: The Devotio Moderna and the World of the Later Middle Ages* (Philadelphia: University of Pennsylvania Press, 2008), 37–44, contextualization of Marguerite Porete at 25–26.

26. Stabler, "Now She Is Martha," 57–61. This picture should not suggest, however, that beguine communities disappeared or that they were ruthlessly hounded without any concern for justice. For example, it is often overlooked that *Ad nostrum* immediately follows two canons that attempted to curb abuses by inquisitors and required inquisitors and bishops to work together more closely. Texts in Friedberg, *Corpus iuris canonici*, vol. 2, cols. 1181–83. Moreover, John XXII tried to clarify who was really targeted in *Cum de quibusdam* with another decree, *Ratio recta*, issued in 1318. There he explicitly quoted from the former text and noted that it would not be fair for the innocent to be punished with the guilty (cols. 1279–80). These mitigating measures, however, were not entirely effective. Elizabeth Makowski has shown that since *Ratio recta* was not part of the Clementines, it was not widely known and in fact was largely ignored by canonists, who tended to represent *Cum de quibusdam* as a blanket condemnation of beguines. See *Pernicious Sort*, 47–50.

27. There is a voluminous bibliography on Eckhart and his condemnation. For the basic trial dossier, see M. H. Laurent, "Autour du procès de Maître Eckhart: Les documents des Archives Vaticanes," *Divus Thomas* 39

(1936): 331–48, 430–47. For recent analysis, see Robert E. Lerner, "New Evidence for the Condemnation of Meister Eckhart," *Speculum* 72 (1996): 347–66, and "Meister Eckhart's Specter: Fourteenth-Century Uses of the Bull *In agro dominico* Including a Newly Discovered Inquisitorial Text of 1337," *Mediaeval Studies* 70 (2008): 115–34.

28. Scholars often seem to assume that a textual dependence by Eckhart on Marguerite has been demonstrated, but the article most often cited, Edmund Colledge and J. C. Marler, "Poverty of the Will: Ruusbroec, Eckhart, and *The Mirror of Simple Souls*," in *Jan van Ruusbroec: The Sources, Content, and Sequels of His Mysticism,* ed. P. Mommaers and N. de Paepe (Leuven: Leuven University Press, 1984), 14–47, does not in fact offer concrete proof. And although the formative article by Grundmann, "Ketzerverhöre des Spätmittelalters," implied the author's belief in such an influence in 1965, it did not claim to offer textual proof. Doubts have recently been raised by Lerner, "New Light," 112, and by Wegener, "Freiheitsdiskurs und Beginenverfolgung." For a fresh argument in favor of Eckhart knowing the *Mirror*, however, see Justine L. Trombley, "The Master and the Mirror: The Influence of Marguerite Porete on Meister Eckhart," *Magistra* 16 (2010): 60–102.

29. Studies that treat Eckhart and Marguerite together include the essays in McGinn, *Meister Eckhart*; Meliadò, "Dottrina mistica della nobilità"; Heidi Marx, "Metaphors of Imaging in Meister Eckhart and Marguerite Porete," *Medieval Perspectives* 13 (1998): 99–108; Hollywood, *Soul as Virgin Wife*; Bérubé, *Amour de Dieu*; Rebecca Stephens, "Eckhart and Sister Catherine: The Mirror's Image?," *Eckhart Review* 6 (1997): 26–39; and De Libera, *Penser au Moyen Âge,* 307 ff.

30. Text in Santi, *Arnau de Vilanova,* 283–89. Convenient brief analysis in Ziegler, *Medicine and Religion,* 32–33.

31. Burr, *Spiritual Franciscans,* 196–206.

32. Ibid., 206.

33. Some sources say it was burned, others that it was thrown into the Rhône. See Burnham, *So Great a Light,* 23–24, and Piron, "Censures et condamnation," 352 (who argues for the latter explanation, indicating that Olivi was not personally considered a heretic at this time).

34. Burr, *Olivi's Peaceable Kingdom,* 202–36, and Piron, "Censures et condamnation," 353–73.

35. This equation is perhaps most dramatically spelled out in the testimony of one of Peter of John's most devoted disciples, Prous Boneta, burned at the stake in 1328. See Burnham, *So Great a Light,* 140–61.

36. Ibid., 189–193.

37. Burr, *Olivi's Peaceable Kingdom,* 202. This was in the bull *Gloriosam ecclesiam,* dated 23 January 1318.

38. Burr, *Spiritual Franciscans,* 205. For the sentence, see Sylvain Piron, ed., "Michael Monachus, Inquisitoris sententia contra combustos in Massilia," *Oliviana* 2 (2006), http://oliviana.revues.org/index36.html.

39. On themes evoked at Vienne continuing through to the consultations under John XXII, see Sylvain Piron, "Avignon sous Jean XXII, l'Eldorado des théologiens," in *Jean XXII et le Midi,* Cahiers de Fanjeaux 45 (Toulouse: Privat, forthcoming). I thank the author for a prepublication copy.

40. Recent work has shown that in 1337 "beghards of poverty" and "beghards of the free spirit" were lumped together in Metz, demonstrating the way the "beguin" label could cross over the geographical boundaries that modern scholarship has often imposed. See Lerner, "Meister Eckhart's Specter," and Courtney Kneupper, "Reconsidering a Fourteenth-Century Heresy Trial in Metz: Beguins and Others," *Franciscana* 8 (2006): 187–227.

41. Though Jacques of Vertus was apparently a serf born out of wedlock (see Jules Viard and Aline Vallée, *Registres du Trésor des Chartes,* vol. 3, pt. 2, *Inventaire analytique* [Paris: Archives nationales, 1979], no. 3212); and Jules Viard, *Documents parisiens du règne de Philippe VI de Valois,* vol. 1 [Paris: Champion, 1899], 267–73), he enjoyed notable success after entering the royal chancellery around 1314; he married, was ennobled in 1320, remained active in the chancery through at least 1329, and finally died before 1335. For traces of Jacques's activity in the royal chancellery, see Fawtier, *Registres,* nos. 1801, 2049, 2118, 2136, 2137 (no. 1801 is dated 1312, no. 2049 is dated 1313, and the latter two are dated 1310, but all seem to be collations made in 1314); Jean Guerout, *Registres du Trésor des Chartes,* vol. 2, pt. 1, *Inventaire analytique* (Paris: S. E. V. P. E. N., 1966), nos. 2077 (December 1318), 3267 (November 1320), 3306 (November 1320); and vol. 2, pt. 2 (Paris: Archives nationales, 1999), no. 4473 (November 1324). He was rewarded for service to Charles de La Marche, who must have been his particular patron. See pt. 1, nos. 3254 (October 1320; ennoblement conceded to Jacques de Vertus, "clerc du roi et familier de Charles, comte de La Marche," for services rendered to the king and Charles) and 3382 (January 1321). See more generally Olivier Canteaut, "Les notaires des derniers Capétiens ont-ils une signature?," in *Hypothèses 2005: Travaux de l'Ecole doctorale d'histoire de l'Université Paris I Panthéon-Sorbonne* (Paris, 2006): 303–14. I am indebted to Prof. Canteaut for many of the references in this note, and to Elizabeth A. R. Brown (whose study of Jacques is eagerly awaited) for correspondence about Jacques and his career.

42. Rudolph Arbresmann, "Henry of Friemar's 'Treatise on the Origin and Development of the Order of the Hermit Friars and Its True and Real Title,'" *Augustiniana* 6 (1956): 93. I owe this reference to Robert E. Lerner.

43. Ibid., 108–9. Henry is here quoting from Joachim's *Expositio in Apocalypsim.* It is true that the word *zona* here is not modified by *pellicea.*

44. See Hasenohr, "Tradition du *Miroir*," for this discovery in Valenciennes, Bibliothèque municipale, ms. 239. Hasenohr shows that fols. 69r–v of the Valenciennes manuscript correspond to chs. 77 and 78 of the Chantilly *Mirror* and further identifies borrowings and reworkings from the *Mirror* in other composite texts found in fols. 63–99. See Lerner, "New Light," for recent analysis of the significance of this find.

45. An observation made by Hasenohr, "Tradition du *Miroir*," 1360.

46. This identification should be credited to Zan Kocher, detailed in "The Apothecary's *Mirror of Simple Souls*: Circulation and Reception of Marguerite Porete's Book in Fifteenth-Century France," forthcoming in *Modern Philology*. I thank the author for a prepublication copy.

47. Hasenohr, "Tradition du *Miroir*," 1360 n. 38 (citing Paris, Bibliothèque de l'Arsenal ms. 3176, fol. 138), and 1352.

48. Ibid., 1349–51. See also Geneviève Hasenohr, "La littérature religieuse," in *La littérature française aux XIVe et XVe siècles*, ed. Daniel Poirion (Heidelberg: C. Winter, 1988), 1:303.

49. Hasenohr, "Tradition du *Miroir*," 1351. The manuscript has been dated to between 1450 and 1530 based on its watermarks.

50. Jean Dagens, "Le *Miroir des simples âmes* et Marguerite de Navarre," in *La mystique rhénane: Colloque de Strasbourg, 16–19 mai 1961* (Paris: Presses universitaires de France, 1963), 281–89; Suzanne Kocher, "Marguerite de Navarre's Portrait of Marguerite Porete: A Renaissance Queen Constructs a Medieval Woman Mystic," *Medieval Feminist Newsletter* 26 (1998): 17–23; Catherine Müller, "La lettre et la figure: Lecture allégorique du 'Mirouer' de Marguerite Porete dans 'Les Prisons' de Marguerite de Navarre," *Versants* 38 (2000): 153–67. Marguerite of Navarre was a patron of this monastery, so her access to the Chantilly manuscript seems certain.

51. Hasenohr, "Tradition du *Miroir*," 1349. Kent Emery Jr., in his foreword to Colledge, Marler, and Grant, *Mirror of Simple Souls*, xxxii n. 58, suggests that Benet of Canfield also may have read the *Mirror* in the seventeenth century.

52. Lerner, "New Light," 103–7, defends this possibility. Guarnieri's "Prefazia storica," 40, also seems to incline toward this position, though other scholars have been skeptical in recent decades.

53. This Middle English version survives in three manuscripts, all made in Carthusian houses in the fifteenth century. See Doiron, "Margaret Porete."

54. Barbara Newman offers thought-provoking comments about how translations into Latin could serve as intermediaries between vernaculars for mystical texts in this period. See "Latin and the Vernaculars," in *The Cambridge Companion to Christian Mysticism*, ed. Amy Hollywood and Patricia Beck-

man (Cambridge: Cambridge University Press, forthcoming). I thank the author for a prepublication copy of this work.

55. According to the descriptions given before Guarnieri and Verdeyen's CCCM edition *(Margaretae Porete Speculum)*, mss. A, B, and C are fourteenth-century copies made in Italy. Justine Trombley's doctoral dissertation at St. Andrews University promises to shed light on the Latin manuscript tradition. See also Michael G. Sargent's forthcoming essay "Medieval and Modern Readership of Marguerite Porete's *Mirouer des simples âmes anienties*: The Continental Latin and Italian Tradition," first given as a conference paper in Padua in the summer of 2010.

56. The claim was put forth by Paul Verdeyen, "La première traduction latine du *Miroir* de Marguerite Porete," *Ons geestelijk erf* 58 (1984): 388–89, while announcing the important discovery of a new Latin manuscript. See, however, the effective refutation by Edmund Colledge, "The New Latin *Mirror of Simple Souls*," *Ons geestelijk erf* 63/64 (1989–90), 279–87, and "Latin *Mirror of Simple Souls*," as well as Lerner, "New Light," 112. The claim nevertheless continues to occasionally resurface (without new evidence)—for example, hampering the analysis of Le Brun-Gouanvic, *"Mirouer des simples ames"* 82.

57. See James Hogg, "Richard Methley's Latin Translations: *The Cloud of Unknowing* and Porete's *The Mirror of Simple Souls*," *Studies in Spirituality* 12 (2002): 82–104; and Watson, "Melting into God," 48–49. An edition of Methley's translation appeared just before the present book went to press: John Clark, ed., *Speculum animarum simplicium: A Glossed Latin Version of "The Mirror of Simple Souls,"* 2 vols. (Salzburg: Institut für Anglistik und Amerikanistik, Universität Salzburg, 2010).

58. Dávid Falvay, "Il *Libro della beata Margherita*: Un documento inedito del culto di Margherita d'Ungheria in Italia nei secoli XIV e XV," *Nuova corniva: Rivista di Italianistica* 5 (1999): 35–45. Three manuscripts of this version survive, and one of the second Italian version (though two traditions may turn out to be versions of a single original translation). The name "Marguerite" here suggests that some Latin manuscripts circulated with the author's name (or at least first name) attached, which was then transferred to a safer "saint" Marguerite in an Italian context. Furthermore, the Bodleian Latin fragment gives an alternative title of "Margareta," which would point in the same direction, and Kocher, "Marguerite de Navarre's Portrait," builds on a suggestion by Guarnieri to observe that Marguerite of Navarre may perhaps have known the name of the *Mirror*'s author, based on her play on the word "pearl" or "Marguerite" in French. I thank Robert E. Lerner and Justine Trombley for discussion on these points.

59. For a survey of the Italian controversy, see Guarnieri, "Prefazia storica," 46–54, and Sargent, "Medieval and Modern Readership . . . the Continental Latin and Italian Traditions" (Sargent points out that Gregorio Correr, writing to Cecilia Gonzaga, assumed the book was by a woman, since he called it "libellum illum nescio cuius mulierculae.") The 1521 copy is Verdeyen's ms. D.

60. Paolo Simoncelli, "Il 'Dialogo dell'unione spirituale di Dio con l'anima' tra alumbradismo spagnolo et prequietismo italiano," *Annuario dell'Istituto Storico Italiano per l'Età Moderna e Contemporanea* 29–30 (1977): 565–601. I am grateful to Juan Marín for this reference.

61. Discovery of a German translation was reported by M. de Corberon in 1957, but no evidence ever materialized, and scholars have generally concluded that this claim was either a hoax or a mistake. See Watson, "Melting into God," 21 n. 7. But a medieval Latin copy was recorded in the library of the Charterhouse of Strasbourg, and the fragment now in Oxford was probably copied in Germany (see Verdeyen's introduction to Guarnieri and Verdeyen, *Margaretae Porete Speculum,* xii), so at least in its Latin version the *Mirror* was known there. The German theologian Jordan of Quedlinburg apparently also knew the *Mirror* in the mid–fourteenth century. See Lerner, *Heresy,* 130.

62. On Ruysbroeck, see Colledge and Marler, "Poverty of the Will," and Paul Verdeyen, "Ruusbroec's Opinion on Marguerite Porete's Orthodoxy," *Studies in Spirituality* 3 (1993): 121–29. For Ghent, see Simons, *Cities of Ladies,* 137, and Lerner, "New Light," 109. Simons believes that the work in question must have been a Flemish or Dutch translation (the inventory in which it was recorded was written in Flemish, and many of the titles were clearly in this language), while Lerner argues for French (the work was written on parchment, indicating it was older, and not all titles in the list were in Flemish). I am unable to offer further elucidation, but I find Simons's argument more compelling than does Lerner. See generally, on Germany and Dutch lands, Guarnieri, "Prefazia storica," 41–43.

63. A plausible hypothesis found in Emery's foreword to Colledge, Marler, and Grant, *Mirror of Simple Souls,* xxiii.

64. Lerner, "New Light," 116.

Appendix A.　Translations of the Trial Documents

1. Verdeyen, "Procès d'inquisition," supplies the word "arrestate" from AN J428 no. 17.

2. Verdeyen, "Procès d'inquisition" (56, line 39), has "salutant" where the ms. and Lerner, "Angel of Philadelphia," read "salutem."

3. Verdeyen, "Procès d'inquisition," amends "nominationes" to "monitiones," as found in J428 no. 17.

4. Verdeyen, "Procès d'inquisition" (57, line 2), has "inquisitoris" where the ms. and Lerner, "Angel of Philadelphia," read "inquisitionis."

5. Verdeyen, "Procès d'inquisition" (57, line 5), again has "inquisitoris" where the ms. and Lerner, "Angel of Philadelphia," read "inquisicionis."

6. On the phrase "*fidei zelatores,*" see Sullivan, *Inner Lives,* 75 ff.

7. Verdeyen, "Procès d'inquisition," supplies "procedendum" from J428 no. 17.

8. Verdeyen, "Procès d'inquisition" (57, line 28), has the correct manuscript reading "continuatis"; Lerner, "Angel of Philadelphia," emends to "contumacis," following J428 no. 17, and I follow this emendation.

9. Verdeyen, "Procès d'inquisition" (57, line 37), has "Actum" where the ms. and Lerner, "Angel of Philadelphia," read "Datum."

10. Verdeyen, "Procès d'inquisition" (58, line 6), has "publice" where the ms. reads "predicte" (Lerner, "Angel of Philadelphia," does not give the full text of the notary's authentication).

11. Verdeyen, "Procès d'inquisition" (58, line 14), has "Cossun" where the ms. reads "Coffini" (perhaps Cossini).

12. Verdeyen, "Procès d'inquisition" (58, lines 14–15), has "in vico novo septem viarum" where the ms. reads "in vico novo beate Marie." I owe this correction to Elizabeth A. R. Brown. See Richard H. Rouse and Mary A. Rouse, *Manuscripts and Their Makers: Commercial Book Producers in Medieval Paris, 1200–1500* (Turnhout: Harvey Miller, 2000), 1:19–23, for consideration of the rue Neuve Notre Dame (on the Île-de-la-Cité) as a book-trade neighborhood.

13. Verdeyen, "Procès d'inquisition" (58, line 15), has "tertia die octobris" where the ms. reads "iiij die octobris."

14. Verdeyen, "Procès d'inquisition" (63, line 12), has "continuatis," where the ms. and Lerner, "Angel of Philadelphia," read "contumaciis."

15. Verdeyen, "Procès d'inquisition" (61, line 1), has "perversitatis" where the ms. reads "pravitatis."

16. The Latin text contains an untranslatable pun on "oriens" and "occidens," which can mean "east" and "west" or (among other possibilities) "arising" and "perishing."

17. Verdeyen, "Procès d'inquisition" (65, line 9 of document), and the ms. have "notabiliter" where Lerner, "Angel of Philadelphia," reads "necabiliter."

18. Apoc. 3:7.

19. Apoc. 3:7.

20. The lower chapel of the Sainte-Chapelle in Paris.

21. Cf. Apoc. 3:8.

22. Verdeyen, "Procès d'inquisition" (66, line 12), has the plural "aliis" where the ms. and Lerner, "Angel of Philadelphia," read "alio."

23. Verdeyen, "Procès d'inquisition" (66, line 18), has "ecclesiastice" where the ms. and Lerner, "Angel of Philadelphia," read "ecclesie."

24. Cf. Apoc. 3:8.

25. Verdeyen, "Procès d'inquisition" (66, line 27), has "dictum" where the ms. and Lerner, "Angel of Philadelphia," read "talem."

26. Verdeyen, "Procès d'inquisition" (66, line 34), has "quia" where the ms. and Lerner, "Angel of Philadelphia," read "quod."

27. Lerner, "Angel of Philadelphia," omits "habitum," which is found in the ms. and Verdeyen, "Procès d'inquisition" (66, line 44).

28. Cf. Gal. 4:31.

29. 2 Kings 1:8; Matt 3:4; Mark 1:6.

30. Lerner, "Angel of Philadelphia," reads "inquisitus" where Verdeyen, "Procès d'inquisition" (67, line 5), and the ms. have "inquisitis."

31. Verdeyen, "Procès d'inquisition" (67, line 12), reads "habita tamen ratione" where the ms. and Lerner, "Angel of Philadelphia," have "habita cum ratione."

32. See "Decretum magistri Gratiani," in Friedberg, *Corpus iuris canonici*, 1:58–60 (Prima pars, dist. 19, c. 1).

33. Ibid., 1:1008 (pt. 2, causa 25, quest. 1, c. 5).

34. Ibid., 1:1016 (pt. 2, causa 25, quest. 2, c. 18).

35. See "Decretales Gregorii P. IX," in ibid., 2:6 (book 1, title 1, cap. 1, §3).

36. Verdeyen, "Procès d'inquisition," (50, lines 1–2 of document) reads "nostrorum" (Langlois, in "Marguerite Porete," read "nostra") and omits the word "publicorum" where the ms. reads "in nostrum notariorum publicorum infrascriptorum." Elizabeth A. R. Brown kindly pointed out to me the misreading of "nostrum."

37. Verdeyen, "Procès d'inquisition" (50, line 3 of document), silently adds in the name "Guillelmi," which the scribe actually omitted (presumably by accident). Langlois, in "Marguerite Porete," had supplied "G."

38. Verdeyen, "Procès d'inquisition" (51, line 7, following Langlois, "Marguerite Porete"), has "supradictos," which would make the meaning "the same above-mentioned masters." The ms. however reads "supradictus," with this adjective therefore modifying "Simon."

39. Verdeyen, "Procès d'inquisition" (51, line 9), has "ab eisdem petite" where the ms. reads "ab eis petite."

40. Verdeyen, "Procès d'inquisition" (51, line 15), has "quarto" where the ms. reads "quinto." Langlois, in "Marguerite Porete," did not transcribe this

final portion of the dating clause (or the following authentication by the notary). He did, however, note that the year 1309 for this document was "old style" and so was aware of the correct date of the document in modern reckoning.

41. Verdeyen, "Procès d'inquisition" (51, line 15), has "personis quibus supra ad haec specialiter evocatis." The abbreviation that he renders as "personis" can only stand for "pres" and presumably should be expanded as "presentibus."

42. Verdeyen, "Procès d'inquisition" (51, line 18), omits the word "presens" where the ms. reads "Eveno Phili notario publico presens, interfui."

43. Verdeyen, "Procès d'inquisition" (78, line 9 of document), has "super processum" where the ms. has "nuper processum" (Lea, *History of the Inquisition,* reads "inque processum"). My reading assumes punctuation should be "nuper processum qui sequitur nobis intimasse, consultationemque nobis fecisse, inferius annotatam." Note also that this document spells Marguerite's name as "Margareta," whereas Verdeyen, "Procès d'inquisition" (following Lea), has "Margarita" each time.

44. Verdeyen, "Procès d'inquisition" (78, line 12), omits the word "in" where the ms. reads "in inobediencia."

45. Verdeyen, "Procès d'inquisition" (78, line 18, following Lea, *History of the Inquisition*), has "fuit condempnatus" where the ms. reads "fuerat condempnatus."

46. Verdeyen, "Procès d'inquisition" (78, line 28), omits the word "idem."

47. William Baufet, physician to Philip IV and canon of Paris before becoming bishop of Paris (from 17 January 1305 to his death on 30 December 1319). See Hauréau, "Guillaume Baufet."

48. Verdeyen, "Procès d'inquisition," has "Fregeris" (Lea, *History of the Inquisition,* read "Forgerio") where the ms. reads "Forgetis." John of Forgetis (or Forgettes) is here designated as "official of Paris" (the bishop's chief administrator). William of Chanac, the next man on the list, had held this office as recently as 1307, but the label here clearly applies to John (the scribe placed a faint but distinct point after "Iohanne de Forgetis officiali parisiensi" and before "G. de Chenac"; moreover, the document consistently lists names before offices). John of Forgetis was archdeacon of Brioude in the Church of Clermont by 1308 (Fawtier, *Registres,* 396, #399), part of a group of royal ambassadors to Clement V relative to the Boniface VIII heresy trial in November 1310 (Coste, *Boniface VIII en procès,* 600), part of a delegation to conclude a treaty with Henry VII, king of the Romans, the following February (755), canon of Paris by 1314 (Fawtier, *Registres,* 471–72, #2245), and archdeacon of Brie in the Church of Paris by 1317 (following William of Chanac). According to the *Corpus Philippicum* (the compilation of documentary evidence on figures from the

court of Philip IV, begun by Robert Fawtier and now held at the Paris branch [recently moved from the Orléans branch, where I consulted it] of the Institut de recherche et d'histoire des textes under the direction of Élisabeth Lalou), he served later as royal *enquêteur* and member of parlement, before his death in July 1326. The biographical portion of the *Corpus,* the *Gallia Regia Philippica,* is scheduled to be made available online by Xavier Hélary and Élisabeth Lalou—both of whom I thank for access to the hard-copy files of the *Corpus* in the meanwhile. I am also grateful to Elizabeth A.R. Brown and Olivier Canteaut for discussion of the careers of John of Forgetis and William of Chanac (below).

49. William, as executor of Hélie of Maumont, handled the sale of several houses to Enguerran of Marigny in June 1306 and was already canon of Paris and royal clerk (Favier, *Roi de marbre,* 556–58). He was labeled "canonicus et officialis Parisiensis" when he appended his seal as witness to Templar confessions made before the university on 26 October 1307 (Finke, *Papsttum und Untergang,* 2:312). Some of his activities as royal enquêteur around 1308 are traced in Brown, *Customary Aids,* 81–82 and 162–63, with evidence for his presence in Paris in March 1310. In 1313 called "clerc du roi," (Fawtier, *Registres,* 388, #1915); by1314 archdeacon of Brie in the church of Paris (Fawtier, *Registres,* 470, #2240); and finally bishop of Paris from 1333 to 1342.

50. Royal revenue collector by 1290, collecting payments to the crown for the war with England in 1294 and accounts for various segments of the army over the next five years; canon of Rouen by 1298; royal enquêteur and master in the Chambre des Comptes by 1301, where he would have associated with both Sanche of Charmoie and Enguerran of Marigny; canon of Chartres in 1310; called "clerc du roi" in 1311 (Fawtier, *Registres,* 252, #1322). Died 1321. See Strayer, *Reign of Philip IV,* 165–66, and Favier, *Roi de marbre,* 591, 612, 720, 797. (Additional info on canonries comes from the *Corpus Philippicum.*)

51. Verdeyen, "Procès d'inquisition," reads "Xaverio" (following Lea, *History of the Inquisition*) where the ms. has "Xanccio." I thank Elizabeth A.R. Brown for this correction. Sanche was a royal clerk of accounts from the 1290s, and master of accounts from 1299 until his death in 1314. Several members of his family maintained positions in the Chambre des Comptes as well, and had ties to Enguerran of Marigny. See Strayer, *Reign of Philip IV,* 185, and Favier, *Roi de marbre,* 532, 591, 612, 662, 797.

52. I have been unable to identity this man.

53. See Glorieux, *Répertoire,* #346. Franciscan regent master of theology at Paris just after this time, from 1312 to 1314. Date of death unknown.

54. Another Dominican who worked closely with William of Paris during the Templar trial. See Kaeppeli, *Scriptores ordinis praedicatorum,* 3:141–42, and Fournier, "Nicolas d'Ennezat."

55. Denifle and Chatelain, *Chartularium universitatis Parisiensis,* 2:85, 123, 269. As provost of Paris, numerous extant acts document his activities from September 1309 to February 1316 (listed up to the end of the reign of Philip IV in the *Corpus Philippicum*).

56. A citizen of Paris who witnessed a number of documents in the Templar trial.

57. Verdeyen, "Procès d'inquisition" (81, line 22 of document), has "indita" (Lea, *History of the Inquisition,* read "ortata") where the ms. reads "monita."

58. Verdeyen, "Procès d'inquisition," has "centempsisti" (81, line 33), presumably a typographical error for the correct reading "contempsisti."

59. Ibid. (81, line 40, following Lea, *History of the Inquisition*), reads "quondam" where the ms. reads "quemdam."

60. Verdeyen, "Procès d'inquisition" (82, line 9), omits the words "pluries habuisti eo" where the ms. reads "contra dictam prohibitionem pluries habuisti eo pluries usa es." Lea, *History of the Inquisition,* read "pluries habuisti et pluries usa es."

61. Verdeyen, "Procès d'inquisition" (82, line 11, following Lea, *History of the Inquisition*), has "Johanne" where the ms. reads "domino Ph."

62. Verdeyen, "Procès d'inquisition" (82, line 22, following Lea, *History of the Inquisition*), reads "finaliter" where the ms. has "sentencialiter." I owe this correction (here and below) to Elizabeth A. R. Brown.

63. Verdeyen, "Procès d'inquisition" (82, line 27), again reads "finaliter" for "sentencialiter."

64. In *History of the Inquisition,* Lea's transcriber incorrectly read "demum excommunicari" instead of "nunc exterminari," leading to confusion and the sense that the inquisitor was directly asking that Marguerite be excommunicated and then burned. It was in fact the book referred to here—to be exterminated and burned.

65. Verdeyen, "Procès d'inquisition" (82, line 31), omits "of Paris."

66. Ibid. again reads "Margerita" instead of "Margereta."

67. Ibid. (82, line 41), has "nuper" where the ms. reads "Parisius" (Lerner, "Angel of Philadelphia," expands to the more classical locative "Parisiis").

68. Verdeyen, "Procès d'inquisition" (82, line 45), has "presentares" where the ms. and Lerner, "Angel of Philadelphia," read "prestares."

69. Verdeyen, "Procès d'inquisition" (82, line 45), has "domine" where the ms. and Lerner, "Angel of Philadelphia," read "dicte."

70. Verdeyen, "Procès d'inquisition" (82, line 47), has "quin" where the ms. and Lerner, "Angel of Philadelphia," read "quoniam."

71. Verdeyen, "Procès d'inquisition" (82 lines 47–48), has "adstiturus pluries excitatus a nobis" where the ms. and Lerner, "Angel of Philadelphia," read "constitutus pluries exortatus a nobis."

72. Verdeyen, "Procès d'inquisition" (83, lines 2–3), has "veraciter edicere" where the ms. and Lerner, "Angel of Philadelphia," read "respondere et dicere."

73. Verdeyen, "Procès d'inquisition" (83, line 8), has "notata" where the ms. and Lerner, "Angel of Philadelphia," read "notificata."

74. Verdeyen, "Procès d'inquisition" (83, line 9), has "obtulimus" where the ms. and Lerner, "Angel of Philadelphia," read "obtulerimus."

75. Verdeyen, "Procès d'inquisition" (83, line 15), has "asseres" where the ms. and Lerner, "Angel of Philadelphia," read "assereres."

76. Verdeyen, "Procès d'inquisition" (83, line 19), has "si" where the ms. and Lerner, "Angel of Philadelphia," read "et si."

77. Verdeyen, "Procès d'inquisition" (83 n. 1), indicates that the ms. reads "condempnandi" and emends to "condempnanda." In fact the ms. reads "condempnanda."

78. Ibid. (83, line 30), has "veritate" where the ms. and Lerner, "Angel of Philadelphia," read "veritati."

79. Verdeyen, "Procès d'inquisition" (83 line 31), and Lerner, "Angel of Philadelphia," both read "finaliter," which should correctly be "sententialiter."

80. Lerner, "Angel of Philadelphia," read "omnibus peractis" where the ms. and Verdeyen, "Procès d'inquisition" (83, line 34), have "quibus peractis."

81. Verdeyen, "Procès d'inquisition" (83, line 34), and Lerner, "Angel of Philadelphia," again have "finaliter" for "sentencialiter."

82. Verdeyen, "Procès d'inquisition" (83, line 36), has "annuendi" where ms. and Lerner, "Angel of Philadelphia," read "minuendi."

83. Verdeyen, "Procès d'inquisition" (83, line 41), has "item" where the ms. and Lerner, "Angel of Philadelphia," read "actum."

Appendix B. Translations of Other Contemporary Sources

1. Spiegel, *Chronicle Tradition,* 98.

2. Pentecost was on 7 June in 1310. The lack of precision on this date shows that a certain amount of time must have elapsed before these events were recorded.

3. Spiegel, *Chronicle Tradition,* 112.

4. Following a reference to Wednesday, 27 May, this produces the correct date of 1 June 1310.

5. The internal logic of the text should indicate that this would refer to the spot outside the walls of Paris where the Templars were burned. See, however, chapter 7 for a discussion of how best to interpret the place of Marguerite's death.

6. This claim is often cited, but it is clearly a misunderstanding of the phrase in the *Grandes chroniques* that says she "transgressed Divine Scripture."

Appendix C. Translation of Arnau of Vilanova's
Epistola ad gerentes zonam pelliceam

1. This manuscript is described in detail in Perarnau, "*Allocutio Christini,*" 10–24.

2. Lerner, "Addenda on an Angel," favors summer 1309 as the date of composition, while I argue (Epilogue II) for summer 1310. Perarnau in "*Allocutio Christini,*" 24, assumes 1310 as the date of copying and seems to prefer a composition date shortly after April 1310 in Cartaregia and Perarnau, "Text Sencer," 17–18.

3. Perarnau, "Problemes i criteris," 78–94, and "Noves dades sobre manuscrits," 415–24.

4. The section includes the *Conflictus Iudaeorum* and *Tractatus contra passagium ad partes ultramarinas,* as well as a copy of the anonymous *Liber de flore.* Perarnau adduces plausible evidence to suggest Arnau's authorship of the first two, while the latter is known to have been produced in Arnau's circle around 1305.

5. Catalan traits include the spelling "tunch" for "tunc," as Robert Lerner pointed out to me. Perarnau, "Noves dades sobres manuscrits," speculates on connections to Valencia. See Robert E. Lerner, "The Prophetic Manuscripts of the 'Renaissance Magus' Pierleone of Spoleto," in *Il profetismo gioachimita tra Quattrocento e Cinquecento,* ed. Gian Luca Potestà (Genoa: Marietti, 1991), 97–116, for Pierleone's "similarities to and reverence for" Arnau.

6. The *Informatio beguinorum* begins, "Tots aquells qui volen fer vida esperitual"; the *Alia informatio beguinorum* has "Als cultivadors de la evvangelica pobrea." See Cartaregia and Perarnau, "Text Sencer," 25 n. 1. It was this similarity, in fact, that caused the *Epistola* to be misidentified for years, with scholars assuming it must be a Latin version of one of these two vernacular works. Compare also a passage in the *Interpretatio de visionibus in somniis Jacobi et Frederici,* "Cunctos volentes in evangelica paupertate vel abieccione vivere." See Menéndez y Pelayo, *Historia de los heterodoxos,* 7:249.

7. The "Presentatio burdigalensis," edited in Finke, *Aus den Tagen,* ccvii–ccviii: "primus est paupertas voluntaria. . . . Secundus lapis est humilitas vera. . . . Tertius lapis est caritas perfecta. . . . Quartus lapis est pudicitia sive castitas integra." Cf. the *Epistola,* where the four virtues (transposed here into the nominative case) are "altissima paupertas, plenissima humilitas, perfectissima

caritas, sincerissima pudicicia seu castitas." See the brief analysis by Manselli, *Spirituels et béguins,* 58.

8. Carreras i Artau, Mercacci, and Morató i Thomàs, *Expositio super Apocalypsi,* 136 (commenting on "Audivit vocem unam ex quatuor cornibus altaris aurei"): " Vox autem illa . . . est concordia quatuor virtutum . . . quae faciunt quatuor ipsius cornua vel eminentias: primum cornu est paupertas voluntaria; secundum est humilitas vera; tertium est caritas perfecta; quartum est castitas integra." Commentary in Santi, *Arnau de Vilanova,* 217.

9. See Miquel Batllori, "Les versions italianes medievales d'obres religioses de Mestre Aranu de Vilanova," in *Archivio italiano per la storia della pietà,* vol. 1 (Rome: Edizioni di Storia et Letteratura, 1951), 411–27, 454–62. See the notes to Cartaregia and Perarnau's edition of the *Epistola* ("Text Sencer") for parallels between these three works.

10. G reads "impatientem"; the reading "patientem" in V is preferable.

11. G reads "ingentibus"; the reading "ignorentibus" in V is preferable.

12. The reading in G "quod portaverit exit deserum" must be corrupt; V must have the correct reading "extra desertum."

13. G reads "qui in proposito dicunt quod nullus rector ecclesie potest inhibere quod Christus concedit et hoc est verum." V omits "in proposito," which seems to make more sense. The previous three notes follow the sound suggestions of the editors of the Latin text. This emendation and that in the next note, however, are my own.

14. G has "templum figuratum adorat." V cannot provide an alternative, since it is incomplete and ends before this point. My translation assumes that this should be amended to read "aderat," based on the sense of the passage.

BIBLIOGRAPHY

Archival and Manuscript Sources

Paris, Archives nationales de France

J306 no. 90 (Letters of Philip IV concerning Toulouse)
J413 B no. 15 (Ralph of Ligny questions two German Templars)
J413 B no. 17 (Templar confessions at Caen)
J413 B no. 18 (Templar confessions at Paris)
J413 B no. 22 (Letters concerning the arrest of Templars)
J416 no. 3 (Letter of Clement V)
J428 nos. 15–19bis (Trial documents of Marguerite and Guiard)
L291 no. 15 (Letter of Clement V)
LL1595 (Cartulary of Saint-Antoine)
S4373 dossier 2, nos. 8, 10–13, 15 (Archives of Saint-Antoine)

Paris, Bibliothèque Mazarine

Ms. 248 (Nicholas of Gorran, *Postillae super Lucam*)
Ms. 900 (John Baconthorpe, Book IV of Sentence Commentary)

Paris, Bibliothèque nationale de France

Ms. lat. 3208 *(Dialogus de septem sacramentis)*
Ms. lat. 3209 *(Dialogus de septem sacramentis)*
Ms. lat. 3210 *(Dialogus de septem sacramentis)*
Ms. lat. 3473 *(Dialogus de septem sacramentis)*
Ms. lat. 3474 *(Dialogus de septem sacramentis)*
Ms. lat. 3987 *(Summa Innocenti abbreviati)*
Ms. lat. 4306 *(Summa Innocenti abbreviati)*

Ms. lat. 5473 (Cartulary of Ourscamps)
Ms. lat. 10731 *(Dialogus de septem sacramentis)*
Ms. lat. 10919 (Register XXIX of the Trésor des Chartes)
Ms. lat. 13451 *(Dialogus de septem sacramentis)*
Ms. lat. 13667 *(Tabula juris)*
Ms. lat. 14523 *(Dialogus de septem sacramentis)*
Ms. lat. 14741 *(Dialogus de septem sacramentis)*
Ms. lat. 14922 *(Dialogus de septem sacramentis)*

Saint-Omer, Bibliothèque municipale

Ms. 283 (Guido of Collemezzo's extracts from St. Bernard)

Vatican City, Biblioteca Apostolica Vaticana

Ms. Borgh. 276 *(Tabula juris)*

Printed Primary Sources

"Anonymum S. Martialis chronicon." In *Recueil des historiens des Gaules et de la France,* 21:802–14. Paris: Imprimerie impériale, 1855.

Arbresmann, Rudolph. "Henry of Friemar's 'Treatise on the Origin and Development of the Order of the Hermit Friars and Its True and Real Title.'" *Augustiniana* 6 (1956): 37–145.

Babinsky, Ellen L., trans. *The Mirror of Simple Souls,* by Marguerite Porete. Preface by Robert E. Lerner. New York: Paulist Press, 1993.

Baluze, Étienne. *Vitae paparum avenionensium.* 2nd ed. Ed. G. Mollat. Vol. 3. Paris: Letouzey et Ané, 1921.

Barber, Malcolm, and Keith Bate, trans. *The Templars: Selected Sources.* Manchester: Manchester University Press, 2002.

Batllori, Miquel, ed. *Obres catalanes,* by Arnau de Vilanova. Vol. 1. *Escrits religiosos.* Barcelona: Editorial Barcino, 1947.

Biller, Peter, Caterina Bruschi, and Shelagh Sneddon, eds. and trans. *Inquisitors and Heretics in Thirteenth-Century Languedoc: Edition and Translation of Toulouse Inquisition Depositions, 1273–1282.* Leiden: Brill, 2011.

Bochert, Ernst, ed. *Die Quaestiones speculativae et canonicae des Johannes Baconthorp über den sakramentalen Charakter.* Munich: Ferdinand Schöningh, 1974.

Bormans, Stanislas, ed. *Ly Myreur des Histors, chronique de Jean des Preis dit d'Outremeuse.* 7 vols. Brussels: Hayez, 1859–87.

Boutaric, Edgar P. "Notices et extraits de documents inédits relatifs à l'histoire de France sous Philippe le Bel." *Notices et extraits des manuscrits de la Bibliothèque Impériale et autres bibliothèques* 20, no. 2 (1862): 83–237.

Brereton, Geoffrey, trans. *Chronicles,* by Jean Froissart. Harmondsworth: Penguin, 1978.

Burr, David, and E. Randolph Daniel, trans. *A Chronicle or History of the Seven Tribulations of the Order of Brothers Minor,* by Angelo Clareno. St. Bonaventure, NY: Franciscan Institute Publications, 2005.

Carreras i Artau, Joachim, Olga Marinelli Mercacci, and Joseph M. Morató i Thomàs, eds. *Expositio super Apocalypsi.* Vol. 1 of *Arnaldi de Villanova scripta spiritualia.* Barcelona: Institut d'estudis catalans, 1971.

Cartaregia, Oriana, and Josep Perarnau. "El text Sencer de l'*Epistola ad gerentes zonam pelliceam* d'Arnau de Vilanova." *Arxiu de textos catalans antics* 12 (1993): 7–42.

Cawley, Martinus, trans. *Send Me God: The Lives of Ida the Compassionate of Nivelles, Nun of La Ramée; Arnulf, Lay Brother of Villers; and Abundus, Monk of Villers,* by Goswin of Bossut. Turnhout: Brepols, 2003.

Clark, John, ed. *Speculum animarum simplicium: A Glossed Version of "The Mirror of Simple Souls," by Richard Methley.* 2 vols. Salzburg: Institut für Anglistik und Amerikanistik, 2010.

Colledge, Edmund, J. C. Marler, and Judith Grant, trans. *The Mirror of Simple Souls,* by Margaret Porette *[sic].* Foreword by Kent Emery Jr. Notre Dame: University of Notre Dame Press, 1999.

Coste, Jean. *Boniface VIII en procès: Articles d'accusation et deposition des témoins.* Rome: L'Erma di Bretschneider, 1995.

Cousins, Ewart, trans. *The Soul's Journey into God, the Tree of Life, the Life of St. Francis,* by Bonaventure. New York: Paulist Press, 1978.

De Loisne, M. le Comte. "Bulles de papes pour l'Ordre du Temple, conservées aux Archives nationales (1155–1312)." *Bulletin philologique et historique (jusqu'à 1715) du Comité des travaux historiques et scientifiques* 5 (1917): 171–236.

De Longchamp, Max Huot, trans. *Le miroir des âmes simples et anéanties et qui seulement demeurent en vouloir et désire d'amour,* by Marguerite Porete. Paris: Albin Michel, 1984.

Denifle, H., and A. Chatelain, eds. *Chartularium universitatis Parisiensis.* 4 vols. Paris: Delalain, 1889–97.

Devic, Claude, and J. Vaissete. *Histoire générale de Languedoc.* Vol. 10. Toulouse: Privat, 1885.

Doiron, Marilyn, ed. "Margaret Porete: *The Mirror of Simple Souls,* a Middle English Translation." In *Archivio italiano per la storia della pietà,* 5:241–355. Rome: Edizioni di Storia e Letteratura, 1968.

Douais, Célestin, ed. *Documents pour servir à l'histoire de l'inquisition dans le Languedoc.* 2 vols. Paris: Renouard, 1900.

———, ed. *Practica inquisitionis heretice pravitatis,* by Bernard Gui. Paris: Picard, 1886.

"Extraits d'une chronique anonyme française finissant en M. CCC. VIII." In *Recueil des historiens des Gaules et de la France,* 21:130–36. Paris: Imprimerie impériale, 1855.

Fawtier, Robert, ed. *Registres du Trésor des Chartes.* Vol. 1. *Règne de Philippe le Bel. Inventaire analytique.* Paris: Imprimerie nationale, 1958.

Finke, Heinrich. *Papsttum und Untergang des Templerordens.* Vol. 2. Munster: Aschendorffschen Buchhandlung, 1907.

Fozzer, Giovanna, trans. *Lo specchio della anime semplici,* by Marguerite Porete. Preface by Romana Guarnieri. Commentary by Marco Vannini. Milan: Edizioni San Paolo, 1994.

Fredericq, Paul. *Corpus documentorum inquisitionis haereticae pravitatis Neerlandicae.* Vol. 1. Ghent: Vuylsteke, 1889.

Friday, Hal. "I Saw Another Angel: An Edition of Two Sermons by Guibert of Tournai for the Feast of St. Francis of Assisi." MA thesis, University of Vermont, 2008.

Friedberg, Emil. *Corpus iuris canonici.* 2 vols. Leipzig, 1879–81. Reprint, Graz: Akademische Druck- u. Verlagsanstalt, 1959.

Gerard de Frachet. *Chronicon Gerardi de Fracheto et anonyma ejusdem operis continuatio.* In *Recueil des historiens des Gaules et de la France,* 21:1–70. Paris: Imprimerie impériale, 1855.

Géraud, Hercule, ed. *Chronique latine de Guillaume de Nangis de 1113 à 1300, avec les continuationes de cette chronique de 1300 à 1368.* New ed. Vol. 1. Paris: Renouard, 1843.

Gerson, Jean. *Oeuvres complètes.* Vol. 3. Ed. Palémon Glorieux. Paris: Desclée et Cie, 1962.

Guarnieri, Romana. "Il movimento del Libero Spirito." In *Archivio italiano per la storia della pietà* 4:351–708. Rome: Edizioni di Storia et Letteratura, 1965.

Guarnieri, Romana, and Paul Verdeyen, eds. *Margaretae Porete Speculum simplicium animarum / Marguerite Porete, Le mirouer des simples ames.* CCCM 69. Turnhout: Brepols, 1986.

Guerout, Jean, ed. *Registres du Trésor des Chartes: Inventaire analytique.* Vol. 2, pt. 1. Paris: S.E.V.P.E.N., 1966; vol.2, pt. 2, Paris: Archives nationales, 1999.

Hart, Mother Columba, trans. *Hadwijch: The Complete Works.* New York: Paulist Press, 1980.

Hobbins, Daniel, trans. *The Trial of Joan of Arc.* Cambridge, MA: Harvard University Press, 2005.

Kirchberger, Clare, ed. *The Mirror of Simple Souls, by an unknown French mystic of the thirteenth century, translated into English by M.N.* London: Burns, Oates, and Washbourne, 1927.

Lalou, Élisabeth. *Les comptes sur tablettes de cire de la chambre au deniers, de Philippe III le Hardi et de Philippe IV le Bel (1282–1309).* Paris: Boccard, 1994.

Lalou, Élisabeth, X. Hélary, C. Jacobs, C. Masset, and Z. Abbadi, eds. *Enquêtes menées sous les derniers capétiens.* Paris: Centre de resources numériques TELMA, 2007. www.cn-telma.fr/enquetes/.

Langlois, Ernest, ed. *Registres de Nicolas IV.* Vol. 1. Paris: Thorin, 1890.

Laurent, M. H. "Autour du procès de Maître Eckhart: Les documents des Archives Vaticanes." *Divus Thomas* 39 (1936): 331–48, 430–47.

Lizerand, Georges, ed. *Le dossier de l'affaire des Templiers.* 2nd ed. Paris: Les belles lettres, 1964.

Louis-Combet, Claude, trans. *Le miroir des simples âmes anéanties et qui seulement demeurent en vouloir et désire d'amour,* by Marguerite Porete. Grenoble: Millon, 1991.

McCready, W. D., ed. *The Theory of Papal Monarchy in the Fourteenth Century: Guillaume de Pierre Godin, Tractatus de causa immediata ecclesiastice potestatis.* Toronto: Pontifical Institute of Mediaeval Studies, 1982.

Meersseman, Gillis, ed. *Laurentii Pignon catalogi et chronica.* Rome: Apud Institutum Historicum Fratrum Praedicatorum, 1936.

Michaëlsson, Karl. *Le livre de la taille de Paris l'an de grace 1313.* Göteborg: Wettergren och Kerbers, 1951.

———. *Le livre de la taille de Paris l'an 1296.* Göteborg: Wettergren och Kerbers, 1958.

———. *Le livre de la taille de Paris l'an 1297.* Göteborg: Wettergren och Kerbers, 1962.

Michelet, Jules. *Le procès des Templiers.* New ed. 2 vols. Paris: Éditions du C. T. H. S., 1987.

Molinier, Auguste, ed. *Obituaires de la province de Sens.* Vol. 1, pt. 2. Paris: Imprimerie nationale, 1902.

Mollat, Guillaume, ed. *Manuel de l'inquisiteur,* by Bernard Gui. 2 vols. Paris: Champion, 1926.

Mulder-Bakker, Anneke B., ed. *Mary of Oignies: Mother of Salvation.* Turnhout: Brepols, 2006.

Newman, Barbara, ed. *The Collected Saints' Lives,* by Thomas of Cantimpré. Turnhout: Brepols, 2008.

Pales-Gobilliard, Annette, ed. and trans. *Le livre des sentences d'inquisiteur Bernard Gui, 1308–1321.* 2 vols. Paris: CNRS Éditions, 2002.

Perarnau, Josep, ed. *"L'Alia informatio beguinorum" d'Arnau de Vilanova.* Barcelona: Facultat de Teologia de Barcelona, 1978.

Peters, Edward, ed. *Heresy and Authority in Medieval Europe: Documents in Translation.* Philadelphia: University of Pennsylvania Press, 1980.

Piron, Sylvain, ed. "Michael Monachus, Inquisitoris sententia contra combustos in Massilia." *Oliviana* 2 (2006). http://oliviana.revues.org/index36.html.

Port, Célestin. "Livre de Guillaume le Maire." In *Mélanges historiques: Choix de documents.* Vol. 2. *Collection de documents inédits sur l'histoire de France,* 189–569. Paris: Imprimerie nationale, 1877.

Potthast, Augustus. *Regesta pontificum romanorum.* Vol. 2. Graz: Akademische Druck- u. Verlagsanstalt, 1957.

Regestum Clementis papae V. Rome: Ex Typographia Vaticana, 1887.

Reichert, B. M., ed. *Acta capitulorum generalium.* Vol. 2. Monumenta ordinis fratrum praedicatorum historica 4. Rome: Ex Typographia Polyglotta S.C. de Propaganda Fide, 1899.

Ripoll, Thomas., ed. *Bullarium ordinis fratrum praedicatorum.* Vol. 2. Rome: Hieronymus Mainardus, 1730.

Schneider, Robert J., ed. *Vincentii Belvacensis, De morali principis institutione.* CCCM 137. Turnhout: Brepols, 1995.

Shirley, Janet, trans. *The Inquisitor's Guide: A Medieval Manual on Heretics,* by Bernard Gui. Welwyn Garden City: Ravenhall, 2006.

Steiner, Arpad, ed. *De eruditione filiorum nobilium,* by Vincent of Beauvais. Cambridge, MA: Mediaeval Academy of America, 1938.

Stroick, Autbert, ed. "Gilbert of Tournai, *Collectio de scandalis ecclesiae.* Nova editio." *Archivum Franciscanum historicum* 24 (1931): 33–62.

Thorndike, Lynn. *University Records and Life in the Middle Ages.* New York: Columbia University Press, 1944.

Verdeyen, Paul. "Le procès d'inquisition contre Marguerite Porete et Guiard de Cressonessart (1309–1310)." *Revue d'histoire ecclésiastique* 81 (1986): 47–94.

Viard, Jules, ed. *Documents parisiens du règne de Philippe VI de Valois.* Vol. 1. Paris: Champion, 1899.

———, ed. *Les grandes chroniques de France.* Vol. 8. Paris: Champion, 1934.

———, ed. *Les journaux du Trésor de Philippe IV le Bel.* Paris: Imprimerie nationale, 1940.

Viard, Jules, and Aline Vallée, eds. *Registres du Trésor des Chartes.* Vol. 3, pt. 2. *Inventaire analytique.* Paris: Archives nationales, 1979.

Vidal, J.-M. *Bullaire de l'Inquisition française au XIVe siècle et jusqu'à la fin du Grand Schisme.* Paris: Letouzey et Ané, 1913.

Vincent of Beauvais. *Bibliotheca mundi seu Speculi Maioris Vincentii Burgundi praesulis Bellovacensis, . . . tomus quartus, qui Speculum historiale inscribuntur.* Douai: Baltazarus Bellerius, 1624.

Warnock, Robert G., and Adolar Zumkeller, eds. *Der Traktat Heinrichs von Friemar über die Unterscheidung der Geister.* Wurzburg: Augustinus-Verlag, 1977.

Watt, J. A., trans. *On Royal and Papal Power,* by John of Paris. Toronto: Pontifical Institute of Mediaeval Studies, 1971.

Zumkeller, Adolar, ed. *Henri de Frimaria O.S.A, Tractatus ascetico-mystici.* Vol. 1. Wurzburg: Augustinus Verlag, 1975.

———. *Henrici de Frimaria O.S.A. Tractatus ascetico-mystici.* Vol. 2. Rome: Augustinianum, 1992.

Secondary Sources

Allirot, Anne-Hélène. "Une *beata stirps* au féminin? Autour de quelques saintes reines et princesses royales." In *Une histoire pour un royaume (XIIe–XVe siècle). Actes du colloque Corpus Regni organisé en hommage à Colette Beaune,* ed. Anne-Hélène Allirot et al., 142–51. Paris: Perrin, 2010.

Allirot, Anne-Hélène, et al., eds. *Une histoire pour un royaume (XIIe–XVe siècle). Actes du colloque Corpus Regni organisé en hommage à Colette Beaune.* Paris: Perrin, 2010.

Ames, Christine Caldwell. *Righteous Persecution: Inquisition, Dominicans, and Christianity in the Middle Ages.* Philadelphia: University of Pennsylvania Press, 2009.

Arnold, John H. *Inquisition and Power: Catharism and the Confessing Subject in Medieval Languedoc.* Philadelphia: University of Pennsylvania Press, 2001.

Arway, Robert J. "A Half Century of Research on Godfrey of Fontaines." *New Scholasticism* 36 (1962): 192–218.

Backman, Clifford R. "Arnau de Vilanova and the Franciscan Spirituals in Sicily." *Franciscan Studies* 50 (1990): 3–30.

———. "The Reception of Arnau de Vilanova's Religious Ideas." In *Christendom and Its Discontents: Exclusion, Persecution, and Rebellion, 1000–1500,* ed. Scott L. Waugh and Peter D. Diehl, 112–31. Cambridge: Cambridge University Press, 1997.

Balasse, Céline. *1306: L'expulsion des juifs du royaume de France.* Brussels: De Boeck, 2008.

Baldwin, John W. *The Scholastic Culture of the Middle Ages, 1000–1300.* 1971. Reprint, Prospect Heights, IL: Waveland Press, 1997.

Bale, John. *Scriptorum illustrium maioris Brytannie catalogus.* Basel: Apud Ioannem Oporinum, 1557.

Barber, Malcolm. *The New Knighthood: A History of the Order of the Temple.* Cambridge: Cambridge University Press, 1994.

———. *The Trial of the Templars.* 2nd ed. Cambridge: Cambridge University Press, 2006.

———. "The World Picture of Philip the Fair." *Journal of Medieval History* 8 (1982): 13–27.

Barcelona, P. Martì de. "Regesta de documents arnaldians coneguts." *Estudios franciscanos* 47 (1935): 261–300.

Bataillon, Louis-Jacques, Gilbert Dahan, and Pierre-Marie Gy, eds. *Hugues de Saint-Cher (d. 1263): Bibliste et théologien.* Turnhout: Brepols, 2004.

Batllori, Miquel. "Les versions Italianes medievales d'obres religioses de Mestre Aranu de Vilanova." In *Archivio italiano per la storia della pietà,* 1:395–462. Rome: Edizioni di Storia et Letteratura, 1951.

Bériou, Nicole. "La prédication au béguinage de Paris pendant l'année liturgique 1272–1273." *Recherches augustiniennes* 13 (1978): 105–29.

———. "Robert de Sorbon, le prud'homme et le béguin." *Comptes-rendus des séances de l'Académie des inscriptions et belles-lettres* (1994): 469–510.

Berman, Constance H. "Cistercian Nuns and the Development of the Order: The Abbey at Saint-Antoine-des-Champs outside Paris." In *The Joy of Learning and the Love of God: Studies in Honor of J. Leclercq,* ed. E. Rozanne Elder, 121–56. Kalamazoo, MI: Cistercian Publications, 1995.

Bertho, Marie. *Le miroir des âmes simples et anéanties de Marguerite Porete: Une vie blessée d'amour.* Paris: Découvrir, 1993.

Bérubé, Camille. *L'amour de Dieu selon Jean Duns Scot, Porète, Eckhart, Benoît Canfield et les Capucins.* Rome: Istituto Storico dei Cappuccini, 1997.

Blumenfeld-Kosinski, Renate. "Satirical Views of the Beguines in Northern French Literature." In *New Trends in Feminine Spirituality: The Holy Women of Liège and Their Impact,* ed. Juliette Dor, Lesley Johnson, and Jocelyn Wogan-Browne, 237–49. Turnhout: Brepols, 1999.

Boeren, P. C. *La vie et les oeuvres de Guiard de Laon, 1170env.–1248.* The Hague: Nijhoff, 1956.

Bollweg, John August. "Sense of Mission: Arnau de Vilanova on the Conversion of Muslims and Jews." In *Iberia and the Mediterranean World of the Middle Ages: Studies in Honor of Robert I. Burns,* ed. Larry J. Simon, 50–71. Leiden: Brill, 1995.

Boureau, Alain. *L'inconnu dans la maison: Richard de Mediavilla, les Franciscains et la Vierge Marie à la fin du XIIIe siècle.* Paris: Les belles lettres, 2010.

————. *La religion de l'état: La construction de la République étatique dans le discours théologique de l'Occident médiéval (1250–1350)*. Paris: Les belles lettres, 2006.

Boutaric, Edgar P. *Clément V, Philippe le Bel et les Templiers*. 1874. Reprint, Whitefish, MT: Kessinger, 2010.

Boyle, Leonard. "The Summa confessorum of John of Freiburg and the Popularization of the Moral Teaching of St. Thomas and Some of His Contemporaries." In *Pastoral Care, Clerical Education and Canon Law, 1200–1400*. London: Variorum Reprints, 1981.

Brown, Elizabeth A. R. *Customary Aids and Royal Finance in Capetian France: The Marriage Aid of Philip the Fair*. Cambridge, MA: Medieval Academy of America, 1992.

————. "Persona et Gesta: The Image and Deeds of the Thirteenth-Century Capetians. The Case of Philip the Fair." *Viator* 19 (1988): 219–46.

————. "The Prince Is Father of the King: The Character and Childhood of Philip the Fair of France." *Mediaeval Studies* 49 (1987): 282–334.

————. "The Religion of Royalty: From Saint Louis to Henry IV." In *Creating French Culture: Treasures from the Bibliothèque nationale de France*, ed. Marie-Hélène Tesnière and Prosser Gifford, 131–48. New Haven: Yale University Press, 1995.

————. "Royal Testamentary Acts from Philip Augustus to Philip of Valois: Executorial Dilemmas and Premonitions of Absolutism in Medieval France." In *Herrscher- und Fürstentestamente im westeuropäischen Mittelalter*, ed. Brigitte Kasten, 415–30. Cologne: Böhlau, 2008.

Brown, Elizabeth A. R., and Robert E. Lerner. "The Origins and Import of the Columbinus Prophecy." *Traditio* 45 (1989–90): 219–56.

Brundage, James A. *The Medieval Origins of the Legal Profession: Canonists, Civilians, and Courts*. Chicago: University of Chicago Press, 2008.

Bruschi, Caterina. *The Wandering Heretics of Languedoc*. Cambridge: Cambridge University Press, 2009.

Bryant, Gwendolyn. "The French Heretic: Marguerite Porete." In *Medieval Women Writers*, ed. Katharina M. Wilson, 204–26. Athens: University of Georgia Press, 1984.

Burgtorf, Jochen, Paul F. Crawford, and Helen J. Nicholson, eds. *The Debate on the Trial of the Templars (1307–1314)*. Farnham: Ashgate, 2010.

Burnham, Louisa A. *So Great a Light, So Great a Smoke: The Beguin Heretics of Languedoc*. Ithaca: Cornell University Press, 2008.

Burr, David. *Olivi's Peaceable Kingdom: A Reading of the Apocalypse Commentary*. Philadelphia: University of Pennsylvania Press, 1993.

————. *The Persecution of Peter Olivi*. Philadelphia: American Philosophical Society, 1976.

———. Review of *Joachim von Fiore, Psalterium decem cordarum,* ed. Kurt-Victor Selge. *Speculum* 85 (2010): 978–80.

———. *The Spiritual Franciscans: From Protest to Persecution in the Century after Saint Francis.* University Park: Pennsylvania State University Press, 2001.

Bussey, Francesca Caroline. "The World on the End of a Reed: Marguerite Porete and the Annihilation of an Identity in Medieval and Modern Representations—a Reassessment." PhD diss., University of Sydney, 2007.

Bynum, Caroline Walker. *Holy Feast and Holy Fast: The Religious Significance of Food to Medieval Women.* Berkeley: University of California Press, 1987.

Cacciola, Nancy. *Discerning Spirits: Divine and Demonic Possession in the Middle Ages.* Ithaca: Cornell University Press, 2003.

Canteaut, Olivier. "Les notaires des derniers Capétiens ont-ils une signature?" In *Hypothèses 2005: Travaux de l'École doctorale d'histoire de l'Université Paris I Panthéon-Sorbonne,* 303–14. Paris: Publications de la Sorbonne, 2006.

Capelle, G. C. *Autour du décret de 1210: III.—Amaury de Bène. Étude sur son panthéisme formel.* Paris: Vrin, 1932.

Carbasse, Jean-Marie. "Les origines de la torture judiciaire en France du XIIe au début du XIVe siècle." In *La torture judiciaire: Approches historiques et juridiques,* ed. Bernard Durand, 1:381–419. Lille: Centre d'histoire judiciaire, 2002.

Cardelle de Hartmann, Carmen. *Lateinische Dialoge, 1200–1400: Literaturhistorische Studie und Repertorium.* Leiden: Brill, 2007.

Carolus-Barré, Louis. *Le procès de canonisation de saint Louis (1272–1297): Essai de reconstitution,* ed. Henri Platelle. Rome: École française de Rome, 1994.

Carpentier, Bernadette. "Le béguinage Sainte-Élisabeth de Valenciennes, de sa fondation au XVIème siècle." *Mémoires du Cercle archéologique et historique de Valenciennes* 4 (1959): 95–182.

Carreras i Artau, J. "La polémica gerundense sobre el anticristo entre Arnau de Vilanova y los dominicos." *Anales de Instituto de estudios gerundenses* 5/6 (1950/51): 5–58.

———. *Relaciones de Arnau de Vilanova con los reyes de la casa de Aragón.* Barcelona: Academia de buenas letras de Barcelona, 1955.

Castan, Auguste. "L'évêque de Paris, Hughes de Besançon." *Mémoires de la Société d'émulation du Doubs,* 4th ser., 1 (1865): 250–70.

Clarke, Peter D. *The Interdict in the Thirteenth Century: A Question of Collective Guilt.* Oxford: Oxford University Press, 2007.

Coakley, John W. *Women, Men, and Spiritual Power: Female Saints and Their Male Collaborators.* New York: Columbia University Press, 2005.

Cohen, Esther. "To Die a Criminal for the Public Good: The Execution Ritual in Late Medieval Paris." In *Law, Custom, and the Social Fabric in Medieval Europe: Essays in Honor of Bruce Lyon,* ed. Bernard S. Bachrach and David Nicholas, 285–304. Kalamazoo, MI: Medieval Institute Publications, 1990.

Cohen, Meredith. "An Indulgence for the Visitor: The Public at the Sainte-Chapelle of Paris." *Speculum* 83 (2008): 840–83.

Colledge, Edmund. "The Latin *Mirror of Simple Souls*: Margaret Porette's Ultimate Accolade?" In *Langland, the Mystics and the Medieval English Tradition: Essays in Honour of S. S. Hussey,* ed. Helen Phillips, 177–83. Woodbridge: D. S. Brewer, 1990.

———. "The New Latin *Mirror of Simple Souls.*" *Ons geestelijk erf* 63/64 (1989–90): 279–87.

Colledge, Edmund, and J. C. Marler. "Poverty of the Will: Ruusbroec, Eckhart, and *The Mirror of Simple Souls.*" In *Jan van Ruusbroec: The Sources, Content, and Sequels of His Mysticism,* ed. P. Mommaers and N. de Paepe, 14–47. Leuven: Leuven University Press, 1984.

Coste, Jean. "Les deux missions de Guillaume de Nogaret en 1303." *Mélanges de l'École française de Rome, Moyen Âge* 105 (1993): 299–326.

Coulon, R. "Guillaume de Paris." In *Dictionnaire de théologie catholique,* ed. Alfred Vacant and E. Mangenot, vol. 6, cols. 1977–80. Paris: Letouzey et Ané, 1920.

Courtenay, William J. "Between Pope and King: The Parisian Letters of Adhesion of 1303." *Speculum* 71 (1996): 577–605.

———. "Une correction au Chartularium universitatis Parisiensis: Le legs de Jean de Thélus et la chapellenie de l'université à Saint-André-des-Arts." *Paris et Ile-de-France: Mémoires* 52 (2001): 7–18.

———. "Inquiry and Inquisition: Academic Freedom in Medieval Universities." *Church History* 58 (1989): 168–81.

———. "The Instructional Programme of the Mendicant Convents at Paris in the Early Fourteenth Century." In *The Medieval Church: Universities, Heresy, and the Religious Life. Essays in Honour of Gordon Leff,* ed. Peter Biller and Barry Dobson, 77–92. Woodbridge: Boydell, 1999.

———. "Learned Opinion and Royal Justice: The Role of Paris Masters of Theology during the Reign of Philip the Fair." In *Law and the Illicit in Medieval Europe,* ed. Ruth Mazo Karras, Joel Kaye, and E. Ann Matter, 149–63. Philadelphia: University of Pennsylvania Press, 2008.

———. "Marguerite's Judges: The University of Paris in 1310." In *Marguerite Porete et le "Miroir des simples âmes": Perspectives historiques, philosophiques et littéraires,* ed. Sylvain Piron, Robert E. Lerner, and Sean L. Field. Paris: Vrin, forthcoming.

———. "The Parisian Faculty of Theology in the Late Thirteenth and Early Fourteenth Centuries." In *Nach der Verurteilung von 1277: Philosophie und Theologie an der Universität von Paris im letzten Viertel des 13. Jahrhunderts,* ed. Jan A. Aertsen, Kent Emery Jr., and Andreas Speer, 235–24. Berlin: Walter de Gruyter, 2001.

———. "Radulphus Brito, Master of Arts and Theology." *Cahiers de l'Institut du Moyen-Âge grec et latin* 76 (2005): 131–58.

———. "Reflections on Vat. Lat. 1086 and Prosper of Reggio Emilia, O.E.S.A." In *Theological Quodlibeta in the Middle Ages: The Fourteenth Century,* ed. Christopher Schabel, 345–58. Leiden: Brill, 2007.

———. "The Role of University Masters and Bachelors at Paris in the Templar Affair, 1307–1308." In *1308: Eine Topographie historischer Gleichzeitigkeit,* ed. Andreas Speer and David Wirmer, 171–81. Berlin: Walter de Gruyter, 2010.

Courtenay, William J., and Karl Ubl. *Gelehrte Gutachten und königliche Politik im Templerprozess.* Hannover: Hansche, 2010.

Crawford, Paul F. "The Involvement of the University of Paris in the Trials of Marguerite Porete and of the Templars, 1308–1310." In *The Debate on the Trial of the Templars (1307–1314),* ed. Jochen Burgtorf, Paul F. Crawford, and Helen J. Nicholson, 129–43. Farnham: Ashgate, 2010.

———. "The University of Paris and the Trial of the Templars." In *The Military Orders,* vol. 3, *History and Heritage,* ed. Victor Mallia-Milanes, 115–23. Aldershot: Ashgate, 2008.

Cré, Marleen. *Vernacular Mysticism in the Charterhouse: A Study of London, British Library, MS Additional 37790.* Turnhout: Brepols, 2006.

Dagens, Jean. "Le *Miroir des simples âmes* et Marguerite de Navarre." In *La mystique rhénane: Colloque de Strasbourg, 16–19 mai 1961,* 281–89. Paris: Presses universitaires de France, 1963.

Dancoisne, l'abbé. "Mémoire sur les établissements religieux du clergé séculier et du clergé régulier qui ont existé à Douai avant la Révolution." *Mémoires de la Société d'agriculture de sciences et d'arts séant à Douai, centrale du Département du Nord,* 2nd ser., 14 (1876–78): 310–12.

Daunou, M. "Simon Duval." *Histoire littéraire de la France* 19 (1838): 385–87.

De Guimaräes, Ag. "Hervé Noël (d. 1323): Étude biographique." *Archivum fratrum praedicatorum* 8 (1938): 5–81.

De Keyser, Walter. "Aspects de la vie béguinale à Mons aux XIIIe et XIVe siècles." In *Autour de la ville en Hainaut,* ed. Jean Dugnoille and René Sansen, 205–26. Ath: Cercle royal d'histoire et d'archéologie d'Ath et de la région et musées Athois, 1986.

De la Selle, Xavier. *Le service des âmes à la cour: Confesseurs et aumôniers des rois de France du XIIIe au XVe siècle.* Paris: École des Chartes, 1995.

De Lépinois, E. *Recherches historiques et critiques sur l'ancien comté et les comtes de Clermont-en-Beauvoisis du XIe au XIIIe siècle.* Beauvais: D. Pere, 1877.

De Libera, Alain. *Penser au Moyen Âge.* Paris: Éditions du Seuil, 1991.

De Montfaucon, Bernard. *Diarium italicum.* Paris: J. Anisson, 1702.

De Moreau, Edouard. *L'abbaye de Villers-en-Brabant aux XIIe et XIIIe siècles.* Brussels: A. Dewit, 1909.

De Wulf, Maurice. *Étude sur la vie, les oeuvres et l'influence de Godefroid de Fontaines.* Brussels: Hayez, 1904.

Deane, Jennifer Kolpacoff. "Beguines Reconsidered: Historiographical Problems and New Directions." *Monastic Matrix,* August 2008. Commentaria 3461. http://monasticmatrix.org/commentaria/article.php?textId=3461.

———. *A History of Medieval Heresy and Inquisition.* Lanham, MD: Rowman and Littlefield, 2011.

Deane, Jennifer Kolpacoff, Hildo von Engen, and Letha Boehringer, eds. *Labels, Libels, and Lay Religious Women in Northern Medieval Europe.* Turnhout: Brepols, forthcoming.

Delattre, Daniel, and Emmanuel Delattre. *Le canton de Saint-Just-en-Chaussée.* Grandvilliers: Éditions Delattre, 2000.

Delcambre, Étienne. *Les relations de la France avec le Hainaut, depuis l'avènement de Jean II d'Avesnes, comte de Hainaut, jusqu'à la conclusion de l'alliance franco-hennuyère (1280–1297).* Mons: Union des Imprimeries, 1930.

Delettre, l'abbé. *Histoire du diocèse de Beauvais, depuis son établissement, au 3.me siècle, jusqu'au 2 septembre 1792.* Vol. 2. Beauvais: Imprimerie d'Ach. Desjardins, 1843.

Delmaire, Bernard. "Les béguines dans le Nord de la France au premier siècle de leur histoire (vers 1230–vers 1350)." In *Les religieuses en France au XIIIe siècle,* ed. Michel Parisse, 121–62. Nancy: Presses universitaires de Nancy, 1989.

———. *Le diocèse d'Arras de 1093 au milieu du XIV siècle.* 2 vols. Arras: Commission départementale d'histoire et d'archéologie du Pas-de-Calais, 1994.

Demurger, Alain. *The Last Templar: The Tragedy of Jacques de Molay.* Updated ed. Trans. Antonia Nevill. London: Profile Books, 2009.

Denton, Jeffrey H. "The Attempted Trial of Boniface VIII for Heresy." In *Judicial Trials in England and Europe, 1200–1700,* ed. Maureen Mulholland and Brian Pullan with Anne Pullan, 117–28. Manchester: Manchester University Press, 2003.

———. "Bernard Saisset and the Franco-Papal Rift of December 1301." *Revue d'histoire ecclésiastique* 102 (2007): 399–427.

———. "Heresy and Sanctity at the Time of Boniface VIII." In *Toleration and Repression in the Middle Ages: In Memory of Lenos Mavrommatis*, 141–48. Athens: Institute for Byzantine Research, 2002.

Des Ormes, A. Trudon. "Liste des maisons et de quelques dignitaires de l'Ordre du Temple." *Revue de l'orient Latin* 7 (1899): 223–74.

Despy, Georges. "Les débuts de l'Inquisition dans les anciens Pays-Bas au XIIIe siècle." In *Problèmes d'histoire du Christianisme: Hommages à Jean Hadot,* ed. Guy Cambier, 71–104. Brussels: Éditions de l'Université de Bruxelles, 1980.

———, ed. *Inventaire des archives de l'abbaye de Villers.* Brussels: Ministère de l'instruction publique, Archives générales du Royaume, 1959.

Diepgen, Paul. *Arnald von Villanova als Politiker und Laientheologe.* Berlin: Rothschild, 1909.

Dondaine, Antoine. "Documents pour servir à l'histoire de la province de France: L'appel au concile (1303)." *Archivum fratrum praedicatorum* 22 (1952): 381–439.

———. "Guillaume Peyraut: Vie et oeuvres." *Archivum fratrum praedicatorum* 18 (1948): 162–236.

———. "Le manuel de l'inquisiteur (1230–1330)." *Archivum fratrum praedicatorum* 17 (1947): 85–194.

Dronke, Peter. *Women Writers of the Middle Ages: A Critical Study of Texts from Perpetua († 203) to Marguerite Porete († 1310).* Cambridge: Cambridge University Press, 1984.

Duba, William O. "Continental Franciscan *Quodlibeta* after Scotus." In *Theological Quodlibeta in the Middle Ages: The Fourteenth Century,* ed. Christopher Schabel, 569–649. Leiden: Brill, 2007.

Dunbabin, Jean. *A Hound of God: Pierre de la Palud and the Fourteenth-Century Church.* Oxford: Clarendon Press, 1991.

Duval, André. "Nicolas de Gorran." In *Dictionnaire de spiritualité, ascétique et mystique, doctrine et histoire,* vol. 11, 281–83. Paris: Beauchesne, 1981.

Elliot, Dyan. *Proving Woman: Female Spirituality and Inquisitorial Culture in the Later Middle Ages.* Princeton: Princeton University Press, 2004.

Etzwiler, James P. "John of Baconthorpe, Prince of the Averroists?" *Franciscan Studies* 36 (1976): 148–76.

Eubel, Konrad. *Hierarchia catholica medii aevi.* Vol. 1. Regensberg: Monasterii Libr. Regensbergiana, 1898.

Falvay, Dávíd. "Il *Libro della beata Margherita*: Un documento inedito del culto di Margherita d'Ungheria in Italia nei secoli XIV e XV." *Nuova corvina: Rivista di Italianistica* 5 (1999): 35–45.

Farmer, Sharon. *Surviving Poverty in Medieval Paris: Gender Ideology and the Daily Lives of the Poor.* Ithaca: Cornell University Press, 2002.

Favier, Jean. *Un conseiller de Philippe le Bel: Enguarran de Marigny.* Paris: PUF, 1963. Reprinted in *Un roi de marbre: Philippe le Bel, Enguerran de Marigny.* Paris: Fayard, 2005.

———. *Philippe le Bel.* Rev. ed. Paris: Fayard, 1998. Reprinted in *Un roi de marbre: Philippe le Bel, Enguerran de Marigny.* Paris: Fayard, 2005.

———. *Un roi de marbre: Philippe le Bel, Enguerran de Marigny.* Paris: Fayard, 2005.

Fenster, Thelma, and Daniel Lord Smail, eds. *Fama: The Politics of Talk and Reputation in Medieval Europe.* Ithaca: Cornell University Press, 2003.

Field, Sean L. "Agnes of Harcourt, Felipa of Porcelet, and Marguerite of Oingt: Women Writing about Women at the End of the Thirteenth Century." *Church History* 76 (2007): 298–328.

———. "The *Dialogus de septem sacramentis* Attributed to William of Paris, O.P.: One Text in Two Versions." *Archivum fratrum praedicatorum* 80, forthcoming.

———. *Isabelle of France: Capetian Sanctity and Franciscan Identity in the Thirteenth Century.* Notre Dame: University of Notre Dame Press, 2006.

———. "The Master and Marguerite: Godfrey of Fontaines' Praise of the *Mirror of Simple Souls.*" *Journal of Medieval History* 35 (2009): 136–49.

———. "William of Paris's Inquisitions against Marguerite Porete and Her Book." In *Marguerite Porete et le "Miroir des simples âmes": Perspectives historiques, philosophiques et littéraires.* Paris: Vrin, forthcoming.

Finke, Heinrich. *Aus den Tagen Bonifaz VIII: Funde und Forschungen.* Munster: Druck und Verlag der Aschendorffschen Buchhandlung, 1902.

Forey, Alan. "Could Alleged Templar Malpractices Have Remained Undetected for Decades?" In *The Debate on the Trial of the Templars (1307–1314),* ed. Jochen Burgtorf, Paul F. Crawford, and Helen J. Nicholson, 11–19. Farnham: Ashgate, 2010.

Fournier, P. "Nicolas d'Ennezat, canoniste." *Histoire littéraire de la France* 35 (1921): 603–5.

Frale, Barbara. "The Chinon Chart: Papal Absolution to the Last Templar, Master Jacques de Molay." *Journal of Medieval History* 30 (2004): 109–34.

Frederichs, Jules. *Robert le Bougre, premier inquisiteur général en France.* Ghent: Librairie Clemm, 1892.

Friedlander, Alan. *The Hammer of the Inquisitors: Brother Bernard Délicieux and the Struggle against the Inquisition in Fourteenth-Century France.* Leiden: Brill, 2000.

Froehlich, Karlfried. "St. Peter, Papal Primacy, and the Exegetical Tradition, 1150–1300." In *The Religious Roles of the Papacy: Ideals and Realities, 1150–1300,* ed. Christopher Ryan, 3–44. Toronto: Pontifical Institute of Mediaeval Studies, 1989.

Galloway, Penelope. "Beguine Communities in Northern France, 1200–1500." In *Medieval Women in Their Communities,* ed. Diane Watt, 92–115. Toronto: University of Toronto Press, 1997.

———. "Life, Learning, and Wisdom: The Forms and Functions of Beguine Education." In *Medieval Monastic Education,* ed. George Ferzoco and Carolyn Muessig, 153–65. London: Leicester University Press, 2000.

Gaposchkin, M. Cecilia. *The Making of Saint Louis: Kingship, Sanctity, and Crusade in the Later Middle Ages.* Ithaca: Cornell University Press, 2008.

Geltner, Guy. *The Medieval Prison: A Social History.* Princeton: Princeton University Press, 2008.

Géraud, Hercule. *Paris sous Philippe-le-Bel, d'après des documents originaux.* Paris: Crapelet, 1837.

Gillerman, Dorothy. *Enguerran de Marigny and the Church of Notre-Dame at Ecouis: Art and Patronage in the Reign of Philip the Fair.* University Park: Pennsylvania State University Press, 1994.

Given, James. "Chasing Phantoms: Philip IV and the Fantastic." In *Heresy and the Persecuting Society in the Middle Ages: Essays on the Work of R.I. Moore,* ed. Michael Frassetto, 271–89. Leiden: Brill, 2006.

———. *Inquisition and Medieval Society: Power, Discipline and Resistance in Languedoc.* Ithaca: Cornell University Press, 1997.

Glorieux, Palémon. *Aux origines de la Sorbonne.* 2 vols. Paris: Vrin, 1965–66.

———. *Répertoire des maîtres en théologie de Paris au XIIIe siècle.* 2 vols. Paris: Vrin, 1933.

Graves, Louis. "Précis statistique sur le canton de St.-Just-en-Chaussée, arrondissement de Clermont (Oise)." 1835. Reprinted in *Cantons de Mouys et de Saint-Just-en-Chaussée,* vol. 9. Paris: Res Universis, 1991.

Grayzel, Solomon. "Popes, Jews, and Inquisition from *Sicut* to *Turbato.*" In *Essays on the Occasion of the Seventieth Anniversary of the Dropsie University,* ed. Abraham Isaac Katsch and Leon Nemoy, 151–88. Philadelphia: Dropsie University, 1979.

Grundmann, Herbert. "Ketzerverhöre des Spätmittelalters als quellenkritisches Problem." *Deutsches Archiv für Erforschung des Mittelalters* 21 (1965): 519–75.

———. *Religious Movements in the Middle Ages.* Trans. Steven Rowan. Notre Dame: University of Notre Dame Press, 1996.

Guarnieri, Romana. "Il movimento del Libero Spirito." In *Archivio italiano per la storia della pietà* 4:351–708. Rome: Edizioni di Storia et Letteratura, 1965.

———. "Prefazia storica" to *Lo specchio della anime semplici,* by Marguerite Porete, trans. Giovanna Fozzer, 7–54. Milan: Edizioni San Paolo, 1994.

————. "Quando si dice, il caso!" *Bailamme: Rivista di spiritualità e politica* 8 (1990): 45–55.

Guyotjeannin, Olivier. "Les méthodes de travail des archivistes du roi de France (XIIIe–début XVIe siècle)." *Archiv für Diplomatik* 42 (1996): 295–373.

————. "*Super omnes thesauros rerum temporalium:* Les fonctions du Trésor des Chartes du roi de France (XIVe–XVe siècles)." In *Écrit et pouvoir dans les chancelleries médiévales: Espace français, espace anglais,* ed. Kouky Fianu and DeLloyd J. Guth, 109–32. Louvain-la-Neuve: Fédération internationale des instituts d'études médiévales, 1997.

Guyotjeannin, Olivier, and Yann Potin. "La fabrique de la perpétuité: Le Trésor des Chartes et les archives du royaume (XIIIe–XIX siècle)." *Revue de synthèse* (2004): 15–44.

Hackett, Jeremiah. "Augustinian Mysticism in Fourteenth-Century Germany: Henry of Freimar [sic] and Jordanus of Quedlinburg." In *Augustine: Mystic and Mystagogue,* ed. Frederick Van Fleteren, Joseph C. Schnaubelt, and Joseph Reimo, 439–56. New York: Peter Lang, 1994.

————. "The Reception of Meister Eckhart: Mysticism, Philosophy and Theology in Henry of Friemar (the Elder) and Jordanus of Quedlinburg." In *Meister Eckhart in Erfurt,* ed. Andreas Speer and Lydia Wegener, 554–86. Berlin: Walter de Gruyter, 2005.

Hasenohr, Geneviève. "La littérature religieuse." In *La littérature française aux XIVe et XVe siècles,* ed. Daniel Poirion, 1:266–303. Heidelberg: C. Winter, 1988.

————. "La tradition du *Miroir des simples âmes* au XVe siècle: De Marguerite Porete (†1310) à Marguerite de Navarre." *Comptes rendus des séances de l'Académie des inscriptions et belles-lettres* 4 (1999): 1347–66.

Haskins, Charles Homer. "Robert le Bougre and the Beginnings of the Inquisition in Northern France." In *Studies in Mediaeval Culture,* 193–244. New York: Frederick Ungar, 1929.

Hauréau, B. *Bernard Délicieux et l'inquisition albigeoise.* Paris: Hachette, 1877.

————. "Guillaume Baufet, évêque de Paris." *Histoire littéraire de la France* 32 (1898): 469–74.

Heid, Ulrich. "Studien zu Marguerite Porète und ihrem 'Miroir des simples âmes.'" In *Religiöse Frauenbewegung und mystische Frömmigkeit im Mittelalter,* ed. Peter Dinzelbacher and Dieter R. Bauer, 185–214. Vienna: Böhlau, 1988.

Hélary, Xavier. "Les testaments de Philippe d'Artois (d. 1298) et la naissance du culte de Saint Louis dans la famille capétienne." Forthcoming.

Hillairet, Jacques [Auguste André Coussilon]. *Gibets, piloris et cachots du vieux Paris.* Paris: Éditions de minuit, 1956.

Hillgarth, J. N. *Ramon Lull and Lullism in Fourteenth-Century France.* Oxford: Clarendon Press, 1971.

Hindley, Alan, Frederick W. Langley, and Brian J. Levy. *Old French-English Dictionary.* Cambridge: Cambridge University Press, 2000.

Hödl, Ludwig. "Die Aulien des Magisters Johannes de Polliaco und der scholastische Streit über die Begründung der menschlichen Willensfreiheit." *Scholastik* 35 (1960): 57–75.

———. "The Quodlibeta of John of Pouilly (d. c. 1328) and the Philosophical and Theological Debates at Paris, 1307–1312." In *Theological Quodlibeta in the Middle Ages: The Fourteenth Century,* ed. Christopher Schabel, 199–230. Leiden: Brill, 2007.

Hogg, James. "Richard Methley's Latin Translations: *The Cloud of Unknowing* and Porete's *The Mirror of Simple Souls.*" *Studies in Spirituality* 12 (2002): 82–104.

Hollywood, Amy. *The Soul as Virgin Wife: Mechthild of Magdeburg, Marguerite Porete, and Meister Eckhart.* Notre Dame: University of Notre Dame Press, 1995.

Hooghe, Filip. "The Trial of the Templars in the County of Flanders (1307–1312)." In *The Debate on the Trial of the Templars (1307–1314),* ed. Jochen Burgtorf, Paul F. Crawford, and Helen J. Nicholson, 285–299. Farnham: Ashgate, 2010.

Jantzen, Grace M. "Disrupting the Sacred: Religion and Gender in the City." In *Mysticism and Social Transformation,* ed. Janet K. Ruffing, 29–44. Syracuse: Syracuse University Press, 2001.

Jones, Chris. *Eclipse of Empire? Perceptions of the Western Empire and Its Rulers in Late-Medieval France.* Turnhout: Brepols, 2007.

Jordan, William Chester. "The Anger of the Abbots in the Thirteenth Century." *Catholic Historical Review* 96 (2010): 219–33.

———. *The French Monarchy and the Jews: From Philip Augustus to the Last Capetians.* Philadelphia: University of Pennsylvania Press, 1989.

———. *Louis IX and the Challenge of the Crusade.* Princeton: Princeton University Press, 1979.

———. *A Tale of Two Monasteries: Westminster and Saint-Denis in the Thirteenth Century.* Princeton: Princeton University Press, 2009.

———. *Unceasing Strife, Unending Fear: Jacques de Thérines and the Freedom of the Church in the Age of the Last Capetians.* Princeton: Princeton University Press, 2004.

Juilfs, Jonathan. "Reading the Bible Differently: Appropriations of Biblical Authority in an Heretical Mystical Text, Marguerite Porete's *The Mirror of Simple Souls.*" *Religion and Literature* 42 (2010): 77–100.

Kaeppeli, Thomas, ed. *Scriptores ordinis praedicatorum medii aevi.* 4 vols. Rome: S. Sabinae, 1970–93.

Kaup, Matthias, and Robert E. Lerner. "Gentile of Foligno Interprets the Prophecy 'Woe to the World,' with an Edition and English Translation." *Traditio* 56 (2001): 149–211.

Kelly, Henry Ansgar. "Inquisition and the Prosecution of Heresy: Misconceptions and Abuses." *Church History* 58 (1989): 439–51.

———. "Inquisitorial Due Process and the Status of Secret Crimes." In *Proceedings of the Eighth International Congress of Medieval Canon Law,* ed. Stanley Chodorow, 407–27. Vatican City: Biblioteca Apostolica Vaticana, 1992.

———. "The Right to Remain Silent: Before and after Joan of Arc." *Speculum* 68 (1993): 992–1026.

Kerby-Fulton, Kathryn. *Books under Suspicion: Censorship and Tolerance of Revelatory Writing in Late Medieval England.* Notre Dame: University of Notre Dame Press, 2006.

Kerby-Fulton, Kathryn, and E. Randolph Daniel. "English Joachimism, 1300–1500: The Columbinus Prophecy." In *Profetismo gioachimita tra Quattrocento e Cinquecento,* ed. Gian Luca Potestà, 313–50. Genoa: Marietti, 1991.

Kieckhefer, Richard. "The Office of Inquisition and Medieval Heresy: The Transition from Personal to Institutional Jurisdiction." *Journal of Ecclesiastical History* 46 (1995): 36–61.

———. *Repression of Heresy in Medieval Germany.* Philadelphia: University of Pennsylvania Press, 1979.

Klepper, Deeana Copeland. "The Dating of Nicholas of Lyra's Quaestio de adventu Christi." *Archivum Franciscanum historicum* 86 (1993): 297–312.

———. *The Insight of Unbelievers: Nicholas of Lyra and Christian Reading of Jewish Text in the Later Middle Ages.* Philadelphia: University of Pennsylvania Press, 2007.

Kneupper, Courtney. "Reconsidering a Fourteenth-Century Heresy Trial in Metz: Beguins and Others." *Franciscana* 8 (2006): 187–227.

Koch, Josef. "Die Magister-Jahre des Durandus de S. Porciano O.P. und der Konflikt mit seinem Orden." In *Kleine Schriften,* 2:7–118. Rome: Edizioni di storia e letteratura, 1973.

———. "Philosophische und theologische Irrtumslisten von 1270–1329: Ein Beitrag zur Entwicklung der theologischen Zensuren." In *Kleine Schriften,* 2:423–50. Rome: Edizioni di storia e letteratura, 1973.

———. "Der Prozess gegen den Magister Johannes de Polliaco und seine Vorgeschichte (1312–1321)." *Recherche de théologie ancienne et médiévale* 5 (1933): 391–422.

Kocher, Suzanne. *Allegories of Love in Marguerite Porete's "Mirror of Simple Souls."* Turnhout: Brepols, 2008.

———. "Marguerite de Navarre's Portrait of Marguerite Porete: A Renaissance Queen Constructs a Medieval Woman Mystic." *Medieval Feminist Newsletter* 26 (1998): 17–23.

Kocher, Zan. "The Apothecary's *Mirror of Simple Souls*: Circulation and Reception of Marguerite Porete's Book in Fifteenth-Century France." Forthcoming in *Modern Philology.*

Koziol, Geoffrey. "Imagined Enemies and the Later Medieval State: The Failure of France under Philip the Fair." In *Identities and National Formation: Chinese and Western Experiences in the Modern World*, 407–33. Taipei: Institute of Modern History, 1994.

Krämer, Thomas. "Terror, Torture and the Truth: The Testimonies of the Templars Revisited." In *The Debate on the Trial of the Templars (1307–1314)*, ed. Jochen Burgtorf, Paul F. Crawford, and Helen J. Nicholson, 71–85. Farnham: Ashgate, 2010.

Krey, Philip D. W., and Lesley Smith, eds. *Nicholas of Lyra: The Senses of Scripture.* Leiden: Brill, 2000.

Krynen, Jacques. *L'empire du roi: Idées et croyances politiques en France, XIIIe–XVe siècle.* Paris: Gallimard, 1993.

La Croix, A. *Annales du Hainaut: Guerre de Jean d'Avesnes contre la ville de Valenciennes, 1290–1297; et Mémoires sur l'histoire, la juridiction civile et le droit public, XI.me–XVIII.e siècle.* Brussels: A. Vandale, 1846.

Labrosse, Henri. "Biographie de Nicolas de Lyre." *Études franciscaines* 19 (1907): 489–505, 593–608.

Lahav, Rina. "Marguerite Porete and the Predicament of Her Preaching in Fourteenth-Century France." In *Gender, Catholicism and Spirituality: Women and the Roman Catholic Church in Britain and Europe, 1200–1900*, ed. Laurence Lux-Sterritt and Carmen M. Magion, 38–50. New York: Palgrave Macmillan, 2011.

Lajard, F. "Gui de Colle di Mezzo." *Histoire littéraire de la France* 25 (1869): 280–83.

———. "Guillaume de Paris, dominicain." *Histoire littéraire de la France* 27 (1877): 140–52.

———. "Nicholas de Gorran, dominicain." *Histoire littéraire de la France* 20 (1842): 324–56.

Lalov, Élisabeth. *Itinéraire de Philippe IV le Bel (1285–1314).* 2 vols. Paris: Boccard, 2007.

Lambert, Malcolm. *Medieval Heresy: Popular Movements from the Gregorian Reform to the Reformation.* 3rd ed. Oxford: Wiley-Blackwell, 2002.

Langlois, Charles-Victor. "L'affaire des Templiers." *Journal des savants* 6 (1908): 417–35.

———. "Marguerite Porete." *Revue historique* 54 (1894): 295–99.

———. "Nicolas de Lyre, frère mineur." *Histoire littéraire de la France* 36 (1927): 355–401.

———. "Les papiers de Guillaume de Nogaret et de Guillaume de Plaisians au Trésor des Chartes." *Notices et extraits des manuscrits de la Biliothèque nationale et autre bibliothèques* 39 (1909): 215–41.

———. *Saint Louis, Philippe le Bel, les derniers Capétiens directs (1226–1328).* Paris: Tallandier, 1901.

Laurent, M.-H. *Fabio Vigili et les bibliothèques de Bologne.* Vatican City: Biblioteca Apostolica Vaticana, 1943.

Lauwers, Michael, and Walter Simons. *Béguins et Béguines à Tournai au Bas Moyen Âge: Les communautés béguinales à Tournai du XIIIe au XVe siècle.* Tournai: Archives du Chapitre Cathédral de Tournai et Association des diplômes en archéologie et histoire de l'art de l'UCL, 1988.

Lawrence, C. H. *The Friars: The Impact of the Early Mendicant Movement on Western Society.* London: Longman, 1994.

Le Boucq, Simon. *Histoire ecclésiastique de la ville et comté de Valentienne (1650).* 1844. Reprint, Marseille: Lafitte Reprints, 1978.

Le Brun-Gouanvic, Claire. "Le *Mirouer des simples ames aneanties* de Marguerite Porete (vers 1300) et le *Speculum simplicium animarum* (vers 1310): Procès d'inquisition et traduction." In *D'une écriture à l'autre: Les femmes et la traduction sous l'Ancien Régime,* ed. Jean-Philippe Beaulieu, 81–99. Ottawa: Presses de l'Université d'Ottawa, 2004.

Le Grand, Léon. "Les béguines de Paris." *Mémoire de la société de l'histoire de Paris et de l'Ile-de-France* 20 (1893): 295–357.

Lea, Henry Charles. *A History of the Inquisition of the Middle Ages.* 3 vols. 1887. Reprint, New York: Russell, 1955.

Lecler, Joseph. *Vienne.* Paris: Éditions de l'orante, 1964.

Lee, Harold. "Scrutamini Scripturas: Joachimist Themes and Figurae in the Early Religious Writing of Arnold of Vilanova." *Journal of the Warburg and Courtauld Institutes* 37 (1974): 33–56.

Lee, Harold, Marjorie Reeves, and Giulio Silano. *Western Mediterranean Prophecy: The School of Joachim of Fiore and the Fourteenth-Century Breviloquium.* Toronto: PIMS, 1989.

Leff, Gordon. *Heresy in the Later Middle Ages.* Manchester: Manchester University Press, 1967.

Leicht, Irene. *Marguerite Porete: Eine fromme Intellektuelle und die Inquisition.* Freiburg: Herder, 1999.

Lejeune, Jean. "Contribution à l'histoire des idées politiques: De Godefroid de Fontaines à la paix de Fexhe (1316)." *Annuaire d'histoire liègeoise* 6 (1962): 1216–59.

Lerner, Robert E. "Addenda on an Angel." In *Marguerite Porete et le "Miroir des simples âmes": Perspectives historiques, philosophiques et littéraires.* Paris: Vrin, forthcoming.

———. "An 'Angel of Philadelphia' in the Reign of Philip the Fair: The Case of Guiard of Cressonessart." In *Order and Innovation in the Middle Ages: Essays in Honor of Joseph R. Strayer,* ed. William C. Jordan, Bruce McNab, and Teofilo F. Ruiz, 343–64. Princeton: Princeton University Press, 1976.

———. "Antichrist Goes to the University: The *De victoria Christi contra Antichristum* of Hugo de Novocastro, OFM (1315/1319)." In *Crossing Boundaries at Medieval Universities,* ed. Spencer E. Young, 277–313. Leiden: Brill, 2011.

———. "Beguines and Beghards." In *Dictionary of the Middle Ages,* ed. Joseph R. Strayer, 2:157–62. New York: Scribner, 1983.

———. "Ecstatic Dissent." *Speculum* 67 (1992): 33–57.

———. *The Feast of Saint Abraham: Medieval Millenarians and the Jews.* Philadelphia: University of Pennsylvania Press, 2001.

———. "Frederick II, Alive, Aloft, and Allayed, in Franciscan-Joachite Eschatology." In *The Use and Abuse of Eschatology in the Middle Ages,* ed. Werner Verbeke, Daniel Verhelst, and Andries Welkenhuysen, 359–84. Leuven: Leuven University Press, 1988.

———. *The Heresy of the Free Spirit in the Later Middle Ages.* 1972. Reprint, Notre Dame: University of Notre Dame Press, 1991.

———. "The Medieval Return to the Thousand Year Sabbath." In *The Apocalypse in the Middle Ages,* ed. Richard K. Emmerson and Bernard McGinn, 51–71. Ithaca: Cornell University Press, 1992.

———. "Meister Eckhart's Specter: Fourteenth-Century Uses of the Bull *In agro dominico* Including a Newly Discovered Inquisitorial Text of 1337." *Mediaeval Studies* 70 (2008): 115–34.

———. "Millennialism." In *The Encyclopedia of Apocalypticism,* ed. Bernard McGinn, John Joseph Collins, and Stephen J. Stein, 2:326–60. New York: Continuum, 1998.

———. "New Evidence for the Condemnation of Meister Eckhart." *Speculum* 72 (1996): 347–66.

———. "New Light on the *Mirror of Simple Souls.*" *Speculum* 85 (2010): 91–116.

———. "A Note on the University Career of Jacques Fournier, O. Cist., Later Pope Benedict XII." *Analecta cisterciana* 30 (1974): 66–69.

———. "The Pope and the Doctor." *Yale Review* 78 (1988): 62–79.

———. "Poverty, Preaching, and Eschatology in the Revelation Commentaries of 'Hugh of St-Cher.'" In *The Bible in the Medieval World: Essays in Memory of Beryl Smalley,* ed. Katherine Walsh and Diana Wood, 157–89. Oxford: Blackwell, 1985.

———. *The Powers of Prophecy: The Cedar of Lebanon Vision from the Mongol Onslaught to the Dawn of the Enlightenment.* Berkeley: University of California Press, 1983.

———. "The Prophetic Manuscripts of the 'Renaissance Magus' Pierleone of Spoleto." In *Il profetismo gioachimita tra Quattrocento e Cinquecento,* ed. Gian Luca Potestà, 97–116. Genoa: Marietti, 1991.

———. "Writing and Resistance among Beguins of Languedoc and Catalonia." In *Heresy and Literacy, 1000–1530,* ed. Peter Biller and Anne Hudson, 186–204. Cambridge: Cambridge University Press, 1994.

Lizerand, Georges. *Clément V et Philippe IV le Bel.* Paris: Hachette, 1910.

———. "Philippe le Bel et l'Empire au temps de Rodolphe de Habsbourg (1285–1291)." *Revue historique* 142 (1923): 161–91.

Loeb, Isidore. "Le role des juifs de Paris en 1296 et 1297." *Revue des études juifs* 1 (1880): 60–71.

Lorentz, Philippe, and Dany Sandron. *Atlas de Paris au Moyen Âge: Espace urbain, habitat, société, religion, lieux de pouvoir.* Paris: Parigramme, 2006.

Makowski, Elizabeth. *"A Pernicious Sort of Woman": Quasi-Religious Women and Canon Lawyers in the Later Middle Ages.* Washington, DC: Catholic University of American Press, 2005.

Manselli, Raoul. *Spirituels et béguins du Midi.* Trans. Jean Duvernoy. Toulouse: Bibliothèque historique Privat, 1989.

Marín, Juan. "Annihilation and Deification in Beguine Theology and Marguerite Porete's *Mirror of Simple Souls.*" *Harvard Theological Review* 103 (2010): 89–109.

Marx, Heidi. "Metaphors of Imaging in Meister Eckhart and Marguerite Porete." *Medieval Perspectives* 13 (1998): 99–108.

McDonnell, Ernest W. *The Beguines and Beghards in Medieval Culture: With Special Emphasis on the Belgian Scene.* New York: Octagon, 1969.

McGinn, Bernard. *The Calabrian Abbot: Joachim of Fiore in the History of Western Thought.* New York: Macmillan, 1985.

———. "Evil-Sounding, Rash, and Suspect of Heresy: Tensions between Mysticism and Magisterium in the History of the Church." *Catholic Historical Review* 90 (2004): 193–212.

———. *The Flowering of Mysticism: Men and Women in the New Mysticism, 1200–1350.* New York: Crossroad, 1998.

————, ed. *Meister Eckhart and the Beguine Mystics: Hadewijch of Brabant, Mechthild of Magdeburg, and Marguerite Porete.* New York: Continuum, 1994.

————. "Pastor Angelicus: Apocalyptic Myth and Political Hope in the Fourteenth Century." In *Santi e Santità: Atti del XV Convegno Internazionale, Assisi, 15–16–17 ottobre 1987,* 221–51. Perugia: Università degli studi di Perugia, 1989.

McNamara, Jo Ann. *Gilles Aycelin: The Servant of Two Masters.* Syracuse: Syracuse University Press, 1973.

McVaugh, Michael. "Arnau de Vilanova and Paris: One Embassy or Two?" *Archives d'histoire doctrinale et littéraire du Moyen Âge* 73 (2006): 29–42.

Meliadò, Mario. "La dottrina mistica della nobilità: Margherita Porete e Meister Eckhart." *Rivista di ascetica e mistica* 33 (2008): 417–61.

Melville, Marion. *La vie des Templiers.* 2nd ed. Paris: Gallimard, 1974.

Menache, Sophia. *Clement V.* Cambridge: Cambridge University Press, 1998.

————. "La naissance d'une nouvelle source d'autorité: L'université de Paris." *Revue historique* 268 (1982): 305–27.

Menéndez y Pelayo, Marcellino, ed. *Historia de los heterodoxos españoles.* 2nd ed. Madrid: Librería general de Victoriano Suárez, 1911–32.

Merlo, Grado Giovanni. "Il senso delle opere dei frati predicatori in quanto *inquisitores haereticae pravitatis.*" In *Le scritture e le opere degli inquisitori,* 9–30. Quaderni di stori religiosa 9. Verona: Cierre, 2002.

Miethke, Jürgen. "Philippe le Bel von Frankreich und die Universität von Paris: Zur Rolle der Intellektuellen am Beginn des 14. Jahrhunderts." In *1308: Eine Topographie historischer Gleichzeitigkeit,* ed. Andreas Speer and David Wirmer, 182–98. Berlin: Walter de Gruyter, 2010.

Moeglin, Jean-Marie. "La frontière introuvable: L'Ostrevant." In *Une histoire pour un royaume (XIIe–XVe siècle): Actes du colloque Corupus Regni organisé en hommage à Colette Beaune,* ed. Anne-Hélène Allirot et al., 381–92. Paris: Perrin, 2010.

Molinier, Auguste. *Catalogue des manuscrits de la Bibliothèque Mazarine.* Paris: Plon, 1885.

Mollat, G. "Chateauvillain (Jean de)." In *Dictionnaire d'histoire et de géographie ecclésiastiques,* ed. Alfred Baudrillart et al., 12:584. Paris: Letouzey at Ané, 1953.

Montaubin, Pascal. "'Avec de l'Italie qui descendrait l'Escault': Guido da Collemezzo, èvêque de Cambrai (1296–1306)." In *Liber largitorius: Études d'histoire médiévale offertes à Pierre Toubert par ses élèves,* ed. Dominique Barthélemy and Jean-Marie Martin, 477–502. Geneva: Droz, 2003.

Mooney, Catherine M., ed. *Gendered Voices: Saints and Their Interpreters.* Philadelphia: University of Pennsylvania Press, 1999.

Morand, Sauveur-Jérôme. *Histoire de la Sainte-Chapelle royale du palais.* Paris: Clousier, 1790.

Müller, Catherine. "La lettre et la figure: Lecture allégorique du 'Mirouer' de Marguerite Porete dans 'Les Prisons' de Marguerite de Navarre." *Versants* 38 (2000): 153–67.

Müller, Ewald. *Das Konzil von Vienne (1311–1312): Seine Quellen und seine Geschichte.* Munster: Aschendorff, 1934.

Mulchahey, M. Michèle. *"First the Bow Is Bent in Study . . .": Dominican Education before 1350.* Toronto: Pontifical Institute of Mediaeval Studies, 1998.

Mulder-Bakker, Anneke B. *Lives of the Anchoresses: The Rise of the Urban Recluse in Medieval Europe.* Trans. Myra Heerspink Scholz. Philadelphia: University of Pennsylvania Press, 2005.

Murano, Giovanna. "Postille perdute e problemi d'autenticità (Nicola di Gorran O.P. e Guglielmo di Melitona Omin)." *Archivum Franciscanum historicum* 92 (1999): 299–327.

Muraro, Luisa. *Lingua materna, scienza divina: Scritti sulla filosofia mistica di Margherita Porete.* Naples: M. D'Auria Editore, 1995.

———. *"Le mirour des simples ames* de Marguerite Porete: Les avatars d'un titre." *Ons geestelijk erf* 70 (1996): 3–9.

Murray, James M. *Notarial Instruments in Flanders between 1280 and 1452.* Brussels: Académie royale de Belgique, 1995.

Nadiras, Sébastian. "Guillaume de Nogaret et la pratique du pouvoir." *École nationale des Chartes, Positions des thèses* (2003): 161–68.

Nahon, Gérard. "Les juifs de Paris à la veille de l'expulsion de 1306." In *Finances, pouvoirs et mémoire: Mélanges offerts à Jean Favier.* ed. Jean Kerhervé and Albert Rigaudière, 27–40. Paris: Fayard, 1999.

Nebbiai, Donatella. "Angèle et les spirituels: À propos des livres d'Arnau de Villeneuve (†1311)." *Revue d'histoire des textes* 32 (2002): 265–83.

———. "Un intellectuel catalan à Marseille: Arnaud de Villeneuve." In *Marseille au Moyen Âge, entre Provence et Méditerranée: Les horizons d'une ville portuaire,* ed. Thierry Pécout, 340–43. Méolans-Revel: Éditions Désiris, 2009.

Newman, Barbara. *God and the Goddesses: Vision, Poetry, and Belief in the Middle Ages.* Philadelphia: University of Pennsylvania Press, 2003.

———. "Latin and the Vernaculars." In *The Cambridge Companion to Christian Mysticism,* ed. Amy Hollywood and Patricia Beckman. Cambridge: Cambridge University Press, forthcoming.

———. "The Mirror and the Rose: Marguerite Porete's Encounter with the *Dieu d'amours.*" In *The Vernacular Spirit: Essays on Medieval Religious Literature,* ed. Renate Blumenfeld-Kosinski, Duncan Robertson, and Nancy Bradley Warren, 105–23. New York: Palgrave, 2002.

————. "*La mystique courtoise*: Thirteenth-Century Beguines and the Art of Love." In *From Virile Woman to WomanChrist: Studies in Medieval Religion and Literature,* 137–67. Philadelphia: University of Pennsylvania Press, 1995.

Nicholson, Helen J. "The Changing Face of the Templars: Current Trends in Historiography." *History Compass* 8/7 (2010): 653–67.

Nirenberg, David. *Communities of Violence: Persecution of Minorities in the Middle Ages.* Princeton: Princeton University Press, 1996.

O'Sullivan, Robin Anne. "The School of Love: Marguerite Porete's *Mirror of Simple Souls.*" *Journal of Medieval History* 32 (2006): 143–62.

Palacios, Arturo Bernal. "La *Summa Innocenti abreviatti* [*sic*] de Guido de Collemedio." In *Cum Vobis et pro Vobis: Homenaje de la Facultad de Teología San Vicente Ferrer, de Valencia, al Excmo. y Rvdmo. Dr. D. Miguel Roca Cabanellas,* ed. Ramón Arnau-García and Roberto Ortuño Soriano, 465–71. Valencia: Facultad de Teología San Vicente Ferrer, 1991.

Paravicini Bagliani, Agostino. *Boniface VIII: Un pape heretique?* Paris: Payot, 2003.

Patschovsky, Alexander. *Die Anfänge einer ständigen Inquisition in Böhmen: Ein Prager Inquisitoren-Handbuch aus der ersten Hälfte des 14. Jahrhunderts.* Berlin: Walter de Gruyter, 1975.

————. "Strassburger Beginenverfolgungen im 14. Jahrhundert." *Deutsches Archiv für Erforschung des Mittelalters* 30 (1974): 56–198.

Paulmier-Foucart, Monique, with Marie-Christine Duchenne. *Vincent de Beauvais et le Grand miroir du monde.* Turnhout: Brepols, 2004.

Pegg, Mark Gregory. *The Corruption of Angels: The Great Inquisition of 1245–1246.* Princeton: Princeton University Press, 2001.

————. *A Most Holy War: The Albigensian Crusade and the Battle for Christendom.* Oxford: Oxford University Press, 2008.

Pegues, Franklin J. *The Lawyers of the Last Capetians.* Princeton: Princeton University Press, 1962.

Pélicier, M. "Une émeute à Chalons-sur-Marne sous Philippe IV le Bel, 1306–1307." In *Bulletin historique et philologique du Comité des travaux historiques et scientifiques: Année 1889* (Paris: Ernest Leroux, 1890), 142–47.

Perarnau, Josep. "L'*Allocutio Christini* d'Arnau de Vilanova." *Arxiu de textos catalans antics* 11 (1992): 7–135.

————. "Noves dades biogràfiques de Mestre Arnau de Vilanova." *Arxiu de textos catalans antics* 7–8 (1988–89): 276–82.

————. "Noves dades sobre manuscrits 'espirituals' d'Arnau de Vilanova." *Arxiu de textos catalans antics* 27 (2008): 351–424.

————. "Problemes i criteris d'autenticitat d'obres espirituals atribuides a Arnau de Vilanova." *Arxiu de textos catalans antics* 13 (1995): 25–103.

———. "Sobre la primera crisi entorn el *De adventu antichristi* d'Arnau de Vilanova: París 1299–1300." *Arxiu de textos catalans antics* 20 (2001): 349–402.

———. "Sobre l'estada d'Arnau de Vilanova a París, 1299–1300: Les dues dates dels textos." *Arxiu de textos catalans antics* 28 (2009): 623–28.

———. "Troballa de tractats espirituals perduts d'Arnau de Vilanova." *Revista catalana de teologia* 1 (1976): 489–512.

Pereira, Michela. "Margherita Porete nello specchio degli studi recenti." *Mediaevistik* 11 (1998): 71–96.

Peters, Edward. *Inquisition.* Berkeley: University of California Press, 1989.

———. *Torture.* Expanded ed. Philadelphia: University of Pennsylvania Press, 1985.

Piétresson de Saint-Aubin, Pierre. *Archives Departmentales du Nord, Répertoire numérique, Série G.* Lille: Douriez-Bataille, 1968.

Piron, Sylvain. "Adnichilatio." In *Mots médiévaux offerts à Ruedi Imbach,* ed. I. Atucha et al., 23–31. Porto: Fédération internationale des instituts d'études médiévales, 2011.

———. "Avignon sous Jean XXII, l'Eldorado des théologiens." In *Jean XXII et le Midi,* Cahiers de Fanjeaux 45. Toulouse: Privat, forthcoming.

———. "Censures et condamnation de Pierre de Jean Olivi." *Mélanges de l'École française de Rome, Moyen Âge* 118, no. 2 (2006): 313–73.

———. "Le métier de théologien selon Olivi: Philosophie, théologie, exégès et pauvreté." In *Pierre de Jean Olivi—Philosophe et théologien. Actes du colloque de Philosophie médiévale. 24–25 octobre 2008, Université de Fribourg,* ed. Catherine König-Pralong, Olivier Ribordy, and Tiziana Suarez-Nani, 17–85. Berlin: Walter de Gruyter, 2010.

Piron, Sylvain, Robert E. Lerner, and Sean L. Field, eds. *Marguerite Porete et le "Miroir des simples âmes": Perspectives historiques, philosophiques et littéraires.* Paris: Vrin, forthcoming.

Pou y Marti, Jose M. *Visionarios, beguinos y fraticelos catalanes (siglos XIII–XV).* Rev. ed. Madrid: Colegio Cardenal Cisneros, 1991.

Principe, Walter H. "The School Theologians' Views of the Papacy, 1150–1250." In *The Religious Roles of the Papacy: Ideals and Realities, 1150–1300,* ed. Christopher Ryan, 45–116. Toronto: Pontifical Institute of Mediaeval Studies, 1989.

Provost, Alain. *Domus diaboli: Un évêque en procès au temps de Philippe le Bel.* Paris: Belin, 2010.

———. "On the Margins of the Templars' Trial: The Case of Bishop Guichard of Troyes." In *The Debate on the Trial of the Templars (1307–1314),* ed. Jochen Burgtorf, Paul F. Crawford, and Helen J. Nicholson, 117–27. Farnham: Ashgate, 2010.

Prutz, Hans. *Entwicklung und Untergang des Tempelherrenordens.* Berlin: Grote, 1888.

Pycke, Jacques. *Répertoire biographique des chanoines de Notre-Dame de Tournai, 1080–1300.* Louvain-la-Neuve: Collège Erasme, 1988.

Quétif, Jacques, and Jacques Echard. *Scriptores ordinis Praedicatorum.* 1719–21. Reprint, New York: Burt Franklin, 1959.

Reeves, Marjorie. *Joachim of Fiore and the Prophetic Future: A Medieval Study in Historical Thinking.* Rev. ed. Phoenix Mill: Sutton, 1999.

Renardy, Christine. *Les maîtres universitaires du diocèse de Liège: Répertoire biographique, 1140–1350.* Paris: Les belles lettres, 1981.

Richard, Jules-Marie. *Mahaut comtesse d'Artois et de Bourgogne (1302–1329).* 1886. Reprint, Monein: Editions Pyremonde, 2006.

Richir, Luc. *Marguerite Porete, une âme au travail de l'Un.* Brussels: Éditions OUSIA, 2002.

Riley-Smith, Jonathan. *Templars and Hospitalers as Professed Religious in the Holy Land.* Notre Dame: University of Notre Dame Press, 2010.

———. "Were the Templars Guilty?" In *The Medieval Crusade,* ed. Susan J. Ridyard, 107–24. Woodbridge: Boydell, 2004.

Robert, Gaston. *Les béguines de Reims et la maison de Sainte-Agnès.* Reims: Monce et Cie, 1923.

Robinson, Joanne Maguire. *Nobility and Annihilation in Marguerite Porete's Mirror of Simple Souls.* Albany: SUNY Press, 2001.

Rouse, Richard H., and Mary A. *Manuscripts and Their Makers: Commercial Book Producers in Medieval Paris, 1200–1500.* Vol. 1. Turnhout: Harvey Miller, 2000.

Rubin, Miri. "Choosing Death? Experiences of Martyrdom in Late Medieval Europe." In *Martyrs and Martyrologies,* ed. Diana Wood, 153–83. Studies in Church History 30. Oxford: Blackwell, 1993.

———. *Gentile Tales: The Narrative Assault on Late Medieval Jews.* Philadelphia: University of Pennsylvania Press, 1999.

Ruh, Kurt. "*Le miroir des simples âmes* der Marguerite Porete." *Verbum et Signum* 2 (1975): 365–87.

Ryan, Christopher. "The Theology of Papal Primacy in Thomas Aquinas." In *The Religious Roles of the Papacy: Ideals and Realities, 1150–1300,* ed. Christopher Ryan, 193–225. Toronto: Pontifical Institute of Mediaeval Studies, 1989.

Santi, Francesco. *Arnau de Vilanova: L'obra espiritual.* València: Disputació provincial de València, 1987.

Sargent, Michael G. "The Annihilation of Marguerite Porete." *Viator* 28 (1997): 253–79.

———. "Marguerite Porete." In *Medieval Holy Women in the Christian Tradition, c. 1100–1500,* ed. Alistair Minnis and Rosalynn Voaden, 291–312. Turnhout: Brepols, 2010.

———. "Medieval and Modern Readership of Marguerite Porete's *Mirouer des simples âmes anienties*: The Continental Latin and Italian Tradition." Forthcoming.

———. "Medieval and Modern Readership of Marguerite Porete's *Mirouer des simples âmes*: The Old French and English Traditions." In *Middle English Religious Writing in Practice: Texts, Readers and Transformations,* ed. Nicole Rice. Turnhout: Brepols, forthcoming.

Schabel, Christopher. "Carmelite Quodlibeta." In *Theological Quodlibeta in the Middle Ages: The Fourteenth Century,* ed. Christopher Schabel, 493–544. Leiden: Brill, 2007.

———, ed. *Theological Quodlibeta in the Middle Ages: The Fourteenth Century.* Leiden: Brill, 2007.

Schenk, Jochen. "Aspects of Non-Noble Family Involvement in the Order of the Temple." In *The Military Orders,* vol. 4, *By Land and by Sea,* ed. Judi Upton-Ward, 155–61. Aldershot: Ashgate, 2008.

Schmidt, Hans-Joachim. *Kirche, Staat, Nation: Raumgliederung der Kirche im mittelalterlichen Europa.* Weimar: Hermann Böhlaus, 1999.

Serventi, Silvia. "Did Giordano da Pisa Use the *Distinctiones* of Nicolas Gorran?" In *Constructing the Medieval Sermon,* ed. Roger Andersson, 83–116. Turnhout: Brepols, 2007.

Sikes, J. G. "John de Pouilli and Peter de la Palu." *English Historical Review* 49 (1934): 219–40.

Simoncelli, Paolo. "Il 'Dialogo dell'unione spirituale di Dio con l'anima' tra alumbradismo spagnolo et prequietismo italiano." *Annuario dell'Istituto Storico Italiano per l'Età Moderna e Contemporanea* 29–30 (1977): 565–601.

Simons, Walter. *Cities of Ladies: Beguine Communities in the Medieval Low Countries, 1200–1565.* Philadelphia: University of Pennsylvania Press, 2001.

———. "The Lives of Beghards." In *Medieval Christianity in Practice,* ed. Miri Rubin, 238–45. Princeton: Princeton University Press, 2009.

———. "Staining the Speech of Things Divine: The Uses of Literacy in Medieval Beguine Communities." In *The Voice of Silence: Women's Literacy in a Men's Church,* ed. Thérèse de Hemptinne and María Eugenia Góngora, 85–110. Turnhout: Brepols, 2004.

Sivery, Gérard. "Commerce et marchands à Valenciennes à la fin du Moyen Âge." In *Valenciennes et les anciens Pay-Bas: Mélanges offerts à Paul Lefrancq,* 71–80. Valenciennes: Cercle archéologique et historique de Valenciennes, 1976.

Smalley, Beryl. "John Baconthorpe's Postill on St. Matthew." In *Studies in Medieval Thought and Learning,* 289–344. London: Hambledon Press, 1981.

———. "Some Latin Commentaries on the Sapiential Books in the Late Thirteenth and Early Fourteenth Centuries." *Archives d'histoire doctrinale et littéraire du Moyen Âge* 18 (1950–51): 103–28.

———. *Study of the Bible in the Middle Ages.* 3rd ed. Oxford: Blackwell, 1983.

Speer, Andreas, and David Wirmer, eds. *1308: Eine Topographie historischer Gleichzeitigkeit.* Berlin: Walter de Gruyter, 2010.

Spiegel, Gabrielle M. *The Chronicle Tradition of Saint-Denis: A Survey.* Brookline, MA: Classical Folia Editions, 1978.

Stabler, Tanya. "Now She Is Martha, Now She Is Mary: Beguine Communities in Medieval Paris (1250–1470)." PhD diss., University of California at Santa Barbara, 2007.

———. "What's in a Name? Clerical Representations of Parisian Beguines (1200–1328)." *Journal of Medieval History* 33 (2007): 60–86.

Steiner, Arpad. "Guillaume Perrault and Vincent of Beauvais." *Speculum* 8 (1933): 51–58.

Stephens, Rebecca. "Eckhart and Sister Catherine: The Mirror's Image?" *Eckhart Review* 6 (1997): 26–39.

Strayer, Joseph R. *The Albigensian Crusades.* 1972. Reprint, Ann Arbor: University of Michigan Press, 1992.

———. "France: The Holy Land, the Chosen People, and the Most Christian King." In *Action and Conviction in Early Modern Europe: Essays in Memory of E.H. Harbison,* ed. Theodore K. Rabb and Jerrold E. Seigel, 3–16. Princeton: Princeton University Press, 1969.

———. *On the Medieval Origins of the Modern State.* 1970. Reprint, Princeton: Princeton University Press, 2005.

———. "Philip the Fair: A 'Constitutional' King." *American Historical Review* 62 (1956): 18–32.

———. *The Reign of Philip IV.* Princeton: Princeton University Press, 1980.

Stroick, Clemens. *Heinrich von Friemar: Leben, Werke, Philosophisch-Theologische Stellung in der Scholastik.* Freiburg: Herder, 1954.

Sullivan, Karen. *The Inner Lives of Medieval Inquisitors.* Chicago: University of Chicago Press, 2011.

Tarrant, Jacqueline. "The Clementine Decrees on the Beguines: Conciliar and Papal Versions." *Archivum historiae pontificiae* 12 (1974): 300–308.

Teetaert, Amédée. "Un compendium de théologie pastorale du XIIIe–XIVe siècle." *Revue d'histoire ecclésiastique* 26 (1930): 66–102.

Terry, Wendy Rachele. *Seeing Marguerite in the "Mirror": A Linguistic Analysis of Porete's "Mirror of Simple Souls."* Leuven: Peeters, 2011.

Théry, Julien. "Allo scoppio del conflitto tra Filippo il Bello di Francia e Bonifacio VIII: L'affare Saisset (1301)." In *I poteri universali e la fondazione dello Studium Urbis: Bonifacio VIII dalla "Unam sanctam" allo "schiaffo" di Anagni*, ed. Giovanni Minnucci, 21–68. Rome: Monduzzi, 2008.

———. "Contre-enquête sur un procès." *Histoire* 323 (2007): 40–47.

———. "Fama: L'opinion publique comme preuve judiciaire. Aperçu sur la révolution médiévale inquisitoire (XIIe–XIVe siècle)." In *La preuve en justice de l'antiquité à nos jours*, ed. Bruno Lemesle, 119–47. Rennes: Presses universitaires de Rennes, 2003.

———. "Une heresie d'état: Philippe le Bel, le procès des 'perfides Templiers' et la pontificalisation de la royauté française." *Médiévales* 60 (2011): 157–86.

———. "Philippe le Bel, la persécution des 'perfides Templiers' et la pontificalisation de la royauté capétienne." In *L'età dei processi: Inchieste e condanne tra politica e ideologia nel '300. Atti del convegno di studio svoltosi in occasione della XIX edizione del Premio internazionale Ascoli Piceno*, ed. Antonio Rigon and Francesco Veronese, 65–80. Rome: Istituto Storico Italiano per il Medio Evo, 2009.

———. "Philippe le Bel, pape en son royaume." *L'histoire* 289 (2004): 14–17.

———. "Le procès des Templiers." In *Prier et combattre: Dictionnaire européen des ordres militaires*, ed. N. Bériou and Ph. Josserand, 743–50. Paris: Fayard, 2009.

Thijssen, J. M. M. H. *Censure and Heresy at the University of Paris, 1200–1400*. Philadelphia: University of Pennsylvania Press, 1998.

———. "Master Amalric and the Amalricians: Inquisitorial Procedure and the Suppression of Heresy at the University of Paris." *Speculum* 71 (1996): 43–65.

Thomas, Louis. "La vie privée de Guillaume de Nogaret." *Annales du Midi* 16 (1904): 161–207.

Trombley, Justine L. "The Master and the Mirror: The Influence of Marguerite Porete on Meister Eckhart." *Magistra* 16 (2010): 60–102.

Trusen, Winfried. *Der Prozess gegen Meister Eckhart: Vorgeschichte, Verlauf und Folgen*. Paderborn: Schöningh, 1988.

Tugwell, Simon. "The Downfall of Robert le Bougre, OP." In *Praedicatores, inquisitores*, vol. 1, ed. Wolfram Hoyer, 753–56. Rome: Istituto Storico Domenicano, 2004.

Ubl, Karl. "*Haeretici relapsi*: Jean de Pouilly und die juristischen Grundlagen für die Hinrichtung der Tempelritter." In *1308—Eine Topographie historischer Gleichzeitigkeit*, ed. Andreas Speer and David Wirmer, 161–170. Berlin: Walter de Gruyter, 2010.

Ullmann, Walter. "The Defence of the Accused in the Medieval Inquisition." In *Law and Jurisdiction in the Middle Ages,* ed. George Garnett, 15:481–89. London: Variorum Reprints, 1988.

———. "John Baconthorpe as a Canonist." In *Church and Government in the Middle Ages: Essays Presented to C.R. Cheney on His 70th Birthday,* ed. C.N.L. Brooke et al., 223–47. Cambridge: Cambridge University Press, 1976.

———. "Reflections on Medieval Torture." In *Law and Jurisdiction in the Middle Ages,* ed. George Garnett, 17:124–37. London: Variorum Reprints, 1988.

Vale, Juliet. *Edward III and Chivalry: Chivalric Society and Its Context, 1270–1350.* Woodbridge: Boydell, 1982.

Valois, Noel. "Jean de Pouilli, théologien." *Histoire littéraire de la France* 34 (1914): 220–81.

Van Engen, John. "Marguerite (Porete) of Hainaut and the Medieval Low Countries." In *Marguerite Porete et le "Miroir des simples âmes": Perspectives historiques, philosophiques et littéraires.* Paris: Vrin, forthcoming.

———. *Sisters and Brothers of the Common Life: The Devotio Moderna and the World of the Later Middle Ages.* Philadelphia: University of Pennsylvania Press, 2008.

Verdeyen, Paul. "La première traduction latine du *Miroir* de Marguerite Porete." *Ons geestelijk erf* 58 (1984): 388–89.

———. "Le procès d'inquisition contre Marguerite Porete et Guiard de Cressonessart (1309–1310)." *Revue d'histoire ecclésiastique* 81 (1986): 47–94.

———. "Ruusbroec's Opinion on Marguerite Porete's Orthodoxy." *Studies in Spirituality* 3 (1993): 121–29.

Verweij, Michael. "Princely Virtues or Virtues for Princes? William Peraldus and His *De eruditione principum.*" In *Princely Virtues in the Middle Ages, 1200–1500,* ed. István P. Bejczy and Cary J. Nederman, 51–72. Turnhout: Brepols, 2007.

Viard, Jules. "Le concile de Paris de mai 1310." *Revue des questions historiques* 115 (1931): 358–61.

———. "L'Ostrevant, enquête au sujet de la frontière française sous Philippe VI de Valois." *Bibliothèque de l'École des Chartes* 82 (1921): 316–29.

Vidier, A. "Le Trésor de la Sainte-Chapelle (suite)." *Mémoires de la Société de l'histoire de Paris et de l'Ile-de-France* 36 (1909): 245–395.

Wakefield, Walter L. *Heresy, Crusade and Inquisition in Southern France, 1100–1250.* Berkeley: University of California Press, 1974.

Ward, John O., and Francesca C. Bussey, eds. *Worshipping Women: Misogyny and Mysticism in the Middle Ages.* Sydney: Department of History, University of Sydney, 1997.

Watson, Nicholas. "Melting into God the English Way: Deification in the Middle English Version of Marguerite Porete's *Mirouer des simples âmes anienties.*" In *Prophets Abroad: The Reception of Continental Holy Women in Late-Medieval England,* ed. Rosalynn Voaden, 19–49. Woodbridge: D. S. Brewer, 1996.

Wegener, Lydia. "Freiheitsdiskurs und Beginenverfolgung um 1308: Der Fall der Marguerite Porete." In *1308: Eine Topographie historischer Gleich-zeitigkeit,* ed. Andreas Speer and David Wirmer, 199–236. Berlin: Walter de Gruyter, 2010.

Wei, Ian P. "The Masters of Theology at the University of Paris in the Late Thirteenth and Early Fourteenth Centuries: An Authority beyond the Schools." *Bulletin of the John Rylands Library* 75 (1993): 37–63.

———. "The Self-Image of the Masters of Theology at the University of Paris in the Late Thirteenth and Early Fourteenth Centuries." *Journal of Ec-clesiastical History* 46, no. 3 (1995): 398–431.

Werner, Thomas. *Den Irrtum liquidieren: Bücherverbrennungen im Mittelal-ter.* Göttingen: Vandenhoeck und Ruprecht, 2007.

Wippel, John F. *The Metaphysical Thought of Godfrey of Fontaines: A Study in Late Thirteenth-Century Philosophy.* Washington, DC: Catholic University of America Press, 1981.

Woods, Marjorie Curry. "Shared Books: Primers, Psalters, and the Adult Acquisition of Literacy among Devout Laywomen and Women in Orders in Late Medieval England." In *New Trends in Feminine Spirituality: The Holy Women of Liège and Their Impact,* ed. Juliette Dor, Lesley Johnson, and Jocelyn Wogan-Browne, 177–93. Turnhout: Brepols, 1999.

Xiberta, B. "De magistro Iohanne Baconthorp, O. Carm." *Analecta Ordinis Carmelitarum* 6 (1927): 3–128.

Ziegler, Joseph. *Medicine and Religion c. 1300: The Case of Arnau de Vilanova.* Oxford: Clarendon Press, 1998.

INDEX

SEAN L. FIELD

is associate professor of history at the University of Vermont.
He is the editor and translator of *The Writings of Agnes of Harcourt:
The Life of Isabelle of France* and the *Letter on Louis IX and
Longchamp* and author of *Isabelle of France: Capetian Sanctity
and Franciscan Identity in the Thirteenth Century,*
both published by the University of Notre Dame Press.